Ethical
Issues in
Psychology

Ethical Issues in Psychology

Marion Steininger
Rutgers University

J. David Newell
Washington College

Luis T. Garcia
Rutgers University

Being published simultaneously by
THE DORSEY PRESS
and
THE DOW JONES-IRWIN DORSEY PROFESSIONAL BOOKS
Homewood, Illinois   60430

Dorsey Library of Congress Catalog Card No. 83-71606
Dow Jones-Irwin Library of Congress Catalog Card No. 83-71734

Printed in the United States of America

1 2 3 4 5 6 7 8 9 0 ML 1 0 9 8 7 6 5 4

MS–To the three most important women in my life: my daughters and my mother.

JDN–To Judith, Jeffrey and Jonathan.

LTG–To the memory of my father.

FOREWORD

A lot has happened in the last 15 years in the ethics of social and behavioral research. The stirring of the field can be conveniently dated at around 1968, when social psychologist Herbert C. Kelman published his pioneering volume *A Time to Speak*. Although developments were less rapid in the ethics of the social and behavioral sciences than in the medical sciences over the next decade, approximately a dozen books were published in these years, and virtually every major professional association of social scientists undertook to write and rewrite codes of professional conduct. The American Psychological Association was the pacesetter.

This general area of interest was brought into prominence by increasing federal involvement and by a number of celebrated cases of abuse by social researchers. While the social and behavioral sciences have a history by no means analogous to biomedical experimentation under the Third Reich, they are not lacking in heated debate over certain ventures. The earliest landmark case in the United States featured problems of confidentiality and secrecy; it is popularly known as the Wichita Jury Study. This case emerged in 1954, when some professors at the University of Chicago performed a study of jury deliberations by secretly recording the discussions of six separate juries. In this way they obtained empirical data by which to test frequent criticisms of the jury system and the assumptions about that system implicit in American law. This project—like many since—generated heated public controversy and eventually led to legislation in 1956 that prohibited the recording of federal grand or petit jury deliberations. Some of the other celebrated controversies surrounding psychology are recounted in the following pages.

However, this book is not abuse-oriented. We are now in a period of constructive thinking about the moral responsibilities of psychologists, and this volume makes a significant contribution to a field growing in this direction. It is important to remember that this turn of events is relatively recent. I can remember debates and testimony in the 1976 and 1977 deliberations of the National Commission for the Protection of Human Subjects of Biomedical and Behavioral Research on topics of social and behavioral research in which commissioners, staff, and witnesses alike were wholly unprepared to grapple with many of the issues considered in this book. The ethics of social research was still an infant. Although such generalizations are fraught with ready counterexample, I believe the general study of ethics in the social and behavioral sciences did not ease into adolescence until approximately 1980–81.

This book, then, will be most welcome to those interested in this now flourishing, but still maturing area of interest. The book is based on what I believe to be the only sound methodology for advancing the field: genuine interdisciplinary collaboration between philosophers and psychologists. A great flaw in most of the work thus far produced is that it is naive to the core about either philosophical ethics or psychology. This book provides a sound, mainstream philosophical framework, while confining the issues to actual problems in psychology—not philosophical visions about the problems that *might* exist in that field. This book is not naive about either field, and it lucidly maps out the terrain of problems and solutions that have been offered in both. It contains matters of essential thinking in psychology, for these problems simply cannot be avoided by the members of that profession.

Tom L. Beauchamp
Professor of Philosophy and
Senior Research Scholar
Kennedy Institute for Ethics
Georgetown University

PREFACE

This book is a critical survey of the activities of psychologists from the joint perspectives of psychology and ethics. As the project progressed, we (two psychologists and one philosopher) found ourselves increasingly intrigued and challenged, and we hope that readers will be stimulated in the same ways.

Our major purpose is to sensitize readers to the pervasiveness of ethical issues in psychology, and to offer conceptual tools for thinking about them. Therapy and social psychology research are not the only activities about which one can ask morally relevant questions. Rather, our major thesis is that all of our activities, including those we perform as professionals, can be viewed from the perspective of ethics. This thesis does not imply that the discipline of ethics is totally separate from and superior to psychology. In fact, in the final section, we argue that the concerns and concepts of these two disciplines overlap considerably, and that both leave many unanswered questions.

Thus, we consider psychology from the perspective of ethics, and ethics from the perspective of psychology. Part I introduces ethics and moral reasoning, using psychologically relevant examples. Part II asks morally relevant questions as it explores the activities of psychologists: choosing an area of research and/or application; conceptualizing and theorizing; gathering information; sharing knowledge; and applying knowledge. Part III considers specific areas of controversy, as psychology is involved with life and death, the powerless, testing, and the law. Part IV explores in greater depth the overlapping concerns of psychology and ethics.

We wish it was possible to say that we answered all the questions we raised, or event that we raised all the important questions, but neither of these claims would be justified. Instead, we hope that readers will understand why the questions raised are important, difficult, and sometimes divisive, and that they will be able to reflect about these questions better than they could before reading the book.

It is always a pleasure to thank those who have touched our lives in a positive way. Our many teachers, colleagues, and students deserve such thanks, especially when they confront(ed) us with hard questions. The final manuscript gained immeasurably from the criticisms of Morton Winston, Desmond Fitzgerald, Andrew Bondy, Genevieve Falciani, Melissa Mullin, and Deborah Kaczka, and above all, the Dorsey reviewers, Salvatore Maddi and Wendell Jeffrey. Marion Steininger spent an exciting and productive summer (1980) in a Summer Seminar for College Teachers sponsored by the National Endowment for the Humanities. The Seminar was organized by Professor Gareth Matthews of the University of Massachusetts (Amherst), and it explored the meanings and implications of *personhood*. J. David Newell worked on the manuscript while participating in a National Endowment for the Humanities Seminar in Bioethics at Indiana University in 1982–83. The seminar was directed by Professor David H. Smith, who along with 10 other National Endowment for the Humanities Fellows, offered much by way of constructive criticism and enthusiastic support. Newell and Steininger met in a provocative bioethics course sponsored by the National Science Foundation and directed by Tom Beauchamp. Discussions and correspondence followed, and eventually work on the manuscript was begun. Luis T. Garcia joined as author after providing helpful criticisms of several chapters.

Special thanks go to Ann Urbanus, who typed the entire final manuscript under pressure without losing her sense of humor. Eve Henry and Betty Zubert typed earlier drafts of several chapters from originals best left undescribed. Alice Cook worked tirelessly on the many small details that are part of any major project.

Rutgers University and Washington College provided opportunity, shelter, and support. We are grateful for all of these.

Finally, we want to thank our families, who enrich our lives by simply being themselves. The intimate relationships they make possible serve as constant reminders of the complexity and value of social life.

Marion Steininger
J. David Newell
Luis T. Garcia

CONTENTS

Ethical
Issues in
Psychology

INTRODUCTION

PART I

The proper place to begin reflecting on ethical issues in psychology, or in any other field, is by considering certain basic questions, concepts, and perspectives in ethics. If we do not start with a shared understanding of those key ethical concepts and theories to which we will be making constant reference throughout this work, our concern with ethical issues will not make much sense. For the reader already well versed in moral philosophy, the material in this section will serve as a quick but adequate review. For those with less awareness of the fundamentals of ethics, we have tried to provide an account of ethical theory that is sufficient for understanding the issues raised in subsequent sections of this investigation.

This book deals with some provocative and important questions that do not admit of easy, straightforward answers. These questions challenge us to think seriously about our own beliefs and values, as well as the beliefs and values of those actively engaged in the field of psychology.

Psychologists teach, do research, and engage in professional (often clinical) practice. Two examples show how some of their activities involve practical and perplexing questions with far-reaching ethical significance.

1. Almost everyone has some familiarity with the controversial study of obedience Stanley Milgram did at Yale University (1963). Milgram placed ads in newspapers inviting people to take part in a learning experiment. Participants were led to believe that they were divided by lot into "teachers" and "learners." The teachers were then instructed to teach lists of words to the learners by administering increasingly strong electric shocks to them for each mistake they made. The real aim of the study, however, was to study obedience to authority. Every participating subject was in fact a teacher. The alleged learners were not genuine volunteers, but persons hired to play the role of learner in the project. They were given instructions on how to respond, including the making of mistakes and distress responses to the pseudoshocks they received as penalties. When teachers wanted to stop administering more severe shocks, they were prodded first with requests and then with commands to continue with the experiment.

Sixty-five percent of the teachers obeyed the experimenter's command to continue, long after the alleged learners complained that they were in pain and wanted to quit, a finding both fascinating and alarming. The fascination came primarily from revelations concerning human motivation. The alarm centered on the fact that the study involved deception of the participants, resulting in considerable discomfort for them, first during the study and later when they were told the truth. This experiment reportedly "contributed to the generating of a public sense that it is not merely medical research that needs regulating: social science needs it too" (Thomson, 1981, p. 359). For our purposes in this book, it introduces a basic conflict in human values: the value of new scientific knowledge versus the values assigned to the methods of obtaining such knowledge. This conflict in human values is typical of the many and varied unresolved value conflicts discussed in this book.

2. In the area of clinical practice, the psychologist is confronted with conflicts in values as fascinating and alarming as those in the Milgram experiment. In 1969, a client of Dr. Lawrence Moore, a psychologist on the Berkeley campus of the University of California, confided his intention to murder an unnamed but readily identified girl, Tatiana Tarasoff, upon her return from a summer stay in Brazil (131 *California Reporter* 14). Moore and two of his colleagues agreed that the client, Prosenjit Poddar, should be committed for observation in a mental hospital. Moore called campus police and followed up with a letter requesting help in securing Poddar's confinement. Campus police picked up the client, decided he was rational, and released him. Notified of their action, Moore and his colleagues withdrew the letter requesting confinement of Poddar and considered the matter settled. Poddar subsequently persuaded Tatiana Tarasoff's brother to share an apartment with him near Tatiana's residence. Soon after Tatiana returned from Brazil, Poddar went to her home and killed her.

The serious nature of this case may not be typical of most clinical cases, but the values in conflict in the Tarasoff case are quite familiar. Quite often in clinical settings the interests of the client may conflict with the public interest, or with the well-being of specific individuals not involved in the therapist-client relationship. In any clinical setting, confidentiality has to be weighed against the preservation of public trust in the profession, with all the benefits this brings, and the threat of actual harm to some innocent victim, as in the Tarasoff case. Each case may have its own unique features, and there may be no single way of dealing with all such value conflicts. But we believe that those who engage in sustained reflection on such ethical issues will be in a better position to deal effectively with them than those who do not. This conviction is a principal motive behind the writing of this book.

Our goal is not so much to provide clear-cut and sparkling answers to the ethical dilemmas facing psychologists, as it is to provoke thought and discussion about them. Our own perspectives are bound to emerge as the book proceeds, but a conscientious effort has been made to allow readers as much freedom as possible in arriving at their own conclusions. But before turning our attention directly to the issues themselves, we must lay the groundwork for our ethical reflection by offering an account of the nature and scope of ethical reasoning.

THE SUBJECT MATTER
OF ETHICS

If the average person is asked what ethics is about, the answer is likely to be that it is about the "right and wrong, good and evil, in human conduct." Although hardly accounting for the many and varied interests of moral philosophers, this response is not too far off the mark. Judgments about what is morally right or morally wrong in human conduct are among the many concerns of moral philosophers. Such judgments are usually called *judgments of obligation* and generally express what someone ought (or ought not) to do—they state what one's duty is. Judgments about what is morally good or morally evil, on the other hand, are usually called *judgments of value,* and generally express those things we think are of value or importance to us. When something is held to be valuable in and of itself, it is said that it has intrinsic or inherent value. When it has value only as a means or way of securing some other end, it is said that it has extrinsic or instrumental value. The average person can be understood to be saying that ethics deals primarily with judgments of obligation, on one hand, and judgments of value on the other.

In ethics, both judgments of obligation and judgments of value point to things, practices, or states of affairs that are in some sense ideal. That is, they are judgments that focus on the way things ought to be in an ideal or morally perfect world. Judgments of obligation tell us how people ought to behave ideally and judgments of value tell us what things or states of affairs one should try to bring about because they would be good to have. Both types of judgment are distinguishable from what might be called judgments of fact—judgments that describe the way things actually are or were. A traditional way of making this point is to say that ethics is concerned with "what ought to be," as opposed to merely "what is, has been, and will be" (Sidgwick, 1902, p. 22). Naturally, since the ideal can become actual, "what ought to be" might be one and the same with "what actually is." Moreover, our thinking about what ought to be will always be limited by considerations of what can be, since it is absurd to say that a person is morally obliged to do what that person cannot do. For example, normally we are morally obliged to be honest, and we can be honest in most situations, perhaps all. In contrast, no one argues that we are morally obliged to fly in the manner of birds, because we are physically incapable of doing so. Moral philosophers put this point simply by saying that *ought* implies *can*. But even when the moral ideal is realized in a particular situation, the moral judgment is still separate and distinct from the judgment of fact.

JUSTIFYING MORAL JUDGMENTS

Ethics is concerned with judgments of value and obligation. But the concern is not simply with finding out what moral judgments or beliefs people actually have. This sort of empirical investigation is the proper business of sociologists and other social scientists. In contrast, the principal concern of moral theory is focused on what moral beliefs people ought to have—the moral beliefs that can be supported or defended by sound argumentation. Hence, the focus of ethical reasoning is on developing ways of justifying moral judgments, whether they are judgments of obligation or judgments of value.

When people say that abortion is morally right or that world peace is good, they are making moral judgments that are open to challenge. We may ask someone why they think that abortions are right or that world peace is good. When we ask why, we have begun to request a justification for the moral belief or judgment that has been expressed. We want evidence to support or defend the claim being made.

Wittgenstein pointed out that "justification consists in appealing to something independent" (1953, p. 93, paragraph 265). We cannot hope to justify our claim that the walls in some particular room are colored aqua by declaring that they just are, or by staring at them over and over again and saying they are aqua. Some help might be gotten by asking others what they think the color is, but this sort of intersubjective confirmation is not convincing, since all might be in error. The use of a color chart by the paint company would be more helpful, since it could be defended as an independent criterion. This simple analogy illustrates the validity of going beyond the situation and people at hand to appeal to an external criterion that would eliminate the pitfalls of mere subjective determinations. It is this kind of going beyond that is being requested when one seeks a justification for a moral judgment.

Suppose that, in response to our demand for a good reason, someone said that murder is wrong because it is wrong to take a human life. Here the appeal is to a criterion usually called "the principle of the sanctity of human life." This response seems to meet the minimal requirements of providing a justification since a formally (logically) valid argument could be offered—all human life is sacred, murder desecrates human lives, hence, murder is immoral. The critic of this argument is apt to challenge the scope and meaning of the sanctity of the life principle itself, and to offer such counterexamples as killing in self-defense, which might require the modification or even abandonment of the principle. It may turn out that the sanctity of life principle itself has application in some circumstances and not others, so that an even higher principle, such as "do whatever God wills" or "maximize human happiness," is needed to justify the sanctity principle, or to determine those circumstances in which it is applicable and those in which it is not. Some of these principles will be examined presently.

Our concern here is with the method of justifying moral judgments. In general, we should follow the process of moving from a specific moral judgment to a somewhat specific moral principle, and, in turn, to some higher or more overarching principle. Such highly abstract general principles are sometimes referred to as *first principles* or, in ethical discourse, *fundamental ethical principles*. In the chapter on moral theories several such basic principles will be examined. They are considered basic because they both serve as foundations for moral reasoning and provide the ultimate and final justification for our moral judgments. Such fundamental ethical principles may be viewed as self-evident propositions that commend themselves to our reason; or as assumptions we make as basic commitments; or as revelations of some sort; or even as postulates that are essential to making sense out of the data of our moral experience. No matter what the grounds we have for accepting particular fundamental ethical principles, they are the highest court of appeal available and lie in one form or another at the heart of all moral reasoning. A rich variety of moral perspectives can be found in the literature, because even reflective persons differ about fundamental moral principles. What is common to almost every moral perspective, however, is the realization that an appeal to principles is central to the process of thinking about ethical issues. The concluding section of this book will return to the nature of ethics and consider in greater detail such problems as disagreements among individuals who subscribe to different moral viewpoints.

THE NATURE OF ETHICAL PRINCIPLES

Since ethical principles are crucial to moral reasoning, a fuller, richer grasp of the nature and scope of such principles is needed than has been provided thus far. It is also useful to look at several of the fundamental ethical principles that are part of a long and distinguished tradition in moral philosophy and still apply to moral problems in our time.

An ethical principle should help determine what we ought or ought not to do when faced with a moral problem. Some people, facing a moral problem, turn to friends, teachers, clergy, or lay moralists writing newspaper advice columns. In such contexts specific moral advice is offered for specific moral problems. Such advice may or may not be based on more general grounds, on principles, but mention of higher or more general principles and a defense of their correctness or acceptability is not usually an explicit part of newspaper advice. The concern is with what one ought to do here and now about this or that particular problem. An appeal to ethical principles, on the other hand, involves much, much more. Rather than merely telling us what we ought to do about a particular situation, an ethical principle is designed to help us decide what to do, or not do, in a wide variety of diverse moral contexts. There is a sense in which it is correct to say that ethical principles help to determine what we ought to do *about everything* that is in the moral sphere.

Genuine ethical principles are universal in their scope or range of application. Statements of such principles contain universal notions such as *whenever, whatever, wherever,* and *everyone.* For example, the utilitarian moral principle discussed below states that whenever and wherever possible, everyone ought to try to do whatever will maximize the greatest amount of happiness. A theist may express the basic principle of theistic ethics by saying that whenever and wherever possible, everyone ought to try to do whatever will be pleasing in the sight of God. Fundamental or ultimate ethical principles, then, are universal principles in the fullest sense of the word.

Notice that in both the utilitarian and the theistic principles mentioned above explicit reference is made to what we ought to try to do. The *ought* clause tells us what is morally required, what we are morally obliged to either do or to refrain from doing. These principles do not, by themselves, tell specifically what we ought to do in a particular situation, but rather, that whatever the facts of the particular case may be we ought to try to maximize happiness, or please God, and so on. Fundamental moral principles tell us, in a very general way, what our moral obligations are, and yet they must, in the final analysis, be relevant or applicable to everyday concrete situations. Thus, in addition to being universal in scope, such principles must meet the criterion of being applicable to actual moral problems.

Another essential feature of a fundamental moral principle is the statement of certain conditions that must be fulfilled in order for a moral obligation or duty to be present. For the utilitarian, the condition to be fulfilled is the production of the maximum amount of happiness. For the theist, the condition to be fulfilled is the pleasing of the Divine Being. The conditions to be fulfilled are always expressed in relation to a notion of the good. That is, some appeal is made to what is thought to be good or of value. The principle also says that we have a moral obligation to try our best to bring about the states of affairs that are good or valuable. It goes almost without saying that the fundamental theory one adopts will be consistent with and expressive of one's own set of values, for the conditions one would want to see fulfilled are the states of affairs one thinks are good.

The distinguishing feature of a fundamental moral principle is the broad scope of the conditions that are to be fulfilled by its application. Consider the principle that "whenever and wherever possible, everyone ought always to tell the truth." The universal notions *whenever, wherever,* and *everyone* reveal the universal nature of this principle. Now even if one considers truth telling to be an inherently good thing, an intrinsic good, no matter what the circumstances or consequences may be, this principle cannot serve as a basic or fundamental moral principle because it only applies to a specific set of circumstances, namely those in which lying or deception are at stake. A moral theory based ultimately on such a principle would tell us nothing about what we ought to do in a whole range of other circumstances in which truth telling is not the issue. Moreover, most people would be unwilling to say that truth telling is always an absolute moral obligation as, for instance, in the case of the military officer who is being interrogated by the enemy. Even staunch defenders of truth telling (such as Bok, 1978; Fried, 1978) allow for exceptions to the rule. Hence, because it does not encompass all the issues, and because there may be circumstances in which the strong(est) presumption in favor of truth telling can be justifiably rebutted, we prefer to say that truth telling is not a genuine fundamental moral principle. Like the sanctity of life principle mentioned earlier, and other important moral principles such as "always keep your promises" and "never treat a person as a mere means to an end," the principle of truth telling is a secondary, rather than a fundamental moral principle.

Secondary moral principles, several of which are discussed below, are vitally important principles of moral reasoning, but they do not meet the requirements of basic or ultimate ethical principle. Their proper place and strategic function in moral reasoning can be best understood in the light of the suggested model of moral reasoning that follows.

A MODEL OF MORAL REASONING

Inherent in what has been said so far is a model or pattern of reasoning about ethical issues that must now be made explicit. This model, presented below in outline form, provides us with a way of reasoning, either from specific moral judgments to fundamental moral principles, or from fundamental moral principles to specific moral judgments.

Step 1: A clearly stated fundamental moral principle.

Step 2: Any relevant secondary principle or principles that seem applicable to the particular case.

Step 3: A sufficiently complete descriptive account of the essential features of the particular case under consideration.

Step 4: A moral judgment or decision concerning how we ought or ought not to act in the particular case at hand.

The use of the term *step* here may be misleading in that the model does not call for an orderly progression from step 1, through 2 and 3, to step 4. Very often our moral reflection begins with step 3: a serious problem which calls for a moral decision or judgment. If the case presented in step 3 is straightforward and we make a moral judgment that goes unchallenged, by others or even by ourselves, the matter may end there. If challenged, we are apt to appeal to any one of a number of secondary principles that apply to the case at hand and say no more. But when the secondary principle is challenged, for instance by a counterexample, the need for a higher court of appeal, a more ultimate principle, presents itself. When all is said and done, however, it should be possible, at least theoretically, to set forth the entire process in terms of the four steps in the model.

The model is not a strictly deductive model in which movement is from premises 1, 2, and 3, to a conclusion, 4, though it appears to be just that. The relationship of fundamental and secondary principles to steps 3 and 4 is one of applying principles to particular cases and specific judgments, in much the same way in which a color chart is applied to the walls of a room or a yardstick to measure the length of a desk.

It is a virtue of this model that it functions in the same way no matter what fundamental and secondary moral principles we plug into steps 1 and 2. The need for step 2 is primarily one of mediating between the highly abstract fundamental moral principle in step 1, such as to maximize happiness, and the facts of the particular case described in step 3 such as where the particular case involves truth telling. This is what was meant earlier when we said that a fundamental moral principle may be used to determine the applicability of secondary principles to a given particular case. Step 1 also serves the purpose of allowing us to range over a wide variety of particular cases without lapsing into inconsistencies. For example, if we reason that killing people is wrong (step 4), because "whenever and wherever possible everyone ought to try to preserve human life" (step 2), how could we justify a belief in capital punishment, killing in combat, euthanasia, suicide, or even self-defense? Unless we are able to show: (a) a reason for accepting the sanctity principle; and (b) a reason for applying it to murder but withholding it from these other cases, we may be drawn into an inconsistency in our moral beliefs.

CHOOSING A MORAL THEORY

A consistent and coherent set of moral beliefs is one of the benefits of having worked out a moral point of view for oneself or adopting a moral theory of some kind. Let us say that a moral theory consists of some fundamental moral principle or other, a set of arguments in support of the principle, as well as a set of replies to objections, actual or imagined, to the principle. If the primary or essential conditions to be fulfilled by the principle are consequences or outcomes of actions, a *consequentialist* theory exists, of which utilitarianism is one example. If the consequences of our actions are not given top priority, our theory is a deontological or *nonconsequentialist* theory. The theistic theory of ethics mentioned earlier, to do what pleases God no matter what the immediate consequences, is an example of such theory.

Since several major moral theories exist, a very difficult question arises: how can we decide which theory to adopt? We suggest some guidelines for the selection of a moral theory that, while neither infallible nor conclusive, will serve a useful purpose for the reader. Consider the following criteria for testing a moral theory:

Universalizability: The fundamental moral principle and the secondary moral principles must be universal in scope and application (along the lines suggested above).

Applicability: All the principles in a moral theory must have application, direct or indirect, to the moral issues we face in life.

Consistency: A moral theory cannot require us to both do and refrain from doing the same thing at the same time, and it cannot justify contradictory conduct at different times.

Possibility: A moral theory cannot oblige us to do what we cannot possibly do, given our best effort.

Accountability: A moral theory that takes the rich data of moral experience into account in the fullest measure is better than one only partially doing so.

Intersubjectivity: A moral theory that accords with the considered moral judgments of competent moral judges is generally to be preferred to a theory which does not do so.

These six standards or guidelines can be disputed, and there may be room for additional suggestions. Moreover, they reflect a slight bias on our part for what is generally considered to be a reasonable, reflective person point of view. Nonetheless, we offer them as suggestions and invite readers to question or modify them as seems appropriate. In Part IV, we will reexamine what has been said. However, some understanding of what moral reasoning is generally thought to involve and some ideas as to how to evaluate various moral theories are necessary at the outset. We now proceed to a consideration of some major moral theories as presented in the vast literature of the field of ethics.

MORAL THEORIES
AND MORAL AGENTS

There is perhaps no substitute for a full blown course in ethics, or at least the careful reading of a text exclusively devoted to moral theories, but we can effectively introduce several major ethical theories in a manner sufficient for our purposes in this inquiry. Chapter 1 presented a conceptual framework for moral reasoning and it was clear that moral principles play a key role in such reasoning. We now present some examples of general moral theories or moral points of view, each of which embodies ethical principles. The theories presented are major moral theories found in the current literature on ethics.

MAJOR MORAL THEORIES

Theism

One moral theory with a very long history and current widespread popularity in a large section of society is *theism*. Theistic ethics has taken several diverse forms over the years, but its central claim has always been that one should please God or do whatever God wills. This is often called the Divine Will theory (Brunner, 1932). It does not matter whether one thinks that God is love and loving is doing God's will, or that God's will is expressed through the course of human events occurring in history, or that God's will is directly revealed to believers. The point is that moral obligation is grounded on what some Divine Being is thought to want. Usually, theists, such as St. Thomas Aquinas, hold that God is the ultimate repository of goodness: God is good, creates good, and provides good things for people. In this way it is fairly clear how a theory of value can be tied to a theory of obligation. It is also important to see that, while obeying or following the Divine Will is the fundamental moral principle of the theist, there can be and often is a set of secondary moral principles in the theory as well. Some theists take the 10 commandments to be secondary principles, while others might include sayings or prescriptions from literature or traditional moral rules of society.

Several problems face this approach to ethics. The sometimes vast and varied interpretations of what it is that God wants us to do, especially when we get down to specifics, is a source of dispute and confusion in this tradition. Of course, it is a moral theory that will have no appeal whatever to nonbelievers, and it seems to be almost irrelevant to many people who claim to be believers as well. That is, many people who say they believe in a Divine Being seem to base their moral conclusions on reasoning that has little or nothing to do with an attempt to discover what God would want in a given situation.

Furthermore, the theistic theory faces a conceptual difficulty that cannot be easily overlooked. For if the theist says that an action is right because God wills it, we may want to know why God wills that action and not some other. If the theist answers that God wills it because it is good or right, this would mean that what is right is already set. If so, God cannot be the determiner, or creator, of rightness. And yet, if we say that these actions are right because God willed them, we are forced to conclude that what is right is a purely arbitrary matter, as far as humans go. That is, even if we see some very horrible event taking place replete with blood, gore, and the slaughter of innocents, we cannot judge the rightness or wrongness of it as far as God is concerned. If God wills or establishes rightness, and there is no way for us to determine rightness independently, then we are left without a means of judging which acts are right and which are wrong.

In spite of these objections, the moral principle that we are obliged to do whatever God wills is not without its supporters, and it remains a viable principle for some moralists. Theists have satisfied themselves that most if not all of the problems with theistic ethics can be met, and this is a matter for individual readers to decide for themselves. Moreover, the theist can adopt any one of the following moral perspectives and claim that what they require is, in human terms, the best we can do by way of following the Divine Will.

Aristotleanism

A second moral theory that has a distinguished history is that of the ancient Greek philosopher Aristotle. The *Nicomachian Ethics* presents a theory of ethics based on the character of persons more than on subscription to an abstract principle. Aristotle held that people are by nature rational beings and are fulfilling their true function or purpose only when they are following the requirements of reason. The good person, for Aristotle, is the rational person, that is, the person who follows reason. If one repeatedly acts in a virtuous fashion, in Aristotle's view, subsequent right actions will build character, and eventually the individual will become morally strong and follow right conduct almost automatically. In this view, the good life is the rationally ordered life. If human beings want to be truly happy, they must follow their true (rational) nature. Aristotle's theory is a theory of virtues. The kinds of actions which are virtuous are discoverable by the use of reason. A good life is then a virtuous life, one in which the virtues are exercised. Some contemporary theorists have defended a current version of virtue theory in ethics (MacIntyre, 1981, Veatch, 1962), and those interested in such theory will want to examine these sources.

The critics of Aristotlean ethics have doubted that humans have the faculty of reason in Aristotle's sense, or at least that such an ability to reason has any moral significance. The dictates of reason seem to be as vague and conflicting as the determinations of Divine Will in the theory previously described. Some writers deny that human beings are by nature rational creatures, and emphasize other features of human nature as essential. Some even deny that there is such a thing as a universal human nature (Sartre, 1957). Furthermore, someone who takes rationality to be crucial and concludes that this is an exclusively human trait, one not possessed by lower forms of animal life, may be tempted to use animals in experimentation in ways that may seem morally objectionable. Even so, Aristotle's emphasis on virtue and character, and on being a good person leading the good life, are notions that might serve us in contemporary contexts and lead to better human conduct. We may still see the need to look elsewhere for guidance on moral decision making, however, and one place to look would be the works of the great 18th century moral philosopher Immanuel Kant.

Kantianism

Kant's most important contribution to contemporary moral thought is his famous categorical imperative. It requires that we act only in such a way as we can will that the maxim or rule covering our action be universally prescribed. That is, when contemplating an action we must always ask whether we are willing to have everyone act that way—especially when the action is one we would not want done to ourselves. Hence, for Kant, stealing is wrong because I cannot will that everyone engage in stealing—especially that others steal from me. I cannot universalize the maxim of an act of stealing, that is, will that stealing become a universal practice. So stealing is morally wrong.

The key elements in this point of view are will and reason. The will is central because it is a matter of my being able or unable to will that everyone act as I am acting. This is why Kant said that the only good thing is a good will. He took this a step further and said that unless I am exercising my will in the performance of my duty, my conduct does not have moral worth. All of us can act in accord with duty if such action is what we want to do anyway, but it takes a great deal of will, morally good will, to do our duty in contexts in which desire pulls us in the opposite direction. Reason enters by telling us what our duty is. We reason about the universal application of the maxim of our action and determine what is right for us to do. Following through is a matter of exercising a strong moral will—at least in those morally praiseworthy cases in which duty and desire are in conflict.

The application of this theory to the question of research involving human subjects would dictate that the scientist must be willing to be a participant in the experiment and be treated in exactly the same way as subjects. If the scientist is unwilling to be a subject-participant or to have loved ones be subjects, the Kantian would say that the experiment is morally wrong.

Few theories have been as influential to the subsequent development of moral thought as Kant's theory, and a great debt is owed to him for our present ideas concerning the moral point of view. Hardly a theory has been developed since Kant's day that does not take the notion of universalizability into account in some way or other. But Kant is not without his detractors. Some critics claim that the notion of the good as the *good will* is itself a murky and elusive concept. Others claim that the Kantian theory cannot account for conflicts arising from too strict an application of its fundamental moral principle. The case of the Jews hiding in my cellar in Nazi Germany comes up frequently. If I cannot will that everyone lie to me, then I cannot lie to the Nazi police, and so my reason tells me I must speak truthfully to them—even though that means certain death for those hiding in my cellar.

In spite of these drawbacks, we may want to keep the formal element of Kant's theory in mind in reasoning about ethical matters. That is, it should always be asked whether we would want our action to be generalized and to have that generalization made into a universal moral requirement to be followed by everyone. This use of the Kantian principle is still valuable as a check on our decisions, though it does not have to be taken and applied in the absolute sense that Kantians seem to have taken and applied it.

The Kantian notion of universalizability is a central feature of the concept of a universal ethical principle. This concept is influential in Kohlberg's (1964) theory of moral development. According to Kohlberg, the ability to reason about ethical matters at the level of universal ethical principles is the highest stage of moral development. He identifies six stages of moral development, through which individuals progress in sequence, though they may never reach the highest stages.

In the two earliest stages, right and wrong are largely matters of responding to punishment and reward, or bargaining concerning these experiences. The next two stages specify right and wrong in terms of accepted norms: social norms about good boys or girls at the third stage, legal norms about good citizens (law and order) at the fourth stage. A small percentage of people reach the next two stages, in which abstract principles are employed in reasoning about right and wrong: political or constitutional principles at the fifth stage, universal ethical principles at the sixth stage. The few who reach this stage reason in the manner of Kantians, though they need not be full-fledged Kantians.

In a recent critique of Kohlberg's theory, Gilligan (1982) argues that it only describes and conceptualizes the development of men, while women speak "in a different voice." In any case, a description or conceptualization of development cannot by itself tell us what is right and wrong. On the contrary, we will argue (in chapter 5) that conceptualizations often contain judgments of right and wrong.

Utilitarianism

A fourth moral theory, one mentioned a few times already, is the utilitarianism of Jeramy Bentham and John Stuart Mill. This theory has many and varied forms, but the general, more basic versions of it can be classified into two types: *act-utilitarianism* and *rule-utilitarianism*.

An act-utilitarian holds that everyone ought to always do whatever will maximize the happiness of all sentient beings affected by the particular act in question. Each and every action has to be scrutinized individually for the happiness-making consequences or pain-producing consequences it will probably have, and the one that maximizes happiness or pleasure is always to be chosen from among the alternatives available, including inaction. Act-utilitarianism gets in trouble in cases where it can be shown that goldbricking (everyone else pushes your car out of the mud while I only pretend to push it out) maximizes happiness; or in cases in which it would seem to maximize happiness to punish an innocent person, such as the feeble-minded beggar in *Les Miserables*.

To solve these and similar problems, some utilitarians have developed a rule-utility calculus in which the consequences of having a rule followed are considered, and acts are thought to be right acts if and only if they fall under a right rule, that is, a rule that maximizes happiness. The goldbricking case and the innocent beggar case are both handled by saying that the result of everyone following the goldbricking rule or the punishment of an innocent person rule would be unhappy, hence any act falling under either of these rules would be an immoral act.

One trouble with the rule-utilitarian approach, which takes up some of the Kantian emphasis on universalizing, is that we would then have a set of rules to follow that would disallow the exceptional cases in which it would seem to be right to waive the rules. Moreover, there are many actions that not everyone would either want to be able to engage in, and it seems ridiculous to have rules governing such actions. Still, it must be pointed out that in spite of these objections, utilitarianism is a powerful influence in present moral debates. In fact, it is not unreasonable to suggest, as Sidgwick did over a hundred years ago, that the moral reasoning of the average person and the highly educated alike is "latently or unconsciously utilitarian" (Sidgwick, 1874, p. 453). That is, most of us most of the time, in facing moral problems and issues, take into account the consequences produced by our actions for all those who are affected by them.

Ethical Egoism

A fifth theory, similar to the consequentialism of utilitarianism but with a much more individualistic emphasis, is ethical egoism. Ethical egoists, such as Medlin (1957), take as a fundamental principle that people ought to do whatever promotes or maximizes their own self-interest. This is not to say that everyone is selfish—for an ethical egoist need not hold that everyone is basically selfish. Nor is it to say that everyone will in fact look out for their own interests, for people sometimes do deliberate harm to themselves. It is rather to say that everyone ought to look out for their own self-interests. The term *self-interest* does not merely mean what one is interested in, or even what one thinks are one's best interests. Rather, it involves an obligation to pursue what is in fact in one's own best interests.

The best interests of an individual may be difficult to determine, but there are things that do count in this regard. One may find out from a doctor that, given the condition of one's body, a five mile walk every day is in one's best interests even though one may hate walking and disbelieve the medical report. Presumably, a case could be made for saying that it would be immoral from the ethical egoist's view for such an individual not to take the recommended daily walk. A similar line of reasoning could be used to determine that one ought not to smoke. On the positive side, we could argue that unless I give generously to charity or pay the full measure of my taxes, I am acting against my own long-range interests (enlightened self-interest), hence I have an obligation to do such things.

Ethical egoism runs into the most difficulty when it tries to handle cases in which one person's interests are in conflict with the interests of another in a deadlocked situation. If "ought" implies "can," and you and I are competing for the same promotion, how can I be obliged to want you to work at your best, which is in my interest as a consumer, while at the same time wanting the promotion myself? The conflict here may not have much significance, however, for the moral theory of ethical egoists it may only curtail their advice-giving activities. Most ethical egoists say that we are only accountable for what we can subjectively determine to be our obligations, given that we have done our best to find out what the outcome of our action will be. This has the odd result, however, of saying that what we sincerely think is our duty, based on the best determination available, may actually turn out to be morally forbidden when all things are eventually considered. On the other hand, ethical egoism does have the merit of taking full account of the individual interests of everyone concerned, including the principal agent. That account might rightfully include our own gains, prestige, position, and pocket-money—though we might hope that such purely selfish personal interests would not be the overriding factors.

The conceptual distinction between selfish and unselfish acts has been blurred somewhat by recent theorizing about *gene selfishness*. Sociobiologists Wilson (1975) and Dawkins (1976) are trying to show that apparently altruistic acts among animals (a bird endangering its own life by squawking warnings of approaching predators to other birds in the flock) are genetically based behaviors, like all other behaviors. Such acts are said to be instances of gene selfishness, that is, the altruistic bird is only doing whatever is most likely to perpetuate its own genetic structure.

This thesis does not entail accepting ethical egoism as the best moral theory. First, all behavior is species specific. We cannot fly like birds, but we can make music. We can learn to trip people or to help those who have fallen. Precisely because of our human genes, we can learn either behavior. Furthermore, regardless of whether Behavior X is easier or harder to learn than Behavior Y, human beings are capable of choosing to learn and to teach their children the harder behavior. Second, it is necessary to make some distinctions between evaluating behavior and theorizing about its causes. While our motives may be selfish in the sense of being ours, all our actions need not be condemned as selfish. Thus, we may do what feels good to us, but sometimes we feel good when we help others, while at other times, we feel good when we hurt them. In Part IV, we will return to some of the morally relevant questions raised by sociobiology and all other explanations of behavior, as we explore the overlapping concerns of psychology and ethics.

Moral Intuitionism

The sixth moral theory has the virtue of seeming to encompass many of the finer points of the previous theories surveyed. This theory might be called moral intuitionism, or more specifically, the prima facie duty theory. It is a theory less formal or reason-oriented than Kantianism and less consequence-oriented than both utilitarianism and ethical egoism. It sees the absolutism of Kant as overly rigorous, and the consequentialist theories as often in conflict with ordinary moral inclinations or intuitions. Instead, it is a theory emphasizing the personal character of our moral responsibilities. We feel, according to Ross (1930), that we have special duties to special persons by whom our own lives have been affected and toward those who have in fact contributed to the betterment of our lives. This means that what we ought to do is determined to some extent by what has actually happened to us. So this theory takes a look backward into the past, in addition to looking to the future, to see what sort of consequences will result.

At the heart of this theory are six moral principles, none of which seems to be more fundamental than any other. At first blush it would seem that this theory has no fundamental moral principle, but one can in fact be formulated. The six duties can be viewed as secondary principles intuited directly or in a prima facie way. According to this theory, we have a duty to fidelity, reparation, gratitude, beneficence, justice, and self-improvement.

The prima facie duty to fidelity is a duty to keep our promises and uphold confidences and trusts. The duty of reparation is the duty to right wrongs and make amends for misdeeds. The duty to gratitude is the duty to show appreciation for what others have done for us. Notice that these three duties are based on the previous actions of others and of ourselves— they are past-looking. The duty to beneficence is the utilitarian duty to maximize or promote the general welfare of others. The duty to justice is the duty to deal fairly and impartially with others. And the duty to self-improvement is a duty to better ourselves intellectually and morally. This is a form of enlightened self-interest or ethical egoism. The duties to be beneficient, just, and self-improving are future-oriented duties, since they emphasize the consequences of our actions. The fundamental moral principle of this theory can be stated as saying that it is always morally right for us to do whatever duty our moral intuition tells is primary or prima facie.

The trouble with this theory lies in its seemingly arbitrary list of duties or secondary principles. Someone might argue that we have a perfectly natural right to want to get revenge on our enemies for misdeeds, for instance, so why is there no duty to vengeance? Or, even if there is a duty to be beneficient, it could be argued that there are contexts in which we would have a duty not to harm—a duty to nonmaleficence. Why not include it on our list? Moreover, how are we to handle cases in which the duty to keep a promise conflicts with an equally compelling duty to self-improvement? Will not the result be a quietism of some sort?

It may even be argued that moral intuitionism cannot provide a satisfactory justification for our particular moral judgments. Perhaps our intuitions are merely the result of socialization or conditioning that we have received in this or that society, as opposed to being inherent in human nature and hence common to all humans. Some philosophers have maintained, however, that moral intuitions are a part of the common sense of all mankind. Reid (1857, p. 363), for example, held that our moral intuitions were "the gift of Heaven" to all humans capable of moral reasoning. And James (1907, p. 170) held that "our fundamental ways of thinking about things are discoveries of exceedingly remote ancestors, which have been able to preserve themselves throughout the experience of all subsequent time." More recently, Gert (1970) has argued that a large part of traditional morality can be justified as a system of rules that it would be irrational for human beings living in society not to adopt. Whether they result from socialization, are the legacy of our ancestors, or are the gift of God, certain moral intuitions, like the immorality of cold-blooded murder, are very widely held, and they do play a role in our ethical reflections. We will return to this issue in Part IV.

An important feature of moral intuitionism, lies in its emphasis on what we earlier called "secondary moral principles" (see Chapter 1). Our model of moral reasoning features secondary moral principles as a vital step, step 2, in most instances of moral reasoning. Since many of our everyday conversations about moral matters involve direct appeals to such principles, rather than the six or so more foundational principles, and since the emphasis throughout this book is on them, an entire section of this chapter is devoted to them (see below).

The Rawlsian Theory

The seventh and final theory in our brief survey of major ethical viewpoints, is the theory presented by John Rawls in *A Theory of Justice* (1971). Rawls is mainly concerned with a satisfactory account of individual rights and liberties, and his principles of social justice are designed to provide such an account. Offering essentially a social contract theory, Rawls argues that his principles of justice would be accepted by any rational and free agent contemplating the optimal conditions for group living from a neutral vantage point outside any actual social context. He calls this "the original position." Shielded by a "veil of ignorance" from the particular features of their actual situations, individuals in this hypothetical situation would endorse principles of justice that would not be biased in their own favor.

Rawls believes that two principles would be accepted in such circumstances: (1) people should have the maximum amount of basic liberty compatible with a similar and equal liberty for all, and (2) given the equal liberty of all, inequalities of income or opportunities are justified only when they benefit all parties and if everyone has had equal access to them. Clearly, the central concept in this theory is the concept of equality. His second principle, for instance, allows unequal distribution of basic goods on the proviso that equal liberty and equal or fair opportunity have been secured first. Such inequalities, Rawls argues, are justified whenever it can be shown that they actually work to benefit those in society who are the worst off. Thus, even though this theory is deontological in tone, calling for the rigorous application of its two central principles of social justice, it also seems to involve a covert appeal to consequences in its attempts to determine right from wrong.

It could be argued that the hypothetical nature of the so-called "original position" does not guarantee a rational, unbiased analysis, because it forces us to rely too much on idle speculation from a viewpoint none of us can assume. Whatever objections we may raise to this theory, there can be little doubt that it has offered a provocative basis for moral reflection in recent years.

SECONDARY MORAL PRINCIPLES

The following principles are considered secondary only in the sense that they can be overruled by a more ultimate or fundamental moral principle, and only because they are content-specific, that is, they refer to a particular class or kind of actions in each case. They are not secondary in the sense of being unimportant or second-rate. Some moral theorists have even tended to treat some of them as ultimate. We should at least look upon them as integral to moral reflection and subsumable under some more general moral principle or principles, such as those described earlier as fundamental moral principles.

The principle of veracity requires that we tell the truth to others.

The principle of privacy requires that we respect the person and property of others by not violating (stealing or damaging) these things.

The principle of autonomy requires that we respect the right of others to determine their own fates and destinies.

The principle of promise-keeping calls upon us to keep the promises we make to others.

The principle of paternalism (or parentalism) requires us to care for and safeguard the interests of those who cannot do so for themselves.

The principle of self-improvement requires us to improve our mental and physical well-being.

The principle of nonmaleficence requires that we do no willful harm to others.

The principle of equality requires that we treat everyone equally unless there is good reason for doing otherwise.

The sanctity of life principle requires us to treat all living things as intrinsically valuable.

The principle of gratitude requires that we respond with appreciation to the good things others do for us.

The principle of reparation requires that we compensate for the evil we may have done to others.

The principle of liberty requires that we grant the maximum amount of freedom (consistent with the liberties of everyone) to other individuals.

There is nothing sacrosanct about this particular list of secondary principles, and some of them surely overlap with each other. But this list will serve as a reasonably good account of the sort of principles we have in mind when we refer to secondary moral principles. It is reasonable to believe that most people who reflect on ethical issues are willing to accept most of the above principles to some extent, even if only in a conditional or provisional fashion.

MORAL DILEMMAS

The attempt to rely exclusively on secondary principles in moral reasoning is likely to produce conflicts or dilemmas. "Today one says somewhat loosely that a person is in a dilemma when the person must choose between two alternatives, both of which are bad or unpleasant" (Copi, 1982, p. 268). When the alternatives are moral ones, and when we have good reasons for choosing or not choosing each of them, we have a moral dilemma. For example, if someone subscribes to the principle of nonmaleficence and to the principle of veracity, then the question of telling a lie to avoid hurting someone's feelings versus hurting someone to avoid telling a lie represents a genuine moral dilemma. Similarly, a psychologist may experience a conflict with the promise to keep all conversations confidential when it appears that the disclosure of certain information will be in the best interests of the client or others. This is the sort of dilemma the Tarasoff case presented.

Some apparent moral dilemmas are dissolved when one sees that the stated alternatives do not exhaust all possibilities. Perhaps the psychologist in the above example could discuss the problem with the client, and the client would agree to a particular disclosure. Other apparent dilemmas are dissolved by showing that the bad or unpleasant consequences are either not the only ones, or that they are not as bad or unpleasant as expected.

In moral reasoning we can sometimes handle a moral dilemma by appealing to a principle higher than the secondary principles that generated the conflict. Depending on which moral theory or fundamental moral principle one subscribes to, and depending on the full facts of the particular case, one may reason that in the interests, of, for instance, maximizing happiness, the principle of veracity can be justifiably overridden in this case because acting on the principle of nonmaleficence will lead to the greatest happiness. In other circumstances, the principle of nonmaleficence may have to be overridden. Consistency is maintained by the application of the fundamental moral principle employed. The model of moral reasoning may not always work this neatly, but it frequently does provide a way of advancing beyond the conflicting (secondary) principles in question. It also illustrates the importance of acquiring an understanding of moral theories and frameworks and, in particular, the moral point of view we as individuals have adopted.

Once we have adopted a particular moral point of view, much of our moral reasoning in psychology, for instance, will involve its application to ethical issues facing anyone interested in the activities of psychologists. There may be moral principles and moral points of view beyond those presented above, or the individual reader may prefer some fresh combination of the major moral theories presented. In any event, the structure of moral reasoning used and the salient notions involved are likely to be very close to those we have considered.

The bottom line is that none of us stands outside the moral world. There is no morally neutral point of view. However muddled and partial it may be in any particular person, there is some moral point of view or perspective involved in everyone's thoughts about ethical issues. The choice of a moral theory itself may be ours to make, but the option of being completely indifferent to moral issues is not available to anyone who engages in the daily activities of even the most ordinary life. We are thus all equals in the sense that we are all moral agents.

MORAL AGENTS

The claim that we are all equals in the sense that we are all moral agents, raises some vitally important questions. The most basic one is about the nature of moral agency itself: are children, babies, fetuses, the insane, the retarded, the senile, and lower forms of animal life moral agents? If they are not, then what is a moral agent? Secondly, how should moral agents treat those who do not appear to be their equals in certain important respects? To what extent and in what fashion are we responsible for those who are presumably nonagents?

The conception of a moral agent implicit in everything we have said is that *a moral agent is a person who is able to make free choices about alternative courses of action and who is capable of knowing the difference between right and wrong.* Such persons can be held accountable for their actions. This is roughly the notion of responsibility used in most legal systems. It assumes that the choices we may be held responsible for making are free choices, at least in the sense that clearly discernible constraints, either external or internal, are absent. An external constraint involves confinement or coercion by

other persons or physical situations, such as being overpowered by someone who is very strong, or being locked in a room. An internal constraint
involves some overwhelming internal obsession or passion over which one
has no control. A moral agent is able to understand the various options
available, and has a sense of their rightness or wrongness (at least from the
agent's viewpoint, if not the general viewpoint of society). Thus, a moral
agent is someone who knows what he or she is doing, has the ability to
choose to do or not do it, and knows the difference between right and
wrong at least from a personal viewpoint. We might add that it is pre-
sumed that the individual is capable of understanding that (but not necessarily why) others think certain forms of conduct are wrong.

Moral agents can be reasonably held responsible for their actions. We
may take criminally insane persons off the streets and place them into
institutions, and, in this sense, we are holding them legally responsible for
their misdeeds, but we do not hold them morally responsible. Moral responsibility involves a morally significant response to situations and it is
virtually impossible for some people to respond morally. Such people are
not moral agents—at least not in certain situations. This way of defining a
moral agent also eliminates fetuses, babies, very small children, some retarded people, and most, if not all, lower forms of animal life. If any of
these agents sometimes appear to meet the standards of a morally responsible agent, we should be willing to say that they acted as moral agents on
such occasions. For example, we might want to say this if a chimpanzee
had rescued a small child from drowning in a swimming pool (in a context
in which the chimp appeared to choose). But such events are very rare, if
they occur at all.

Moral responsibility, like legal responsibility, admits of degrees. The
minimal conception of a morally responsible agent involves knowing what
one is doing, making choices, and knowing the difference between the
rightness or wrongness of one's actions. It does not require the ability to
give moral reasons, or to produce moral principles of some sort, as justification for such actions. A minimal moral agent may know, for example,
that shoplifting is wrong, but may not understand why it is wrong. Presumably, we would hold a minimal moral agent less responsible than
someone who is capable of the sort of moral reasoning outlined in Chapter
2. This is why judges, lawyers, professors, physicians, psychologists,
clergy and teachers are held more accountable, morally speaking, than the
untrained and the illiterate.

Corresponding to the degree of moral responsibility is the degree of
moral praise or moral blame, and perhaps degree of reward and punishment, applied to the actions of moral agents. Obviously, there are problems with notions that admit of degrees, since at some point or other the
elements must shade into each other. For example, it might be very difficult to discern a child's degree of accountability. It would not follow from

such difficulties, however, that we are completely preempted from assigning praise and blame, reward and punishment in every context. Moral praise and blame are notions that we do in fact wield in everyday discourse, however uncertain we may be about some of the gray areas.

MORAL EQUALS

In arguing that, barring very exceptional circumstances, fetuses, babies, and lower forms of animal life are not genuine moral agents, we are saying that they are not moral equals with moral agents. But while the inequality in question bears on the issues of agency and responsibility, it does not settle the vitally important issue of equal treatment. If someone holds that there is a right to life, for example, it would not follow from our view of moral agency that only genuine moral agents have this right. Similar remarks could be made about harmful treatment of subjects used in scientific experiments, many of whom are the weak and the helpless (see Chapter 10).

The principle of equality, as Aristotle understood it 2,000 years ago, and as it is still generally understood in our own times, is that "equals should be treated equally, and unequals should be treated unequally" (*Aristotle,* 1941, p. 1006). This rather abstract formulation of the principle of equality says nothing about how to determine who the equals or the unequals are, nor does it tell us what differences of treatment should be between these two groups. Such a principle is meaningless apart from a context in which such issues are answered. The equality principle cannot serve as a fundamental moral principle because it contains absolutely no specification of the conditions to be fulfilled for a moral obligation to obtain. But the principle is vitally important as a component part of a moral theory or point of view.

The concept of equality in ethics, as in geometry, is a purely *relational* concept. Nothing is equal all by itself, but always equal to something else. And two things that are equal in one sense (John and Mary are both college students) may be unequal in many other respects (height, age, religion, hobbies). So the notion of equality, in ethics at least, also requires that we state the respect or sense in which the items compared are said to be equal. Moreover, treating people as equals requires that the persons involved are determined to be equals in some clearly relevant respect. For example, that John and Mary are equal as college students is relevant to their right to vote in a student election. In contrast, their being unequal in height is not relevant to this right.

One final point about the principle of equality. If we decide that genuine moral agents are equals with respect to ability, intelligence, and responsibility and that others (nonmoral agents) are not their equals in these respects, what follows? One obvious thing is that in treating equals equally and unequals unequally, we will often hold moral agents responsible for doing the very same thing that nonmoral agents do, while treating the latter in some entirely different fashion. Thus, it is one thing when a two-year-old hurts someone, quite another when a scientist does so. Some people unfortunately seize upon the differences between the agents in question in order to engage in abusive practices. Thus, children, the unborn, and the mentally incompetent may sometimes be exploited as subjects of research by scientists who would never dream of trying these experiments with subjects who are not as weak and helpless. This might even occur when the experiments have nothing to do with intelligence or social adjustment, such as in the case of dermatological experiments at a mental hospital.

At the opposite extreme, ethicists like Ramsey (1975) insist on the principle that we must always protect and preserve the weak and helpless. This principle, taken by itself, may lead to a blanket prohibition against such practices as experimentation on babies. Consequently, we may want to limit its application by appeal to some higher, more fundamental moral principle. The main virtue of Ramsey's principle, however, is that it calls attention to the need for special care in dealing with those unable to fend for themselves. If special care is warranted, the principle of equality requires that it be given to all those to whom it is due—that equals be treated as equals. If it is argued that the weak and the helpless are not deserving of special care or treatment, then the equality principle requires us to treat them on a par with everyone else. To take this a step further, we might want to insist that all research involving human subjects involve an application of the principle that researchers treat research subjects as their own moral equals. In the Milgram experiment, it would require Milgram and his colleagues to ask themselves whether they would want to be treated in exactly the same fashion in which they treated the subjects in the experiment. The principle of equality has an important role to play in ethical reflection, and its consistent application accords very well with our sense of fair play.

SUMMATION

In this chapter, several major moral theories and their fundamental moral principles have been considered. The reader will want to reflect on these theories in the light of the guidelines for adopting a moral theory presented at the end of Chapter 1. We do not provide a single coherent moral theory in this book, but no matter which moral theory the reader adopts, that moral point of view will have to take into account the dozen or more secondary moral principles underlying everyday moral discourse. We saw how these secondary principles, by themselves, often form the basis of moral dilemmas, the resolution of which may require an appeal to fundamental moral principles.

Adopting a moral theory, complete with secondary moral principles, and applying it along lines suggested in our model of moral reasoning, makes us moral agents. Our analysis of moral agency, in this chapter, pointed out the fact that some human beings are not moral agents in the full-blown sense of the term, and most nonhuman animals are also non-agents in this sense. But that does not mean that they are insignificant or unimportant in the reflections of genuine moral agents. On the contrary, we will have special obligations toward them in certain circumstances. The principle of equal treatment of moral equals, and special treatment of those not our moral equals, has an important role to play in the reflection of those who are conscientiously taking the moral point of view.

But not everyone takes the moral point of view. In the next chapter, we consider three ways in which the whole idea of taking the moral point of view has been called into question.

3

CHALLENGES TO
THE MORAL POINT
OF VIEW

What can we say about those members of society who decide not to play fair? Suppose someone says "I know what it means to adopt the moral point of view, to act on principle and engage in moral reflection, but that's a losing game. Good guys finish last! Everyone would act immorally if they could get away with it." Let's call this the immoralist's challenge and see if it can be met. This challenge was presented in story form by Glaucon, a philosophical opponent of Plato, in Plato's *Republic* (1945, part II, book II, chapter 5).

THE IMMORALIST'S CHALLENGE

Glaucon tells the story of a shepherd, Gyges, who is employed by the king to tend his flocks. One of Gyges' sheep goes astray and Gyges sets out in search of it. Along the way he comes upon a great opening in the earth and, looking down into the opening, he sees a large dead horse. Gyges climbs down into the hole and approaches the dead animal. As he nears it, he notices a large opening in the side of the dead horse. Looking inside, Gyges sees a man lying still and straight (either dead or unconscious). The man is naked except for a ring on one of his fingers. Gyges removes the ring and places it on his own finger. Later, in a gathering with his friends, Gyges notices that the others begin to speak about him as if he were not present. This phenomenon, he observes, occurs whenever he has turned the newly acquired ring around on his finger so that the crown is not visible to the others. This discovery makes Gyges very happy, and he leaves his flock, heads straight for the palace, where he seduces the beautiful queen, murders the king, and takes over the wealth and power of the kingdom.

Glaucon's point is that the only reason people behave morally is fear of reprimand or punishment from others, and once that fear is removed (by the magic ring) human beings are going to throw away the moral standards they normally follow and serve their own selfish interests and advantages. All people are fundamentally immoral, in other words, and there is no good reason for acting morally if one does not have to. The immoralist is simply asking: Why be moral?

The question, Why be moral? is not as simple and straightforward as it looks. In fact, it contains a fundamental ambiguity, as was pointed out by Frankena (1973). He argued that this question might be taken as either a request for a motivation, on the one hand, or a justification, on the other. The answer given to it will be quite different depending on the sense we attach to the question.

As a request for a motivation for being moral, the inquirers are asking for essentially psychological reasons that will motivate them to act the way they believe they ought to act. If their request is for a motivational reason, not a moral reason, there is little else we can do but show them that there are various prudential as well as nonprudential reasons for being moral. They may face the alienation of others, lose their jobs, or be denied the sorts of advantages that go with having a good reputation. If they are not motivated by any of these punishments and rewards, there is not much chance of success with them. Moreover, it would be difficult to convince persons in Gyges' position (as king) that it would be to their personal advantage to have remained as pauper-shepherds. Most people are likely to respond to threats and inducements in much the same way Gyges did before finding the ring. But the threat of punishment does not fulfill the standards of justification introduced in Chapter 1. It is not the sort of reason that would satisfy the reasonable, reflective individual. Consider someone who says, "I don't commit murder only because I do not want to go to prison. If I weren't afraid of that, I wouldn't think twice about murdering people."

What is usually sought, in asking why one should be moral is for some sort of rationale that would justify adopting the moral point of view, when rejecting it would be clearly to one's advantage. In requesting a justification for being moral, the inquirer may be seeking either a moral justification, or a nonmoral justification for being moral. If one is asking for a moral justification, one is really only asking, Why morally ought I to do what I morally ought to do? If this is what is being asked, the answer is that the very fact that a certain piece of conduct is morally right is all the moral reason one needs and can hope for to do that thing. But usually it is a nonmoral reason that is wanted. So our question—Why choose to be moral—comes down to a request for a nonmoral justification, not a motivation, for adopting the moral point of view.

At this level we may want to divide the question into two stages: one applying to society as a whole, and one applying to the individual in society.

If our question is, Why should society adopt the moral point of view? the answer is that doing so is a necessary condition for human beings living together in groups. A shared morality is the basis for social order, and its absence would result in chaos and grief for all members. The state of affairs of no morality at all was vividly portrayed by Hobbes (1651). With no morality and no legal system, society would consist of a loose amalgamation of individuals constantly at each other's throats. It would be a state of "the war of every individual against every individual" (Hobbes, p. 101). There would be no right and wrong, no justice, no civilization, and no art or culture. Distrust and greed would be the cardinal rules of thumb, and insecurity and fear would be the order of the day. To quote Hobbes, life in such a state would be "solitary, poor, nasty, brutish, and short" (p. 100).

But what if some hypothetical individual, say Tom Owen, upon hearing these words, says that he agrees 100 percent that society should adopt the moral point if view, but wants to know why he should adopt it? (Keep in mind that, at this point in our analysis, he is asking for a nonmoral justification). Owen may go on to say that the adoption of a moral point of view by society is exactly what he is counting on, because when he goes to the bank he wants to find that trusting souls have been naive enough to leave their money there for him to steal, and when he gets that money home he is glad that his neighbors are too honest to enter his house and steal it from him. So why should he be moral, when being immoral is so much more to his advantage?

Again, we cannot hope to show Tom Owen that being moral will always be to his advantage, or even that it will almost always be so. What we can do is ask him to decide what sort of life he wants: one that is open and honest, or one that is based on deception and secrecy? We can try to appeal to his sense of fair play by asking him why he thinks that others should make sacrifices for the good of all—and for his good specifically—when he makes no sacrifices at all for their good. We should try to get him to think of the consequences of everyone doing what he does, and the inconsistency of his not wanting these things done to him. If he acknowledges that these are reasons for being moral, but asks why he should follow such reasons—be reasonable—we can point out to him that if he will not accept some such reasons for being moral he has no business asking for them in the first place. When Owen begins with "Why should . . . ," he is requesting reasons, and to reject all reasons as counting against his immorality is to lapse into inconsistency and irrationality. If we are no longer dealing with a rational person (see Part IV) argumentation is rendered useless. We might as well try to convince paranoids that everyone is not out to get them. In other words, the problem we are faced with is psychological rather than philosophical at this point, and psychological help is the sort of help he will have to have. Moral thinking, after all, is a type of thinking, and those for whom reasons no longer count are persons who have stepped outside the arena of reasoning about ethical questions— though not outside the domain of making moral judgments in their personal lives.

THE RELATIVIST'S CHALLENGE

A second challenge to the moral point of view comes from the moral relativist, who challenges the objectivity of moral conclusions. Moral or ethical relativism can be understood in a number of different ways or at various levels of application. Properly speaking:

> The relativist recognizes: first, the importance of the social environment in determining the content of beliefs both about what is and what ought to be the case; and, second, the possible diversity of such social environments. To be a relativist about value is to maintain that there are no universal standards of good and bad, right and wrong. (Flew, 1979, p. 281)

The concept of ethical relativism that is featured in this definition is one that we can call *cultural normative moral relativism*. It is what social scientists have in mind when they describe the nature of morals in a particular society in terms of socially approved and socially learned habits of conduct. Each society has a shared set of acceptable behavior patterns it teaches the younger members of its group. Different societies or cultures have different social habits, and one interpretation of this is to call it moral relativism. What is considered right in Saudia Arabia (polygamy) is not considered right in most Western countries.

That different cultures have different moral standards cannot be denied, once it is established by empirical observation. In fact, the essential notion of this form of relativism can be extended to an intramural relativism within particular societies. In one and the same social setting there might be a diversity of backgrounds, ethnic orientations, economic influences, and religious commitments. These diverse elements may bring moral influences to bear on individuals belonging to subgroups within the society, even though the morality of that society as a whole might be singular and intact. Under the generally accepted moral standards of the American people, for example, there is the morality of the ghetto, the morality of the business world, and the morality of this or that religious group.

Going a step further, we could extend the phenomenon of moral relativism to each and every individual in any given society. Moral relativism is no longer a social doctrine at this level, but a notion taken to describe the individual differences among persons in any given society. *Individual moral relativism* holds that right and wrong are not only relative to societal conditions, or even to groups within society, but to this and that individual in every society. This point of view is usually expressed by saying that as long as you do not interfere with me or harm me, you can do whatever you please. Unlike cultural normative relativism, this form of relativism rejects all rules or norms of conduct as applicable to everyone, even everyone in a particular society, as long as no one gets hurt. The individual may have rules of right conduct for himself or herself, but these rules do not apply, indeed must not be applied, to other individuals. The fear might be that others will apply their rules to us, if we dare impose ours on them. Individual moral relativism, then, is the attempt to secure as much personal freedom from the meddlesome interferences of others as possible. To the individual moral relativist that would seem to be a good thing.

What then is wrong with moral relativism? Perhaps nothing, but we won't know that unless we first ask ourselves some questions about it. Let us begin with individual moral relativism and move beyond it to consider cultural moral relativism. Perhaps there are difficulties both forms of relativism face in common, but that is a conclusion to which we can only come piecemeal.

Individual Moral Relativism

This form of relativism leaves open the possibility, however remote, that every member of society may have a different moral viewpoint, and hence there would be no shared morality. If this occurred, it would mean that a legal system would not be possible, since there would be no common beliefs for it to express and enforce. Since most members of society participate in a common or nearly similar set of learning experiences or socialization, however, a genuinely individual form of moral relativism is not very probable.

If the individual moral relativist says that people should be allowed to do or believe whatever they wish when it comes to moral matters, so long as no one gets harmed either physically or mentally, what we have is not really moral relativism after all. That is, the person holding this point of view has adopted a very definitive moral principle: the principle of nonmaleficence (do no harm). This principle itself is sometimes viewed as the flip side of the utilitarian principle of maximizing happiness. It requires that all persons refrain from doing harm to others at all times, for to do harm is to do what one ought not do. Of course, proponents of this principle very often do not even take it literally, for if they did, they would have to refrain from defending themselves against assailants, in the interests of not harming them.

What is usually behind the "you do your own thing and I'll do mine" ethical relativism is just that: a laissez-faire attitude. We don't really think that "anything goes," and would be quick to say so if threatened by a gang rape. We don't really think that everyone should refrain from harming everyone in all situations, and we show this by calling a policeman when threatened by a gang of thugs. What we really hope to stake out by insisting on individual relativism is a region of personal life space into which no uninvited guests may intrude. Usually, the types of actions included in this private region are items appearing to affect the individual alone—taking drugs, getting drunk, engaging in sexual activities with other consenting parties. As long as relativists see these acts as bringing no harm to others, they want to tell society to keep hands off. A little serious reflection, however, will show that there are very few acts that do not affect others in some way. One could secure the sort of individual liberty needed to justify allegedly self-regarding actions by appealing to Mill's principle of liberty, or the principle of privacy, and ultimately to the principle of utility or some such fundamental moral principle. To make appeals to such universal ethical principles is de facto to have moved beyond ethical relativism.

Cultural Normative Relativism

The social scientist can tell us whether it is true that different moral norms are to be found in different cultures around the world, and in the same culture at different periods of time throughout its history. The matter is purely empirical and can be settled by observation. The fact that a man can have many wives in one culture, but only one in another is sufficient to illustrate the kind of relevant cultural differences at issue.

Let us say that cultural variation in moral norms is a fact and simply accept it. We can then say that cultural differences in the way people are raised will help to explain their reasons for doing what they do, but explanation, as we saw earlier, is not justification when it comes to evaluating moral matters. If we accept cultural normative relativism as the last word in ethics, we are likely to make the mistake of confusing what is with what ought to be. Hume (1740) pointed out a long time ago that one cannot get an *ought* conclusion from premises which are entirely *is*. A value cannot be deduced from a fact. To do so is to confuse *prescription* with *description*. So, from the fact that the many nations of the world might embrace very different moral values and standards, it does not follow that it is morally right for them to do so.

Moreover, there may not be as many differences among cultures throughout the world as first appear (Kroeber & Kluckholn, 1952). Just as in our society there is much more moral solidarity than individual moral relativism would at first seem to suggest, so, too, there is a great deal more agreement than we might imagine among the world's cultures. For example, it is widely believed that certain acts of assault and aggression, at least among equals, are wrong. Acts of kindness, on the other hand, are widely accepted as right or praiseworthy. It does not follow that such judgments are absolute, or that they have some sort of basis in the nature of things, or in the divine mind. Rather, it means only that in fact there is a certain degree of moral solidarity among the peoples of the earth, and this may be as close to moral absolutism as we can ever expect to get. It was suggested earlier that this moral solidarity might have its roots in common sense moral intuitions that the members of all civilized societies, past and present, seem to share. We will return to an examination of common sense thinking in Part IV.

Of course, we are asking a factual question when we ask whether there is moral solidarity (and how much, if there is any) in the world. But ethics does not deal with empirical issues as such. We must always be careful not to confuse description with prescription, "what is, has been and will be" with "what ought to be," or fact with value. Ethics is not concerned with the way the world is, per se, but with the way the world ought to be. Ethical reflection produces ideals toward which we should move if we are not already there, so that cultural normative relativism could be acknowledged as a correct description of the world in which we live without our accepting that this is the way things should be. Acknowledging the truth of cultural ethical relativism does not preclude the transcendence of this perspective to a more sophisticated level of thought in terms of which we can make moral judgments, moral decisions, and moral evaluations that are universal in scope and applicability. If we can defend the possibility of universal ethical principles, not universal in the sense that everyone accepts them, but in the sense that they apply to all ethically significant situations equally, we will have come a long way from ethical relativism as ordinarily conceived. It may be that such universal ethical principles are self-chosen, and peculiar to the individuals who have chosen them, but this does not mean they are narrow, provincial, individualistic principles that cannot be applied to a wide range of situations in widely divergent times and places. These questions are confronted in greater detail in Part IV.

THE SUBJECTIVIST'S CHALLENGE

The third challenge to the moral point of view comes from those who hold that moral matters are highly subjective and emotional features of human experience. In the interest of being an unbiased and objective as possible, scientists try to keep these subjective and emotional features at a minimum. There is, in principle, nothing wrong with the attempt to eliminate emotion, prejudice and bias from our investigations—including in psychology, where the subject matter is often human behavior. But these critics of the moral point of view tend to take this ideal to its extreme. They argue that, since emotional ethical issues cannot be objectified and quantified, they are totally irrelevant to the activities of scientists, including psychologists qua social scientists.

The roots of this scientism in psychology can perhaps be traced to the influence of the logical positivists. They insist that all factual claims that cannot be empirically verified (those based on observations or sense perceptions) are meaningless and, hence, unknowable, in the strict sense of knowing. Since ethical statements make claims that cannot be verified and quantified in a scientific or at least empirical fashion, the positivists conclude that such statements have no place in considerations of what can be known. Such claims may be meaningful in some other way, but they are not meaningful in the sense needed for genuine knowledge. Thus, in the interest of being scientific, many psychologists may try to ignore or eliminate from their investigation any claims that have to do with morality.

We do not wish to enter here into the philosophical debates about the nature of knowledge, since these would take us too far afield from our subject matter. For our purposes, it does not matter which view of the possibility of moral knowledge one takes. In subsequent chapters we will simply try to demonstrate the importance of ethical considerations for the activities of psychologists. In fact, we maintain that their attempt at moral neutrality is doomed to failure.

Moreover, psychologists who are seduced by the positivistic paradigm are likely to ignore some very fruitful dimensions of human behavior, including their own, if they try to rule all ethical considerations out of court. The reader who does not find these claims convincing at this point is asked to withhold judgment until the end of the book before dismissing them as nonsense. In the meantime, we will try to show that much is to be gained, and very little is lost, by allowing our ethical reflections to have full rein as we enter the world of the psychologist.

THE
ACTIVITIES
OF
PSYCHOLOGISTS

PART II

It is hard to delineate the field of psychology without revealing what kind of psychologist one is. In general, psychologists are interested in why living creatures do what they do under a variety of circumstances and conditions. More specifically, psychology includes such areas as learning, perception, cognition, motivation, emotion, development, personality, behavior problems, psychobiology, testing, and attitudes.

SCIENCE AND ETHICS

Most psychologists attempt to be as scientific as possible in trying to answer questions in their area. That is why Milgram, for example, in studying obedience, tried to observe behaviors under a variety of conditions instead of either assuming that everybody already knew about as common a phenomenon as obedience, or that people are able to predict and understand their own behaviors accurately. In other words, psychologists ask questions rather than assuming they already have the answers, and try to be scientific in their research.

Psychologists tend to be particularly interested in mammals, though research subjects include birds, worms, and roaches. Some psychologists say that they are mainly, if not exclusively, concerned about human beings.

Most psychologists are also concerned about the usefulness of the knowledge in their field. Information can have a great impact on both our thinking and our actions. Freud's ideas, like Darwin's, transformed our ways of thinking about ourselves. Some psychologists are more involved with using what is already known (in schools, business, industry, architecture, clinical practice, courts of law, prisons, nursing homes, mental institutions) than in searching for further knowledge. For others, the reverse is true. Since new applications are continually emerging (such as genetic counseling) the search for knowledge and the process of applying it are often intimately intertwined.

Both in terms of subject matter and methods, psychology overlaps with biology in the natural sciences, and with sociology in the social sciences. A study of the physiological mechanisms for learning, emotion, motivation, and psychopathology requires that psychologists understand and investigate the biological foundations of human behavior. An understanding of affiliation, person perception, aggression, attitude change, and conformity is essential to an accurate assessment of interpersonal or group behavior.

In terms of its subject matter, psychology shares concerns with several areas of the humanities as well. For example, literature and philosophy, especially applied areas of philosophy such as ethics, also deal with interpersonal relationships, attitudes, and emotions, although not necessarily in the same ways or for the same reasons or purposes (see Part IV).

As the Milgram and Tarasoff examples cited earlier make clear, psychologists are embroiled with ethical issues in many and complex ways. In fact, as we shall soon see, all activities of psychologists raise ethical questions. Whether choosing an area for research or practice, conceptualizing, gathering and sharing information with others, or applying what is already known, the psychologist engages in ethically significant matters—however unwittingly or unwillingly. Increasing and developing our awareness of these ethical issues is one of the central goals of this book.

PSYCHOLOGISTS' PROFESSIONAL CODE

Psychologists are aware that their profession has a moral dimension. They have an ethical code, EPP (*Ethical Principles of Psychologists*, 1981), and a book analyzing specific situations in order to guide them in interpreting and using the code (*Casebook of Ethical Principles of Psychologists*, 1974). In this section, we take a brief look at professional codes in general, but with special reference to EPP.

Individuals may support their professional code for practical reasons like respect and reputation among colleagues, but most basically, they support it because they believe that it is a good code containing principles they consider morally justified. The fact that many professionals accept a code does not demonstrate that its principles are morally sound. Conceivably, though not typically, an immoral code could be adopted, as has happened with laws (such as those formerly mandating discrimination against black people). The question, then, is neither, What do professionals say and do? nor, What motivates professionals?, but rather, Are the guidelines in this professional code consistent with moral principles? For EPP, the answer is clearly yes. Consider the code's *Preamble:*

PREAMBLE

Psychologists respect the dignity and worth of the individual and strive for the preservation and protection of fundamental human rights. They are committed to increasing knowledge of human behavior and of people's understanding of themselves and others and to the utilization of such knowledge for the promotion of human welfare. While pursuing these objectives, they make every effort to protect the welfare of those who seek their services and of the research participants that may be the object of study. They use their skills only for purposes consistent with these values and do not knowingly permit their misuse by others. While demanding for themselves freedom of inquiry and communication, psychologists accept the responsibility this freedom requires: competence, objectivity in the application of skills, and concern for the best interests of clients, colleagues, students, research participants and society. In the pursuit of these ideals, psychologists subscribe to principles in the following areas: (1) responsibility, (2) competence, (3) moral and legal standards, (4) public statements, (5) confidentiality, (6) welfare of the consumer, (7) professional relationships, (8) assessment techniques, (9) research with human participants, and (10) care and use of animals.

Acceptance of membership in the American Psychological Association commits the member to adherence to these principles. Psychologists cooperate with duly constituted committees of the American Psychological Association in particular, the Committee on Scientific and Professional Ethics and Conduct, by responding to inquiries promptly and completely. Members also respond promptly and completely to inquiries from duly constituted state association ethics committees and professional standards review committees.

This general statement of the code reveals that the American Psychological Association is concerned with each individual's sense of self-worth and dignity; with coming to understand people (human behavior and human personality traits); with the general welfare of citizens, and of its research subjects (humans and others); with abuses of whatever power or authority might belong to psychologists; and with a free but responsible approach to all professional activities. As might be expected, the 10 specific principles of EPP, together with elaborations of each, offer general guidelines for making morally relevant decisions about research, teaching, consulting, and clinical work.

What EPP does not do, nor does it claim to, is to explore the philosophical issues related to its principles. It relies on psychologists to interpret problematic concepts like duty, rights, responsibility, and the dignity and worth of the individual, each of which raises profound and troubling questions. Some of these questions are discussed in this book. In addition, EPP guidelines may conflict with each other. For example, one may be able to increase knowledge about a certain phenomenon only by causing subjects some psychological or physical pain. How shall one decide what to do then? Finally, EPP seems to alternate between utilitarian and Kantian theories (Blackstone, 1975), and these theories sometimes lead to different resolutions of moral dilemmas.

The EPP was never intended to resolve theoretical ethical questions. Rather, it is a statement about psychologists' moral concerns, and as such, can be helpful to psychologists, students of psychology, and lay people. This book does not try to defend, criticize, or modify EPP. Rather, it discusses in detail the ethical issues psychologists face as they choose an area, conceptualize, gather information, share information, and apply their knowledge. We hope this book clarifies the terms and principles stated in EPP, and provides a deeper understanding of the moral issues confronting psychologists.

Part II reviews the basic activities of psychologists—what they actually do as professionals. These activities are interrelated in any given project, but for the sake of clarity, they are explored in separate chapters.

Chapter 4 investigates how psychologists choose an area or domain in which to work, how they become school or social or physiological psychologists, and/or they choose one research project rather than another.

Chapter 5 discusses the way psychologists conceptualize and theorize about such concepts as intelligence, figure-ground perception, adjustment, right hemisphere dominance, internal locus of control, and retro-active inhibition.

Chapter 6 recognizes that all psychologists gather information, not only researchers. In research, this is called data collection. Its counterpart in direct services includes observation, interviewing, and testing.

Chapter 7 explores the process by which psychologists make decisions about sharing their knowledge: what, for what purpose or reason, when, how, and with whom.

Chapter 8 discusses ways in which psychologists put their knowledge to use, perhaps as a basis for further research, or for influencing public policy, or for direct services.

Most of these activities do not sound as though they are related to moral questions at all. The main purpose of the chapters in Part II is to demonstrate how and why they are. Part III will then explore specific controversies about such areas as testing and psychology and the law in greater detail.

4

CHOOSING AN AREA

People who are exposed to psychology informally rather than in the classroom tend to identify it mainly with treatment (psychotherapy) and with testing. "Pop" psychology books often support this image, as they analyze what is wrong with people and/or society, and then explain how to deal with or treat the current situation. Such books try to provide readers with some psychological knowledge, and encourage them to apply it to their own lives.

This popular conception omits many activities that psychologists perform, and many settings where they work. While some psychologists do testing and therapy, this is not true for all of them. Psychology is used in many settings: schools, industry, correctional systems, the armed services, health care settings, as well as in mental health agencies and private practice. The psychological knowledge used has to come from somewhere. It comes from research, an activity rarely included in the popular conception of psychology. Research takes place in many settings, including the ones cited above, as well as in university laboratories. Finally, psychologists do not work exclusively with human beings. Animals are sometimes trained or treated by psychologists, and sometimes used as research subjects. This is so for several reasons: we want information about them, too; they are more convenient to use (they do not break appointments!); and research procedures are legal for animals that are proscribed for humans (such as removing part of the brain.)

Psychology is thus far broader in scope than most people realize: it deals with behavior and/or mind in all kinds of organisms (even worms and roaches!). As a result, a variety of descriptive words are used that preceed "psychologist": animal, research, clinical, physiological, applied, experimental, and social. For our purposes, it will be helpful to group psychological activity in two ways:

1. According to the purpose or intent of the psychologist. One psychologist may want to contribute to knowledge about the behavioral effects of some drug, another to develop a new test, yet another to try to increase morale in some organization. Thus, some psychologists intend to do basic or pure research, some to do research in specific settings in order to introduce improvements there, others to apply what is already known.
2. According to the content domain. This can be described in broad categories (social, physiological, clinical, developmental, school), or narrower ones (hearing, prejudice, intelligence testing). In any case, these categories inform us about the specific behaviors and/or mental processes with which the psychologist is dealing.

In some content areas, (school psychology), application is the predominant intent or purpose, while in others (physiological psychology), research is.

Most people, psychologists and nonpsychologists alike, react to particular purpose-content choices. Sometimes these reactions are gut level, sometimes they are carefully reasoned analyses. For example, nonsense syllables have been used in research ever since Ebbinghaus developed them in the 1880s. People sometimes dismiss such research as unrealistic or useless as soon as they find out that nonsense syllables are involved—no matter what its purpose or content. On the other hand, they may be eager to read something if a word like *anxiety* or *personality* appears in the title. Most of us have ideas about what psychologists *ought* to be doing as they try to increase our knowledge and/or improve our lives. While some of these oughts are technical or pragmatic, some are moral.

The following analysis stresses the division based on purpose, but content areas are automatically included, since every research project and/or application must have content. Research areas are stressed in this chapter, while application is discussed in Chapter 8.

PURE RESEARCH

One of the oldest traditions in psychology is doing basic or pure research: choosing a project because it establishes a new program of research or fits into an ongoing one that explores unanswered theoretical and/or methodological questions. Pure research does not inevitably deal with the kind of content or materials that some people consider to be dull or socially unimportant. The purpose of doing pure research on attitude change, for example, may be served by comparing people's comprehension of literature that deals with socially important topics with their comprehension of less provocative literature. Quite apart from its content and the interest it arouses in different readers, the research is intended as pure research: the basis for choosing it is not potential application but rather, the potential gain in knowledge or understanding. Careful examination of this tradition and alternatives to it reveals that several complex morally relevant issues are involved: the right to know; the obligation to find out; the merit of the research project; and the principle of nonmaleficence (Do not harm). It is difficult to specify what each of these means or involves in this context. In addition, moral dilemmas occur when two or more of these conflict.

It is helpful to begin with an article by Smith (1978), which is revealingly entitled "Scientific knowledge and forbidden truths." It opens with the following words:

> Two hundred years ago Rousseau raised an issue that biomedicine has forced on us all: whether there are things we should not know. Some moral critics of science and medicine assert that particular kinds of knowledge, for instance about human genetics and evolution, are dangerous and therefore forbidden; those involved in the research in such fields "raise the flag of Galileo" and appeal to an abstract and absolute right to know. In some quarters, proposed restrictions on research are treated not only with the condescension normally extended to the stupid but also with the intolerance usually reserved for the moral pervert. (p. 30)

In this article, Smith examines the scientist's "right to know" within a larger social perspective. He considers arguments based on *(a)* the potential abuses in applications of knowledge (splitting the atom and Hiroshima); *(b)* the use of immoral procedures for obtaining knowledge (obtaining data by harming human guinea pigs, often without their informed consent); and *(c)* the potential destructiveness of some knowledge for personal and social life (the undermining of character and social customs). Smith's deliberations deal essentially with the tension between the right to know and the obligation to do no harm (nonmaleficence).

This same tension is explored somewhat differently by Luria (1976), who argues that human beings are biologically committed in two ways: to facing reality as intelligently as possible, which includes adding to knowledge; and to human solidarity, which includes employing empathy to avoid adding to the suffering of others. Thus, Luria argues that while acquiring knowledge is a biological and moral imperative, it should not be pursued regardless of consequences: some truths may not be worth their cost in suffering.

In the abstract, the arguments of Smith and Luria are neither novel nor exciting, since they appear to be only further elaborations of the thesis that no single right is absolute. Thus, "knowing" is positively valued in human life, and can be defended as an expression of our highest and most human tendencies and capabilities (Luria), and/or on the grounds of social utility. When specific details are included, however, (for example, about methods and applications) many morally relevant questions are raised, because knowing may conflict with other moral values. The detailed deliberations of Smith and Luria are important precisely because they go far beyond clichés, and because they help us to think about and evaluate what transpires in the real world.

Let us begin with one of Luria's examples, which at this time refers to pure research, but for which "believers" envision eventual application. Luria writes, "the believers in extrasensory perception or telepathy insist on their right to be funded for their meaningless research on nonexistent phenomena in their field of unreality" (p. 332). In other words, Luria is saying that there is no right to know about and to do research on that which doesn't exist! Three issues are raised in this brief quotation: (1) the scientific or other merit of a particular research area of project; (2) the nature of input from the public, that is, from nonspecialists, in deciding about such merit; and (3) the weighing of merit, however judged, against other considerations such as taxpayers' money, social repercussions, or minor discomforts for subjects.

Merit

The merit of a research area or project is very relevant morally, since it would be difficult to justify deliberately choosing a research area or project that seemed to be theoretically, methodologically, and/or practically worthless. If a project were that worthless, how could one justify anyone's time and salary or the time and/or comfort of subjects?

Although the scientific merit of a pure research project is morally relevant, judging such merit is problematic, since it is evaluated very differently by psychologists with different prescriptions for psychology (Watson, 1967). For those whose most basic concern is that psychology be based on moral values and action like reducing suffering (beneficence), a project is meritorious if, for example, it deals with developing different teaching strategies for children with different reading problems. These psychologists emphasize utility and helpfulness. When they are accused of doing research that isn't scientific but rather technological, since it makes no lasting contributions to theory or knowledge, they respond in at least two ways: (1) Nonbiological psychology resembles history and biography more than science, and it is therefore an error to expect lasting theoretical structures. In other words, regardless of whether the generalizations are about reading or about positive reinforcement, they are culturally and historically bounded, and are not scientific theory comparable to that in the natural sciences (Gergen, 1973; Cronbach, 1975; Scheibe, 1978). (2) In any case, what moral, social, or esthetic values would lead one to say that only lasting contributions are worthy? From the most extreme expression of this vantage point, traditional pure research (such as on the learning of lists of words or nonsense syllables) is virtually in the same category as ESP is for Luria. The learning of nonsense syllables exists, after all, only in the laboratories of psychologists! Such research is therefore viewed as having little or no merit.

But what about those who do the research on verbal learning or discpecking in pigeons? What might their ideas be about scientific merit? They believe that developing a science of psychology is both possible and desirable, and contributing to that science is their basic purpose. They therefore consider a project meritorious if, for example, it contributes to our scientific knowledge of the specific ways in which positive reinforcement shapes behavior—any behavior. As for utility and helpfulness, they make at least two points:

1.   There is an important place for pure science as there is for other seemingly useless human activity. While some specialists help us to appreciate and enjoy 18th century French poetry, others help us to understand the nature of living organisms. If humans really are curious, creative, intelligent beings, then pure psychology needs no more defense than pure art or pure physics. All of these are expressions of what is best in humankind.
2.   Most complex projects, as on reading, are likely to be methodologically or ecologically flawed, and conclusions drawn from them are therefore at best tenuous, if not downright unwarranted. It is therefore better, if one has eventual application in mind, to do pure well-designed research on basic processes and perhaps use its results later than to use questionable results from ill-designed studies or from nongeneralizable experiments. This strategy worked for the natural sciences and is expected to work for psychology as well.

The debate between proponents of these different perspectives is not easily settled, and is as old as psychology itself. Coan (1973) may be correct in saying that such debates are not resolvable by reason and fact, and that the perspective chosen reveals above all one's personality. Psychologists do not enter the field as blank slates and later become convinced by fact or reason that one prescription is correct. Rather, they find one or another prescription attractive, and then study and work within it (though they may occasionally have conversion experiences!).

One's ideas about the merits of pure psychological research are part of one's entire outlook on the discipline of psychology, and it becomes difficult to characterize any one set of arguments as more or less flawed morally than another set. The accusation that "You are ignoring human suffering" gives rise to the counteraccusation that "You are a charlatan, dabbling in human affairs without sufficient knowledge" (Bordin, 1966). There may be a grain of truth in both assertions, but the point to be stressed here is that while scientific merit is repeatedly used to justify or attack choice of research area or projects and methods, such merit can be difficult to evaluate in psychology. It is especially difficult at a time when many social-personality psychologists are arguing, along with some philosophers, that much of psychology, by its very nature, is not and cannot be a scientific discipline at all. Insofar as establishing the merit of a research area is difficult, so is resolving any dilemma in which such merit figures as one consideration. Given the current situation in the discipline of psychology, arguments involving the right to know will quickly focus on the right to know *what*.

Input from the Public

By using the word *funding*, Luria raises a second issue: who shall decide about the scientific or other merits of any research project, and who wants to know what? Several years ago, groups of 8–10 of our introductory psychology students were asked to pretend that they were review boards deciding about new projects presented by psychologists. We chose students because (a) they are not psychologists; (b) they are rational, informed citizens; (c) they are present or future taxpayers; and (d) they are often subjects in psychological research. Their vested interests are therefore different from those of psychologists. One proposal dealt with the effects of different reinforcement schedules on pigeons, and students repeatedly asked, What good will it do? Unimpressed by "pure research" and/or "eventual utility" answers, one group finally concluded, somewhat grudgingly, that if the research wouldn't cost any money (because it would use already available equipment and pigeons) and if the psychologists weren't wasting anybody else's time, it would be all right to do the research.

Their answer was of course unrealistic. Research facilities are always funded, by public (tax) funds and/or by private moneys such as tuition or alumni gifts. Research always costs money! And while the psychologists might not have been wasting anybody's time, they apparently were not planning to use their time in ways that impressed the students as useful.

The discussion of the debate about merit in psychology leads one to expect that, like psychologists, students and other groups representing the public would not always agree on the merit of proposed projects. While there was disagreement among our students, more of them preferred the prescription that emphasizes utility and helpfulness than the one emphasizing the development of scientific psychology. For comparable results among graduate students, see Lipsey (1974). What, then, might happen if people who are rational and informed but not experts regularly reviewed research proposals along with experts, as suggested by Bok (1978)? To return again to Luria's ESP example, such research would probably receive considerable public support, since public interest and belief in ESP-type phenomena is always sizable (Greeley & McCready, 1975), while support for pure research in psychology might be significantly lower.

What if a psychologist did seek to justify a pure research project to a lay group? The public has its ups and downs about esoteric studies (including 18th century French poetry), and so might react like the students mentioned earlier. Furthermore, the public may have little information to bring to the content of the proposal. People thus may have no basis for evaluating the potential contribution of a pure proposal to theory, method, or even eventual application. Two kinds of decisions seem to be involved. First, one can ask whether pure research is justified now. Nonpsychologists can reasonably ask, for example, Why don't you do research on reading problems instead? In other words, Why don't you address yourself to a pressing human problem?

To take an extreme example, if it appeared to others that you could save a life right now but were instead continuing to paint, these others would not need to know much about the merit of your art to make moral judgments about your choice. But the second kind of decision is difficult, at times perhaps impossible for nonexperts. When a pure research project is justifiable (it does no harm and leads, or may lead, to later good theory and/or application), then its evaluation on its own terms requires a great deal of knowledge about a particular area of research. If scientists sometimes succumb to the question-begging, biased view that their area is obviously worthy, it surely is not more reasonable for nonchemists to judge a pure chemistry proposal when they know nothing about the major theoretical issues in chemistry!

Thus, researchers must acknowledge that in fact, they always enjoy support from others (the rare exception might be a successful amateur scientist), even when doing pure research. Therefore, when proposing new studies, they should be able to convince somebody that they are worthy of such support, though it is far from clear from whom, above all in psychology: the public? psychologists? psychologists doing research in the area of the proposed study? But nonspecialists have a companion responsibility: to acknowledge that they cannot make informed judgments in specialized areas of knowledge without first learning extensively about those areas.

Weighing Conflicting Factors

For psychologists and public alike, both establishing merit and weighing conflicting factors present very real difficulties. Some of these conflicting factors have already been included in our discussion, notably pressing social problems. Merit and other considerations will continue to be explored as we consider applied research. Finally, one particular research example (race-IQ) will be presented to illustrate the difficulties confronted in weighing and balancing the many considerations involved.

APPLIED RESEARCH

A consideration of applied (rather than pure) research highlights other problems. For example, in 1978, Snyder and Mentzer wrote an article about the possibility of developing a "psychology of the physician." They pointed out that physicians engage in two activities upon which psychologists could shed light: they make judgments, and they communicate with patients. Research has identified both systematic errors in judgments and reluctance to communicate bad news. The authors ask for further research, and conclude with this paragraph:

> And if we really wanted to know whether it is better to leave the terminally ill uninformed, an experiment could be done randomly assigning patients to be informed or not. Outcomes to be measured include longevity, anxiety, depression and the quality of social relationships. Of course, there are ethical issues surrounding the conduct of such research, but in the absence of a convincing rationale for the current predominant practice of not informing, perhaps it is unethical not to do the research. The general idea is to try to resolve dilemmas by replacing speculation with fact. (p. 547)

This paragraph is very provocative. First, it speaks not of the right to know, but rather, of the obligation to know, to find out. It does not raise the flag of Galileo, but rather, argues that there is a moral obligation to do research when current practice has no convincing rationale, when research results could replace speculation with fact. Thus, in choosing a research area, a psychologist may appeal not to a right, but to an obligation. In applied areas, the obligation to know rests on the superiority of acting with knowledge to acting without it.

Pure researchers can of course make similar statements: as long as we are ignorant about how people think, learn, or develop, psychologists, with their special training, have a special obligation to dent that ignorance. Some might prefer this version: ultimately all knowledge has utility, since human beings are eternally curious. This means that they want to understand, among other things, the functioning of living creatures. Psychologists are not the only ones who are intrigued when apes are taught "language" or rats are taught far more complicated tricks than anyone would have believed possible. Such research sheds light for everyone on the continuities and discontinuities in all mental life, and this utility obligates the appropriately trained psychologists to do such research.

Some psychologists and nonpsychologists consider pure research morally indefensible on the grounds that it is not intended to be useful or helpful. The paragraph quoted above shows that in the case of applied research, moral problems arise precisely because it is intended to be useful. The morally concerned applied researcher will therefore ask, Who would find useful, and for what purpose(s), the information gained from my research in this area?

In choosing pure research, the psychologist may be biased toward a theoretically significant outcome. For example, the researcher may hope that Group I will learn more rapidly than Group II because that would illustrate a theoretically significant point. Such bias can be a technical problem, since the experimenter's hopes may affect the outcome of the research, but it need not be a moral problem. In contrast, in choosing an applied area, the researcher may be biased toward a socially significant outcome—a very different matter. As the above quotation shows, applied research is typically directed at diagnosis and intervention. Other examples include determining why children cannot read, and what can be done to improve reading; why workers are late so often, and what can be done to decrease lateness; why adolescents are prejudiced, and what can be done to decrease prejudice; why women are so conforming and what can be done to increase independence; and why men are so Machiavellian, and what can be done to make them less so.

The above examples were deliberately arranged to move from apparently innocuous areas to more controversial ones. If pure research at times elicits the question, Don't you feel obligated to do something useful? applied research elicits approval about usefulness only when we agree with the moral values implied by the project, outrage when we don't. This becomes even clearer when we add to the list of examples possible interventions for suicide and homosexuality. Thus, as stated previously, the basic question becomes, Who wants this information, and for what purpose(s)?

Consider applied research on dyslexia (severe reading disorders). It will meet with much approval because the people who want the information are the dyslexics and/or those who care for and about them. The research is thus directed at finding ways to help people who view themselves and who are viewed by others as having a serious problem. There is agreement here because one could defend one's choice to help others, but could not defend making life even harder for them. In the absence of compelling reasons to the contrary, one ought to respect their wishes, and one ought not to unjustly treat them in an unequal way by ignoring their suffering while helping others with different problems. All moral theories, all specific moral principles, lead to the same conclusion in this case. Contrast this with the example on conformity-independence. Quite apart from the possible sexism, lively debates center on the question, How much and what kind of individual independence from group values is compatible with moral behavior and/or human survival? (Campbell, 1975).

Thus, choosing applied instead of pure research does not automatically solve all moral problems. To the contrary, that choice guarantees being deeply enmeshed with them. This has been true since the earliest days of psychology when Sir Francis Galton concluded that intelligence was inherited, and helped establish the eugenics movement!

Tyler, whose presidential address to the American Psychological Association in 1973 was clearly in the "do no harm" or "do good" tradition, asked psychologists to remember in all that they do that psychology is the discipline in which researcher, subject, and consumer are all members of the same species. Who, then, should decide whether or not race-IQ research should be continued? (This combination pure and applied area is discussed in detail later in this chapter.) Tyler argued that since one cannot control the crucial variables (for example, each person's environment), the major questions cannot be resolved anyway, and so it is better not to pursue, and thus keep stressing, the difference between blacks and whites. Furthermore, the results of such research are used by some psychologists and nonpsychologists to support immoral racism. Therefore psychologists, who should be aware of both of these points, should view the starting of a new race-IQ research project as a morally relevant choice. There are alternatives, since one can either do it or some other research or no research at all, and what is chosen will make a difference in the lives of many people. Luria (1976), pitting "knowing" against "solidarity," expressed this idea even more forcefully:

> If a single person black or white or yellow, should suffer because of the social consequences of the right claimed by some psychologists to find out what a 15-point mean difference in IQ "really means," then maybe we should forsake that knowledge. That truth may not be worth such a price. (p. 333)

OTHER MORALLY RELEVANT FACTORS

Expectations about Other Activities

Choosing an area is only one of several choices psychologists make. They conceptualize, collect information, share their findings with others, and contribute to the application of psychological knowledge. The choice of research area, be it pure, applied, or a combination, is thus also influenced in ethically relevant ways by the expectations psychologists have about such considerations as necessary data collection techniques or uncontrollable distortions of results in the media. For example, some psychologists might decide not to do research in the area of cheating on tests because they have moral and other reservations about all available methods. The only way to experiment in this area involves deceiving the subjects. They may consider this similar to cheating, and may be morally opposed to both. Field research using interviews and/or questionnaires may seem of dubious merit to them (whether or not these judgments are justified is irrelevant here: it is their view), and so they decide not to do research in this area at all. This is a decision based in part on moral considerations, and involves weighing the scientific merit and/or utility of the research against the deception of subjects.

Pragmatic Considerations

Thus far, the discussion has stressed the ethically relevant considerations in the choice of a research area. In actual fact, it is likely that psychologists often choose their research area on pragmatic grounds as much as on ethical ones. Considerations of time, money, and energy guide choices at least as much as moral considerations. Choosing in this manner is itself ethically relevant. One often hears it said in private, "I would like to do X, but it is difficult and a poor investment of my time when I must have my eye on publications and/or promotion." These are, of course, practical, realistic considerations. In morally relevant terms, however, the question would be, Would you make and defend the same choices, and on the same grounds, if the pragmatic considerations for all the research alternatives open to you were identical? Why or why not? The answers might reveal that psychologists sometimes feel compelled to put ethical values into second place. For example, if they said that work on X would make a greater contribution to understanding and/or would be of greater benefit, but work on Y was chosen because it would more rapidly lead to publications, those psychologists have chosen on the basis of pragmatic rather than moral values. They felt compelled to choose on the basis of what was good for them personally, rather than on the basis of what was good in a more universal sense. Thus, such pragmatic decision making is morally relevant, not somehow outside of or beyond ethics.

Personal Preferences

Pragmatic considerations (time, money, and energy) are not the only bases for choosing an area; personal preferences or tastes are also important. Psychologists choose the content and purpose they find "interesting," an overused word that does not do justice to the intense excitement psychologists often feel about intellectual and other challenges provided by one or another area of their discipline. While psychologists certainly talk about families, cars, music, and politics, it is a rare lunch that doesn't find them talking shop! They do not differ from other people who know what grips them, and who are fortunate enough to have the opportunity to develop their talents and inclinations.

Here again, the comment applies that was made about pragmatic considerations: choosing on the basis of one's interests is itself ethically relevant. One could conclude that the pursuit of one's interests was morally unjustified under particular circumstances. Examples of this are familiar among the career choices made by young adults.

Content Domains

Content domains (cognitive development in children, the effects of punishment on maze learning, reactions to jobs lost under various conditions) are chosen partly on pragmatic grounds such as availability of jobs and partly as a matter of personal preference. Moral judgments are sometimes made about content choices per se. Thus, Luria argues that trying to study ESP is morally unjustifiable, since it doesn't exist. Others argue that the major personal and social problems of our era should take precedence over sensation, perception, and other traditional content areas.

The moral justification of content areas is as problematic as that of purpose (pure research, applied research, application). Questions about what exists and what does not exist arise in psychology not only for ESP, but also for abstractions like intelligence, love, factor, trait, and happiness. It is one thing to make a personal statement about one's preferences ("I don't find any of this particularly interesting"), quite another to judge somebody's commitment to one of these areas as moral or immoral (psychologists should or should not study X for such and such morally relevant reasons.). The next section discusses one content area that has been explored for all possible purposes of research and application, and about which there has been considerable debate in recent years. (The ethically relevant aspects of applying psychology are discussed in greater detail in Chapter 8.)

AN EXAMPLE OF CONTROVERSY: RACE–IQ

One controversial content area deals with the relationship between race and IQ. This area has theoretical, methodological, *and* applied aspects, and thus might seem to be especially defensible morally, since it potentially makes both scientific and practical contributions. Nonetheless, strong reservations have been expressed about the choosing of this area.

Different ideas about the relative potency of heredity and environment in determining human attributes and behaviors go back to antiquity. It is not surprising, therefore, that discussions about the determinants of IQs developed almost as soon as IQ tests were created. Discussion is perhaps too mild a word. Intense feelings and acrimonious debate have at times been involved, since IQ tests were designed and often taken to measure a dimension of great theoretical and social significance: intelligence. The social aspect of this debate is related to attacks on or defenses of existing social hierarchies: do they exist because they must inevitably exist, or can they be altered or even eliminated? If intelligence is already fixed at birth, there is little point in attempting to develop remedial programs to help people move upward on one or another hierarchy, since we would then be as unable to remedy low intelligence as eye color! If intelligence is significantly affected by learning, however, existing social hierarchies can be viewed as the products of historical forces, can be altered by improving and equalizing educational opportunities for all children, and cannot be defended as inevitable or eternal.

The psychologist who in recent years has rearoused many passions in this area is Jensen, who wrote in 1969 that the empirical evidence convinced him that genetic variations among people accounted for approximately 80 percent of the variation among them in intelligence (Jensen, 1969). He extended this interpretation to the observed difference in IQ between whites and blacks. Both his basic interpretation and its extension were quickly attacked by others (for example, Block & Dworkin, 1974, and Gomberg, 1975). In the present context, we consider the ethical aspects of choosing this research area. The parties to the controversy repeatedly deal with one or more of the principles and issues explored in the first part of this chapter: the nature of meritorious research; the right to do such research; the obligation to do such research; nonmaleficence; and beneficence.

Tyler's presidential address to the A.P.A., mentioned earlier, includes the following suggestion:

> Long after they [researchers] have moved on to other hunting grounds, in this world or the next, people may be citing their results in support of policies and programs they know nothing about. We need to remember this in making research plans. While it is to be expected that ambiguous results will often turn up, especially in work on new and complex problems, if it becomes clear that the results of a line of research are going to continue to be ambiguous no matter how many successive studies are made because of the impossibility of controlling or correcting for the influence of a crucial independent variable, it would be better not to pursue it further. I have heard arguments in recent years over the question of whether ambiguous findings should be published, as in the case of racial differences in intelligence. I think such arguments miss the point. Many ambiguous findings have been stimulating and productive. But in cases where it appears that there is no way to resolve the issues raised, investigators should give serious thought at the outset to whether the research should be *done* [italics hers]. (p. 1026)

Although the next paragraph proceeds to another point, its opening sentence is also important here:

> The thinking that is done at the outset about what the experience will mean to participants will tend to rule out some alternatives and increase the attractiveness of others. (p. 1026)

Jensen's position differs strikingly. In his view, science has no dogma; every question may be asked, and if possible, answered (Jensen, 1974). His is an appeal to the right to know. Since his research is seen as having an applied aspect (Jensen, 1969), an appeal is also made to the obligation to know: to plan educational programs on the basis of knowledge is more defensible than to continue to do so on the basis of ignorance or faulty information. Finally, he proposes essentially that equals should be treated equally (principle of justice): children who are alike intellectually should receive similar educations. Different educational programs should exist for children with different talents, not races. Thus, action is to be based on morally relevant inequalities (IQ or specific intellectual talents), not on irrelevant ones (eye color, the charm of a smile, or race).

Ireland (1974) defended race research on several grounds, in part echoing Jensen. He said that Jensen's attackers seem to think "that if significant differences between racial groups do exist, it follows that members of different races should be treated differently on that account" (p. 140). This, says Ireland, is nonsense: people should be treated individually, according to their abilities, not on the basis of the average for a group of which they are members.

He also argued that the extensive disputes in this area about what is fact and what is not are partly due to the lack of research, since many people have considered this area taboo since the time of Hitler. We need information, however, and researchers therefore should not be attacked for asking questions and trying to answer them.

> Without making any judgment as to whether the black race is genetically different from the white in intelligence, one can argue that knowledge of racial differences in intelligence, if such differences exist, should be a benefit and not a detriment to either race. If such differences do exist, perhaps, as with sickle-cell anemia, research may lead to improvements for the weaker race. In this respect, it seems obvious that race research is useful even in the area of intelligence. (p. 143)

Somewhat later, he wrote:

> The problem here is bias, among people who should know better, against any racial genetic research on the assumption that research *will* [italics his] produce evidence of black racial disadvantages in intelligence and that this evidence will be used effectively to deprive blacks of basic rights. This is prejudging the case, and it is extremely dangerous in that it indicates an unexamined assumption that evidence showing that blacks are genetically disadvantaged according to one measure of intelligence would be proper basis for racial discrimination. (p. 144)

Finally, Ireland discussed the fear of eugenics:

> If eugenic ideas are left to the underground, they may be appropriated by those who would subordinate human freedom to a simple-minded program

of eugenics. It would be far better to have the theoretic and practical problems of eugenics openly discussed by the intellectual community at large.
Suppressed ideas do have a way of becoming extremely potent. (p. 145)

He concluded that more such research is needed, and that intimidating
people like Jensen is not helpful to anyone.

Gombert (1975) responded to Ireland in several ways, some of which
lead into topics that will be discussed in later chapters.

1. People like Jensen are attacked not for the questions they ask, but for
    their views. Controversy revolves around both the correctness of Jen-
    sen's hereditarian explanation of intelligence and the impact of these
    views on the public.
2. Jensen's critics do not assume that racial differences would actually
    justify differential treatment; they fear that stressing racial differences
    will lead to more differential treatment than already exists, and that the
    research results and their interpretation would provide rationalizations
    (not reasons) for prejudice and discrimination.
3. Race research can be beneficial, as in research on sickle-cell anemia.
    The critical question is, "Would more and better race-IQ research be
    equally beneficial?" Gomberg argued that it would not, since the tests
    do not measure *intelligence*. Furthermore, they are inherently biased,
    by virtue of their content, against blacks and the poor. Research using
    these tests can only generate more hatred, and therefore cannot be
    compared to research on sickle-cell anemia.
4. Because Jensen's research was scientifically flawed (as Ireland con-
    ceded), it should not have been published. Public debate is not helpful:
    it legitimizes the issue. One cannot plead free speech. The political and
    social factors behind the debate (for example, Jensen becomes rich and
    famous, and therefore is not open to rational discourse; racists find
    support in media reports of his "facts" and "theories") justify mili-
    tancy against people like Jensen.

Block and Dworkin's (1974) detailed analysis of race-IQ research makes
clearer than Ireland's and Gomberg's that competing values are involved.
"We recognize the great value in encouraging the freest possible use of
scientific intelligence and the great benefits that have been gained from it.
. . . [but] at some point the harmful consequences for human welfare of
one's research must enter into the decision whether to pursue it" (p. 81).
Before their argument is pursued in a formal way, it will be helpful to
consider a common sense example that is less emotionally involving. (This
example should not be taken as proof that common sense is always best
either technically or morally.)

If society thinks that children should have certain skills (for example, in
athletics), then resources (time, energy, money) must be given to trying to
develop these skills, whatever the sources of individual differences among

children. These sources are clearly many: the degree of parental encouragement; boredom-interest; the teaching technique's suitability for the child; or genetic endowment. Let us consider five-year-old Joe who wants to master bike riding but is having great difficulty. If his parents at once went to a tester to find out Joe's "athletic quotient," we would surely consider them strange. In these situations, there is much wisdom in traditional parenting, which automatically combines diagnosis and intervention. Even if Joe's parents (erroneously) believe that Joe has inherited his Uncle Charlie's clumsiness (note that they are attributing an innately low athletic quotient to him), they will first try to help Joe in every way they can until (we hope!) he can finally ride his bike. Why? Because they believe that mastering the bike is important for their child (for his self-esteem, for his relationships with other children), and probably also because they need or want to see their child as a winner and not as a loser. In other words, no matter what the parents think causes Joe's difficulty, they will first do everything to help him. How? They will carefully observe him, and address themselves to specific things he does right and wrong: "Don't lean forward so much"; "Try to pedal just a little faster"; "That was great!"

Overall, black children have not been treated similarly in relation to academic skills. When a black child did not learn to read easily, rather than someone trying to pinpoint the problem and then help, the child was tested ("intelligence quotient" rather than "athletic quotient") and often relegated to a special class—a teaching situation which offered less help, in part because of the label permanently attached to the child: stupid, or "scientifically" speaking, IQ= 82.

Can one realistically expect to teach everything to every child? No, nor is that a necessary assumption for anyone entering into this debate. Some children will never draw well, some will never do math well or even at all. But the best way to find that out is to teach each child as well as possible (because it has been decided that drawing and math are important for the child to learn). This is precisely what parents do when they help their children master bikes, or when they give them art or swimming lessons.

The point should be clear by now that no research on race-IQ has any bearing on this humane, commonsense, traditional approach. That research cannot help a single child to learn to read, write, and think as well as possible. This does not mean that a particular child cannot be helped by selective testing. It may indeed be the case that Joe has a specific physical defect that makes it difficult for him to ride a bike, or a specific perceptual problem that makes it difficult for him to read.

Block and Dworkin's argument begins with this last point, and then proceeds to the conclusion that race-IQ research should be discontinued.

1. They share Jensen's goals of finding different curricula for different children. "Where we disagree is in supposing that promoting these goals has anything to do with finding out more about racial genetic

differences" (p. 83). Nor does Jensen ever explain this link. If information about genetic makeup is important, "it would be knowledge of the individual's genetic make-up and not that of any group of which he is a member" (p. 83).

2. They are concerned about educational policies that might be developed on the basis of such research data. "It seems unlikely that the type of educational effort expended in order to change IQ would be very different from the type of effort that would be expended to produce educational (not IQ) gains. If it turns out that there are black-white genetic differences, and this becomes known, one ill effect might be a mistaken cessation of efforts to find new types of intervention aimed at raising IQ" (p. 85).

3. The media try to simplify the information, and in this case, the distortions are harmful to millions of people. They quote from a 1969 (March 31) article in *Newsweek*, that opens with the headline, "Born Dumb?" and then interprets Jensen's work as follows: "Dr. Jensen's view, put simply, is that most blacks are born with less 'intelligence' than most whites. . . . Since intelligence is fixed at birth anyway, he claims, it is senseless to waste vast sums of money and resources on such remedial programs as Head Start which assume that a child's intellect is maleable and can be improved." Such media interpretations permit society to ignore or rationalize "the structural faults of society which condemn large segments of the population to radical inferiority" (p. 89). (This excerpt from *Newsweek* distorted Jensen's views greatly, and was thus unfair both to black citizens and to Jensen, who has never stated that intelligence is fixed at birth.)

4. Jensen, and others, make no effort to guard against such misinterpretations. In as sensitive an area as this, which affects the lives of so many people, extra care is necessary to prevent erroneous and harmful interpretations.

5. Since individual assessment consumes time and money, information about group averages may (erroneously) be used in making decisions about individuals, such as in hiring decisions.

6. Given social reality, "one has a responsibility to cease such investigations while the above circumstances obtain" (p. 95). They are not persuaded by Jensen's right to know position, nor by his argument that all knowledge can be used for good or evil. "What is important is not whether such discoveries *could be* misused, but whether, on the best available evidence, *they are likely to be*. [italics ours] (p. 96).

What about research that uses Jensen's techniques but comes to different conclusions, notably Scarr-Salapetek's work (1971), from which she concluded that the "heritabilities" of intelligence differ in advantaged and disadvantaged children? "In attempting to prevent damage due to one-sided work in the field one is usually implicitly endorsing both the importance of the questions that are being asked and the methods used to arrive at answers" (p. 98).

Block and Dworkin differ from Gomberg in one important respect: "nothing we have said implies that it is legitimate to interfere with the teaching, research, or speaking activities of researchers who act irresponsibly. The fact that individuals may be acting wrongly does not, by itself, justify the use of coercion against them" (p. 98).

Several major questions discussed earlier are involved in this debate about whether or not race-IQ research should be continued. First, what merit has it? What, if any, information do we get from such research? Does it begin to answer questions about the hereditary and environmental determinants of intelligence? Does it bear on educational planning for children? Jensen clearly believes that this research is meritorious, since it helps to answer important theoretical and practical questions. On the other hand, others have raised many questions about the validity of Jensen's research and his interpretations, and according to these critics, this research has no merit: it does not answer any questions at all. Ireland seemed to argue that the main lesson is that more and better research is needed: the area is meritorious, but the research done so far is not very good. Thus, there is universal respect for knowledge, but there is disagreement about whether any knowledge is forthcoming from this research, and especially knowledge relevant to educational planning.

It does not follow from the analyses of critics that no child should ever be tested, nor does it follow that research on intelligence should never be done. Animal experiments on heredity-environment interactions are illuminating, as are correlational studies of changing or constant IQs in children exposed to different parenting styles (Moriarty, 1966; Rosenzweig, 1966).

Second, questions are raised about how to balance the right to know or the obligation to know and concerns about harming people. Thus, many arguments are made that such research is inevitably going to be harmful to black people. One might want to add that insofar as prejudice and discrimination exact a price from everyone, such research is also harmful to white people. Jensen is somewhat vulnerable here, since he, too, links educational planning not to race, but to IQ, or more specifically, to Type I (associative) and Type II (abstract) intelligence. It is thus not clear how any results pertaining to race can be helpful, or to whom. Questions about group differences in IQ are mainly of theoretical interest; studies dealing with social class, age, and family size raise many challenges for the theoretician. But aside from eugenicists, surely nobody would defend discrimination against children with six siblings, even though their IQs are in fact lower than children with only one sibling.

Third, difficult questions are raised about communicating statistical analyses and technical results to those not technically trained. To understand the most telling technical arguments about Jensen's research one would need a good understanding of statistics. Members of the community could judge some issues related to doing this research, but not all, especially not those related to scientific merit. What are the obligations of psychologists in this situation? This question is discussed in Chapter 7.

Fourth, when, if ever, are efforts to suppress research or research results justified? Singer (1979) has argued that at times one may do less harm or more good if one tries to prevent the doing of certain research than if one continues to pursue obviously time-consuming and often destined-to-fail debate or legal tactics. Others, like Ireland, argue that open debate is the best safeguard against social evils.

Finally, this debate raises the troubling question: how can we resolve the conflict between or among competing values? When Luria worries about harming even one person, is he holding up a model of human decency for us, or is he merely being absurd (since most research would have to cease at once by that standard)? We return to this question again and again, since no formulas are available for weighing this amount of merit against that amount of harm to some person or group. In some cases, moral priorities seem clear; for example, psychologists do not search for better ways to demean people. In other cases, however, what factors should receive most weight will not be readily apparent, nor are measures available for merit, harm, and other morally relevant factors.

THEMES AND VARIATIONS: CHAPTER 4

The Different Perspectives within Psychology

Chapter 4 states that the worth of a research project will be judged differently by psychologists with different prescriptions for psychology. In 1967, Watson argued that psychology has no paradigm, a term he took from Kuhn (1962):

> That psychology lacks this universal agreement about the nature of our contentual model that is a paradigm, in my opinion, is all too readily documented. In psychology there is still debate over fundamentals. In research, findings stir little argument but the overall framework is still very much contested. There is still disagreement about what is included in the science of psychology. In part, at least, it is because we lack a paradigm that one psychologist can attack others who do not agree with him as being "nonscientific" or "not a psychologist," or both. Schools of psychology still have their adherents, despite wishful thinking. And an even more telling illustration, because it is less controversial, is the presence of national differences in psychology to such an extent that in the United States there is an all too common dismissal of work in psychology in other countries as quaint, odd,

or irrelevant. National differences, negligible in paradigmatic sciences such as physics and chemistry, assume great importance in psychology. (p. 436)

He then presented 18 trends or themes in contrasting pairs that continue to be important in psychology (for example, methodological objectivism-methodological subjectivism; peripheralism-centralism; purism-utilitarianism) and called these *prescriptions.*

> The overall function of these themes is orientative or attitudinal; they tell us how the psychologist-scientist must or should behave. In short, they have a directive function. They help to direct the psychologist-scientist in the way he selects a problem, formulates it, and the way in which he carries it out. The other essential characteristic is that of being capable of being traced historically over some appreciable period of time. On both counts, the term *prescription* seems to have these connotations. It is defined in the dictionaries as the act of prescribing, directing, or dictating with an additional overtone of implying long usage, of being hallowed by custom, extending over time. (p. 437)

He concluded his article with this sentence:

> Since psychology seems to lack a unifying paradigm, it would seem that as a science it functions at the level of guidance by prescriptions. (p. 433)

In 1974, Lipsey factor analyzed the questionnaire responses of a group of faculty members and students in graduate psychology departments (Lipsey, 1974). He, too, found different prescriptions, and described the two main factors as follows:

> Social concern: Combined concern for promoting human welfare, a sense of special obligation to solve social problems, belief in man's capacity for self-fulfillment, need to demonstrate psychology's value to society, and a feeling of responsibility for the use society makes of psychological findings.
>
> Experimentalism: An affirmation of confidence in the problem-solving potential of experimental psychology and laboratory methodology, support of operationism, satisfaction with psychology's past efforts to study learning, and disagreement that the discipline only mimics the physical sciences. (p. 544)

By splitting each factor at the median, Lipsey created four groups. "Basic researchers" were high on experimentalism, low on social concern, "human activists" were the reverse, and "social engineers" were high on both factors. Low on both factors were the "pure researchers" who rejected experimentalism. Many were working in the areas of perception and cognition.

It is helpful to consider Lipsey's categories in conjunction with Bordin's (1966) analysis of "the dilemma of the psychologist" (his subtitle):

> I propose that these differences and tensions within our profession are best understood not solely as tensions among psychologists but rather as including tensions within psychologists. (p. 116)

He argued that all psychologists share curiosity, compassion, and doubt, though in different proportions:

> This curiosity about others and this need to understand human behavior and experience surely are accompanied by and probably reflect curiosity about ourselves. Why else have we as scientists chosen this area for study rather than the many other physical and natural phenomena which provoke epistemic curiosity? It is my hypothesis that most varieties of psychologists share this curiosity and that this is not a major issue among them, nor is it a great source of tension within them.
>
> It is in the other two motivations that we find the seeds for tensions among and within psychologists. It seems evident to me that compassion and doubt can exist side by side only in a volatile state. . . . By compassion I mean the capacity to reverberate to the feelings of others, particularly to their distress. An empathic response stimulates readiness to play a facilitating role in the relief of distress. It is likely to include some feeling of urgency about making such a contribution, and an unwillingness to postpone action in the service of certainty.
>
> The tendency to doubt is a very significant feature of the scientist. Most of what we designate as scientific method refers to specific means of controlling our observations for bias and distortion in the interest of testing the tenability of conclusions about the nature of various phenomena (p. 117)

> Compassion fosters the thought, "here are a great many persons in distress, we need to bend our efforts to relieve them with whatever knowledge, intuition, or experience we have." Doubt says, "Here are a great many persons in distress, we must develop theories and engage in research so that we will come to understand what has created the anguish and how it can be relieved. If we devote our energies to direct action grounded in ignorance and emotional response to the misery of others, we will have no assurance that we can relieve the distress and at the same time have dissipated energies best devoted to the necessary process of accumulating the knowledge." Thus we find practicing clinicians adopting the activist's stance. They have little patience with the experimenter's response, "Let's make a study," when faced with some human problem. Conversely, the research-oriented psychologist finds alien the practicing psychologist's seemingly unrealistic certainty in the absence of proof. This is to him a form of quackery. (p. 118)

Although both social engineers and humanist activists are high on social concern (compassion), they resolve their inner tensions between doubt and compassion in different manners. Given both our ignorance about many important and interesting psychological phenomena, and the many pressing problems in the world today, at least some of which involve psychological phenomena, it seems indefensible to point to any one prescription as immoral. It is far more reasonable to take one research area or project at a time (for example, differences between racial or gender or age groups; language development in children) and to evaluate it for its potential contributions to compassionate action and/or reducing our doubts. It is clear that Tyler, Gomberg, and Block and Dworkin view the search for racial determinants of IQ scores as failures in both respects: they argue that this line of research does not satisfy our curiosity, reduce our doubts, or qualify as scientific research—nor does it involve or lead to compassionate action.

Luria's article (1976) views curiosity, compassion, and doubt as "expressions of the unique biological destiny of humankind" (p. 334). We therefore may not ignore them. Because he treats them as ethical principles, he calls them "the ethic of knowledge" and "the ethic of innocence." He views race-IQ research as having ignored the latter entirely, and argues that we must always follow both ethics. Unfortunately, he does not say how, and he sometimes seems close to neglecting the ethic of knowledge.

> The ethic of knowledge is often embraced by some who interpret it as the right to pursue the quest for knowledge whenever one so wishes, irrespective of consequences. We are all familiar with the abuses of this principle.
>
> Thus, for example, the believers in extrasensory perception or telepathy insist on their right to be funded for their meaningless research on nonexistent phenomena in their field of unreality. More seriously, it was sufficient for some self-styled educational geneticist to assert that the lower mean IQ scores of black youngsters are genetically determined for a whole pack of racists and intellectual profiteers to generate a bandwagon of so-called genetic research on race differences in intelligence. The right-to-knowledge becomes the analogue of the right-to-life: the right to affect and possibly blight the life of others for the satisfaction of being proved right. If one points out that, before drawing conclusions from measurement of IQ tests, one should know what it is that the tests measure and what kind of genetic analysis can be done on such data, one is accused of wanting to suppress the pursuit of knowledge. More important still, the concern that doing and advertising this kind of "research" will have serious social consequences, irrespective of its findings, is discounted as irrelevant by the champions of the right-to-know.

*   *   *   *   *

> What is wrong with the claim of an unfettered right-to-know, whether in the social or medical research field? I believe that the main pitfall is the failure to balance the right-to-know value, that is, the ethic of knowledge, with what I shall call the ethic of innocence. What I mean by the ethic of innocence may be stated metaphorically in the words of Dostoevski put in the mouth of Ivan Karamazov: "If the suffering of children serves to complete the sum of suffering necessary for the acquisition of truth, I affirm that truth is not worth such a price."
>
> The ethic of innocence is simply the ethic of human solidarity. Morality does not exist in a vacuum. Human pursuits should always be judged in terms of what their consequences are for other human beings. Values are but norms for human interaction. If the ethic of knowledge urges us to strive to add new knowledge to the intellectual patrimony of mankind, the ethic of

innocence prescribes that we must refrain from doing anything that has a forseeable chance to cause suffering.

* * * * *

The ethic of knowledge and the ethic of innocence are two complementary aspects of morality. Both are expressions of the unique biological destiny of humankind. The development of the human brain and the acquisition of consciousness in the course of evolution have given to us human beings the power to organize and transmit knowledge, as well as the power to identify ourselves with the feelings and the sufferings of other human beings. They have forced upon us the need to know and the need to be innocent, both biologically rooted values. We may not legitimately follow either one and ignore the other. (p. 332–334)

One thing that makes it hard to judge the merit of a research area is that we often cannot know in advance what impact work in it will have in relation to either ethic. In an illuminating article on historic trends in the study of women, Shields (1975) leaves one perplexed as to which, if any, studies of gender comparisons she might consider to be morally viable.

And what has happened to the issues of brain size, variability, and maternal instinct since the 1930's? Where they are politically and socially useful, they have an uncanny knack of reappearing, albeit in an altered form. For example, the search for central nervous system differences between males and females has continued. Perhaps the most popular form this search has taken is the theory of prenatal hormonal "organization" of the hypothalamus into exclusively male or female patterns of function (Harris & Levine, 1965). The proponents of this theory maintain an Aristotlelian view of woman as an imcomplete man:

> In the development of the embryo, nature's first choice or primal impulse is to differentiate a female. . . . The principle of differentiation is always that to obtain a male, something must be added. Subtract something, and the result will be a female. (Money, 1970, p. 428)

The concept of maternal instinct, on the other hand, has recently been taken up and refashioned by a segment of the woman's movement. Pregnancy and childbirth are acclaimed as important expressions of womanliness whose satisfactions cannot be truly appreciated by males. The idea that women are burdened with "unreasoning tendencies to pet, coddle, and 'do for' others" has been disposed of by others and replaced by the semiserious proposal that if any "instinctive" component of parental concern exists, it is a peculiarly male attribute (Stannard, 1970). The variability hypothesis is all but absent from contemporary psychological work, but if it ever again promises a viable justification for existing social values, it will be back as strongly as ever. Conditions which would favor its revival include the renaissance of rugged individualism or the "need" to suppress some segment of society, for example, women's aspirations to positions of power. In the first case the hypothesis would serve to reaffirm that there are those "born to lead," and in the latter that there are those "destined to follow." (p. 753–754)

Can Psychology Be a Science?

Much debate exists about whether or not psychologists following the ethic of knowledge are scientists, partly because they must also follow the ethic of innocence, but also for other reasons.

According to Gergen (1973), social psychology resembles history more than it does science, since the discipline itself alters the very behavior it seeks to systematize via transhistorical laws. For example, as people read studies dealing with conformity and prejudice, they inevitably learn that psychologists consider conformity and prejudice to be "bad" (see Chapter 5), and they may therefore alter their behavior, thus negating the findings of the studies. Therefore, it is senseless to exalt pure social psychology research on the grounds that it helps us to develop transhistorical laws, and neither pure nor applied research can be justified on the grounds that it will lead to the prediction and control of behavior.

> A pervasive prejudice against applied research exists among academic psychologists, a prejudice that is evident in the pure research focus of prestige journals and in the dependency of promotion and tenure on contributions to pure as opposed to applied research. In part, this prejudice is based on the assumption that applied research is of transient value. While it is limited to solving immediate problems, pure research is viewed as contributing to basic and enduring knowledge. From the present standpoint, such grounds for prejudice are not merited. The knowledge that pure research bends itself to establish is also transient; generalizations in the pure research area do not generally endure. To the extent that generalizations from pure research have greater transhistorical validity, they may be reflecting processes of peripheral interest or importance to the functioning of society.

* * * * *

> The central aim of psychology is traditionally viewed as the prediction and control of behavior. From the present standpoint, this aim is misleading and provides little justification for research. Principles of human behavior may have limited predictive value across time, and their very acknowledgment can render them impotent as tools of social control. However, prediction and control need not serve as the cornerstones of the field. Psychological theory can play an exceedingly important role as a sensitizing device. It can enlighten one as to the range of factors potentially influencing behavior under various conditions. Research may also provide some estimate of the importance of these factors at a given time. Whether it be in the domain of public policy or personal relationships, social psychology can sharpen one's sensitivity to subtle influences and pinpoint assumptions about behavior that have not proved useful in the past. When counsel is sought from the social psychologist regarding likely behavior in any concrete situation, the typical reaction is apology. It must be explained that the field is not sufficiently well developed at present so that reliable predictions can be made. From the present standpoint, such apologies are inappropriate. The field can seldom

yield principles from which reliable predictions can be made. Behavior patterns are under constant modification. However, what the field can and should provide is research informing the inquirer of a number of possible occurrences, thus expanding his sensitivities and readying him for more rapid accommodation to environmental change. It can provide conceptual and methodological tools with which more discerning judgments can be made. (p. 317)

Schlenker's rebuttal (1974) defended social psychology as a scientific discipline. His major point was that Gergen didn't understand the nature of scientific laws. Such laws, Schlenker argued, don't deal with specific details, as in, "A promise of a lollipop will get a child to finish his spinach at suppertime" (p. 3); it is true but irrelevant that children may not like lollipops 200 years from now. Rather, scientific laws are conditional abstract formulations by means of which we try to account for specific details, as in, "Expectations of positive reinforcement will increase the probability of a contingent response" (p. 3). In other words, under conditions ABC, XYZ will occur. In any specific instance, we must first observe whether or not conditions ABC exist, whether or not positive reinforcement is in fact expected. Then we observe whether XYZ occurs.

The striking thing about Schlenker's examples of transhistorical generalizations is that they include precisely those terms that have traditionally presented the greatest difficulties for a *science* of psychology: *expectation* (p. 3) and *perception* (p. 8). This is not to argue that psychologists shouldn't use theoretical constructs: science is always theoretical. Rather, it is to argue that the theoretical constructs of psychologists have been harder to anchor simultaneously in theory and observation than those in chemistry or physics; and success in doing so is critical to Schlenker's argument. It is potentially no less scientific to speak about the effects of hypothetical cognitions and perceptions than about the effects of hypothetical subatomic particles, but can psychologists specify the conditions under which they would reject or modify Schlenker's transhistorical generalization involving expectation on the grounds that it was inconsistent with the facts?

Cronbach's views (1975) were closer to Gergen's than to Schlenker's. He agreed with Schlenker that scientific generalizations were true only for the conditions to which they refer (nor would Gergen disagree), but then pointed out that in the social sciences even complex factorial designs cannot eliminate the many important variables even a series of studies cannot include.

> This puts construct validation (Cronbach, 1971; Cronbach & Meehl, 1955) in a new light. Because Meehl and I were importing into psychology a rationale developed out of physical science, we spoke as if a fixed reality is to be accounted for. Events are accounted for—and predicted—by a network of propositions connecting abstract constructs. The network is patiently revised until it gives a good account of the original data, and of new data as they

come in. Propositions describing atoms and electrons have a long half-life, and the physical theorist can regard the processes in his world as steady. Rarely is a social or behavioral phenomenon isolated enough to have this steady-process property. . . . The atheoretical regularities of the actuary are even more time bound. An actuarial table describing human affairs changes from science into history before it can be set in type.

Our troubles do not arise because human events are in principle unlawful; man and his creations are part of the natural world. The trouble, as I see it, is that we cannot store up generalizations and constructs for ultimate assembly into a network. It is as if we needed a gross of dry cells to power an engine and could make one a month. The energy would leak out of the first cells before we had half the battery completed. So it is with the potency of our generalizations. If the effect of a treatment changes over a few decades, that inconsistency is an effect, a Treatment X Decade interaction that must itself be regulated by whatever laws there be. Such interactions frustrate any would-be theorist who mixes data from several decades indiscriminately into the phenomenal picture he tries to explain (p. 123).

If social scientists would give up trying to do what, as Cronbach sees it, cannot be done, they could make important contributions:

Though enduring systematic theories about man in society are not likely to be achieved, systematic inquiry can realistically hope to make two contributions. One reasonable aspiration is to assess local events accurately, to improve short-run control (Glass, 1972). The other reasonable aspiration is to develop explanatory concepts, concepts that will help people use their heads.

*   *   *   *   *

Social scientists are rightly proud of the discipline we draw from the natural-science side of our ancestry. Scientific discipline is what we uniquely add to the time-honored ways of studying man. Too narrow an identification with science, however, has fixed our eyes upon an inappropriate goal. The goal of our work, I have argued here, is not to amass generalizations atop which a theoretical tower can someday be erected (Scriven, 1959, p. 471). The special task of the social scientist in each generation is to pin down the contemporary facts. Beyond that, he shares with the humanistic scholar and the artist in the effort to gain insight into contemporary relationships, and to realign the culture's view of man with present realities. To know man as he is is no mean aspiration. (p. 126)

What, Then, Might *Merit* Mean?

While there is considerable disagreement on the matter of psychology as a theoretically sophisticated science, there is far more agreement on the virtues of detailed, careful ("scientific") observation that strives to eliminate the personal biases likely to creep into casual, everyday observation. This suggests that the merit of a psychology proposal may be more easily evaluated with regard to the methods chosen than with regard to the ultimate goals of the researcher (to build a better theory and/or world). While some of the most important criticisms of the race-IQ area pertain to the goals of the research, others deal with the suitability of the methods for reaching whichever goal the researcher has chosen. We may, then, view *merit* in two ways: an area may or may not lend itself to the goals of the researcher (for example, theory building); and/or its nature may be such that no methods can be found that would achieve the aims of the researcher, or only methods that are by their nature damaging to the "subjects" and/or others. Agreement among psychologists in the first category will be all but impossible to achieve at this time, but in the second category, there might be considerable agreement. Since the merit of a research area or project usually figures extensively in deliberations about the justifications for choosing it, it is important to try to pinpoint the sources of disagreements and to consider carefully the possibility of resolving them.

CHALLENGES

1. Think about Bordin's presentation of the tension between *doubt* and *compassion*, and then develop arguments pertaining to the question, "Is psychological research low on Lipsey's social concern factor immoral?"
2. Select several lines of research in psychology. First consider the prescription each seems to represent, and then consider what you would say to someone who wanted to do research in each area.
3. Read several studies whose area is gender comparison (notably Benbow & Stanley, 1980) and then develop arguments pertaining to the question, Is it immoral to choose this research area? (See also Schafer & Gray, 1981).
4. Discuss your views about Challenge three with several other people. What specific agreements and disagreements emerged in your discussion about choosing an area?
5. Present arguments to justify one form of each thesis, supplying details (conditions) as necessary:
   a. It is (always) (never) (sometimes) ethical to do research on the learning and forgetting of nonsense syllables.
   b. It is (always) (never) (sometimes) ethical to do research on the learning and forgetting of anxiety-provoking experiences.

5

CONCEPTUALIZING, THEORIZING, AND/OR EVALUATING

All psychologists conceptualize, regardless of their area. Whether all psychologists also *theorize* depends on one's interpretation of that word. Not every psychologist creates new theories, as did Freud and Hull, but every psychologist does think within some theoretical framework, however loose it may be. Psychology has a striking number of theories, even within subareas. There are many theories about learning, personality, therapy, social behavior, physiological processes, and language development. Along with the many theories come even more concepts, so many that psychologists keep reminding each other that naming a perplexing phenomenon is not the same as explaining it! (See, for example, Hilgard, 1980, p. 21.) The morally relevant question, however, is whether psychological concepts and theories inevitably reveal our moral concerns and judgments.

THREE SOCIAL-PERSONALITY PERSPECTIVES

This chapter argues that theories that deal with human conduct inevitably include values. Therefore, we begin by considering theories in the social-personality areas. Theories in these areas differ from each other in two ways relevant to the issue of whether values are expressed in psychological theories. First, some theorists stress causes, taking what is called a *hard determinism* position, while other theorists stress choices. The latter either argue a free will position, or try to reconcile free choice and causes of behavior, thus taking what is called a soft or *reconciling determinism* position. The freedom-determinism position is considered in greater detail in the next chapter. It concerns us here because theories in the social-personality areas invariably take a position on this issue, and that position enters into their values.

Second, some theorists stress what goes on inside a person confronting a situation, while others stress the impact of the situation outside the person. Freud's theory is an example of the former, Skinner's of the latter. For Freud, behavior is the resultant of inner forces. For Skinner, it is a function of environmental contingencies. Social psychology, too, has typically stressed the immediate social environment. Positions on this issue also enter into the values implied by theories.

Psychological Freedom

Szasz (1970) has made freedom the cornerstone of his theory, and the link between theory and values is very clear as he moves (perhaps too readily) from one meaning of that word to another. Individuals are and should be able to make choices. We have free will, and to that extent, are unpredictable. Those who try to predict behavior are therefore likely to try to constrain and control it. Thus, those who view people as complex but determined mechanisms are likely to favor social and political systems low on social and political freedoms. *Statism* refers to government efforts to control people, and insofar as these succeed, people become more predictable. (Laws make us more predictable, as when they contribute to our choosing to stop for a red light or to send our children to school.) Szasz prefers a minimum of state control and a maximum of individual freedom. For him, laws about stealing are necessary, but laws about suicide and laws regulating the sale of drugs are not.

Szasz conceptualizes people as choosing all of their roles and behaviors in particular situations. He even speaks of psychotics as, for example, choosing the role of pretending to be Christ (Szasz, 1970, p. 195). He argues that the concept of mental illness is a modern myth: nothing in social relationships is comparable to pneumonia or hepatitis. Rather, people have always had, and still do have, problems in living together. In the above example, the psychotic's family has difficulty dealing with him and he with them. This is a moral problem, not a medical one. Our modern solution to it is to label people mentally ill, and thus to justify depriving them of their freedom by locking them up in mental hospitals. Yet hallucinations and delusions are not against the law, and the people involved have no trial. Therefore, they are and will continue to be unjustly deprived of their freedom by various groups working for the state (such as psychiatrists). What does Szasz recommend instead? That we return to taking seriously the moral and personal challenges of living with each other responsibly.

It must be emphasized that Szasz is not opposed to the seeking of advice if we choose to do so. Thus, even if all drugs were available over-the-counter, we might still decide to consult a physician. Similarly, we might seek out a family therapist. What he does oppose is our being forced by the state to go to physicians and other therapists when we have not chosen to do so. We are forced because so many drugs are available by prescription only and because, for example, our child might otherwise be expelled from school. Such state force is on the increase, *in part because of our modern conceptualization of human beings.* This conception guides psychologists' activities, which is one of the things that theories always do.

How are theory and evaluation intertwined in Szasz's views? He is not only saying, "Other hypotheses about human beings contradict facts." He is also saying, "The way we think about human beings (constructs, theories) is related to the most basic moral concepts: rights, responsibilities, freedom." Conceptualize one way, and you reflect and support statist psychology: enforced interviewing, testing, and adjusting for the sake of the state and its institutions. Conceptualize another way, and you reflect and support individual freedom from government control: the right to request or not to request help in solving the problems of social living.

Psychological Determinism

Szasz's views are striking to us because they differ from some of the Freudian and post-Freudian concepts which have by now been absorbed by almost everybody. In this view, not everyone is free; in fact, depending on how close to Freud one stays, one might say that no one is free. Rather, people differ in degrees of mental health or illness: precisely what Szasz calls a "myth." The healthiest people strike a personally satisfying and socially acceptable or even admired balance among id, ego, and superego. Their contact with reality is good; this includes approximately realistic self-perception. The least healthy have a distorted perception of reality, including themselves. Thus, a man might believe that he is Christ (to use Szasz's example), or that he is a despicable person who deserves nobody's love. Such people can only be cured if their unconscious motives, which control their thoughts, feelings, and actions, become conscious. These then lose their potency or are dissipated in some way.

In this view, one might observe a family who are living together well, and yet conclude that all of them are less healthy than they might be. Furthermore, one would not hesitate to treat psychotics, even if they were protesting: they are so sick (they have lost contact with reality to such an extent) that they do not know they need help. One deprives them of freedom while they are hospitalized only long enough to help them; if they cannot be helped, then clearly one ought to act responsibly toward those who cannot deal with the realities outside the hospital. In this view, then, statism and/or parentalism is justified, one might even say demanded, under certain conditions.

Social Determinism

Some of the values implicit in the Freudian perspective are clear from the contrast with those of Szasz. Others become clear only as a third perspective is considered. In this regard, it will be helpful to consider Ryan's *Blaming the Victim* (1971), the central thesis of which is more than hinted at in the title of his book. When social scientists theorize, argues Ryan, their social values are revealed. Most of the time they defend the status quo by blaming the victim. Thus, people are poor because . . . and the causes explored and "discovered" reflect badly on the poor: they are stupid, they cannot delay gratification, they cannot keep their families together, they do X, they do not do Y. Ryan's sympathies lie with the disadvantaged rather than with those who usually theorize about them: people are poor because they do not have enough money—and that is a broadly social phenomenon with social causes, not the fault of the poor's personalities and behaviors.

Here again, theory and evaluation are intertwined. Ryan alerts us to the negative evaluation of the disadvantaged inherent in theorizing that views their "weaknesses" as causing their disadvantaged status, theories distinctly to the advantage of the advantaged. His own sympathetic attitudes toward the disadvantaged are revealed in his theorizing about the effects of the (morally wrong) distributions of wealth and power in our society.

Ryan's social determinism and his social-political sympathies reveal that for all of their other differences, the Freudian and Szaszian views share an emphasis on what Ryan calls the victim—the person. It is the person who should change, though differently for Freud and Szasz. On Ryan's view, changes should be made in society.

DESCRIPTION AND PRESCRIPTION

It should be clear by now that concepts and theories reveal values and thus prescribe; they also refer to something, they also describe. When someone says, "That cake is delicious," we certainly cannot conclude that the cake doesn't exist. Similarly, when someone (erroneously) says, "Prejudice is neurotic," we cannot conclude that prejudice doesn't exist, though it may exist in some sense other than cake (see below). Thus, both statements conceptualize (foods, attitudes, tastes, personalities), but they also evaluate (delicious, neurotic). The evaluation implied by *neurotic* may, as we have seen, be intended to mean no more than that health is preferable to illness. It is also the case, however, that this label carries a social stigma, and that one may feel insulted when called neurotic, as one does not when told one has pneumonia. Furthermore, one difference between "cake" and "prejudice" is that prejudice is also value-laden. Both good and bad cakes are still called "cake," but prejudice is viewed by many psychologists as inherently bad (Collins, 1970), so that "good prejudices," if there are any, may end up with another name!

COULD PSYCHOLOGY BE NEUTRAL?

So far, the intertwining of theorizing and evaluating has been considered on a relatively abstract level, but the critical role of evaluation may be seen in descriptions of the most ordinary situations. These, too, are of great interest to psychologists. Consider the following. Z and X are discussing topic T. Z makes a point, X makes a point. This continues for 15 minutes. At that time, we hear Z say, "You really are rigid!" to which X replies, "If you mean that I stick to my guns, you bet I do!" Note that in this case, they are in agreement about the outcome: that at the end of the discussion, both of them are saying what they said at the beginning. The difference between them is that Z labels X "rigid" (bad), while X is essentially boasting that "I have the courage of my convictions" (good).

The most value-neutral description we could achieve would look like this: "Z and X are discussing topic T. Z makes a point, X makes a point. This continues for N minutes. At the end of the discussion, both of them are saying what they were saying in the beginning." The most striking thing about this summary of a large group of common human situations is that it permits no further thought or action unless details are provided, and that would immediately introduce a social context and a value framework. What might a psychologist say then? "We must discuss this some more." This would imply that some sort of resolution could perhaps be reached, that discussion is preferable to violence, and that it would be desirable to resolve the matter. Or perhaps, "This is another example of X's inability to get along with people, to compromise." This implies that it is good to get along with others, perhaps even if this means giving up or silencing important beliefs. Finally, consider, "This is another example of Z's resorting to name-calling when angry." Same point: name-calling is bad. These descriptions imply values and prescriptions, the nature of which becomes clearest whenever change is considered.

In other words, the most nontheoretical and nonsocial description possible permits no one to take sides because of the absence of detail. Such a description also makes one wonder why anyone would want to take sides, why anyone would even be interested in the entire matter! The episode described, however, touches on some of the most important theoretical and practical questions in several areas of psychology. Under what conditions do people change their minds? How can we know whether only verbalizations changed or also beliefs? How can and do people (psychologists and others) decide what changes, if any, would be desirable in a particular situation? The importance of this episode becomes clear as soon as we put some flesh on the bones. Z and X are husband and wife and they are discussing whether or not to purchase an expensive new living room set. Z is a student, X is a professor and they are discussing the grading of one of Z's essays. Z is an alienated member of a church, X is the church's minister and they are discussing Z's nonattendance at church. If we are honest, we will admit that films of such discussions would make it difficult for us not to take sides—that is, to put "good" and "right" into a moral framework. Have we any reason to believe that psychologists are exempt from this human tendency?

According to several recent observers (Gergen, 1973; Haan, 1977; Campbell, 1975; Sampson, 1977), the answer is no. Gergen argues, for example, that the values of psychologists show clearly in their studies of prejudice, rigidity, dogmatism, conformity, and authoritarianism; as any reader will have guessed, these are all "bad." One could almost say that any reader of Maslow's writings who does not grasp that *self-actualization* is (the ultimate) good simply does not understand Maslow's sentences. Campbell has called attention to possible negative consequences of the great value psychology as a discipline places on individuality and self-expression; these are viewed as good, conformity as bad. His concern is that "psychology may be contributing to the undermining of the retention of what may be extremely valuable social-evolutionary inhibitory systems which we do not yet fully understand" (Campbell, 1975, p. 1120).

Some psychologists are sensitive to this problem, but sensitivity, while helpful, does not provide an escape. For example, in their book about Machiavellianism, Christie and Geiss (1970) relate that in the beginning they had a negative attitude toward high Mach people but, in the end, they are expressing different values: different social slots are best filled by different personalities. Perhaps that is so, in a pragmatic sense, but this view implies that all or most personalities are potentially good because they are useful in some context. In addition social roles or slots as they exist seem to be accepted rather than questioned. Someone else might wish to argue that both high Machiavellianism and the slots high Machs fill should be abolished.

SHOULD PSYCHOLOGY BE NEUTRAL?

Some psychologists, notably Maslow (1969), are convinced not only that psychology is inevitably a value-laden discipline, but that the striving for neutrality is itself immoral, because it turns psychology away from its responsibilities to humanity. Maslow stresses the interaction between good people and a good society: only good people can create and appreciate a good society, only in a good society can people become the best they are capable. Psychologists should not create and test theories in a detached, morally neutral way. Instead, they should begin with a clear commitment to helping humanity, and that commitment should remain paramount in all professional activities.

WHY ARE DESCRIPTION AND PRESCRIPTION RELATED?

Several links exist between the psychologist's use of *good* and morally relevant concepts. Psychological concepts and theories do indeed imply moral *oughts,* and this consideration applies to all the areas of psychology that deal with human activities: developmental, personality, social, industrial, abnormal, clinical, counseling, and school. Physiological concepts per se have no morally relevant content. Thus, the physiological processes involved in eating or thinking are morally neutral. Haan (1977) has suggested that this is because they refer to physical reality, while concepts dealing with human social activities do not. The latter, she suggests, are constructions of the human imagination. It does not seem likely that this can be the critical factor, since scientific knowledge of physical reality involves as much "construction" as knowledge of social reality.

Two other possible explanations deserve consideration. First, some constructs are closer to perceptually obvious segments of reality than others. Compare tree, artery, and rock throwing to autumn, frictionless planes, and achievement motivation. Second, people normally have little vested interest in the social hierarchies of animals and physiological bases of behavior, but there are instructive exceptions to this statement. Thus, physiological approaches to the study of psychosis are not value-free merely because they are physiological, since they hypothesize about psychosis and, potentially, its cure by means of drugs. As pointed out above, this involves us with the social hierarchies among people and the uses of power.

To give another example, we have a vested interest in the hierarchies that exist in the animal world whenever we humans are viewed as part of it, and when questions arise about the uses and abuses of human power. Thus, we either don't question human superiority and our use of animals in psychological research, or we rationalize (or do we reason?) our way to these (see Chapter 6). If we valued *kindness* more than *intelligence,* could humans still be viewed as the top of the animal hierarchy? As a final example, consider Gould's (1978) concept of *finagling.* Gould described the work of Samuel Morton, an early 19th century physician who searched for physical differences among races and therefore collected and classified more than 1,000 human skulls between 1830 and 1851. He tabulated their relative capacities in such a way that the races were ranked in line with the racist hypotheses of his time. This finagling of data was guided by the unquestioned thesis of Caucasian superiority, and was unconscious, not deliberate. Since Morton was not covering his tracks but, on the contrary, saved all his raw data, Gould was able to discover the finagling and to reconsider his interpretations.

SUMMARY AND IMPLICATIONS

Most fundamentally, a psychologist who conceptualizes or (as we have just seen) touches on human social activities and concerns inevitably does so within a moral values framework. The different conceptions of optimal personality or mental health and illness accept the social status quo in varying degrees. *Well adjusted* usually means adjusted to social reality as it exists. Emphasizing the statistically normal (modal personality) all but explicitly argues that what is ought to be. At the other end of the continuum are the views emphasizing self-fulfillment. As Haan (1977) introduces these, "happiness minimizes social concern and optimizes personal salvation, irrespective of social context, and by so doing places society, either as a force for good or bad, in an unimportant role" (p. 75). Haan points out that those views that emphasize being symptom-free reveal no striving for growth in a positive sense. Thus, she suggests that behavior modification is the therapy of the poor, since "the poor cannot afford to expect more" (p. 73) and only go for help when their situation is desperate. They therefore settle for the removal of the major problems. To give an example from a different area, the industrial psychologist is forced while conceptualizing and hypothesizing to choose the value framework of management or labor, since the two are not identical, though they may overlap. Or again, stage theories implicitly or explicitly view some stage(s) as optimal. The same can be said about psychologists who conceptualize physiological and/or animal processes that have implications for human social activities.

Second, how are the value framework and specific values chosen? Psychologists may assume that their expertise permits or obligates them to choose, since they know what mental health or optimal adjustment is, while other people do not. Thus, Freud knew that neurotic and psychotic people could not be blamed for their condition because they were ill. In both behavior modification and humanistic therapies, the goals to be reached are more nearly chosen jointly by therapist and client. The difference between these two perspectives is clearly revealed in the different prescriptive, evaluative (and also descriptive) words used: *patient* and *client*. If the client of any therapist wanted to reach a goal considered immoral by that therapist, the latter either would not accept the former in therapy (hopefully explaining why not), or would hope to cure this symptom.

Thus, the continued existence of any therapeutic relationship implies either that the therapist chooses the values or that both parties accept the agreed goals of therapy as moral rather than immoral. Strupp and Hadley (1977) point out that three parties are actually involved, clients, therapists, and society, and their moral perspectives do not always agree. To give just one example, both client and therapist may consider homosexuality morally acceptable, while many members of the community may consider it morally reprehensible. How shall the therapeutic good be chosen? Whose values shall concepts reflect?

Third, psychological concepts have implications for the morally relevant concept of *acting responsibly*. The Freudian therapist would take responsibility, yielding relatively little to the patient and, as we have seen, this notion has been vigorously attacked by Szasz. In behavior modification, joint responsibility is accepted and sometimes even formalized in a contract. As both philosopher of science and theoretician, Skinner (1971) has argued against traditional meanings of *responsible* altogether, at least insofar as these imply freedom of choice. All choices, according to him, including so-called moral ones, are under environmental control. Therefore, what is called acting responsibly can only happen in an environment designed according to behavioral science knowledge.

Fourth, when psychologists conceptualize some good, is it desirable that everybody have this good, if possible? If so, what obligations do psychologists have for making it possible for everyone to have it? If it is good in some sense to be free of toothaches or psychosis or reading problems or hyperactivity, then surely (and this is a moral judgment) this good should either be available to everyone, or cogent moral reasons given why it should not. Thus, the good stated or implied by psychologists in their theorizing raises questions about citizen and professional rights and obligations. The other side of this coin is that at times, it appears that the psychologist's good is available to everyone almost too rapidly, at least according to psychologists like Campbell (1975), who is concerned about a proper balance between individual and group needs. There is the further question of what happens when the good represents different things in different value frameworks. What happens in society when everybody is influenced by Freud and/or Maslow and/or Skinner? The moral aspects of sharing psychological theories and their values are discussed in Chapter 7.

It is instructive to look at a final example, this time from research. It is almost nontheoretical but not without content. As we will see, it would be delusion to insist that the concepts used are without morally relevant values.

Let us begin with the major finding, which might be reported as follows: Scores on Test X correlate N with behavior Y under conditions (or in situation) Z. Now let us attach meaning to X, Y, and Z. Y is a measure of *absenteeism* (the number of days absent from work per month). Z is the situation: a particular industrial plant. X is an attitude scale, the items of which sound like affirmations and denials of the Protestant Ethic. How is conceptualization involved here with morally relevant values?

1. Absenteeism has been selected out of the totality of behavior of some of the people employed at the plant: the workers. It is a concept created by people with certain social values rather than being a perceptually obvious unit like a tree. We intuitively sense or know that high absenteeism is the bad end of the continuum, low absenteeism the good end. This is of course not the only possible interpretation of this continuum; consider the viewpoint of a strike organizer!

   It is also important to note that absenteeism has many causes, and a sophisticated study will deal with these. Thus, one person is absent because of a strep throat, another because of alcoholism, a third because a day at the shore seems considerably more inviting than a day at the plant. The point here is not the complexity of absenteeism, but rather that it was chosen and operationalized rather than alcoholism or boredom. Of course, if one of those had been selected instead, this, too, would represent certain values. In the one instance, we tend to think that management interests might be paramount, in the other, that worker welfare is of either major or at least incidental interest.

2. We also evaluate when we look at the personality continuum. It will probably turn out that if there is a significant correlation at all, people displaying more Protestant Ethic on the attitude scale are absent less than those displaying less of this ethic. Even before we know this, however, we have identified low, medium, or high scores as good, depending on our social values and our ideal personality.

3. Personality variables are no easier and no harder to conceptualize than environmental ones (Barker, 1968; Brunswik, 1947; Bem, 1978). The people at the plant are a sample of people. Similarly, the social environments at the plant are a sample of social environments! Thus, moral values will also be involved in conceptualizing either the personalities or the social environments or both, and this will ultimately affect how the findings are used. Will this be a case of blaming the victim, with the result that only high or low scorers will be hired, or will the working environment be changed to make it more attractive to more people?

This fairly typical research example clearly reveals again, in a different domain, the value-laden nature of conceptualization in psychology. We create our concepts or our hypotheses, as do all thinkers. Whenever we touch on human affairs, it does not seem to matter whether our creations deal with gender differences in aptitude for mathematics, absenteeism among workers, or cures for mental illness. Explicitly or implicitly, our morally relevant values will be involved.

This does not mean that hypotheses should be stated, or that research can not or should not be done. When we acknowledge, however, that our initial formulation represents one possibility among several within a very complex situation, then we can begin to consider alternate value perspectives as we explore psychological concepts and hypotheses. Doing this has become routine in those areas where recent power struggles have been involved. Women and blacks have sensitized us to the sexism and racism latent (and occasionally obvious) in our theories and we are currently being similarly sensitized about ageism (see Chapters 9 and 10). Perhaps a time will come when theoretical perspectives are scrutinized not only for their fruitfulness in generating ideas for research and/or application, but also for the value-framework they present.

THEMES AND VARIATIONS: CHAPTER 5

The traditional view is that psychology, as a science, is value-free or value-neutral, and that psychological concepts only *de*scribe—that *retroactive inhibition* doesn't *pre*scribe or imply moral values any more than *photosynthesis* or *mass*. In recent years, this view has been challenged repeatedly. Essentially, its critics argue that we cannot and should not avoid the moral values inevitably implied in all concepts and generalizations which deal with *human affairs*.

Do Concepts and Theories Imply Moral Judgments, Moral "Oughts"?

According to Szasz (1966, chap. 12),

> We can be sure of this: only man creates symbols and is influenced by them. Accordingly, being placed in certain classes affects people, whereas it does not affect animals and things. You call a person "schizophrenic," and something happens to him; you call a rat "rat" and a rock "granite," and nothing happens to them. In other words, in psychiatry and in human affairs generally, *the act of classification* is an exceedingly significant event. (p. 191)

> Those who have considered the prediction and control of human behavior logically possible and morally desirable have, in general, tended to advocate its coercive social control. . . . In contrast, those who have been skeptical about the range of the predictability of human behavior, and about the moral desirability of making such predictions, have tended to advocate freedom from arbitrary or personal social restraints. . . .
>
> Where do psychiatrists, especially nosologists, stand on this issue? On the whole, they are mechanomorphists of the first rank: they view man, especially mentally ill man, as a defective machine. (p. 200)

> As modern science progressed in its conquest of nature, it became clear . . . that, among all the unpredictable events in the universe, human behavior was one of the most baffling. Nor is this surprising. Among all the objects and creatures in the world, man is the only one endowed with free will: his

behavior is not only *determined* by antecedent events but is also *chosen* by him, in accordance with his view of himself and of the goals he seeks to attain. Or is this an illusion? Is personal freedom an ethical concept, unworthy of inclusion in the vocabulary of science?

To classify human behavior is to constrain it. (p. 201)

Human behavior may be regarded as a unique achievement of which only man is capable. Personal conduct is based on the free choices of a sign-using, rule-following, and game-playing person whose *action* is often largely governed by his future goals rather than by his past experiences. This view of man casts efforts to predict his behavior in a new perspective. For, to the extent that man is free to act—that is, free to choose among alternative courses of action—his conduct is, and must be, unpredictable: after all, this is what is meant by the word "free." Trying to predict human behavior is, therefore, likely to result in efforts to constrain it. (p. 203)

"The psychiatric patient" is a person who fails, or refuses, to assume a legitimate social role. This is not permitted in our culture, nor, for that matter, in any other culture. A person unclassified is unpredictable and not understandable and hence a threat to the other members of society. This is why people who choose this path to personal freedom pay dearly for it: although they succeed in breaking out of their particular cells, they do not remain long at liberty. They are immediately recaptured, first symbolically, by being classified as mentally ill; and then physically, by being brought to the psychiatrist for processing into formal psychiatric identities and for psychiatric detention. (p. 210)

According to Ryan (1971, chap. 1),

Consider some victims. One is the miseducated child in the slum school. He is blamed for his own miseducation. He is said to contain within himself the causes of his inability to read and write well. The shorthand phrase is "cultural deprivation," which, to those in the know, conveys what they allege to be inside information: that the poor child carries a scanty pack of cultural baggage as he enters school. He doesn't know about books and magazines and newspapers, they say. (No books in the home: the mother fails to subscribe to *Reader's Digest*.) They say that if he talks at all—an unlikely event since slum parents don't talk to their children—he certainly doesn't talk correctly. (Lower-class dialect spoken here, or even—God forbid!—Southern Negro.) (Ici on parle nigra.) If you can manage to get him to sit in a chair, they say, he squirms and looks out the window. (Impulse-ridden, these kids, motoric rather than verbal.) In a word he is "disadvantaged" and "socially deprived," they say, and this, of course, accounts for his failure (his failure, they say) to learn much in school.

*   *   *   *   *

Pointing to the supposedly deviant Negro family as the "fundamental weakness of the Negro community" is another way to blame the victim. Like "cultural deprivation," "Negro family" has become a shorthand phrase with stereotyped connotations of matriarchy, fatherlessness, and pervasive illegitimacy.

Is it any wonder the Negroes cannot achieve equality? From such families! And, again, by focusing our attention on the Negro family as the apparent *cause* of racial inequality, our eye is diverted. Racism, discrimination, segregation, and the powerlessness of the ghetto are subtly, but thoroughly, downgraded in importance.

The generic process of Blaming the Victim is applied to almost every American problem. The miserable health care of the poor is explained away on the grounds that the victim has poor motivation and lacks health information. The problems of slum housing are traced to the characteristics of tenants who are labeled as "Southern rural migrants" not yet "acculturated" to life in the big city. The "multiproblem" poor, it is claimed, suffer the psychological effects of impoverishment, the "culture of poverty," and the deviant value system of the lower classes; consequently, though unwittingly, they cause their own troubles. From such a viewpoint, the obvious fact that poverty is primarily an absence of money is easily overlooked or set aside. (pp. 3–5)

Should the Discipline of Psychology Strive for Moral Neutrality?

Maslow (1969) argued that we cannot be neutral when dealing with human questions, and that furthermore, we should not be. Neutrality would make us too passive with regard to the future, when we should be studying how to achieve a good society composed of good people.

> I think the question of a normative biology cannot be escaped or avoided, even if this calls into question the whole history and philosophy of science in the West. I am convinced that the value-free, value-neutral, value-avoiding model of science that we inherited from physics, chemistry, and astronomy, where it was necessary and desirable to keep the data clean and also to keep the church out of scientific affairs, is quite unsuitable for the scientific study of life. Even more dramatically is this value-free philosophy of science unsuitable for human questions, where personal values, purposes and goals, intentions and plans are absolutely crucial for the understanding of any person, and even for the classical goals of science, prediction, and control. (p. 725)

> It is now quite clear that the actualization of the highest human potentials is possible—on a mass basis—only under "good conditions." Or more directly, good human beings will generally need a good society in which to grow. Contrariwise, I think it should be clear that a normative philosophy of biology would involve the theory of the good society, defined in terms of "that society is good which fosters the fullest development of human potentials, of the fullest degree of humanness." I think this may at first sight be a little startling to the classical descriptive biologist who has learned to avoid such words as "good" and "bad," but a little thought will show that something of the sort is already taken for granted in some of the classical areas of biology. For instance, it is taken for granted that genes can be called "potentials" that are actualized or not actualized by their immediate surroundings in the germ

plasma itself, in the cytoplasm, in the organism in general, and in the geographical environment in which the organism finds itself. (p. 726)

The classical conception of objectivity came from the earliest days of scientific dealing with things and objects, with lifeless objects of study. We were objective when our own wishes and fears and hopes were excluded from the observation, and when the purported wishes and designs of a supernatural god were also excluded. This of course was a great step forward and made modern science possible. We must, however, not overlook the fact that this was true for dealing with nonhuman objects or things. Here this kind of objectivity and detachment works pretty well. It even works well with lower organisms. Here too we are detached enough, noninvolved enough so that we can be relatively noninterfering spectators. It does not matter to us to any great degree which way an amoeba goes or what a hydra prefers to ingest. This detachment gets more and more difficult as we go on up the phyletic scale. We know very well how easy it is to anthropomorphize, to project into the animal the observer's human wishes, fears, hopes, prejudices if we are dealing with dogs or cats, and more easily with monkeys or apes. When we get to the study of the human beings, we can now take it for granted that it is practically impossible to be the cool, calm, detached, uninvolved, noninterfering spectator. Psychological data have piled up to such a point that no one could conceivably defend this position (p. 730)

Therefore I would urge all biologists, as I would urge all other people of goodwill, to put their talents into the service of these two Big Problems. [For Maslow these are how to create Good People and a Good Society.]

The above considerations have strongly supported my feeling that the classical philosophy of science as morally neutral, value free, value neutral is not only wrong, but is extremely dangerous as well. It is not only amoral; it may be antimoral as well. It may put us into great jeopardy. (p. 733)

Why Is It Hard or Impossible to Have Morally Neutral Concepts, Hypotheses, and Theories in Psychology?

Note again the selections from Szasz and Maslow (especially the paragraph from p. 730).

According to Haan (1977),

Since personality has no known material, physical basis, scientific description must proceed by initially choosing constructs that are based on common meanings and then advancing to defining possible inter-connections among the common meanings with the result that new, more general or supraordinate, constructs may be identified. All of these are acts of creative imagination that acquire reality only as they conform to others' reality. In other words, social agreement is one kind—social scientists' kind—of truth. As a result, the models we construct inevitably imbue our varying value suppositions in different ways and in different degrees. Under the sway of the ultralogical positivists, we pretend that these circumstances did not need to obtain if psychology would strictly confine itself to sense data. If value intrusion were admitted, it was regarded as nonscience. Now, neither pretense nor embarrassed admission is necessary. Still, we do need to be clear and, for the sake of science, vigilant, and we need greater sophistication about the precise nature of value intrusions and how they can and should be handled.

*   *   *   *   *

Many areas of psychology research do not require a close examination of value assumptions because the immediate targets of investigation rest on material realities that may have nearly invariant relations with the behavior of some species, for example, the link between sex behavior and hormonic balance in birds. Work in still other areas of psychology is based on the supposition that physical systems that underlie and determine psychological action will be eventually discovered, for example, studies of some aspects of perception or early ideas that intelligence might be related to cortical myelinization. However, as soon as words like "more intelligent" are used, a social-psychological construct is created by an active effort of imagination. People are not only individually selective about the acts that they regard as intelligent but they are even more so about what they call "more intelligent." For instance, there is an incipient argument brewing between the Piagetians and the psychometricians as to whether a high test IQ is more intelligent and better than being able to reason with formal operations. Only eventual inter-subjective agreement can save such concepts.

*   *   *   *   *

To summarize the implications of the discussion to this point, we can note that these matters are not pressing issues in the minds of some psychologists: (1) because their targets of research, even though not materially based, are clear and consensual (e.g., industrial psychology's acceptance of the research criteria of greater efficiency and more production with greater work satisfaction), or (2) because they think they have identified durable and universal psychological elements, such as cognitive, moral, or linguistic structures, that can be described both synchronically and diachronically in terms of development. The empirically verified description of the maximized, developed form of these structures can be an operational definition for criteria of "greater maturity," a kind of goodness that could guide both research and social policy, or (3) because value intrusion goes unnoticed and the model of personality is constructed by the psychometric mariner at sea, and the technician's values are unwittingly optimized.

At the present time personality-social psychologists have neither criteria of consensus (as do industrial psychologists) nor universal structural elements (as do the cognitive stage theorists) to form their taxonomies of personalities. (pp. 64–68)

After categorizing Morton's "finagling" while analyzing the skull capacities of different races, Gould (1978) concluded:

Yet, through all this juggling, I find no indication of fraud or conscious manipulation. Morton made no attempt to cover his tracks, and I must assume that he remained unaware of their existence. He explained everything he did, and published all his raw data. All I discern is an a priori conviction of racial ranking so powerful that it directed his tabulations along preestablished lines. Yet Morton was widely hailed as the objectivist of his age, the man who would rescue American science from the mire of unsupported speculation. I regard Morton's saga as an admittedly egregious example of a common problem in scientific work. Without a priori preferences, we would scarcely be human; and good science, as Darwin noted so often, collects data to test ideas. Science has long recognized the tyranny of prior preference, and has constructed safeguards in requirements of uniform procedure and replication of experiments. Gross flouting of procedure and conscious fraud may often be detected, but unconscious finagling by sincere seekers of objectivity may be refractory. The culprit in this tale is a naive belief that pure objectivity can be attained by human beings rooted in cultural traditions of shared belief—and a consequent failure of self-examination.

One may argue that lying with statistics is easier than fudging an experiment and that a direct intersection with contemporary politics makes for a more passionate a priori, but I think that most scientists pursue their private battles with as much ardor and as much at stake. I propose no cure for the problem of finagling: indeed, I write this article to argue that it is not a disease. The only palliations I know are vigilance and scrutiny. (p. 509)

CHALLENGE

Carefully read or reread several articles or books that represent a variety of psychological concepts and theories. Which, if any of these, contain morally relevant values? How did you become aware of the values? Would you try to recast the conceptualizations so that they are value-free? Could you? Why or why not?

6

GATHERING INFORMATION

All psychologists gather information, no matter where they work. Furthermore, in doing so, they have an overall purpose, plan, and/or design, and they use particular techniques. A counseling psychologist may suggest that a client take an interest test for the purpose of gathering information relevant to the client's career choice. An experimental design may involve exposing several groups of animals to the same stimuli but for different lengths of time, in order to clarify a particular point about their sensory systems.

Both the purposes of gathering information and the particular techniques used involve the psychologist with ethical issues, with the same issues arising in many settings. For example, questions about telling the truth while gathering information can arise because certain experimental designs include deceiving people, or because a client might be harmed by knowing certain things about the information gathering procedures. Several interrelated ethical issues will be discussed: hurting or harming people and animals; conceptualizing organisms; parentalism; truth telling and deception; informed consent; privacy and confidentiality; and the state of the organism at the end of the information-gathering process.

IDENTIFYING THE ETHICAL ISSUES IN SPECIFIC SITUATIONS

As Part I indicated, "Do no harm" is one of the most basic normative ethical principles, but it is often not the only one relevant in a particular situation. Furthermore, "Do no harm" cannot be taken as an absolute. For example, one may be justified in hurting or harming someone if one thereby prevents even greater hurt or harm to that person. Thus, you are morally justified in momentarily hurting somebody with a strong push if you thereby prevent that person from being hit by an oncoming car. In that situation, your push (the lesser harm) prevents death or serious injury (the greater harm), and you have no time to explain the situation and then ask permission (informed consent), but you are in essence assuming that the person would agree to being saved in this way. (That legal difficulties can arise from such behavior does not alter its moral justifiability.) Similar considerations apply to physicians giving preventive shots to children. *Harm* and *hurt* need not refer to physical acts; most of us are familiar with pain caused by attacks on our character and achievements. Furthermore, harm and hurt need not refer to intense pain; inflicting even mild pain may or may not be justifiable.

Because nonmaleficence is such a basic principle, let us begin with the following observation: it is often impossible to gather information without risking making people uncomfortable—that is, without hurting some people at least slightly for a short time (for instance, by causing them to doubt their capabilities). This observation will be analyzed first in the context that provides the maximum justification for the psychologist to hurt someone, then in more problematic contexts of gathering information. The ethical issues mentioned above will be used in a preliminary way in these analyses and explored in greater detail later in this chapter. As you read the following example, remember that nothing should be viewed as obvious.

Ten-year-old Joe's parents have brought him to a psychologist for evaluation and advice. He is cheerful and cooperative, and his description of the problem parallels that of his parents. He finds it hard to sit still, sometimes has trouble understanding things at home and in school, does uneven school work, and is often chastised by his teacher and tormented by other children. Joe and his parents are easily convinced that the information obtained so far suggests that psychological testing would be desirable (that is, that a special kind of further information is needed). In fact, they may have arrived requesting such testing.

As the testing proceeds, Joe has several experiences of failure (for example, he simply cannot draw a diamond, even with repeated efforts and with a model before him), and these clearly make him anxious. It is true that he also has success experiences, but the psychologist will explore everything that Joe does. The testing session was not designed to maximize his immediate pleasure, but rather to gather information which could lead to his eventually being helped.

Although almost everyone will immediately conclude that testing Joe is morally permissible, even obligatory, it is important to articulate the considerations that bear on this intuitive conclusion.

1. The psychologist's goal is to help Joe, to try to decrease the pains of his daily life, to try to increase his successes and his sense of well being.
2. It is impossible to do this testing without making Joe anxious in the manner described above, and testing is the best available information-gathering technique here (to determine whether he is retarded, brain-damaged, or something else), although psychological procedures are not as certain (valid) as are comparable ones which physicians use when, for example, they draw blood for a test.
3. Joe came voluntarily and is consenting to the testing. He knows that he has some problems, and he suffers from them; he came in the hope or belief that he would find help here.
4. The psychologist will try to arrange the situation so that when Joe leaves, he will feel at least as good as, if not better than, when he came. They will have discussed the testing before, during, and after it takes place. The idea will be to help Joe feel appropriately hopeful yet realistic, and he may even leave with some specific suggestions (such as, for coping with the restlessness).
5. It is not possible to inform Joe in advance about exactly what pleasures and discomforts await him. The psychologist can only give him an approximate overview, and then reassure him (by pointing out that some of the test material is very hard). Thus, the psychologist deals with Joe without any deliberate deception, but on the other hand, cannot anticipate for him his experiencing of the testing, nor can he tell Joe the truth about tests in the sense that college students are told (about reliability and validity).
6. To some extent, the psychologist is parentalistic: I know (not you) what must be done and how to go about it in a manner which is beneficial for you overall.
7. Privacy and confidentiality in this case would probably extend to the family unit rather than to the child. Thus, Joe and his parents would be assured that his teacher would only find out what they wanted the teacher to know. On the other hand, it would probably be made clear to Joe that his problem and possible interventions would be discussed with his parents. (Special problems could arise if Joe said, "Don't tell my parents, but . . .").

If any specific details are changed, so is the analysis of his situation, even though the concerns remain the same. For example, suppose that Diane is three years old; what would it mean then to talk about informing her and asking her consent? Suppose that Robin is an adolescent accused of theft whose testing has been mandated by a court of law. What about consent then? For whom would this testing be helpful? What would happen to privacy and confidentiality? Thus, the particular example chosen should not be interpreted to mean that psychologists have no morally relevant problems while gathering information through the use of tests (on the contrary: see Chapter 11). Rather, that example was chosen to show that even an apparently obvious case deserves careful analysis.

It is instructive to compare this most justifiable case with data collection in research, noting both similarities and differences.

1. The researcher's major goal is not to help the subjects or participants in an immediate sense, but rather, to learn about the functioning of animals or people, sometimes with hopes of later applicability, sometimes not. In totally applied research, the psychologist is typically working within or for (that is, to help) an organization (perhaps an industry or the armed services). This may or may not benefit the individual participants in the end, which raises questions about respect for individuals.

2. In research, the best data collection techniques are also sometimes impossible to use without making the participants somewhat uncomfortable. For example, in order to study rats under the condition of 22 hours of food deprivation, one obviously has to deprive them of food for 22 hours! Similarly, in order to experiment on the effects of success and failure experiences on children, one has to create such experiences for them. One cannot judge beforehand to what extent a particular research project will prove important, and as pointed out in Chapter 4, such judgments vary as a function of the psychologist's perspective on the entire discipline of psychology. Furthermore, such judgments unfortunately also seem to depend on the results. For example, judgments about the importance of the research on language in apes is inevitably affected by one's knowledge of the striking and much-disputed results.

3. Animals cannot be said to have come voluntarily in the hope of being helped. In fact, the harshest critics would contend that the animals didn't have any problems until they were forced to come! Whether and when people can be said to come voluntarily and to give consent is a complex question (see below). In any case, they rarely come into a research situation to be helped with a problem, though when they come to learn about psychology (rather than to flirt with the lab assistant), they come to benefit from the situation (though they had no problem).

4. Psychologists try to arrange the research situation so that when human participants leave, they will feel as good as, or better than, when they came. They do this by discussing the purposes and procedures of their studies, and by dealing with residual discomfort as necessary, such as, with the almost inevitable concern, How well did I do? Questions arise about whether, when, and how psychologists succeed in these efforts.

In the case of animals, hungry rats are fed, and thus presumably returned to their initial state. On the other hand, when psychologists have removed parts of the animals' brains or other body parts, they try to make them as comfortable as possible throughout the study or series of studies, and typically kill them when the research has been completed.

5. One cannot inform or deceive animals in the sense that one can people. Perhaps, then, *informed consent* is a meaningless concept when applied to animals. Then again, it may be pertinent that we know that no animal would consent to being seriously harmed if it could be informed and then asked to consent. This idea may apply to infants and the comatose, and perhaps also to animals. Animals can be viewed as being similar to children. Someone with their best interests in mind could be asked to give informed consent on their behalf. In the case of children, this usually refers to their legal guardians or to somebody acting in loco parentis, while in the case of dogs or abandoned senile adults, it is less clear who might be asked to consent. In any case, these examples raise the issues of conceptualizing organisms (including the questions of animal and children's rights) and parentalism.

   With normal adults, deliberate deception has been so persistently used in certain research areas (for instance, in social psychology) that informed consent has become a major issue. Sometimes, psychologists give incomplete information rather than erroneous information. Suppose a study deals with sex differences in attitudes toward capital punishment. If people were asked their sex at the beginning, they might answer with a certain set ("Oh, so this tests my masculinity!"); therefore, the psychologist asks their sex only at the end. This means that they were not fully informed about the study while answering the questionnaire.

6. Researchers continually face questions about privacy and confidentiality. A researcher might want to observe people unobtrusively in their own homes; questionnaires sometimes probe religious beliefs and sexual behavior, both of which many people consider private. Ideally, participants would be informed in advance about who, if anybody, would be able to match data with individual identities ("Only I will know the identity of each person" or "This questionnaire is completely anonymous"). Any later changes would also require the consent of the participants.

As these introductory analyses show, the complex ethical issues related to gathering information arise in many contexts. Having considered two such contexts briefly, we now turn to more detailed analyses of the issues themselves.

THE CONCEPTUALIZATION OF ORGANISMS

How psychologists conceptualize different organisms (rats, chimpanzees, infants, adults) is fundamental to their relationships with them in general, and in the gathering of information, in particular. Who, for example, is capable of giving informed consent to being tested or to participating in a research project? Who has rights (to privacy, to freedom from torture)?

Psychologists have drawn the traditional sharp line between humans and (other) animals where information gathering is concerned: much that is morally forbidden with any human being is morally permissible with most or all animals. The posture toward those who, relative to normal adults, are considered handicapped in some way (the retarded, psychotic, or senile) is essentially protective. Although animals are also handicapped relative to normal adults, protectiveness applies to them only within limits.

Animals are anaesthetized before surgery, in part because they are usually conceptualized as able to feel pain. Psychologists who do not admit to attributing such experiences to animals may argue instead that they anaesthetize animals because animal cries are aversive to human beings (including psychologists). Even if one thinks of animals as able to feel pain, however, it does not necessarily follow that animals have a right not to be pained, or that one has obligations toward them. One could defend the use of anaesthesia with animals on the basis of human relationships: people would be hardened if they turned a deaf ear to animal pain, and would then be more likely to treat each other cruelly. Passmore (1975), in his history of our treatment of animals, argues convincingly that overall, we have not moved toward extending rights to animals, but rather, have begun to restrict human rights vis-à-vis nature, including animals.

There are important exceptions to this general trend, notably among those arguing for "animal liberation" (Singer, 1979). They argue that *speciesism* is comparable to racism and sexism. Individual differences (in friendliness or school achievement) are not inherently morally relevant in this view. Only the equal consideration of interests (in being without pain) is morally relevant. If our reason for not hiring a person were the sex of the person, we would be sexists; if our reason for indifference to the suffering of a cat were its species, we would be speciesists. The belief that humans may or even should dominate or use other animals is explicitly speciesist. It is also part of the Western world view.

The use of animals in psychological research and practice is clearly within this tradition. The application of psychology to the training of animals to do stunts and to be obedient is related more to human interests than to the interests of the animals involved. The same is true for the use of animals in psychological research. Rats get around well in their natural habitat. It is we who want to know how they do so, and study their sensory processes or maze learning under a wide variety of organismic and environmental conditions. While some research in veterinary medicine is intended to be helpful to future animals, this is rarely the case in psychological research.

Psychologists who work with animals point to many continuities between animals and humans. In fact, a particular species is often chosen because it resembles humans in a particular respect (Bowd, 1980). But it is infrahuman nonetheless, as becomes clear when one thinks about informed consent in relation to animals: one cannot inform them, and they cannot consent after careful deliberation. An animal rights protagonist would quickly point out that this is morally irrelevant. Being caged and having body parts removed is contrary to the interests of the animals used in research, and this is the major or only morally relevant consideration. Insofar as psychologists agree that certain procedures are harmful rather than beneficial to animals, the justification for using them comes down to the rights of humans to use animals to increase human knowledge because animals are (conceptualized as) inferior to humans: they have no souls, they can never be as intelligent or knowledgeable as people, or they are unable to defend themselves against our using them. In this view, the interests of humans (the scientific merits of the research) have a greater claim on us than the interests of the animal subjects not to be caged or hurt.

There may, then, be limits to the ability of human beings to take seriously the idea that those who differ from us greatly (for example, those belonging to different species) have rights, or that we are obligated to them. Our gut reactions or moral intuitions may reveal our species-specific propensities: most people, put into the hypothetical dilemma of saving either a very retarded child or a far more self-aware chimpanzee from a fire, feel that they should save the child. That we do feel this way does not make it right for us to feel this way. It does, however, raise the question whether this is a species-specific human tendency that places such limits on behavior that a moral principle against it could be acted on only with great difficulty or not at all. (Consider a moral injunction against blinking when a cinder enters the eye.) We must be careful with this argument, however: it is also natural for people to want to eat when hungry, yet people have shared their food with others under conditions of great deprivation. Thus, two questions confront us on animal rights: how defensible is the animal rights position, and, if it is defensible, to what extent are we able to act on it?

The psychologist's relationships with human beings are very different from those with animals in the matter of gathering information. No matter what the mental or physical condition of human beings, one may not remove parts of their brains, and one may not inflict pain on them (such as, with electric shocks) without their (or their guardians') prior informed consent. Different psychologists have different conceptions of human beings, and therefore different rationales for favoring such restrictions on their information gathering with human beings. Why shouldn't one harm people? Why should one respect privacy? Why shouldn't one deceive other people? These questions are dealt with later in this chapter. For now, we will relate different rationales to different conceptualizations of human beings, especially in the matter of autonomy.

Some psychologists are hard determinists; they do not justify their ethical codes on the basis of relationships among autonomous moral agents, since they do not believe that any human beings are autonomous or free. Rather, they stress that all behavior is caused by genetic and environmental factors. For such psychologists, *free* refers to *an environment that presents options to a particular organism.* Thus, tied to a chair, and with a particular amount of strength, you can only remain seated; you are not free to get up, and so you have no option. Sitting in a chair normally, you are free in the sense that your strength and your situation permit sitting or standing up; you do have an option. Hard determinists do not justify informed consent or privacy in terms of relationships among free or autonomous agents. Rather, they consider some social environments to be better than others in enhancing individual and group survival, ends which they assume to have evolved or been programmed into organisms. For these ends, a social environment stressing truth telling is generally superior to one stressing deception, except under clearly specifiable conditions.

Other psychologists are soft or reconciling determinists. They agree that heredity and environment together shape development, but they single out certain human attributes as having special moral relevance: being aware of oneself within one's situation; being able to think before acting (as opposed to acting reflexly); and/or having a moral sense or being capable of moral reasoning. It is in one or more of these attributes that soft determinists see freedom or autonomy and (mutual) responsibility. Thus, insofar as people (psychologists and others) have these attributes, they are autonomous moral agents who should think about their rights and obligations, and who should act in accordance with their considered principles, notably, respect for the autonomy of others.

Hard and soft determinists alike must consider which information-gathering procedures are morally justifiable with animals, infants, and psychotics—with those to whom informed consent or other protective principles do not seem to apply. These are discussed below.

PARENTALISM

To treat people parentalistically is to make decisions for them on the assumption that they cannot make these decisions themselves or that they will make dysfunctional decisions. Parentalism refers to relationships between or among unequals, like parents and children; otherwise (if one person among equals makes decisions for the others without having been instructed to do so), we talk about an unjustified usurpation of power or a domineering person. Parentalism also implies nonmaleficence or beneficence. The decisions are made for the benefit of the incompetent ones, or else we use terms like manipulation and selfishness.

Parentalism in information gathering is exemplified by some of the psychologist's decisions in the hypothetical case of Joe's testing (discussed at the beginning of this chapter). Joe and the psychologist are not equals within this situation. The psychologist (not Joe) knows what needs to be done and how to do it with a minimum of discomfort for Joe, and the decisions are being made for the sake of Joe's long-range welfare. Thus, in gathering information about a client through testing or interviewing, the psychologist will sometimes be either parentalistic or unable to gather information at all. Psychologists should err on the side of caution in this matter and explore the competence of their clients to be sure that parentalism is justified.

The hard cases are unwilling clients, who did not ask for this psychologist's services but were forced into testing or other information gathering. The critical questions in such cases are whether or not such clients can make their own decisions about what would be helpful to them, and if not, whether or not the psychologist is making decisions for the sake of the clients, rather than (for example) for a school system.

Parentalism should not be involved in information gathering in research with normal adults. When a psychologist tells participants about a study, they are in a position to make their own decisions about participating. When psychologists deceive participants, they are not acting parentalistically, since the deception is done neither for the sake of the participants, nor because they are incompetent. Parentalistic decisions (for example, how best to debrief at the end) are then necessary only because participants were being deceived in the first place. When people with limited comprehension are studied (children, the retarded, the senile) parentalism may be involved in two ways: in the process of their becoming participants (see "informed consent," below) and in dealing with them during the information gathering procedures. If their participation is justified, parentalism during information gathering will be inevitable.

DECEPTION

According to Bok (1978), both deceit and violence assault people, both can get them to act against their wills. Those who have been deceived feel wronged, suspicious, and robbed of power. Furthermore, if we couldn't trust anybody, society couldn't survive; truth telling is basic to social life as we know it. A liar does not respect people's autonomy or equality or rights. Liars either justify their lies on the grounds of inequality and beneficence (parentalism), or they are using others as means to their own ends.

The former is exemplified by parents who tell their child that the bitter medicine is delicious, the latter by sellers who tell potential buyers that defective merchandise is in perfect condition.

Four possible arguments about deception will be examined here:

1. Most psychological research proceeds without deception and there is entirely too much fuss about a little deception here and there; what counts is the state or condition of people at the end. This argument implies that one person may do or say anything to another provided only that at the end the other is in good shape. First, the other wouldn't be in good shape if we all took that as a guiding moral principle. Since it cannot be universalized, and since psychologists shouldn't have special privileges in the matter of lying, this argument is indefensible. Second, the argument implies that only later actions or conditions are subject to moral scrutiny, not earlier ones. The psychologist's condition or action now (lying) isn't—only the subject's later condition or action is, in two hours or weeks. This is also indefensible: how could we select time periods or states or actions or persons to be exempt from moral scrutiny?

2. Deception in research will not destroy anyone's trust in people generally; suspicion directed at psychologists will not generalize to everybody. It is not a question of generalization, however. Mistrust among people is already high in our society. Therefore, any plan for deception, especially by a trusted and respected person, should be very carefully considered and justified before it is implemented. One possible solution to this problem is to ask people to volunteer for research after they have been told that some of them may be deceived or not fully informed about the research so that the reason (need) for such deception would have been explained. If they agree under those conditions, the deception probably will not increase their mistrust of people. (This solution raises methodological problems: do those who volunteer under these conditions differ in important ways from those who don't?)

3. The morally competent people being deceived would consent to the deception if one could first explain the study to them and then remove this explanation from their minds. The problem with this argument is that it is difficult to test; furthermore, psychologically, it could cut two ways. That participants in research often say at the end that they gained more from the experience than they lost (Asch, 1952; Milgram, 1964) may, perhaps, reveal that they are still trying to deal with having been deceived. One's discomfort is surely less if one's having been deceived was helpful rather than damaging. On the other hand, people's statements in advance that they would not resent being deceived may reveal that they want to appear heroic in some sense (I can tolerate pain for the sake of science), and as Milgram (1963) went to great

lengths to demonstrate, many people do acquiesce to ideas proposed by scientists. It may therefore be an easy out for psychologists to accept what people say; at the same time, it may be patronizing, even parentalistic, not to accept what they say.

4. Respect for persons is a basic value, but it is not the only one. Everyone's need for a greater understanding of people is also basic, and if a particular study is meritorious enough, this universal need for knowledge may in this situation briefly override respect for persons, thus justifying using them. They are being used, furthermore, only in the temporary sense that they don't know about the nature of the study, and therefore its significance for them and others at the time they are "subjects." Respect for them once again receives top priority as soon as that part of their participation is completed, at which time their participation is turned into a learning situation for them, as they are fully informed about the study. This argument deserves to be taken seriously, even though it should be remembered that the results of psychological research rarely if ever have the potential impact of results of medical research. The question must also be answered whether any results, great or small, justify "using" people.

INFORMED CONSENT

Introduction

This is undoubtedly one of the most complex concepts in all information gathering with human beings. Each of the words ("informed" and "consent") presents its own problems of interpretation and application. What is involved is a conjoining of the issues involved in conceptualizing the organism, especially autonomy, and deception.

The need for informed consent grows out of the facts that information gathering procedures can be harmful to people, and that those using them know this, and the principles of nonmaleficence and autonomy. Let us consider an example before we analyze informed consent in greater detail.

Suppose that a research design includes a group to be exposed to failure (for example, by being given unsolvable problems). Such an experience of failure risks varying degrees of psychological pain for almost all participants, and the researchers know this. They are thus acting against the principle of nonmaleficence. They are also planning to deceive the participants, since they will let them assume that the problems are solvable. If it were known that they were unsolvable, there would be no experience of failure! As pointed out in the section on deception, lying goes against the principle of autonomy; each participant is being used as a means to the researchers' own ends, and has no say about being exposed to this failure experience.

What, then, does informed consent involve? Most fundamentally, it refers to carefully considered agreement, given without external coercion, to participate in particular information gathering procedures after having been informed about them and about the voluntary nature of the participation. More specifically, people are to be informed about the purpose or rationale of the study, the procedures, possible risks and benefits, safeguards to minimize possible harms, and the voluntary nature of the participation. One may refuse to begin participating, and one may leave at any time. Furthermore, the consent must be given freely. Free is used here in the sense that one has considered the matter carefully and does not feel coerced to participate by rewards or punishments instituted by the information gatherers or those for whom they are working. Under such conditions, the concerns about autonomy and nonmaleficence have been addressed: people are freely choosing to participate after weighing the potential harms and benefits.

Let us consider in greater detail this interpretation of consenting freely. Suppose that you have been informed that you have a small cavity, and that it has to be filled, or else it will become larger, causing pain and greater damage to the tooth. Although you don't like having teeth filled, you make an appointment without further ado with your dentist. The question is whether you are making it freely. You surely did not consent to have the cavity, but now that you have it, and now that you have been informed about what could happen with and without filling, you are consenting freely in the senses specified above: you have been informed about the procedure to be done (its rationale, its risks and benefits, and the safeguards to be taken), and your consent is voluntary in the sense that you have not been coerced by your dentist. You are thus making a considered decision without external coercion. You may want to argue that the consent was inevitable in this case, since the cavity was coercive (compelling) in its own way, but the coercion was not applied by someone else, and that, as we shall see, is the kind of coercion which is critical in informed consent.

Furthermore, such an argument would lead to the conclusion that you are always being coerced. If you are being coerced either by your dentist or by the condition of your teeth, then obviously all situations are coercive. What this argument erroneously does is to confuse determinism or causal analysis with the specific meaning of free intended here. No one wants to say that informed consent is impossible unless determinism is false! One does want to say that a person consented to taking a battery of psychological tests after understanding the purpose of this information gathering procedure and without positive or negative consequences having been imposed by the psychologist. Positive or negative consequences could surely result from taking or not taking the tests, but these are related to the problems this person wants to resolve, and contributed to the person's coming to the psychologist in the first place. If the testing was court-mandated, on the other hand, then noncooperation clearly could be expected to have negative consequences (harsher treatment by the judge), and in that case, consent is not freely given, since it is coerced by someone else.

When Informed Consent Cannot Be Used

Many groups of human beings cannot be asked for informed consent, because they are not competent enough to understand the information offered them. Examples are infants and young children, very retarded people, very senile people, and some psychotics. What are the ethically relevant considerations in these cases?

First, the nature of the incompetence must be considered. Suppose a psychologist asks parents about having their infants or small children participate in perceptual development research, and suppose the parents consent. Under these conditions, the children will not feel used: they are incapable of understanding that idea. Certain psychotics, however, might be exceptionally sensitive to such matters, even those who on the surface seem to have little or no contact with their social environment. The senile, too, may vary in unpredictable ways in their social perceptiveness. In fact, one needs to be sure that the incompetence of so-called incompetent adults is of such a nature that informed consent is impossible. A person hospitalized for depression, for example, may temporarily be unable to cope with job and family responsibilities, but may nonetheless be able to understand study X and the meaning of refusing or consenting to participate.

Second, those who cannot be asked for informed consent should not be used—just as competent people should not be used. One occasionally hears someone say about psychotics or the retarded, "Of course they should be used in research; they're not doing any good otherwise, so here's their chance to earn their keep." Nonmaleficence applies to everyone, not just to those capable of saying, "Don't hurt me." But suppose the research didn't involve any hurting or harming, as most psychological research does not. Should the means-ends distinction apply to human beings who are not or cannot be autonomous agents?

Research on sensation in schizophrenics can be defended on better moral grounds than forcing schizophrenics to be useful to others. The best defense is the obligation to learn about schizophrenia, for both theoretical and practical reasons. We do not normally speak of using people or of forcing them to be useful to others; we would not include such forcing in our blueprint for a moral utopia. While the words retarded or schizophrenic suggest rigid boundaries, humanity instead presents us with gradations. To be sure, some people are so retarded that they can never even learn to eat by themselves, but beyond that lie variations that move us ever so slowly into the range of normality. Rarely is a slippery slope more slippery than here! But even if that were not so, we would be choosing between the moral ideal of treating human beings as objects (which we feel free to use for our own purposes, or to force into usefulness—or else we throw them out), and the moral ideal of never treating human beings like that. Thus, the argument that the uselessness of certain people justifies using them is morally indefensible.

Third, we must distinguish between information gathering done for the sake of the incompetent person and information gathering done for the sake of knowledge and/or to help other similar people. Testing a retarded adolescent in order to make some helpful decisions about schooling is an example of the former, sensation research with schizophrenics an example of the latter.

We cannot inform the retarded adolescent in the way that we can inform a normal one; is the testing justified in the absence of informed consent? Two principles are relevant in these situations: nonmaleficence, or perhaps beneficence, and parentalism. If the adolescent is very retarded, psychologists and parent-figures alike should care for this adolescent. They should be guided by what is in the best interests of the adolescent, and should make decisions the adolescent cannot make. The best justification for parentalism in such cases is that letting them make their own choices (for example, about taking psychological tests) is more likely to result in harm to them than if the parents make these decisions, precisely because they cannot understand (be informed about) the procedure and its rationale.

What about information gathering as part of research? Let us assume that the research results will not be immediately helpful, since otherwise we would again be discussing the kinds of situations described in the previous paragraph. An example might be pure research with or without implications for eventual application, like research on the development of visual perception. Psychologists can obtain informed consent from adults, but they also want to study infants and young children. May parent-figures give informed consent for their children? Nonmaleficence, beneficence, and parentalism will again be the relevant principles: the children will not be harmed by the perceptual test, and may, in fact, enjoy it. The parent-figures are able to understand the procedure, its rationale, and its complete safety: furthermore, they are volunteering in the total absence of rewards like money or threats of punishment. The problem is that they are giving consent not for themselves but for someone else! Is that morally justifiable?

Before we consider the position of the parents, we must consider the position of the researcher. Much has been written about parents consenting for their children, but what is the ethical situation of the researcher considering asking parents to bring their children to the laboratory? This depends on whether or not the researcher believes that is ethical for the parents to consent or refuse for the children who cannot do so for themselves. Researchers who believe this are being true to their moral convictions when they approach parents about children's participation. Those who do not believe this face a dilemma. On the one hand, they shouldn't be asking parents to do something they (the researchers) consider immoral. On the other hand, by not asking the parents, by not even telling them about the study, they are depriving parents of the opportunity to decide for themselves; they are in essence deciding for the parents. This seems to be the weaker side of the dilemma. If Jones believes that dogs should not be put through dog shows, is Jones obligated to tell Smith about an up-coming dog show to be sure that Smith has the choice of either participating or not doing so?

Now let us return to the parents. Suppose the researcher studying the development of visual perception does ask parents to give informed consent for their children to participate. Wellman (1978) has argued (in the context of medical research) that parents are obligated to care for their children, and that they couldn't do this if others were continually interfering with them. In fact, interfering with parents is permissible socially and legally only when they are clearly violating the principle of nonmaleficence. You may not interfere with your neighbors because you think that their children are watching too much TV. You do feel obligated to interfere if you see your neighbors deliberately burning their child's hand. Thus, goes the argument, parents may volunteer their children for perceptual tests. In fact, the parents could even use the occasion to talk to their four-year-olds about helping someone (even though the psychologists did not intend to gather the information in order to benefit these particular children).

In medical research, the problem of possible risks to infants and children can be a serious one. In most psychological research, risks are virtually nonexistent. Suppose, however, that the research design includes a group who are to be exposed to an anxiety-provoking situation such as being told that they did not do well on some task. One might be tempted to argue that this experimental variation would be morally unjustified, and that the parents' obligation is to keep their children from such unnecessary harm, that to expose them to it is comparable to burning their hands. However, an argument can be made that this exaggerates the impact of the experimental situation. The children who are briefly made anxious will soon be happy again, and some argue that the end state of the children is what counts. In other words, as long as the children leave the research project feeling as good as or better than when they arrived, they were not really harmed.

Some readers may already have felt uneasy about Wellman's interpretations even when the information gathering procedure was fun for the child. They may feel even more concerned when any mental or physical pain is to be deliberately inflicted. It may then seem that the psychologists are violating both the principle of not using people and the principle of nonmaleficence. Is the psychologist not morally obligated to give up doing the study, instead of searching for children, especially since it is clear that psychological research, in contrast to some medical research, never produces a life-saving breakthrough? Under these circumstances, deontological theories would lead to the conclusion that doing the research was morally unjustifiable. Utilitarian interpretations are less clear, since they would depend on the weighing of the morally good and morally bad consequences in this situation. For a psychologist to ask a guardian to consent for an incompetent human being to help that human being is one thing; asking for guardian consent so that the incompetent person may participate in research which is fun is already different; asking for guardian consent for participation in research that inflicts pain is different again.

When People Go to Psychologists Voluntarily

When people consult psychologists about their problems, the initial step is an exchange of information. Clients may want to know, What's wrong with me? and How much will it cost?; psychologists want an overview of the problem so that they can advise clients about further information gathering (interviews, tests) and possible interventions.

In these situations, informed consent presents fewer problems, since we are now talking about competent people coming for help voluntarily. They are usually eager to talk about their problem, so that the psychologist is not only gathering necessary information, but is also providing a willing ear. At times, people may be in an "anything you say" frame of mind. In such cases, one cannot say that they are consenting after careful deliberation, of which they may be temporarily incapable. In such situations, the psychologist will try to help the client resolve the immediate sense of desperation, or if necessary, will proceed parentalistically for the welfare of the client.

Problems may arise when a psychologist believes that the client's case could clarify a theoretical or therapeutic issue. The psychologist may then feel obligated to view this person's problem as a research opportunity, in addition to its being an opportunity to help, since other psychologists could learn from this case. Thus, the psychologist would be thinking about gathering research information even while doing therapy. Questions arise about when the client should be informed about this. How sure does the psychologist have to be that this is an important case? What kind of consent is needed? Very critical is the obligation to the client during therapy: the welfare of the client must be primary, in the event that this conflicts with what one would do to gather information for research. In university clinics, clients may be asked to sign a consent form at the very first meeting that states that they are participating in research in addition to receiving help. In some instances, they may be asked to consent to the taping or filming of diagnostic and therapeutic sessions.

When People Go to Psychologists Involuntarily

Psychologists sometimes see reluctant clients: prisoners are referred by guards; students are referred by teachers; people accused of crimes are referred by judges. In these situations, the people to be interviewed and tested are clients even though they did not come voluntarily. To view them any other way would be to view them as means or objects meant to serve the purposes of others. Such involuntary clients can be informed about information gathering procedures but they cannot be said to consent freely: they are coerced by punishment threatened not by their problems, but rather by powerful others (parole boards, principals, judges).

Psychologists face a true dilemma in such cases. On the one hand, they may believe that testing and/or interviewing is in the best interests of the client, and that anger or suspicion make it impossible for the client to understand that. It is thus tempting to justify parentalism (as for incompetent persons). On the other hand, the client is able to understand what is going on, and is thus clearly competent. The situation is further complicated by the fact that the psychologist also has moral obligations toward the legitimate interests represented by a prison administration or a school board, insofar as these represent the legitimate interests of the larger society. Finally, questions arise about interpreting information obtained under coercive conditions, since reluctant clients may deliberately and/or unconsciously deceive the psychologist and/or themselves. Children who know they are being forced to "talk to that nice lady" have little reason to trust anyone at that moment!

This complex problem obviously cannot have a simple solution, but the several horns of the dilemma suggest some guidelines. The final point mentioned above should be considered first. When, after attempted interviewing, psychologists have good reasons to believe that they cannot obtain usable information, they may well decide not to proceed further. In such situations, they will try to explain to the clients in what way(s) testing could help them, but if the clients continue to be uncooperative, it may be unreasonable to continue trying to obtain usable information.

Some clients may become persuaded that cooperation may benefit them. In that case, coercion has been decreased, usable information may be obtained, and both clients and institutions or society may be helped. It is easy to be suspicious about sudden cooperation in a previously reluctant or even rebellious client. The psychologist has both moral and methodological reasons for interpreting such changes very cautiously. On the other hand, some of these changes may be genuine, and in these cases, the dilemma is resolved.

Research

Probably more has been written about informed consent in relation to gathering information for research (data collection) than in relation to any other information gathering psychologists do. The reason for this is not hard to find: many research designs cannot be executed unless participants are either misinformed or not fully informed (see *Deception*). Thus, the participants are consenting to erroneous or incomplete descriptions of the procedures in these instances.

Most of the violations of informed consent in data collection violate the obligation to give full information. Sometimes, however, consent is also violated, as when participants are coerced or feel they are being coerced. Milgram's (1963) research on obedience is a good example. Not only did he clearly misinform the participants, but in addition, he pressured them to continue with four verbal prods ranging from "Please continue" to "You have no other choice, you must go on." While very participant could have said, "Of course I have a choice!," these verbal prods represent some degree of attempted external coercion. Milgram (1964) was correct in pointing out that he did not have the coercive powers of a dictator (which fact, he argued, made the results all the more striking and the research all the more meritorious), but his not being able to coerce on the scale of a dictator does not prove that no coercion at all took place.

Consent is often violated in dealings with captive groups. An example is requiring research participation for college students; depending on how this requirement is handled, it may or may not be coercive. Far more serious are questions about informed consent among prisoners. Suppose a psychologist has fully informed prisoners about the study to be done, and suppose further that 70 out of 300 then volunteered. Did they consent freely or under external coercion? This may be a hard question to answer, even if nobody explicitly said that volunteering would be rewarded or refusing to participate would be punished. Prisoners often have good reasons for being mistrustful (which is not to say that they can always be trusted), and psychologists doing research in prison would certainly be aware of that. Assurances from psychologists may not carry as much weight with prisoners as rumors circulating within prisons. In such a situation, it would be naive to argue that informed consent was obtained, since it is unfortunately highly improbable that consent was freely given after careful deliberation. Psychologists may decide to do research in prisons anyway, mainly because of the obligation to obtain pure and applied knowledge, but also, perhaps, because they have done what they could not to be coercive in any way.

Informed consent is totally bypassed when unobtrusive observation is used in data collection. The virtue of such observations is that people are behaving naturally, that is, without reacting to the presence of a psychologist. The ethical dilemma then is that unobtrusive observation may contribute greatly to the merit of the research, and psychologists are obligated to do the best research they can. On the other hand, psychologists are unobtrusive only if they don't get informed consent!

Unobtrusive observation sometimes takes place in staged situations, sometimes in naturally occurring situations. The latter is exemplified by Allport's classic study of behavior at traffic lights. The psychologist did nothing but record a few aspects of driver behavior and the conditions under which these occurred (Allport, 1934). Some degree of staging would be involved in a study on superstitions if ladders were placed against several walls in different locations, and then records kept of the ages and genders of the people walking under a ladder or around it; the ladders would be there only for the sake of the study. Informed consent is necessary because information gathering procedures can be harmful to people, and not obtaining it violates the principle of autonomy. In what ways might unobtrusive observation violate these principles?

Consider these arguments: Behavior in public places is observable, and we are all aware of that. Since everyone is free to people-watch at any time, psychologists also have that same freedom. Furthermore, the ladders (or other staging) were only put in place after appropriate permission was obtained from property owners. Finally, no one was harmed by being observed: no one even knew about being observed!

These arguments ignore several morally relevant points:

1. We do indeed assume or know that passersby may occasionally look at us, but we do not assume or know that somebody is systematically observing our actions and recording them in some way. If we knew that members of the secret police were doing this, we would become very frightened, to say the least. Thus, the critical moral issue is what these observations of public behaviors mean. Similarly, you might be angry if you discovered that a neighbor was spying on your public behaviors. Your moral outrage would hinge only in part on your concerns about what the neighbor plans to do with all this information. Also involved in your sense of being violated: had you known you were being observed, you might have chosen to act differently. Our normal assumption that no one is spying on us contributes immeasurably to our happiness or peace of mind, and therefore should not be rendered false. It is an open question whether people would consent to a revised society in which one might periodically be on a social science version of "Candid Camera!" Videotaping, in particular, might raise questions about privacy and confidentiality (see below).

2. In such research, the people observed benefit only, if at all, in the form of gains in knowledge. Once psychologists go into the field, they deal with people who are not at that time college sophomores, and some of

these people might well feel that they have been used and deceived, and that their privacy has been invaded (though in a public place). Furthermore, they may see no benefit for themselves. This raises again the issue of who should decide about the merit of research. Furthermore, if the study were applied research, questions might arise about using the results without public discussion of the matter—as though the study of people's real behavior circumvented the need for discussion, or highlighted the artificiality or invalidity of mere discussion.

3. The argument assumes that since nobody was hurt (neither by having been observed nor by the props), no other moral considerations apply. This assumes that the end state of the people observed is the only morally relevant consideration, which is incorrect. It also assumes that the only people who will ever be informed are the owners of the staging locations, that one will never inform the people who have been observed. In fact, to inform them at the end (to debrief them) would change their end state considerably. Is there an obligation to debrief each person who was observed, or not to do so?

4. Taken together, these points alert one to the potential dangers of **1984** or "Big Brother is watching you" psychology. It is true that on the surface, many such studies sound harmless. How could one possibly fuss about a psychologist recording that this person, female and approximately 40 years old, walked under the ladder at location X at time T? But in doing this, psychologists either assume that they have special privileges (compared to the rest of the population) that include observing and recording people's activities, or that such actions are morally defensible for everyone, meaning that they would be willing to be observed systematically (perhaps with videotape) by other people for their purposes (for example, reporters). Furthermore, people other than only those observed may be harmed by knowing about such research techniques, which may make them feel that their privacy is being invaded more and more (see below). Anything that adds to the mistrustfulness and suspiciousness already rampant in our society needs to be very carefully scrutinized and balanced against the merit of some of this research. The observed people were not informed at all, and one wonders how many would consent if they had been—without external coercion, after careful deliberation.

PRIVACY AND CONFIDENTIALITY

The right to privacy involves the right to keep information for ourselves, the right not to share it with others unless we choose to. The related notion of confidentiality enters when we do choose to share information with somebody: it will not be shared with additional others without our consent.

According to Diener and Crandall (1978) and Smith (1978), privacy is an important value for several reasons. Every society has areas of privacy, though not all societies value privacy about the same things. Privacy may thus be a basic human concern, need, or interest, and therefore should be respected. Furthermore, privacy bears an important relationship to friendship and other intimate relations since intimates are people with whom we choose to share what is private. Privacy is also related to our interest in maintaining uniqueness among persons. Greater freedom of thought is possible when thoughts can remain private, since deviant thoughts might be punished if they were made public, and we would all be more alike if we all had only permissible thoughts. Finally, we might be vulnerable to manipulation by others if they had access to some private information.

Psychologists can invade privacy in a number of different ways. Personality tests are sometimes criticized as being invasions of privacy, since they may ask very personal questions, and/or because those tested may reveal themselves far more than they realize (and therefore consented to). Unobtrusive observation is sometimes criticized as an invasion of privacy, whether it occurs in a person's home or in a public place. In either location, people's actions or conversations are being recorded, and thus are no longer kept for themselves alone. Research practices can involve an invasion of privacy when participants are told that the study deals with situational influences on learning or perception when in fact it also deals with individual differences in learning or perception.

The best safeguard for privacy is informed consent. Those who consent are either willing to give up some privacy in a particular situation (for research purposes, or for personal benefits gained from interviewing or testing), or they do not feel that a particular information gathering procedure involves a domain which they consider private (some people have little need to keep their religious or political beliefs private). The best safeguard for confidentiality is anonymity or assurance that only the practicing psychologist or researcher will have access to the information gathered unless the person consents to share it with others. The important exception to this is conflict between confidentiality and an even more basic value. The best known example of such a conflict occurs when a client confides plans to harm or kill somebody.

HURTING AND HARMING: RECAPITULATION

We started this chapter by saying that nonmaleficence is a basic moral principle that is sometimes violated by information gathering procedures. One justification for hurting somebody is the prevention or correction of greater long-range harm to that person. We can now add another justification: the person has consented (for example, to enduring mild electric shocks in a study on pain or to the discomforts which can be a part of being tested or interviewed).

The hard questions pertain to those who cannot be asked for informed consent, notably animals, and those who are not asked for informed consent though they could be, notably those deceived in research. The latter might be hurt, for example, by being randomly assigned to an experimentally created failure group rather than to a success group, and they might also be hurt by the deception itself. In both instances (animals and the deceived), the major justification will be in terms of the scientific merit of the research: that the knowledge gained justifies the minor, temporary discomfort of the human participants, and almost any discomfort to animals (except that which can be minimized without spoiling the study). Not everyone will be persuaded by this justification. First, the results of psychological research rarely have the potential importance of medical research results; second, psychologists have not, until quite recently, searched for alternate information gathering procedures and designs; and, finally, not everyone accepts utilitarian justifications for moral choices.

THEMES AND VARIATIONS: CHAPTER 6

How Should We View and Treat Animals?

In his historical overview of the treatment of animals, Passmore (1975) defended the traditional human domination of the world. One historic tradition stresses that "rational creatures have the right to govern irrational nature" (p. 201). Animals are not moral agents; they have neither rights nor duties. Compassion to animals is of some importance because those who are kind to animals are more likely to be compassionate toward their fellow human beings. However, if people have *good* reasons for using animals, animal suffering per se is unimportant. This view is rooted in a theology which opposes naturalism and insists on an absolute distinction between humans and animals.

He also traced the view that animals share reason with humans in some degree, as well as the argument that the morally relevant consideration is not the capacity for reasoning, but rather, the capacity for suffering. This last view contributed to new laws regulating the treatment of animals, but such regulation does not mean that animals have rights: we do not "give rights to a river by withdrawing somebody's right to pollute it" (p. 212). While discussing the question of animal rights, Passmore wrote,

> Ecologically, no doubt, men form a community with plants, animals, soil, in the sense that a particular life-cycle may involve two, three, or even all four of them. From the point of view of a virus—if I may be permitted this way of talking—men are hosts in which they can develop, hosts which, regrettably, sometimes die before the virus has a chance to pass on to other hosts. But if it

is essential to a community that the members of it have common interests and recognize mutual obligations then men, plants, animals, and soil do not form a community. Viruses and men do not recognize mutual obligations, nor do they have common interests. In the only sense in which belonging to a community generates ethical obligation, they do not belong to the same community. And it can only create confusion to suppose that they do, or ought to. (pp. 212–13)

He concluded as follows:

Let us now try to sum up. We have been tracing the process by which Western men have divested themselves of certain rights to treat animals as they please. We have seen that throughout the intellectual history of the Western world there have been occasional philosophers or theologians who have condemned such cruelty as intrinsically wrong. Other moralists, however, have sought to show that it is wrong only indirectly, in so far as cruelty to animals encourages cruelty to man. There can be little doubt that they favored this indirect approach because they began from the theological presupposition that man, in his treatment of Nature, was completely at liberty to deal with it as he pleased, except in so far as his doing so adversely affected himself or his fellow-humans.

It was not only animals, however, who were thought of as things rather than as animate beings; slaves and barbarians were put in the same class. Man's treatment of animals was no worse than his treatment of a great many of his fellow human beings. The attack on slavery at the hands of the evangelicals and of Bentham, ran hand-in-hand with the attack on cruelty to animals. Susceptibility to suffering, rather than rationality, was thought of as the dividing line between what could, and what could not, be dealt with as Western man thought fit.

In the East, moralists have condemned the killing of animal life rather than cruelty to it. But cruelty to beasts of burden, at least, was regarded as reprehensible and at times compassion for animals was carried beyond that point. Such compassion met with no resistance from theology.

Once a definite social movement got under way in the West with its objective the restricting of man's treatment of animals, it moved with relative rapidity. Moral philosophers began to regard it as an obvious truth that is wrong to treat animals cruelly. So the history we have been tracing is at once discouraging, in so far as it took two thousand years for Western men to agree that it is wrong to treat animals cruelly, and encouraging in so far as it suggests that man's opinion on such matters can change with considerable rapidity. This is especially true nowadays when the critic of man's treatment of Nature no longer has to contend with a general persuasion that in this respect man's conduct must be left unconfined. It should be observed, however, that if our analysis of the situation is correct, then this change in moral attitude resulted in a restriction of rights rather than an extension of them.

The degree of restriction placed on human behavior, furthermore, is relatively slight. Whereas it once used to be argued, as by Newman, that the least human good compensates for any possible amount of animal suffering, the current doctrine is that it requires a considerable good to compensate for such suffering. There is far from being a precise analogy, however, between the importance attached to animal and to human suffering. So while it is generally agreed that it is wrong to experiment on human beings without their consent in the expectation of making scientific discoveries, there is no such general opposition to animal vivisection. Biological warfare against human beings is generally condemned but not biological warfare against animals. Man-hunting is ruled out as sport but not, at least with the same degree of unanimity, fox or bird hunting. In all these cases, of course, a minority opinion would support laws which go further than the present laws in limiting the circumstances in which men are entitled to cause pain to animals. But not so far as seriously to limit man's domination of the world. (pp. 216–18)

Singer is one of the current philosophers who stress the capacity for suffering and the undesirability of pain, no matter whose. His basic principle of equality is the principle of equal consideration of interests (Singer, 1979). When two people suffer equal pain, differences between them (in height, eye color, or race) are morally irrelevant. "The principle of equal consideration of interests acts like a pair of scales, weighing interests impartially. True scales favor the side where the interest is stronger or where several interests combine to outweigh a smaller number of similar interests; but they take no account of whose interest they are weighing" (p. 19). Singer applied this principle not only to people, but also to animals. If pain is undesirable, then it is morally irrelevant that this particular pain is being experienced by a dog rather than a human being. The intellectual differences among the species sometimes cause humans to suffer more (because their current suffering may be intensified by the anticipation of similar future suffering), sometimes less (when, for example, they can anticipate an early, specific moment when their pain will end, while animals cannot). Singer applied this analysis to the use of animals in research:

> Perhaps the area in which speciesism can most clearly be observed is the use of animals in experiments. Here the issue stands out starkly, because experimenters often seek to justify experimenting on animals by claiming that the experiments lead us to discoveries about humans; if this is so, the experimenter must agree that human and nonhuman animals are similar in crucial respects. For instance, if forcing a rat to choose between starving to death and crossing an electrified grid to obtain food tells us anything about the reactions of humans to stress, we must assume that the rat feels stress in this kind of situation. (p. 57)

He then made two further points. First, little research can be justified on the grounds that its results will produce greater benefits than its procedures will cause harm. In this connection, he singled out some psychological research for special attention. Second, if researchers would not "perform their experiments on orphaned humans with severe and irreversible brain damage if that were the only way to save thousands" (p. 59), they are discriminating on the basis of species alone, since many animals are more aware, intelligent, and sensitive than the humans described.

Suppose someone said, "Look at the animal world. Strong animals always overpower weak ones, so it is natural for human researchers to use mice and rats." Discussing our eating of meat, Singer wrote, "it is odd that humans, who normally think of the behaviour of animals as 'beastly' should, when it suits them, use an argument that implies we ought to look to animals for moral guidance" (p. 61). Furthermore, that which occurs naturally under one set of circumstances isn't necessarily morally right under other circumstances. A lion overpowering a deer is different from a human overpowering a deer—precisely because humans can think in ways that deer and lions cannot.

Singer weakened his entire argument considerably in the chapter on killing. He concluded that "it would not necessarily be speciesist to rank the value of different lives in some hierarchical ordering" because "[i]n general it does seem that the more highly developed the conscious life of the being, the greater the degree of self-awareness and rationality, the more one would prefer that kind of life, if one were choosing between it and a being at a lower level of awareness" (p. 90). If, as he then said, "that is the best that we can hope to say about this issue" (p. 90), we aren't saying much except that self-aware, rational humans prefer to be what they are. How or why this can or should be a basis for ranking "the values of different lives" isn't clear at all, nor is it even clear that his generalization is true for all humans.

Nonetheless, this line of argument challenges our thinking about moral agency, rights, duties, and equality, and even about the possibility of developing a rational basis for ethical principles (see Part IV).

Freedom, Determinism, and Autonomy

Hard determinists believe that behavior is part of the natural world, and that it therefore can be explained by scientific laws, as can other natural phenomena. Why did these particular people do X? If we knew enough about their genetic makeup, their past environments (both physical and social), and their present environment, and if psychological theory were sufficiently advanced, we would be able to answer the question. X could be anything: refusing to eat something, voting for a particular candidate, stealing hubcaps—anything. As Skinner put it (1975, p. 47), "I submit that what we call the behavior of the human organism is no more free than its digestion, gestation, immunization, or any other physiological process." This view denies that behavior is ever autonomous, at least in the sense of coming out of nowhere, of occurring without causes.

That behavior is lawful is assumed even by some of those who question the possibility of developing transhistorical laws of social behavior. As

Cronbach wrote (1975, p. 123), "Our troubles do not arise because human events are in principle unlawful; man and his creations are part of the natural world. The trouble, as I see it, is that we cannot store up generalizations and constructs for ultimate assembly into a network." (See Themes and Variations for Chapter 4.)

Can we reconcile the lawfulness of behavior with any meaning of *autonomous choosing?* According to Schlenker (1974), we can.

> To maintain that given certain knowledge about the individual (e.g., his past learning history, his attitudes and values, his genetic constitution, etc.) we can make predictions about his behavior is not to maintain that the person could not help behaving the way he did. Modifying an example from Kemeny (1959), suppose that you know that your best friend was invited to a party this weekend. You know your friend's preferences for parties compared to other activities, you know who will be at the party and how your friend feels about each of them, you know whether or not your friend was planning another affair on the evening in question, etc. To be able to predict whether or not your friend will actually go to the party does not in the least imply that he had no choice about attending or not attending. All that it means is that you know how your friend goes about making decisions. You have conceptualized the kinds of things which he takes into consideration, you have "guessed" how he weighs each one, and you know a little bit about the mechanisms of the decision. In short, you have developed a naive theory useful in understanding, explaining, and predicting behavior. Thus, to state that social psychology is indeed a science is not to claim that humans are pushed around by inexorable forces which they are helpless to counter. Rather, it is to affirm that human actions are understandable and explainable—the context and method flowing from these assertions are what is called science. The notion of *determinism* in science really means nothing more than this. *Indeterminism,* on the other hand, refers to a situation where events appear to be in a constant state of flux and man's ability to understand is sufficiently limited that understanding and explanation is impossible. Our present state of knowledge is an indication that an assumption of indeterminism probably is incorrect. (p. 12)

This paragraph is interesting for two reasons. First, it seems to externalize or physicalize *choice:* that the friend was able to either attend or not attend the party can mean only that neither possibility was physically impossible, that physically speaking, the friend could have done either one. For if we know how our friends make decisions of this sort, then we know that Tom won't go because his dislike of parties is greater than any feelings of obligation he has in this case, and that Sue will go because she likes parties in general and the people expected at this one in particular. In other words, if we know how Tom and Sue weigh the various relevant factors, we know whether or not they will go. If we expected Sue to go to the party and yet she didn't, determinists (including Schlenker) would attribute this error to our lack of knowledge about Sue, not to her inner freedom, autonomy, or indeterminate behavior.

Second, what Schlenker called indeterminism is what Cronbach was talking about: although human social behavior is lawful, psychologists may never be able to develop transhistorical laws about it.

The critical question here is whether it is necessary to anchor "autonomous choice" in either a denial of causality in the psychological domain or in psychology's problems in the area of theorizing. Soft or reconciling determinists would say this is not necessary, since they view autonomy as a personal attribute developed in different degrees in different people. Soft determinists equate autonomy with certain cognitive processes. Bandura (1974), for example, described the reciprocal influence between the person and the environment: each influences the other. This view differs from Skinner's not in denying that "selection of particular courses of action from available alternatives is itself determined" (p. 867), but in singling out the possibility for people to exercise intentional control over the environment:

> People may be considered partially free insofar as they can influence future conditions by managing their own behavior. Granted that selection of particular courses of action from available alternatives is itself determined, individuals can nevertheless exert some control over the factors that govern their choices. In philosophical analyses all events can be submitted to an infinite regression of causes. Such discussions usually emphasize how man's actions are determined by prior conditions but neglect the reciprocal part of the process showing that the conditions themselves are partly determined by man's prior actions. Applications of self-control practices demonstrate that people are able to regulate their own behavior in preferred directions by arranging environmental conditions most likely to elicit it and administering self-reinforcing consequences to sustain it. They may be told how to do it and initially be given some external support for their efforts, but self-produced influences contribute significantly to future goal attainment.
>
> To contend, as environmental determinists often do, that people are controlled by external forces and then to advocate that they redesign their society by applying behavioral technology undermines the basic premise of the argument. If humans were in fact incapable of influencing their own actions, they could describe and predict environmental events but hardly exercise any intentional control over them. When it comes to advocacy of social change, however, thoroughgoing environmental determinists become ardent exponents of man's power to transform environments in pursuit of a better life.
>
> In backward casual analyses, conditions are usually portrayed as ruling man, whereas forward deterministic analyses of goal setting and attainment reveal how people can shape conditions for their purposes. Some are better at it than others. The greater their foresight, proficiency, and self-influence, all of which are acquirable skills, the greater the progress toward their goals. Because of the capacity for reciprocal influence, people are at least partial architects of their own destinies. It is not determinism that is in dispute, but whether it is treated as a one-way or a two-way control process. Considering the interdependence of behavior and environmental conditions, determinism

does not imply the fatalistic view that man is but a pawn of external influences. (p. 867)

We can see now why psychologists don't generally attribute autonomy to infrahumans. Either they don't attribute it to any living creature, human or otherwise, or they are stressing precisely that degree of cognitive development which is uniquely human.

Moral autonomy, then, or any other kind of autonomy, is not a matter of uncaused behavior, neither for hard nor soft determinists, though the causes of any particular instance of autonomous behavior may be difficult indeed to establish. Autonomy, furthermore, is possible even when (or especially when?) there are external constraints on behavior, since we may decide to ignore or defy these. For example, you may make a conscious, deliberate decision to go through a stop sign at 3:00 A.M. after seeing that yours is the only car on the road. Furthermore, all behavior, whether impulsive or carefully considered, may be viewed from the perspective of ethics, and, given more detail about your behavior at the stop sign, we could analyze it using moral principles and theories. That it was caused doesn't make it more or less harmful to others, for example, than if it had been uncaused. The prospects for your improving your behavior are better, however, if you can find its causes (inner and outer) than if you can't.

Informed Consent

One moral conflict psychologists may face in planning their research is between two obligations: to contribute to knowledge and to make possible "informed consent." After considering several attempted resolutions of this dilemma, Soble (1978) suggested a combination of *prior general consent* and *proxy consent.* In prior general consent, a group of potential research participants is informed about psychological research procedures generally, including the occasional use of deception. Only those who say that they agree to participate in projects involving deception would later be recruited for such projects. Soble argued that this procedure would raise new problems. It would restrict the participating group to those volunteering to be deceived, and would leave us with the major problem of generalizing the results. Furthermore, we would not know to what extent, if any, expectations about deception affected the behavior being studied. Researchers would have to address themselves to these serious questions, so that their projects remain worth doing; the only way to do this, however, would probably involve deception! Soble therefore proposed the following:

Prior General Consent and Proxy Consent

I have so far rejected all but one of the more complicated ways of resolving the dilemma. In addition to the method that I am about to describe, then, the only positions left are the two extreme views. According to one, no experiments involving ineliminable deception are permissible; according to the other, all such experiments are permissible. This latter alternative wants to decrease substantially the significance of the "informed" condition of the principle of informed consent. But there is very little that can be said in favor of doing so. I have already suggested that paternalistic and utilitarian arguments for exceptions to the prohibition on the use of deception are inadequate. But paternalistic and utilitarian reasons are the only one we could have for decreasing the significance of the "informed" condition. The second extreme solution, then, is in practice no different from the solutions proposed by the paternalist or by the utilitarian. There are simply no other arguments to use in defending the second extreme solution.

There are of course perfectly good reasons for accepting the first extreme solution. Experiments without deception respect those individuals who have already volunteered to be subjects at least in part for the sake of other people. Conversely, experiments with deception show disrespect for these persons who have willingly undertaken the risks of an experiment so that other persons might benefit. Deceiving an experimental subject who has volunteered is an acute expression of ingratitude. And it deserves the scorn that we ordinarily give to the person who passes through the cafeteria line twice but pays only once. There is, however, one final method that seems to satisfy our requirements; it allows some ineliminable deception, and so preserves the search for knowledge, without (1) expressing ingratitude to the subjects and (2) undermining the epistemological status of the data collected during the experiment. In this method prior general consent is combined with proxy consent.

I suggest that we make the method of prior general consent applicable to the whole realm of experimental science employing human subjects. If the method of prior general consent is employed for any and every subject pool, the likelihood that forewarning of deception will disrupt the experimental illusion is greatly decreased. In this method, furthermore, the experimental bias introduced in Milgram's proposal (only those subjects who consented in general to deception would be used in deceptive experiments) is overcome in the following way. Subjects are *not* told that only those who approve of deception will be used in experiments utilizing deception; rather, all subjects are candidates for participating in deceptive experiments. But the usual objection to doing this is vitiated by the use of an additional procedure: proxy consent. Each subject in the pool designates some relative or friend as one who will inspect the experiment in which the subject might participate. This relative or friend is empowered by the subject to reject or accept experiments on the basis of whether they posed too much risk, employed deception that was too devious, or was aimed at providing knowledge that might be misused. The proxy makes these judgments from the point of view of the subject who has empowered him or her to do so. It is important to note that combining the method of prior general consent with that of proxy consent combines what is acceptable from both Milgram's and Veatch's proposals. From Milgram's it takes the idea that consent to deception is compatible with the principle of informed consent; from Veatch's proposal it takes the idea that we can resolve the dilemma by consulting persons other than the subjects themselves. But the method of proxy consent used as a conjunct to prior general consent has an obvious advantage to Veatch's proposal: the necessity of having to argue from the approval of mock subjects to the hypothetical approval of real subjects is eliminated by consulting persons empowered by the real subjects to give consent for them.

A procedure employing both prior general consent (as standard for all subject pools) and proxy consent is very far removed from what exists at the present: the use of deception in experiments without the protection for subjects of either prior general consent or proxy consent. For this reason many changes will have to be made in the structure of experimental science using human subjects; so many changes, in fact, that I suspect that the initial reaction of experimental scientists will be that the proposal is impractical, that it will create too many bureaucratic impediments to the conduct of research. Indeed, the experimental scientist could argue that the method, in solving the original dilemma, gives rise to a new dilemma. Either we employ the method of prior general/proxy consent (and abandon a large part of the research enterprise because the method is too costly in terms of time, effort, and money), or we retain the large bulk of the research enterprise (but employ a less ethically satisfying method of obtaining the approval of the subjects). My response to this argument would be to say that as long as we reject the paternalistic and utilitarian arguments for the use of ineliminable deception because those justifications could very well justify deception required only for pragmatic reasons, then we must also be prepared to embrace the relative inefficiency of the method of general proxy consent. Pragmatic considerations, we had decided, are not compelling enough to warrant the less-than-full satisfaction of the principle of informed consent. (p. 45)

In a comprehensive overview of ethical issues in social psychological research, Carlsmith, Ellsworth, and Aronson (1976) pointed out some similarities between field research and research with children.

In field research, people often don't even realize that they are participating in a study. This may add to the merit of the research project, since the people are then behaving naturally, but on the other hand, it means that informed consent has been bypassed completely. In some cases, field research permits greater assurance of confidentiality than any laboratory study, since no one at all may know the identity of any participant. This would not be true if videotaping were involved. Special care is required with regard to introducing unpleasant experiences into the research, since total anonymity, while preserving confidentiality, would probably also preclude debriefing.

For different reasons, young children are also unaware that they are participating in a study; their naivete, in fact, may be one reason why psychologists consider them desirable research participants. Furthermore, they typically cannot be debriefed any more than they can be informed, since the idea of participation in a study is beyond their comprehension.

Instead, researchers try to make sure (for instance, by playing with them) that the children leave the research situation feeling contented and adequate.

Because young children have limited understanding, psychologists must use what Soble called *proxy consent*. According to Carlsmith, Ellsworth, and Aronson (1976),

> The issue of informed consent is typically met by obtaining consent from the parents and/or from the person in charge of a university-administered nursery school, when the parents have delegated the responsibility of providing informed consent to this person. This second system is often a very good arrangement, since the nursery school administrator usually has enough knowledge of psychological research and enough concern for the welfare of the children to make "informed consent" a meaningful term, and in addition the experimenter can be assured that the parents do not object to having their children participate in experiments. It is a good idea for the investigator to take steps to make sure that the parents really are informed about the particular experiment, however, since they are in a position to know whether a given manipulation might have unexpected undesirable effects on their child. If the real reason for deceiving the subjects is that it is necessary that they be ignorant of the true purpose of the experiment, there should be no reason for withholding this information from the parents. In the interests of both the child and the psychologist, the parents should be informed in advance.
>
> But of course no one except the child knows what it is really like to go through the experiment, and the child has not given any informed consent. As with field experiments, then, the experimenter should use only very low levels of arousing experimental manipulations and should watch the child at all times so as to be able to terminate the experiment immediately if the child shows any signs of untoward distress. As with field situations, one useful rule of thumb for choosing stimulus situations for research with child subjects is to choose the sorts of situations which most children are exposed to anyway, in their everyday life. For example, in attempting to arouse fear in a nursery school setting, Carlsmith, Lepper, and Landauer (1974) showed children a clipping from the Walt Disney cartoon *The Legend of Sleepy Hollow*. Although the sequence shown was frightening, it was assumed to involve a kind and level of fear that the children could cope with, since it was from the same movie that large numbers of children have seen and enjoyed on their own.* (pp. 115–16)

At times, the nature of either the research design or the participants makes it impossible or difficult for psychologists to use informed consent in a straightforward manner, telling each potential participant the whole truth and nothing but the truth, and creating a noncoercive situation in

---

* Carlsmith, Ellsworth, Aaronson, *Methods of Research in Social Psychology.* © 1976, Addison-Wesley, Reading, Mass., pp. 115–16. Reprinted with permission.

which each potential participant could say no if so inclined. In such instances researchers should be alert to the temptation to rationalize deceptions and violations of the principle of autonomy. They want to do this study, and they are sincerely convinced that it is both important and well designed, and they may be right on both counts. But they are also members of one of the groups (of scholars, scientists, artists) that have sought to sensitize people to their potential strengths and weaknesses. We all recognize human tragedy when parents know that the only way to raise "good children" is to beat them bloody regularly, when soldiers know that the only way to get critical information out of these captured enemies is to torture them. Do researchers want to be viewed, correctly, as the psychologists who know that the only way to study this or that behavior is to deceive other human beings and to violate their right to choose knowledgeably whether or not to participate in their study? When in doubt, we do well to err on the side of caution, ever sensitive to our human capacity for justifying almost any behaviors.

Deception

In this section, rather than discussing further the activities of psychologists, we will try to defend the moral superiority of truth telling over lying, which Bok called the *principle of veracity* (Bok, 1978; see also Margolis, 1971).

Both truths and lies can hurt people. Facing unpleasant truths is painful, though the long-range harm from not facing them may be even greater. Thus, in a way Sue doesn't want to know that she can never, for whatever complex reasons, become a great bassoonist, yet over a period of years, she will probably be better off if she accepts that painful truth than if she does not. Lies hurt people for many reasons. One is that when people are deceived, they might do something to their own disadvantage which they wouldn't do if they knew the truth. If Sue were looking for a good used car, she wouldn't buy this one if she knew that it needed $700 worth of repairs, but deceived into believing that it is in perfect condition, she buys it. She has clearly been deceived into doing something she was planning not to do—spending $(N + 700).

Most people are tempted to lie at least occasionally, typically to gain a personal advantage, sometimes as an act of kindness toward somebody else. Why would it be morally wrong for you to deceive Sue into buying your car? After all, you want to get rid of it, and if you told her the truth, she would refuse to buy it, or she would insist that you either pay for the repairs or lower the price by $700. Why is it morally wrong for you to do what is best for yourself? Isn't that what everyone does?

First of all even if everyone did precisely that, it might still be morally wrong. That a behavior is universal cannot be taken as proof that it is moral. Second, the argument that we should all take care of Number One is usually a phony: deceivers want to do the deceiving, but they don't want to be deceived! Even as you deceptively seek a buyer for your defective car, you may admit that you don't want anyone to deceive you into buying damaged goods. If you admit that, you have only two options: to justify why you may deceive while others may not, or to admit that what you are doing is immoral. But you may want to make a different argument. Even though you don't want to get stuck with an old lemon, you may nevertheless believe that its owners should try to do what you are doing. In other words, they should try to palm it off on you, and you should constantly be alert to all the deception which is inevitable in this world. Whenever you get stuck, your betters bested you; whenever you don't, you bested them.

It should be noted that both of these arguments take the moral point of view, at least insofar as both involve the notion of universalizability. Either you are acknowledging that you acted against the universal principle, "Tell the truth," or you can justify a modified principle like, "Everyone should tell the truth except people with brown hair." Alternately, you might be guided by the principle, "All individuals should do what is best for them—even when I am injured by others acting on that principle" (for otherwise you are again seeking special privileges just for yourself). Since all of us are social beings, of necessity and from birth on, self-interest is likely to be enlightened, long-range self-interest; taking the short view is likely to cost us dearly in low respect or liking from others.

Suppose that you acted on self-interest, and got away with a lie that was beneficial to you but harmful to someone else. Suppose further that no one ever finds out that you lied—you don't go to jail, and your friends still like and respect you. Most people seem to have an intuitive reaction that what you did was nonetheless immoral, just as committing a perfect murder would be. The basis for this reaction is your having hurt somebody else in order to achieve a personal gain. On the other hand, suppose that you acted on the principle of veracity, and that this was to your disadvantage. Suppose nobody finds out that you were truthful. Then again, pretend that everyone finds out. It seems to make no difference: most people's intuitive reaction is that you behaved morally. Even those who tell you that you were stupid for behaving so morally are thereby granting that they, too, think you did act morally! The basis for this reaction is that you did not harm someone else in order to gain an advantage for yourself.

Both adherence to enlightened, long-range self-interest and to the principle of veracity may result in similar actions in many ordinary situations. Our intuitions, guided by the principle of nonmaleficence, seem to suggest, however, that the principle of veracity is morally superior.

Although telling the truth is always a moral obligation, it may not be the only one in many complex human interactions, nor even the most compelling one. Suppose a lie could save a human life? This brings us back to the question of deception in research, though perhaps we now want to pose it this way: "What obligation of this researcher is more compelling than telling the truth?"

Privacy

We live in the age of computers, and some of us have become understandably concerned about our privacy. If I sign an attendance sheet at this meeting of the XYZ Club, will I end up on 32 new mailing lists? On some government agency's list of unacceptable citizens? We may find it hard to believe that human beings have not been concerned about privacy since time immemorial, but then, humans haven't always lived in the 20th century.

In May 1967, the *American Psychologist* was devoted entirely to the issue of privacy. In a provocative article titled, "What price privacy?", Bennett argued that "the moral imperative is more often allied with the surrender of privacy than with its protection" (p. 371). Thoughts, he argued, can always be kept private: one can refuse to answer questions, and no devices exist for tuning in on one's mind directly. "The real issue is not the right to experience privately, but the right to communicate selectively" (p. 371). Most human beings want to communicate with others from earliest childhood on, and cooperation among people typically demands this.

Privacy emerged as a concern only with the development of city living, and the word, not used in the U.S. Constitution, was used in the legal literature beginning only in 1890. The law typically deals with the surrender of privacy, as when one ought to report that one has witnessed a murder. "When the right to privacy is invoked, I find it appropriate to examine the motives of those who would withhold information" (p. 375). Specifically, Bennett mentioned hermits, prudes, paranoiacs, and rascals, and suggested that we seek "a rational evaluation of the relative propriety of privacy and communication" (p. 375) as we consider specific examples.

Unfortunately, in dealing with such specifics, Bennett's analysis sometimes ignored important moral values. For example, he questioned whether privacy in one-on-one therapy is overemphasized, since people so often talk about their problems to almost anyone. This made him wonder "whether confidentiality is so necessary to the privacy of the patient as to the comfort of the therapist" (p. 374). Privacy in assessment and therapy may indeed sometimes serve to protect therapists who are rascals, and may indeed support a form of prudery in our society (about personal problems), but the main point is that people who share their problems do so voluntarily. A tester may report to a third party provided that the client has agreed to or requested this. Is Jeff really morally remiss if he doesn't want the school psychologist discussing his occupational counselling testing (interest and aptitude) in the hall?

Bennett made an important point, however, about obligations that psychologists ought to assume because they are in a unique position to do so. He used the familiar example of job applicants who keep private (lie about) the fact that they were once in a mental hospital. It is indeed a tragedy that such job applicants must realistically fear that this truth may be used against them, but given our current social reality, the insistence on privacy here resembles not forcing people to testify against themselves. But the valid half of his idea was about psychologists: "On balance, the moral imperative is not to protect this particular secret, but to educate the employer. Perhaps, this is where the psychologist should bend his efforts" (p. 376).

In that same issue of the *American Psychologist* (1967), Lovell addressed an important point that Bennett assumed: privacy of thoughts can always be maintained, because one can refuse to answer questions. But can one, when a psychologist is gathering information by means of interviews or tests? Suppose a test is part of a promotions or hiring procedure?

Lovell distinguished between the *personnel function* of testing, in which there is "a potential conflict of interest between assessor and respondent" (p. 383), and the *client function,* in which there is not. He also described three "test contracts" that implicitly or explicitly described what is "understood between assessor and respondent" (p. 384):

1. *The client contract* described the tests and their purposes. It promised confidentiality, and it asked the respondent to answer honestly or not at all, lest there be a mutual waste of time. A decision not to take the tests would be fully respected.

2. *The strong personnel contract* stated that there was no time to explain the tests, but that the procedures were being "done for sound reasons" (p. 384); that test results would be part of the permanent record and might be used in making decisions about the respondent; and that efforts at impression management would be "apparent to us when we score your test, and will reflect badly on you" (p. 384).

3. *The weak personnel contract* resembled the strong one but viewed good impression management as a potential asset, and told respondents that they could refuse to take the tests, but that the assessors would make it hard for them to do so.

Lovell stressed that psychologists should be explicit about which contract is being used.

Which contract actually respects what Bennett called "the right to communicate selectively"? Lovell argued that only the client contract does:

> If the reader has followed the argument thus far, three questions are likely to come to mind. First, what sort of contract with the respondent is most consistent with the ethical practice of psychology? Second, what sort of contract is most likely to lead in the long run to the valid measurement of

personality? And third, what contract will allow us to offer the community the broadest range of psychological services?

In the remainder of this essay, I shall argue for a client contract on all three counts. I shall further take the view that our three questions cannot ultimately be considered independently from one another, because ethics, science, and services are all outcomes of a single activity, and this activity is one of many interdependent components of a unitary social process. One cannot do something ethically, if one cannot do it at all. We cannot use our personality tests to provide psychological services if we are unable to construct valid measures. And, as I have already tried to suggest comparing sample contracts, the validity of our tests is not independent of our ethics, because our ethics supply the social context in which our tests are administered, and in which they are validated. (p. 386)

Lovell later differentiated between tests of character and tests of capacity; one can "fake good" on the former but not on the latter. Most tests of personality traits are tests of character: you can answer the test questions so as to fake friendliness or broadmindedness or whichever end of the particular trait continuum seems to be the "good" one. It is doubtful, empirically speaking, that psychologists can catch you, and it is clear, morally speaking, that they have no business trying. That would be an invasion of your privacy, statism, and/or parentalism. Lovell concluded:

> My position is that tests of character should never be used for any kind of personnel function, whether it be selection or placement. They should be used only for unbiased research, subject to the restrictions implicit in the client function, and to provide psychological services in situations where the assessor's first professional loyalty is to the respondent. I have argued this position on ethical grounds and on scientific grounds. (p. 392)

CHALLENGES

1a. Pretend you are the person on a review board most opposed to the use of animals in medical research. A team of scientists seem close to finding a new drug which will kill one form of cancer cell with a minimum of side effects for the patient. They have come for approval to further test this drug on pigs and gorillas before they test it on (volunteering) cancer patients. Develop the best argument(s) you can for not granting them permission to do the study.

b. Pretend that you favor the use of animals in medical research. Make the best argument(s) you can for granting the scientists permission to do the study.

2a. Analyze several lines of psychological research in which animals are used (such as learning, psychopharmacology, psychobiology), paying close attention to both the purposes and actual procedures of specific studies. Which studies would you have approved? Which ones not? Make the best possible argument(s) you can for your position.

b. Did your arguments differ for medical and psychological research? Why or why not?

3. Is there too much emphasis on privacy today? Does it increase our alienation from each other even as it protects us from one another? If you were a school psychologist doing individual assessments, what would you consider yourself morally obligated to say to your clients before you began interviewing and testing? Why?

4a. Make the best possible case you can for using Lovell's (1967) strong personnel contract in industry, mental hospitals, and schools.

b. Make the best case you can for using the client contract in these settings.

c. Pretend that you are a school psychologist using the strong personnel contract. A group of parents is morally outraged by this. Try to defend your position to them. Is it consonant with moral principles? Role play this with other students.

d. Pretend you are an industrial psychologist who has been persuaded by Lovell. You are refusing to use personality tests in assessments related to promotional decisions about executives. The personnel department of the XYZ Corporation is incredulous. Try to explain your position to them. Is your explanation consonant with moral principles? Role play this with other students.

7

SHARING KNOWLEDGE

New psychological facts and theories are capable of producing change in individuals and in society. As a result, psychologists face difficult moral questions about sharing their knowledge with others.

The variety of people with whom psychologists share knowledge is as great as the variety within the field of psychology. Research tends to be shared by means of books, professional journals, meetings, and informal conversation. Written reports, staff conferences, and informal interaction are the vehicles for sharing information in clinics, hospitals, schools, and industry. The professionals involved include teachers, nurses, psychiatrists, personnel directors, psychologists, social workers, and others. In direct services (testing, counseling) psychologists share information with clients and their families orally and in writing. Psychologists teach many thousands of undergraduate and graduate students annually and such teaching is yet another way of sharing knowledge. Finally, psychologists make contact with the public through the media, popular books, and adult education.

Each of these contacts with other people presents psychologists with a unique pattern of ethical problems, but certain themes emerge in all of them. The most basic is truth telling.

Telling the truth is one of the most important normative values in society generally, and in professional relationships and science in particular. The *truth* doesn't refer to some mythical absolute truth, nor to truth acquired later. Rather, it refers to the truth that a person knows now. Thus, it is truthful to say, "According to the radio, it will rain today," if that is what one heard and one has not been turned into a liar at the end of the day if the sun was shining until nightfall, since one didn't know that truth until the day was over (Bok, 1978).

Our social relationships would be strikingly different if we could not generally trust one another to tell the truth. Try to imagine, for a moment, having friends who lie at unpredictable times to serve their own purposes. In fact, many complaints that people have about situations in their daily lives do involve matters of truth telling, as when complaints are made about misrepresentations in business deals or family arrangements. People do not always tell the truth, but telling the truth is morally superior to lying, and the statement that "People should tell the truth" is a moral ideal.

What is true of our daily relations with each other is also true when one or more persons are professionals. Our lawyers, dentists, physicians, and psychologists should be honest with us, and we in turn should be honest with them. Some readers may be familiar with debates in bioethics about, for example, physicians telling the truth to patients with a terminal illness. Such debates do not negate the value of truth telling. Rather, they reveal that in particular situations, other values are also operative (such as non-maleficence). This, as we shall see, is true also when psychologists share their knowledge.

Truth telling is critical to the human enterprise known as science. Bronowski (1956) explained in detail that each scientist relies on what others report to be true. If scientists falsified data for their private purposes, science could not proceed as now, and might ultimately be completely impossible. It is for this reason that hoaxes are still rare (most scientists are committed to the value of truth telling) and severely criticized and punished, though there is increasing concern about falsification in natural science research, especially in medicine (Hunt, 1981).

Thus, one value to which all psychologists are committed is truth telling, no matter with whom they are sharing their knowledge. More specifically, psychologists believe that they should report findings in as unbiased a manner as humanly possible, whether or not it was what they expected, hoped for, or wished for. This ideal is not always easy to reach, but it is and should be always kept in mind.

Several things can complicate efforts to act on the ideal of truth telling. The most important one is another basic value: do not hurt or harm others. Consider an example comparable to those in medical ethics. When one must inform parents that their child is retarded, one is inevitably both telling them the truth and hurting them (by killing their last lingering hopes). How much of this truth do they want, when and in what form? What are the obligations of the psychologist in this situation?

A second complication has to do with the nature of psychology's truths.

Most true in one sense are isolated details (for example, after N trials, n percent of the animals were doing X; the child scored IQ 67 on this test), but such truths are meaningless by themselves. This creates a dilemma. On the one hand, if psychologists didn't provide a framework for such details to give them meaning, their listeners would, thus increasingly the probability of serious misunderstandings; these represent failures in the communication of the truth. On the other hand, the frameworks psychologists provide for their observations raise questions about how true psychological interpretations, hypotheses, or theories are. To offer an interpretation of a particular child's IQ of 67 is a very different matter from merely reporting it. Similarly, to offer an interpretation of animal learning is very different from merely reporting the animal behavior observed in a particular study. In both of these examples, different psychologists will probably have different theoretical interpretations. Furthermore, they will probably have observed different facts because of these different theoretical orientations.

Under these circumstances, what are psychologists' responsibilities with regard to truth telling in the different contexts mentioned above (direct services, teaching, informing the public)? Because of the complex issues involved in sharing knowledge, it seems best to consider these contexts one at a time.

SHARING RESEARCH KNOWLEDGE

Sharing with Professionals

The typical pattern for psychologists is to write a research report, and to submit this report to a professional journal or for presentation at a professional meeting. The manuscript is sent out to one or more reviewers who later send it back with detailed comments and recommendations about whether or not it should be published or presented (with or without revisions). Most manuscripts are, in fact, rejected. Thus, wanting to share information doesn't necessarily lead to the opportunity to do so. Many of the comments that arrive from editors' offices are helpful, and may deal with anything from methodology to writing style. Nonetheless, this well-intentioned process sometimes raises major issues about responsibilities for the sharing of knowledge within the field.

Consider the following scenario. Intrigued by a study reported in a journal, a psychologist plans first to replicate it, and then to do a theoretically and/or practically important variation. When this psychologist completes the replication, the data turn out to be notably different from those reported in the original study! Perplexed, the psychologist repeats the study again, but still does not find what was first found. It is easy enough to begin to generate hypotheses when such an apparently astonishing situation arises. Perhaps the sex of the researcher was important; perhaps it was the rat chow. In any case, one thing is clear: the original description and explanation were (inadvertantly) incomplete, and so far, it has not even been possible to repeat the procedure and thus find the same results. The psychologist who did the two replications is committed to telling the truth, whether one finds what one expected or not, and therefore sends a brief note to the appropriate journal. Unfortunately, there is a rather good chance that this note will not be published. Reports that such-and-such did not happen (the null hypothesis could not be rejected) are less likely to be published than reports that it did happen (where $p < .05$). This scenario is not fictional, nor even improbable, though a journal of *Replications in Social Psychology* does exist. Since any one dependent variable is always complexly caused, it is highly probable that innocent variations among researchers are of critical, though initially unsuspected importance (Cronbach, 1975).

This example raises questions about the responsibilities of those who shape the policies of professional journals, the major organs for sharing the truth in psychology. Perhaps every journal needs a section of "Replications." If both studies were well done, the second results are just as significant (in the nonstatistical sense) as the first, and therefore should not be rejected, since such rejection distorts the truth within the field of psychology. (Journal policies are not the only culprit. Before reports of replications can be published, they must be done, but as Smith (1970) observed, many factors contribute to the paucity of such research, only one of which is "the reluctance of some journals to publish replication studies" (p. 970).)

According to Garcia (1981), many psychologists, including journal editors, share with most human beings an inability to appreciate the novel, the creative, the provocative. He writes wryly, "I have studied editorial behavior for years, but I have come to the conclusion that journal editors are neophobic creatures of our own kind" (p. 147).

The sharing of knowledge in journals and at professional meetings seems to avoid the other potential problems mentioned. Normally, the audience for research reports consists of those working in a particular area of psychology. Since the information shared among researchers isn't personal, the possibility of harming someone is minimized. The possibility for misunderstanding is also minimized. Facts aren't presented in isolation; they are always generated and interpreted within a conceptual framework. Furthermore, the audience may not share the views of the researcher, but this cannot be said to harm either of them. On the contrary, professional journals and meetings exist mainly to provide opportunities for sharing and modifying the different viewpoints in the field.

There are important exceptions to this typical situation. Occasionally, public interest is aroused by a research report, either because of media coverage of professional meetings, or because a written report is or seems to be of great social significance (such as Jensen's article in the *Harvard*

Educational Review, 1969). Psychologists know that their professional meetings receive media coverage, and that the public is interested in certain topics (love, violence, heredity-environment debates). Questions can therefore be asked about their moral obligations vis-à-vis their colleagues and the public; these will be discussed below.

Teaching

Psychologists are not the only ones who read journals and books. Students also do, reluctantly or otherwise! Sharing psychology with students, however, is far more problematic than sharing it with colleagues. The variety (not number) of textbooks in every field bears testimony to this statement. Given the different viewpoints in the field, any given course will reflect the truth as conceived by a particular book selected by a particular professor. Some authors and professors use an eclectic approach in order to give every view a fair hearing. Others present one particular point of view, most probably because they believe that it is the closest approximation to the truth, or because they believe the course demands some degree of simplification. Teaching from one perspective does not mean that controversies will be ignored altogether, but it does mean that students will be exposed to a particular version of truth.

This problem can become acute when the professor is a "true believer"; student complaints about having to learn "The Gospel according to Professor X" are not always unjustified. Evaluating this situation from an ethical standpoint is difficult, however. Professors are obligated to tell the truth, like all psychologists, but does that mean they are obligated to assign reading matter they believe to be flawed, perhaps not even worth bothering with? To give just one specific example, how much and in what detail should Freudian theory be covered in the introductory psychology course? A psychodynamically oriented professor might cover Freud in some detail, since so much of that orientation originated with his ideas. A behavioristically oriented psychologist, in contrast, may dispose of Freud, Jung, and Adler in 10 minutes or less as examples of archaic mentalism. Furthermore, including material (whether about Freud, ESP, or anything else) merely because it would interest students is often frowned on as "pandering to students." This expression conceals an important point about the moral obligations of professors: their primary obligation is to share with students their knowledge of the field, not to entertain them. It is not at all clear, therefore, that only eclectic courses are morally defensible. The critical point is not whether courses are eclectic, but whether the psychologists teaching them are teaching the best truth they know. No one can possibly know what psychology will be like in 50 or 100 years. As we pointed out above, early in the morning one can only quote the weather forecast; one cannot report the day's actual weather.

At times, professors with strong views choose texts or readings contrary to their own views because they believe that exposing students to two or more views will provide intellectual challenges and will also be the most truthful thing to do given the current state of the field of psychology. Like all other attempts to solve the problems inherent in truthfully sharing knowledge with students, this approach works well only for those students who can cope with such challenges. For others, it results mainly in confusion and misunderstanding, since right to the end, they want to know the "real answers."

A related issue is that texts, articles, and class lectures and discussions can disturb students, especially in a field like psychology. As we have seen, some psychologists, notably Campbell (1975), have argued that psychology affects people's values and behavior, notably by implicitly endorsing certain personality and behavior patterns. In addition, the philosophic assumptions psychologists inevitably make (whether they recognize them or not) are bound to be troubling to some students, especially thoughtful ones. In fact, college is meant to provide intellectual challenges, and it would be sad indeed if psychology courses could offer none of these. But challenges to one's central beliefs can be genuinely disturbing, as when students think seriously, perhaps for the first time, about their belief in free will or the mental differences and similarities between humans and animals. One cannot deny the pains of such challenges, but they are necessary and justified, since they are an inherent part of higher education. Furthermore, students can and do fight back: while they are not as knowledgeable as colleagues, they can think for themselves and selectively accept and/or reject what they are taught. Research suggests that this is what happens (Steininger & Voegtlin, 1976).

Bakan once argued (1965) that the appropriate role for the psychologist is that of teacher, not technologist. Psychologists will not produce technologies comparable to those related to the natural sciences. (Thus, one can talk about building bridges but ought not talk about building people, since one may control steel and concrete but should not similarly control people.) What psychologists can and should do, argued Bakan, is to teach what they know, since it is characteristic of people to use their knowledge to guide their behavior. This underscores Campbell's point about the potential impact of psychology. How for example, will current students raise any children they may have? Misunderstanding of Freud's ideas may have contributed to a certain kind of excessive permissiveness. What might correct or incorrect understanding of Piaget and Skinner lead to? Professors cannot control what students do with their learning many years after they leave college, but they should be responsive to the fact that students will use it. Thus, practical implications of what is taught should be explored critically. Whether professors like it or not, this is what many students take to be the most (or even only) important course content.

May has criticized modern education for leaning too much in the direction of trying to stuff meaningless details into (therefore) reluctant heads (May, 1967). Students who ask why they are expected to learn what certain cats did in certain puzzle boxes are asking an important and legitimate question. But at the other extreme are found vacuous paragraphs that can be summarized in one sentence ("Each person is unique," or "The environment is important"). Truth in psychology necessarily involves both detailed observation and highly specific interpretations. One cannot teach or write about learning or personality without talking about observations and research in great detail, yet detail alone is truly meaningless (consider: "I drank a cup of coffee at 9:47 A.M."). In any case, even choice of detail reveals one's framework, so one cannot avoid theory (though hopefully one can avoid vacuous theory). Thus, regardless of whether or not a course is approached eclectically, it should help students to think critically (which means creatively) about the material in the course. This is impossible when courses approach either the extreme of empty words or the extreme of disjointed detail.

Finally, what happens when students misunderstand course material? The most obvious answer is that they do poorly on papers and exams, and during class discussions. Our educational system does little to help students learn better what they have not yet mastered. With laudable exceptions, all grades are simply averaged together for a final grade, as though assigning grades were the only purpose of giving tests and papers. This situation wasn't created by psychologists, nor is it unique to psychology courses, yet one might argue that with their special knowledge about learning, psychologists may have a special obligation to try to make sure that all concerned and interested students leave the course with some truth as well as a realization of how much they don't know, and how much nobody knows. The best students are those who are both pleased about what they have learned and excited by what we don't know and have yet to learn. The value judgment involved here is that cognitive complexity is better than cognitive simplicity. In fact, many professors would probably consider change in the direction of cognitive complexity to be the major goal of education.

DIRECT SERVICES

Although some courses are taught on television, most teaching still involves direct contact between professors and students. In testing, counseling, and psychotherapy, psychologists also have direct contact with people when they share their knowledge, but this sharing is very different. In direct services, psychologists share information with clients and their families that is narrow in scope and personal in nature. Clients don't come to learn about personality theory and research. They come to learn about themselves, or even more specifically, about the areas of their lives with which they aren't coping well.

In this context, truth telling is again very important, as it is in all contexts, but the concern about hurting clients is also very salient. Consider some of the specific problems clients bring to different kinds of psychologists: Which careers should I consider? How can I save my faltering marriage? How can we decide whether or not to institutionalize our very retarded child? Why can't I lose weight even though I am dieting carefully? Why doesn't anyone like me? The possible answers clients explore will inevitably involve painful self-confrontation, whether about one's abilities, one's ambivalence toward loved ones, or one's lack of will-power.

In many instances, psychologists do not tell clients the truth in the sense of presenting them with information; rather, they facilitate the discovery of truth by clients. (That's why counseling and therapy are included in this chapter on sharing information.) The people trying to lose weight who are initially convinced that they are carefully following a diet may discover, by keeping careful records, that they are in fact ingesting an extra 500 calories per day (10–15 calories at a time, which is "nothing"). The parents wondering about the severely retarded child may discover, when finally discussing the matter fully and openly, that they agree with each other more than they had anticipated, and that they feared each other's reactions as much as making a decision for and about the child.

At times, then, the truth is being explored or shared under exceptionally benign circumstances. First, clinical and counseling psychologists have been trained to observe carefully any and every cue that their clients provide. Furthermore, depending on the setting, the psychologist may spend one hour or more with the client on as many occasions as are deemed necessary by mutual consent. One of the most important consequences of these two aspects of the sharing of information is that clients can therefore explore fully their angers, hopes, fears, joys, and wishes, and that misunderstandings can be corrected, either immediately with direct information or slowly during the course of further meetings, probably therapeutic in nature. Finally, due to the influence of social psychology and humanistic psychology, as well as to the rejection of the medical model, attention will be given to client strengths as well as problems, and to situational factors as well as personal ones. When psychologists ask clients to keep records of their eating or smoking, or to talk about their family situations, they are also beginning to help those clients take seriously the important truth that most of the so-called solutions for their problems, including the realistic assessment of situations, reside within themselves.

Under the most benign conditions, then, psychologists can help clients to explore and face the truth (that is, can share information) in a sensitive, patient, and thoroughgoing manner. Such conditions do not always exist, however, and at times, psychologists treat clients in a parentalistic manner—they do not tell the truth, or hold parts of it back, because they believe that these clients cannot deal with the truth at that time or ever, for intellectual and/or emotional reasons. Such parentalism is justified only insofar as the client is intellectually and/or emotionally incompetent, and this may vary from situation to situation or from day to day. A severely retarded person may always be incompetent with respect to dealing with certain truths, a depressed person only during the most acute attacks of depression. Parentalism (not sharing information for the sake of the client) always runs the risks of demeaning the client and of proceeding without the informed consent of the client. It is justified only when the client seems incapable of being informed, incapable of acting autonomously.

A particularly troubling matter in this context is that different psychologists believe in different truths. Sometimes these deal with specific matters, as for example, the worth of the Rorschach for learning about personality, and sometimes they deal with broader matters, including moral values. One current example comes from the debates about therapy and counseling for women. Traditional and feminist therapists (who are not necessarily men and women, respectively) will have very different ideas about appropriate goals for women, or about what would constitute successful therapy (Chesler, 1972; Williams, 1976).

Two basic kinds of issues are involved: those dealing with what is known in psychology (that is, what are the correct facts and theories?), and those dealing with social and moral values. Under these circumstances, psychologists are obligated to recognize that theirs is one view among many, even when they believe it to be the correct one morally and/or scientifically. They are obligated to be explicit about their view, both for themselves, so that they may continually put their view to the tests of experience and judgment, and for their clients, so that their clients may choose psychologists with whose views they are comfortable. Unfortunately, clients often do not find out for some time that they do not share the values of their psychologists, not because they are being defensive, but because they would not agree with anyone holding such views.

This matter can be as serious for differences about fact and theory as for differences about moral views. Clients are hard put to evaluate the worth of the Rorschach, or of behavior or psychodynamic therapies. Unfortunately, the proof of the pudding is not in the eating in this case. It has been known for a long time (Forer, 1949) that people are easily convinced about the correctness of descriptions of their personalities supposedly based on this or that personality test when in fact the descriptions are merely the same generalities handed to everyone—hardly proof that the tests are valid! Likewise, every therapy promises hope, making one feel that someone cares and can help—again, hardly proof that this particular therapy is the best one for this particular problem (Frank, 1961).

Someone might ask, "If something works or provides information, why does it matter that something else may also inform or seem to work?" The answer is clear. If it is the case that three tests or therapies actually work, then surely the client should have some ideas about the relative assets and liabilities of each, and should be permitted choice in the matter. On the other hand, if nothing is actually working or providing information, except in the eyes of true believers, then the test or therapy should not be used at all, since it builds false hopes and takes time and money from clients. Consider an extreme hypothetical example. A 10-question test is created and immediately used in counseling, without its first having been subjected to validation studies. It later turns out that test scores are not related to any other behaviors, but the test's creator is still convinced that the test measures X, and continues to use it. This conviction is a sound basis for doing more research; it is not a justification for charging people money and building up their hopes about getting helpful information about themselves on the basis of having taken this new test.

Tests are hard enough to evaluate, and arguments about their worth and/or appropriate use abound in the literature (see Chapter 11). The situation is even more complicated for therapies, since disagreements exist about both the ends to be reached (behavior or personality change? which behavior or traits? for how long?) and how best to reach them. The psychologist faces a severe moral dilemma here: how to inform clients about the incompleteness of our knowledge so as not to misrepresent the situation, without making them feel that real help is unavailable, which isn't true.

INSTITUTIONAL SETTINGS

Sometimes, psychologists see people, especially for evaluation, who are referred by someone else. School psychologists evaluate children referred by their teachers; prison psychologists evaluate prisoners referred by prison administrators; hospital psychologists evaluate patients referred by psychiatrists. In these cases, the most basic question is: who is (are) the client(s)? For whose benefit is the person being evaluated—for the person's, or for the institution's? These do not necessarily conflict: the same course of action could benefit both the person and the institution. Sometimes they do conflict, however, notably when long-range gains for the person are incompatible with institutional needs. It will be argued here that the person being evaluated is always a client, even when institutional personnel are also clients. Were this not so, psychologists would be in the position of contributing to the using of one person by others.

Consider a specific example. Mary is referred to a school psychologist for evaluation because she is very assertive and stubborn. A good student in the past, she is no longer doing her assigned work, and instead, spends time making trouble with an admiring clique of fellow-students. Who are the clients here? The interests of the teacher are compelling: it is difficult enough to teach 20–25 children with different preferences and talents without having to devote time regularly to a subgroup of "difficult" children. But Mary's interests are equally compelling, regardless of whether a difficult home situation, a boring classroom situation, or both are involved in her school behavior. What are the obligations of the school psychologist in this situation?

One may be tempted to reply that whatever would benefit the teacher and the other children would also benefit Mary, but real life is not always that simple. The particular case may represent one of those unfortunate combinations of personalities that can be found in all institutions. For example, we might have a bright, self-directed child in the class of an equally bright, law-and-order type of teacher. Mary has done well with a variety of other teachers; the teacher has done well with a variety of other children. With whom should the psychologist share what truths about the situation and about Mary? The teacher referred Mary; one could therefore say that the teacher is asking for help, but then again, Mary also needs help, and she is automatically a client.

Part of the evaluation will involve trying to predict, on the basis of available information, whether Mary has started on a dysfunctional pattern that will bring her into conflict with most present and future authorities and/or peers, or whether her current behavior will turn out to be specific to this classroom situation. Perhaps she is bright, bored, and hungry for admiration, so that she finds irresistible her new popularity among some of the other children. Perhaps she achieves below the level of most of the other children, and her mischief is both an expression of her frustration and anger, and a source of admiration from peers. The psychologist's evaluation must clearly take into account Mary's current situation. How flexible is the teacher? How will the teacher interpret and use the information which the psychologist has acquired?

In sharing information with Mary's teacher, the psychologist is obligated to try to prevent and/or to clear up misunderstandings, to ensure that the information is helpful to both the teacher and Mary. For example, a high IQ should not be taken out of the context of the whole child coping with a current situation, and should not be taken to mean that Mary can instantly be expected to get A's. Sharing information means being alert to such potential misunderstandings, since they could obviously contribute to harming the person being evaluated. Most teachers want to help the children in their classes; psychologists are obligated to share information in such a way that it will be possible for them to do so. This does not mean distorting or hiding the truth, but, as in direct services, sharing it clearly, thoroughly, and patiently.

At times, it is impossible to even get close to this ideal, let alone reach it. A rare teacher might spend the year hating Mary and making school intolerable for her if she were not switched to another teacher. Some rare hospital or prison professionals might insist on pulling out of the psychologist's evaluation whichever details fit in with their views or plans. In such cases, the psychologist has two conflicting moral obligations: to tell the truth; and to avoid contributing to one person being used by others for their convenience and/or unconscious needs. A particular teacher or prison guard who is out to "get" a particular pupil or prisoner presents a very different situation from a teacher or guard trying to be helpful. The obligation to prevent (even greater) harm to others is stronger than the obligation to tell the truth. If an authority figure seeks to destroy someone (a pupil or a prisoner), then a psychologist should not knowingly provide information to the authority figure which, it is clear to that psychologist, will be used to try to destroy another human being. In such cases, it may be necessary to involve other institutional personnel or even, in extreme cases, people outside the institution.

SHARING INFORMATION WITH THE PUBLIC

Two questions are raised in this context. Should psychologists tell the truth (that is, share their information with the public)? If so, how? The first question is not outrageous, since information affects people, and particular information might have more adverse than helpful impact. Nonetheless, the mere statement of the problem provides the answer: since psychologists should not be an elite, parentalistic group controlling the flow of information to others, they should share their information. They must do so, however, with the awareness that they may be contributing to the changing world views of their audiences. Bakan (1965) is not the only person who has observed that psychology's impact will not come from new technologies, but rather from new ways of thinking about people, which are both causes and effects of social change (Miller, 1969).

Many students and some psychologists sometimes argue that psychologists are still too isolated from the public—that they still do not share sufficiently the knowledge they have. For example, one of the lessons that comes from several areas of psychology is that people's immediate social situations contribute far more to their thoughts, feelings, and actions than they commonly believe. While this is a sweeping generalization, it can be supported with evidence from many areas. We seem willing to believe that heredity, prior learning, or will power contribute to what we are doing. For various reasons, we seem to be astonished or offended by the idea that, for example, the objects lying around in whatever room we happen to be in, or the people there, can make comparably potent contributions. Being aware of this in a particular situation is being in a psychologically different state from being unaware of this. Such awareness is based on knowledge or information. Convinced that acting with information is superior to acting without it, students argue that psychologists have an obligation to share their information. Why should only psychologists be aware of X or Y or Z, but no one else?

The other side of the coin is expressed by writers like Campbell (1975) and Smith (1978). They do not favor hiding the truth, but they are concerned about its impact. As we saw earlier, Campbell is concerned that the values implicit in personality theories and their popularizations are contributing to the destruction of valuable social norms that have evolved through centuries of human social interaction. Smith is concerned that certain kinds of information can be destructive of character: "some virtues—humility, creativity, spontaneity—are destroyed when their subject is made aware of them" (p. 34). Public information can also create new anxieties: Smith points out that knowledge about human sexuality can be beneficial, but it has also created worries about adequate performance and painting by number rather than on one's own. Public information involving group comparisons may adversely affect one or the other group and contribute to dissention among the many groups in society; consider the debates about research on gender and race differences.

Nonetheless, no one argues that psychologists should cease to inform the public. To the contrary, since at least some of psychology is of great interest to everyone, journalists, newscasters, and others will bring psychology to the public no matter what psychologists do. At the very least, then, psychologists are obligated to try to minimize misunderstandings and harm to individuals and social life. Beyond that, psychologists may want to share truths that others don't actively seek, like the generalization about the immediate environment discussed above. It seems reasonable, then, to say that psychologists should share information actively and directly rather than to leave to others the telling of psychological truths. The question is: how?

Two kinds of difficulties confront psychologists writing popular articles, books, or appearing on radio or TV. The first has to do with making complicated matters comprehensible without thereby distorting them through oversimplification. Fortunately, not everything in psychology is complicated. For example, given the opportunity to explain a less punitive (than typical) way of relating to children, a psychologist can do so clearly and with an eye on predictable misunderstandings (for example, less punitive does not mean without discipline). Some psychology is very technical, however, and even slightly technical information seems to be indigestible for some people. For example, even after completing an introductory psychology course, some students can be heard to say that someone with an IQ of 140 is twice as intelligent as someone with an IQ of 70. This is of course sheer nonsense. Assuming that the mean for the test was arbitrarily set at 100 and the standard deviation at 15, the meaning of the two IQs is that one person's performance was 2.67 standard deviations above the mean, the other's 2.0 standard deviations below the mean. Without a "zero IQ," a ratio scale does not exist, and it is therefore meaningless to think of one IQ as twice as high as another. If a given proportion of college students cannot understand that much during their course (in which they are typically exposed to both text and professor and study for exams), what would the proportion be on a radio or television talk show if this matter came up? It is easy to grasp what *Newsweek* said about Jensen's research (see Chapter 1); it is far more difficult to grasp the important technical criticisms of that research. (For a good example, see Gould, 1980.) This statement is not intended as intellectual snobbery. Even educated people cannot understand each other's specialities, and the simple but troublesome fact is that most of the people in any national audience are nonspecialists.

What can psychologists do in such situations? They can try to explain things as clearly as possible. They can communicate in different degrees of detail or at different levels of complexity by using a variety of magazines or talk shows, and keeping their particular audiences in mind in each case. They can recognize this as an ongoing, inherently unsolvable problem which they are nonetheless obligated to attack head-on rather than ignore. As difficult as the problem is, attempts to deal with it cannot always be somebody else's responsibility.

The second difficulty stems from the presence of different viewpoints in psychology in all areas, regardless of technical level. It was pointed out earlier that telling the truth can only mean the truth as I best know it, and not what turns out to be true one hundred years from now. When Skinner, for example, appears on national television, he most assuredly is telling the truth in the former sense: he speaks of his research and the interpretations to which it has led him. Many psychologists think that his interpretations are true for only a limited body of observations, not for all behavior, but people who arrange talk shows are typically more interested in generating excitement among their audiences than in airing alternate theoretical interpretations in psychology. A somewhat different situation exists for radio programs on which psychologists answer calls from listeners, since they are in a position similar to those sharing information in the context of direct services (see below); simultaneously, however, they are giving information to their thousands of listeners. As in the classroom, psychologists have an obligation to present the truth as they know it; but they are also obligated to consider what harm it might do when shared with reporters or by means of a microphone.

Consider studies that seem to show that more men are mathematically talented than women. Such research quickly becomes news, the fate of the report by Benbow and Stanley (1980). Since psychologists know that such information might unjustifiably be used to discriminate against women or to justify already existing discrimination, they are obligated to follow up news reports about such research with supplementary information about alternate theoretical and social interpretations of these data. Above all, the most basic point needs constant repeating: *group characteristics have no bearing on one's responsibilities to individuals.* Even if fewer girls than boys were born mathematically gifted, every child should have good math instruction and the opportunity to display and develop any and all talents in this area. Psychologists cannot and should not prevent the media from reporting their work, but they can make every effort to ensure that the implications of their work are not misunderstood. As pointed out above, it is not always possible to prevent misunderstandings, but it is always possible to try.

Media Therapy and Self-Help

The newest form of sharing psychology is through the media, mostly in the form of advice or therapy on talk shows and call-in shows, but also via popular articles and books. The characteristics of media psychology make its sharing of information different from that occurring in the classroom or during longer therapy or assessment.

Portuges (*APA Monitor*, 1981), has discussed several features of media therapy and advisement as currently practiced. Only one contact occurs between psychologist and client, and it is typically only a few minutes long. This means that the assessment of the problem is minimal; clients are not informed about the suitability, limits, and risks of this kind of intervention as it applies to them, and no follow-up is planned to assess the results of this brief intervention. In addition, any one caller or client is in reality only one among thousands or millions, since as Portuges also points out, a program may "influence how millions think about their lives" (Portuges, 1981, p. 2). This is large scale group therapy with unknown clients! Similar points can be made about popular books and articles that advise readers how to improve their personalities (by becoming more assertive) and how to deal with a crisis (divorce).

What are the moral concerns in such sharing of psychology? The most fundamental question is whether such sharing can help anyone. If each of us is unique, how can advice to this or that person, or about this or that crisis, help anyone, since such advice isn't based on a detailed study of a particular client? In other words, if such advice is always based on incomplete information, is it not inherently immoral? This criticism overemphasizes the uniqueness of individuals and situations: although each is unique, they also have much in common. Readers and listeners may share shyness or constant self-blame or abuse of their children. Furthermore, readers and listeners can often assess themselves: they have some sense of the extent to which the chapter or program on self-blame pertains to them. It would be parentalistic indeed to assume that most or all people are incapable of dealing with their own lives at all.

Such parentalism may be justified in relation to some members of the audience, but not in relation to all, and psychologists should assume that most listeners are competent. Therefore, rather than pretending to offer instant, simple solutions to complex problems, they should and often do provide relevant information and sometimes a different perspective on a problem. Thus, worry that my child is the only one who behaves in a certain way can sometimes be alleviated by the information that such behavior is typical of a certain stage of development. Or someone's search for the "right answer" may be replaced by a realization that each alternative will have both good and bad consequences. The basic problem is neither the uniqueness of each problem nor near-universal incompetency, but rather, that media psychologists cannot easily or at all deal with those few who are truly overwhelmed by their problems. Reaching this latter group is always a moral concern, but this is not an argument against all media psychology.

A second moral concern is that what is shared in the media is typically value-laden, yet it is often presented as "objective" or "scientific" advice. The reader of a book that provides information about how to be more assertive probably shares with its author the value that it is good to be (more) assertive, at least in certain situations. Media psychology shares values even as it shares information. For example, the psychologist may make the point that it is more important to be comfortable with oneself than to live up to somebody else's standard of normality. In other contexts, the psychologist may stress the consequences of behavior. Thus, "too aggressive" may mean that that amount of aggression has resulted in being without friends. In either case, values are involved: self-acceptance and friendships are good. Psychologists may be offering some members of the audience support for their values; others may be exposed to what are for them new values or new ways of thinking about values. One of the responses to Portuges' article deals explicitly with this matter. Russo (*APA Monitor*, 1982), protested that some psychologists depict homosexuality as "faulty development," thus continuing to stigmatize it as mental illness. This, he pointed out, is contrary to a 1970 APA resolution, and he therefore urged the APA to take a stand against the dissemination of such misinformation. But, as pointed out in Part II, in matters of faulty development or living, or "mental illness," we are touching on value differences, not on disagreement about facts. This point should be shared with listeners along with information. Thus, it should be clearly stated that *good adjustment, mental health*, and other such terms are value-laden, and that what one psychologist considers faulty another may view positively. This will be a continuing project, since at least some listeners, perhaps many, think that anything a doctor says is the truth.

Finally, whether or not they want to be, media psychologists are both *entertainers*, subject to the whims of the marketplace, and *professionals* (Larson, 1982). Books and talk shows must walk a fine line between sensationalism, that often sells, and thoughtful caution, that may not sell but which professionalism dictates. The choice of topics is also influenced by this. Sex and assertiveness make for more exciting books or programs than does cognitive development in children, yet the public gets a distorted sense of psychology from such imbalance. Furthermore, not striving for or even insisting on better balance is de facto acceptance of this presentation of psychology. It is possible to share even touchy ideas in an honest, informative manner. Bush's *When a child needs help* (1982) is an excellent example of this point. Bush respects and trusts parents, and gives them a balanced overview of what might be a problem and why, when, and how to seek professional help, and what the nature of such help is. He makes it very clear that therapists are not magicians, and that different therapies are suitable for different problems. Unfortunately, some parents may find Bush's thorough and evenhanded coverage somewhat confusing, even upsetting, since he demystifies therapy rather than presenting therapists as gurus or saviors. In this regard, psychologists face the same dilemma as other professionals writing for lay people: if the presentation is too complex, the audience misunderstands it, but if it is too simplified, it distorts reality. No one book or program can strike a good balance for everyone in the audience, but, with this dilemma in mind, psychologists can plan their choice of presentation carefully, monitor it, and revise it in the light of information about its impact.

CONCLUSION

We started this chapter by stating that knowledge can contribute to change, and that psychologists therefore face difficult moral questions about sharing their knowledge. Difficulties arise for several reasons. First, truth telling may conflict with nonmaleficence. In a variety of settings, the psychologist may face the problem of what to do about truths that can hurt. Second, some information is difficult to communicate at times because recipients lack the knowledge and/or intellective skills needed to comprehend it or they may misconstrue or deny it because of the complex emotions it arouses. The communication difficulties are very real. Psychologists must be cautious, however, about using them as an easy excuse for elitism and/or parentalism: we will share psychology with those who are educated, bright, mature, or normal but sharing it with anyone else is a hopeless task. Third, debates about what is and what is not knowledge present difficulties for sharing "knowledge." How, for example, should parapsychology be shared with students in an introductory psychology course? Not at all? In a debunking lecture which begins, "Some people claim"? Through a series of readings? What percent of class time should be devoted to the topic? While there is no specific answer, teachers can combine truth telling with respect for the students' autonomy, welcoming, for example, a challenge from the student who says, "You said psychology is a science. I think the studies demonstrating that ESP exists are as well controlled as any others in psychology, so why do you say that there's no such thing?"

THEMES AND VARIATIONS: CHAPTER 7

The Values Inherent in Science

In a 1956 essay titled *Science and human values,** Bronowski argued that both art and science involve creativity, although in different ways. While creating is an individual activity, it is also social:

> And in practice, he [the logical positivist] could not verify the rate of expansion of the Crab nebula and the processes which might cause it to glow without the help of a sequence of instrument makers and astronomers and nuclear physicists, specialists in this and that, each of whom he must trust and believe. All this knowledge, all our knowledge, has been built up communally; there would be no astrophysics, there would be no history, there would not even be language, if man were a solitary animal. (p. 73)

> Suppose then that we give up this assumption and acknowledge that, even in the verification of facts, we need the help of others. What follows?
>   It follows that we must be able to rely on other people; we must be able to trust their word. That is, it follows that there is a principle which binds society together, because without it the individual would be helpless to tell the true from the false. This principle is truthfulness. If we accept truth as an individual criterion, then we have also to make it the cement to hold society together. (p. 73–74)

He pointed out that the logical positivists claim that "only those statements have meaning which can in principle be verified and found to be so or not so." (p. 74) A social axiom follows from this:

> We OUGHT to act in such a way that what IS true can be verified to be so. (p. 74, italics in the original)

Under what social conditions can scientists follow this axiom?

> The men and women who practice the sciences make a company of scholars which has been more lasting than any modern state, yet which has changed and evolved as no church has. What power holds them together?
>   In an obvious sense, theirs is the power of virtue. By the wordly standards of public life, all scholars in their work are of course oddly virtuous. They do not make wild claims, they do not cheat, they do not try to persuade at any cost, they appeal neither to prejudice nor to authority, they are often frank

---

* J. Bronowski, *Science and Human Values.* Copyright © 1956, 1965 by J. Bronowski. Reprinted by permission of Julian Missner division of Simon & Schuster, Inc.

about their ignorance, their disputes are fairly decorous, they do not confuse what is being argued with race, politics, sex or age, they listen patiently to the young and to the old who both know everything. These are the general virtues of scholarship, and they are peculiarly the virtues of science. (p. 75)

To be sure, individual scientists have their human foibles, but the main point is:

The values of science derive neither from the virtues of its members, nor from the finger-wagging codes of conduct by which every profession reminds itself to be good. They have grown out of the practice of science, because they are the inescapable conditions for its practice. (p. 77)

What is necessary to support the process of searching for truth?

Independence and originality, dissent and freedom and tolerance: such are the first needs of science; and these are the values which, of itself, it demands and forms. (p. 80)

The society of scientists must be a democracy, and tolerance must be based on respect. The hypotheses of some scientists may turn out to be wrong, but respect for scientists is based on their being good scientists, not on their being right. Many specific scientific ideas have been modified very rapidly.

Yet the society of scientists has survived these changes without a revolution and honors the men whose beliefs it no longer shares. No one has been shot or exiled or convicted of perjury; no one has recanted abjectly at a trial before his colleagues. The whole structure of science has been changed, and no one has been either disgraced or deposed. Through all the changes of science, the society of scientists is flexible and single-minded together and evolves and rights itself. In the language of science, it is a stable society. (p. 87)

He applied this analysis to the larger social arena:

Men have asked for freedom, justice and respect precisely as the scientific spirit has spread among them. The dilemma of today is not that the human values cannot control a mechanical science. It is the other way about: the scientific spirit is more human than the machinery of governments. We have not let either the tolerance or the empiricism of science enter the parochial rules by which we still try to prescribe the behavior of nations. Our conduct as states clings to a code of self-interest which science, like humanity, has long left behind. (p. 90)

Direct Services

The information obtained through testing, counseling, and therapy is both personal and specific; in order to share such information in a moral way, the psychologist must deal with both of these aspects.

Some of the information is not readily understood by clients. School testing programs, for example, often share test results through the use of forms that not only present scores, but also attempt to explain their meaning. These forms are typically well designed and clearly written, but understanding them requires a fairly high level of reading comprehension. Those who confuse the 70th percentile with the more familiar 70 percent will not ask for help in interpreting the information, since they think that they understand it. Those who realize that neither scores nor explanation make sense to them may nonetheless resist asking for help, since they may unfortunately believe that such an action would expose them as being stupid. One possible solution to this problem might be to thoroughly train all teachers in the interpretation of test scores, and return all test scores during individual conferences, since these permit mutual observation and questioning.

Anastasi (1976) warns about the many ways in which psychologists' numbers can be misinterpreted, and makes the wise but typically unheeded suggestion that they be avoided or carefully placed into a proper context:

> Broad levels of performance and qualitative descriptions in simple terms are to be preferred over specific numerical scores, except when communicating with adequately trained professionals. Even well-educated laymen have been known to confuse percentiles with percentage scores, percentiles with IQ's, norms with standards, and interest ratings with aptitude scores. But a more serious misinterpretation pertains to the conclusions drawn from test scores, even when their technical meaning is correctly understood. A familiar example is the popular assumption that an IQ indicates a fixed characteristic of the individual which predetermines his lifetime level of intellectual achievement. (p. 56)

But it isn't just the technical aspects of specific information that are troublesome; just as important is the potential emotional impact of the individual's interpretation of information. In the following paragraph, Anastasi alerts us to problems which can arise in any sharing of information in direct services:

> Last but by no means least is the problem of communicating test results to the individual himself, whether child or adult. The same general safeguards against misinterpretation apply here as in communicating with a third party. The person's emotional reaction to the information is especially important, of course, when he is learning about his own assets and shortcomings. When an individual is given his own test results, not only should the data be interpreted by a properly qualified person, but facilities should also be available for counseling anyone who may become emotionally disturbed by such information. For example, a college student might become seriously discouraged when he learns of his poor performance on a scholastic aptitude test. A gifted schoolchild might develop habits of laziness and shiftlessness, or he might become uncooperative and unmanageable, if he discovers that he is

much brighter than any of his associates. A severe personality disorder may be precipitated when a maladjusted individual is given his score on a personality test. Such detrimental effects may, of course, occur regardless of the correctness or incorrectness of the score itself. Even when a test has been accurately administered and scored and properly interpreted, a knowledge of such a score without the opportunity to discuss it further may be harmful to the individual. (pp. 56–57)

No one is suggesting that psychologists are morally obligated to "molly-cuddle" clients; in fact, that would be the height of condescension, not respect. Rather, in direct services, psychologists are gathering information in order to help the particular individuals who are their clients; the question then becomes how best to share information (not to hide it!) while minimizing pain and misunderstanding, maximizing comprehension and realistic, constructive use of the information. Anastasi's examples point to the obligations of psychologists in this context. Suppose parents are concerned about a child doing poorly in school. Interviewing and testing indicate that the child is exceptionally bright but struggling in dysfunctional ways with a variety of interpersonal relationships. Unnecessary and tragic consequences would follow for everyone in the family from a failure of communication in which the parents clung to the 137 IQ, denied all other information, and began to punish the child for every grade below 90. The psychologist's obligation is to help this family; clearly, the proper sharing of information is an integral part of such helping.

Sharing Information with the "Public"

By far the most bedeviling problem that arises in sharing information is sharing it with the public. As must be clear to anyone who has ever read such outstanding "interpreters" as Bronowski, Sagan, Gould, and Bernstein, even well-written popularizations of science require knowledge, concentration, and critical thinking. The same is true of philosophical writings intended, at least in part, for the general reader. Consider such writers as Skinner, Szasz, May, and Bok.

Let us look at the problem of sharing research in the areas of race and gender differences. Consider the simplest (most easily understood) point which Gould (1980) made in his review of Jenson's *Bias in mental testing* (1979), the important point that the vernacular and statistical meanings of *bias* are different. The verbal explanation of the statistical meaning became cumbersome enough for Gould to supplement it with two graphs! The vernacular meaning, according to Gould, stresses "fairness-unfairness":

> The vernacular charge of bias (I shall call it V-bias) is linked to the idea of fairness and maintains that blacks have received a poor shake for reasons of education and upbringing, rather than of nature. (p. 38)

The statistical meaning (S-bias), in contrast, refers to whether or not a given test score predicts the same nontest behavior for two groups. Does a score of 30 predict job success for Group I but job failure for Group II? In that case, there is S-bias. On the other hand, if test scores predict job performance for both groups in the same way, but Group I performs better than Group II on both test and job, the test is not S-biased. Note, however, that it could still be unfair to use the test (V-bias). If Group II members have been deprived of the opportunities to learn the skills required by both test and job, fairness demands that they be given such opportunities, not that the test be used to further damage their opportunities.

Gould argued that Jensen understands this distinction, but "after making clear distinctions between S-bias and culture fairness, then proceeds to confuse the issue completely by using 'bias' in its ordinary vernacular sense over and over again" (pp. 39–40). Having made this important point, Gould proceeded to give his readers a brief overview of correlation coefficients and factor analysis in order to answer the question, "Is Intelligence a 'Thing'?":

> In sum, there remains a fundamental difference between g as the first principal component (Spearman-Burt) and g as a second-order correlation of oblique simple structure axes (Thurstone): g is usually dominant in the first and very weak in the second—while Jensen's argument requires that it be dominant. Since principal components and oblique simple structure represent two equally valid methods of factor analysis, we are forced to conclude that the dominant g required by Jensen (which appears only in principal components) is not a fact of nature, but an artifact of choice in methods. (p. 42)

Paragraphs of this sort share information about the interpretation of data with only a limited segment of the population! In effect, Gould was arguing, as have others before him, that psychologists attach a name to a set of culturally valued behaviors whose interrelationships can sometimes be clarified through the use of certain statistics. Questionable interpretations are made when this name is assumed to refer to a "thing" that can be inherited like eye color.

Intensely prejudiced persons look for and believe "bad" information about the objects of their prejudice, while they forget or reinterpret "good" information. Lesser prejudice is not so intractable. We may be uneasy about our first encounter with X's, but will quickly conclude that they are just another group of human beings, some of whom we like more, some of whom we like less. Less prejudiced people don't assume or rigidly cling to lesser degrees of intelligence or mathematical aptitude in any group. Their major problem will be to make sense of the relatively sophisticated interpretations found in such publications as the *New York Review of Books, Science 81,* and *Human Nature,* and/or to avoid accepting simplistic yet understandable and convincing statements in the popular media.

The April 10, 1981 issue of *Science* published several letters commenting on the Benbow and Stanley (1980) article on gender differences in mathematical ability. Repeated references were made to the many potentially important differences in the socialization of boys and girls. Critical here, however, were the concerns expressed about the treatment this article received in the media, given the complexity of the topic. For example, Stage and Karplus wrote, "Unfortunately, the hypothesis of superior male ability, favored but not substantiated by the authors, received widespread distribution in the popular media, which did not call attention to the complexity of the problem" (p. 114). Egelman, Alper, Leibowitz, Beckwith, and Leeds (1981) pointed to complexity when they wrote, "An underlying fallacy that has been largely responsible for the unwarranted publicity in the popular media which the study by Benbow and Stanley has received is the notion that, if a trait is under genetic control, the expression of that trait is immutable" (p. 116). In their reply to the letter writers, Benbow and Stanley wrote, "We deeply regret that press coverage of our brief report confused the issues, rather than alerting people to the *magnitude* of the sex difference. The situation is far worse than most persons realize" (p. 121). Regardless of their interpretations, then, these scholars were dismayed by media coverage: it simply did not do justice to the complex problem of presenting the data and the several ways of interpreting them! One need not belong to the groups aptly called "racists" and "sexists" to go astray in these situations; one need only belong to the group called "lay people."

There is no simple solution to this huge and important social problem. It would help considerably, however, if all media had social science coverage at least on a par with current sports and weather coverage. Perhaps psychologists who can write and speak plain English should be more insistent in trying to convince newspapers, radio, and television that accurate coverage of psychological research is morally obligatory, and that such coverage should be a daily feature rather than an occasional, melodramatic one. One can only hope that physical scientists are or will be striving for the same kind of coverage.

CHALLENGES

1. Try to design a society based on the values of science which are, according to Bronowski, "the inescapable conditions for its practice." In such a society, what might be the relationships between parents and children? What might its government be like? Its economic system? Would you move there? Why or why not?

2. Do this with three others. One of you will role play a client, and one a psychologist; the other two will serve as observer-recorders. Rotate roles as you proceed.

    a. A therapist notices occasional psychotic episodes in a 14-year-old client. Role play the sharing of information about this when the psychologist is talking to the client and then with the parents. What moral problem does the psychologist face while sharing information? Discuss as a group the observations of the recorders.

b. Mr. Jones has done heavy physical labor for most of his working life. He left high school after two years, has had no further education, and is now 47. After a car accident, he can no longer do the same work, but he is eager to find a different kind of job. He welcomed the opportunity to take a battery of tests, and is now sitting with the psychologist waiting for information and advice. Role play Mr. Jones and the psychologist, making up details as necessary. What moral problems does the psychologist face while sharing information? Discuss as a group the observations of the recorders.

3. Write a brief newspaper article that clearly yet without oversimplification summarizes a psychological study which you consider important. How did you make your article comprehensible? Interesting? Did you present alternate interpretations of the data? Why or why not? Exchange articles with other students, and discuss possible revisions which you might all make. After you have revised your article, ask someone to read it who has not attended college. Did the reactions differ from those of your fellow students? Are further revisions desirable? Why or why not?

8

USING PSYCHOLOGY

Strictly speaking, psychologists always use their knowledge of psychology, whether they are administering a personality test, comparing the sensory acuities of different species, or doing therapy. Thus, using psychology involves everything discussed so far: choosing an area, conceptualizing, gathering information, and sharing information. One cannot function as a psychologist without using psychology!

But this phrase also has another, more commonly used meaning: applying what we know in new, real-life situations. Thus, having learned something about the internal and external factors related to prejudice, driving behaviors, reliability on a job, we might be in a position to use this knowledge for good. In the examples given, "good" would presumably mean less prejudice, safer driving, and greater reliability, while more prejudice, more accidents, and decreased reliability would be "bad." Clearly then, the application of knowledge always involves decisions about the moral good, about who should use what knowledge when, how, for whom, and in what context.

It may help to start with an example. What in the rebellion of a particular adolescent is "good," what "bad"? What kind of adjustment should the adolescent be helped to make to a violent father who regularly beats his family? How about a strict father who believes in corporal punishment? As we go through life, each of us decides what we will accept and what we will try to change, and even if we do not make speeches, our actions speak for us. *Whenever psychologists apply psychology in a real life setting, they are inevitably acting on their decisions about what should and what should not be changed and why.* These decisions about application are morally relevant ones, even though esthetic, prudential, and other values are also involved.

This chapter will address the morally relevant concerns common to all applications of psychology, whether in classrooms, industry, or counseling centers.

ARE VALUES "RELATIVE" TO THE INDIVIDUAL?

Must we accept the thesis that since one person's "good" is sometimes another person's "bad," that all values are relative to the individual? As was pointed out in Part I, the answer to that question is "no," and we must now explore this matter in greater detail.

First, conflicting rights and obligations are involved in many specific situations. At the moment of voting on a traffic light, for example, one official may weigh the obligation to reduce accidents somewhat more heavily than the obligation not to spend more than a preestablished amount of money, and in the end, is therefore slightly more pro than con; another reverses these weights, and therefore is slightly more con than pro. As a result, even though their views about the obligations involved in this situation are actually quite similar, they vote differently. These obligations are not relative to the individual in the sense of being whimsical or arbitrary. On the other hand, no formula for combining different moral factors is universally acceptable or the only rational one.

This example also highlights another very basic point: empirical questions are often involved in such situations, not only philosophical ones. For example, what impact have traffic lights had on the accident rate at similar corners? The same point pertains to applications of psychology. Consider the goal of decreasing prejudice. Those who are prejudiced against the X's because (all) X's are liars will deny that their belief is prejudice: they will say that it is a fact, and they will act toward X's accordingly. The question, "Should people believe that X's are liars?" can be answered after we know whether or not all X's do indeed lie, and this is best established empirically, not by argument. This example may seem extreme in that it involves condemning, in a very simple-minded and improbable way, an entire group of people, the X's. Surely most of us do not think that way! But suppose that you read about a training-counseling program designed to prepare some retarded adults for marriage. Your first reaction might well be, "Those people marry? They're retarded! How would they manage money? Wouldn't they accidentally burn down their homes while cooking?" If someone suggested that you were making unjustified generalizations of the all-X's-are-liars variety, you might well say, "Oh, no; I'm stating the facts about retarded people." But the question, "Which people can shop for groceries, or can learn to?" is best answered by observation, not by prejudgment or argument, and the answer is not relative to each individual.

At times, then, we think too loosely, too broadly, too generally, as we try to simplify a complex situation by pulling conclusions out of a word like "retarded." It will be more helpful to identify the empirical questions involved, and to answer these with facts. To be sure, facts alone will not resolve questions about what we should or should not do, but they will enable us to make decisions based on information.

The example of the program for the retarded is instructive in another respect. A proposal may be very different from our well-established personal opinions, and we may then react negatively, saying that is absurd, revolting, ridiculous, irrational, or nonsensical. Our personal lives, as well as the history of humankind, can surely remind us that such an initial reaction to a novel proposal does not mean that its goals are bad. They may be—but surely not because we were momentarily shocked when we first heard about them. Many proposals for new inventions were initially greeted in this way. Horseless carriages and flying machines indeed! Most proposals for social reform outrage one group or another. It is helpful to remember periodically that young children used to work in factories for long hours every day, and that the mentally ill used to be chained in dungeons. Such examples do not prove that every application suggested by every psychologist is good. Rather, they remind us that our moral decisions, in this case about application, should be based on something other than immediate, emotional reactions, be they pro or con.

That some empirical questions may be buried at the heart of a debate about application is encouraging in one sense, in that such questions may be answered by careful observation. On the other hand, this raises an interesting dilemma. Consider a proposal for a program designed to help retarded adults learn to manage money. How can we know whether or not the program will work? Obviously by trying it out! But that is what the argument is all about in the first place: is this a good application of psychology?

Careful analysis, rather than a flight into some kind of relativism, will reveal that the dilemma exists in part because the word "good" has several meanings here: well intentioned, nonabusive, workable (the program could be set up for a trial run), successful (it would produce the hoped-for results), and affordable (it would save more money than it would cost to run). We will probably conclude that the program is well intentioned, not abusive of the adults involved, and, if its designers were competent, workable. We cannot know in advance whether or not it will be successful. With hindsight, remember, we smile about the people who knew that no machine would ever fly. Judgments about the program's affordability depend on the many other claims on our resources, but they also depend on its guessed-at, predicted or estimated chances of success. If these chances seem slim, we will be loathe to commit any resources to it, but if we anticipate success, we may be eager to try it out, especially if success would enable us to save time and money later by substituting the new program for more costly current practices such as institutional care.

While this situation is complex, both the factors involved and the limits of our interpretations can be identified. We will not be able to make exact predictions (that exactly 63 percent of the trainees will learn to shop), but our observations can inform our deliberations. We can understand the several meanings of good, and which moral and/or prudential values conflict. Since institutional care is usually very expensive, a less costly alternative will seem very attractive. If we know on the basis of prior research that retarded adults can learn more skills than many people had expected, and that the self-esteem of these newly skilled adults increases, then the proposed training program will become positive on moral grounds.

In arguing that decisions about application are not relative to the individual, we have stressed the following points:

1. Our first emotional reaction to a proposal is not a satisfactory basis for decision making.
2. Careful analysis may reveal that good has several meanings in a particular situation. Furthermore, some questions may be empirical ones, and these should be treated accordingly. Although predictability is limited in the human domain, facts can and should inform our decisions.
3. Knowing the facts is not enough, since actions are guided also by values. In real-life situations, several values may conflict. Finding a balance among these can be difficult and agonizing, but that does not mean that they are matters of personal taste, preference, or whimsy.

INDIVIDUAL AND/OR ENVIRONMENT

The question of relative values is not the only fundamental one. Another important one in applying psychology is whether to concentrate on individuals, their environments or both.

Unemployment provides a good example for exploring this question. All too frequently today, people find themselves unemployed, and within realistic constraints, unemployable. Their ages and/or family considerations may make it unrealistic for them to move to another state (perhaps a spouse has a secure job) or to go to school; no jobs may be available for people with their skills within a 100-mile radius of their homes. In this very stressful situation, they may experience rage, depression, fear, lowered self-esteem, perhaps a total sense of doom for themselves and their families. What can a psychologist offer people in this predicament? What should a psychologist offer?

If they went for counseling because they felt depressed and unworthy, the psychologist could help them to experience the truth that they are not unworthy; rather, their factory closed. Such a changed perspective would be of great benefit to them, and is in that sense a morally good application of the psychologist's knowledge.

Yet one must also point out that such an application seems to accept the situation rather than to try to change it. Perhaps the unemployed workers should be encouraged to try to run the factory themselves, and toward this end, need a discussion facilitator, or training in running fruitful discussions. Their sense of unworthiness might be reduced just as much by participation in such planning as by counseling, and such planning might lead to a restoration of their jobs—in other words, to a removal of the precipitating crisis.

As has been pointed out repeatedly (see, for example May, 1967 and Beit-Hallahmi, 1974) psychologists can help people to adjust, but they can also, either in addition or instead, choose other goals. Two factors are involved here. The first is of major concern in medical areas, and should be of equal concern in applications of psychology: the balance between prevention and cure. Those with specialized knowledge should indeed help those who already have a problem, but insofar as their knowledge pertains to environmental causes of the problem, they should also try to control or remove those causes. Thus, psychologists should help to alleviate problems that already exist, but insofar as possible, should also use that knowledge to prevent new cases. Such a commitment will inevitably draw at least some psychologists into the political arena. This does not mean that all psychologists will join the same party or support the same candidates. First, they will differ from one another on which social changes would be good. Second, even those who have the same goals may differ on how best to achieve them.

The other factor is the balance between acceptance and change. The well-known Alcoholics Anonymous prayer pleads for acceptance of what one cannot change, courage to change what one can, and wisdom to know the difference. It is a difficult balance, to say the least. To return to the example of unemployment, what actually can be changed? What must one learn to accept? Values are not the only determinants of the resolutions of such problems. Also involved are knowledge of cause and effect, and predictions of the future: if I do thus and such, X, Y, and Z will occur, and on balance, my situation will then be somewhat better (or worse) than it is now.

GOALS IN THE ABSTRACT AND IN REALITY

Whenever we set goals, we need to think about them realistically, as embedded in a larger social context. The new state of affairs we are seeking to attain would generate its own set of consequences, not all of them positive, not all of them predictable. Furthermore, we have to get from here to there!

Consider your bill for health insurance. It might seem desirable to charge you according to your health-related behaviors. Then, if you smoked three packs of cigarettes per day, you would pay far more than would nonsmokers. This might be desirable for at least two reasons. First, it is fairer to charge you for your illness-provoking behaviors than to charge others for them. Second, the prospect of high premiums might motivate you to smoke less—that is, to decrease your illness-provoking behaviors. Thus, the proposal to relate your premiums to such behaviors would seem to deserve serious consideration.

But there is an important catch. How would insurance companies know what each of us is eating? How much we exercise? How much alcohol we consume? In other words, what would it take to change the current system to the new one? The answer is troubling: it would apparently take a police state which would permit us little or no privacy. What sounded attractive in the abstract sounds frightening in reality.

Not only must we consider the path or means to a goal, but we must also consider the many possible consequences of the goal. It is a truism that every solution to a problem brings its own set of problems. The saving of life and the enhancement of its quality are among the worthy goals of medical research. New medical technologies and techniques often permit us to attain these goals, yet they have also raised new problems of their own. When is a person dead? When is it morally right, when wrong, to pull the plug? The state of affairs we create as we answer such new questions is also sure to raise its own problems.

These two points certainly do not imply that all change is undesirable, and that psychology (or other knowledge) should therefore never be used to effect change. Rather, they imply that we ought to be as concerned about means as about ends, and that we ought to expect new problems to grow out of our applications, even as they resolve current problems. For example, consider applications of psychology to the process of selecting jurors. Suppose it was concluded that current procedures sometimes result in miscarriages of justice. What we are saying is that possible alternative procedures need to be considered concretely, realistically. What would we actually need to do to find and to implement alternatives? What would be their short-term and long-term consequences? (This topic is explored in Chapter 12.)

WHOSE GOALS?

Psychologists will sometimes encounter value systems truly different from their own. For example, as more has been learned about moral development in children, one application has been programs designed to help children become more thoughtful about their moral values (Simon, Howe, & Kirschenbaum, 1978). While many parents have been pleased with these programs, others have been angered, because they believe that in actual practice, *im*moral values are being taught, and/or because they believe that morality, as part of religion, is a matter of faith rather than thought or reason. Disputes of this kind are almost impossible to resolve, and elicit two kinds of responses: a plea for pluralism (with mutual respect and a live-and-let-live attitude), or efforts to oust the bad (people and belief systems) from the schools so that the good may prevail.

Our view is that pluralism is necessary in a world where people from diverse cultures are both increasingly interdependent and desirous of surviving. Those who want their one and only Truth to prevail will nonetheless repeatedly encounter others with very different truths. They can try to convert these others, but what if they do not succeed? Will they then resort to annihilation? Suppression? Such use of death and force does not sound like a prescription for human survival. In our nuclear age, it may mean that no one survives, not even those who have the Truth. It is also worth pondering what human life would have been like if every new idea had been rejected and its creator silenced.

How can people with different world views approach each other? Ethical concepts and principles may be helpful here because they are acceptable to many people, though perhaps not to all. Consider the question: what should children be taught in school? In principle at least, parents are giving informed consent to their children's curriculum. Reading instruction is almost universally accepted, but values clarification may not be, even after one and all have accurate information about this program. Insofar as values are involved in psychologists' applications in schools, in therapy, and in other settings, the same considerations apply that have been discussed in previous chapters: informed consent, parentalism, statism, nonmaleficence.

Since children grow up to be adult citizens, it is doubtful that parents may refuse to have their children learn to read, and compulsory education laws express and support this view. Those who cannot read are stigmatized and handicapped both as children and as adults, so that the parents would be choosing something harmful for their children. Furthermore, because of this handicap, illiterate adults are often burdens to others in society, so that the parents would in essence be committing these others without their consent.

However, the same points cannot be made for values clarification programs. Parents who want their children to become familiar first or only with a particular set of values and/or world view rather than with many, often and appropriately send their children to religion-affiliated schools. Furthermore, if they are truly convinced that their world view is the only correct one, they will feel obligated to try to have all children exposed to it, regardless of the expressed wishes of the (to them) unenlightened parents. Those who believe that their world view is the only correct one tend to find statism, and/or parentalism very attractive. Their interpretation of "informed consent" tends to be that dissenters from their view are obviously misinformed people who will consent as soon as they grasp the truth.

At this time, we live in a pluralistic society, and are free to find psychologists (and educators) with views compatible with our own. This means that in the many settings where psychologists apply their knowledge and skills, they and their clients should be aware of each other's values, and should try jointly to resolve any existing differences before they do anything else. When those differences cannot be resolved, the clients should be helped to find psychologists with values like their own. *The expertise of professional psychologists does not permit them to make moral choices for other people,* anymore than does the expertise of physicians, lawyers, carpenters, or salespersons.

What do experts mean when they say to us, "You should do X"? They may mean, "If you are (morally) committed to Y, then X will help you toward that goal." They may mean that they are trying to coerce us: "Do X, or else." Finally, they may mean that in this instance, parentalism is appropriate: "I can show you what to do, but I cannot explain to you why it is helpful to you." Sometimes it is appropriate to treat a client parentalistically. If so, the application of psychology should increase that client's later options (Kelman, 1965). For example, a child who has a swimming phobia can only avoid lakes and pools, since going near or into them elicits overwhelming anxiety. A child who has been helped over such a phobia has the option of going into the water or staying out, both without anxiety.

The question, Whose goals? pertains not only to dramatically conflicting world views, but also to lesser but nonetheless important differences between psychologists and their clients in the assessment of the problem. These differences are often related to differences in values.

For example, consider very strict parents, one of whose three children is in their eyes "unmanageable—heading straight for trouble"; the psychologist may have reasons for judging that child to be the "healthiest" member of the family! Or perhaps a homosexual asks to be helped toward heterosexuality—or, alternately, a heterosexual asks to be helped toward homosexuality.

These examples should make clear that psychologists will inevitably respond partly on the basis of personal values to clients' problems. *Good child* may connote different characteristics and behaviors to the parents and the psychologist. And every psychologist has views about good and bad sexual behaviors. Psychologists are as committed to their values as other people are. A particular psychologist may find it difficult, for example, to support parents disciplining their children to be "seen but not heard" or "good little soldiers." In that case, this psychologist could refer the family to someone else.

When clients are incompetent, others choose goals for them, but strict parents and individuals dissatisfied with their sex lives are not incompetent. Why might a psychologist nonetheless hesitate to accept their requests as they first state them without, however, imposing values on them? First, the psychologist may believe that the parents would best deal with their problems if other meanings of "good child" were first explored. For example, what kind of child is most likely to grow up to be a law-abiding, responsible person? Perhaps the parents had not thought about their children as future adults, or perhaps they had incorrect information about what kind of discipline is most likely to help children to become the kinds of adults they admire. Discussing such questions with clients and providing them with accurate information does not mean imposing alien values on them.

Another reason for not taking a client's request at face value may be the hypothesis that the request is based on negative and unconscious motives. This would seem clear to most of us if a healthy person walked into a hospital and said, "I want you to cut off my arms." Although usually less extreme, some requests made to psychologists are comparable: people do not make such requests when they are aware of their needs and their anxieties about satisfying them. In such instances, the client is in essence viewed as incompetent within a certain domain and for a short time period.

APPLICATION AND BEHAVIOR CONTROL

In one sense we are always controlled. Insofar as heredity, past environments, and the current situation affect our beliefs, feelings, desires, and actions, we say that they are controlling factors: if they were changed, we would be changed. However, this is not what most people mean when they express concern about behavior control, and it is misleading and unnecessary to use ominous-sounding phrases when we only mean "causes" (Bandura, 1974).

What people do worry about is control in the sense of manipulation— whether by psychologists, government officials, business people, or neighbors. The relevant dictionary definition of *manipulate* (Webster, 1961) is "to control, manage, or play upon by artful, unfair, on insidious means especially to one's own advantage." Specifically, we are afraid, often with good reason, that efforts will be made to get us to act in ways we would not normally choose or that are contrary to our beliefs or desires. How? By means of bribes (a promotion or raise), physical force (overpowering a violent patient to administer drugs), threat (loss of love), or misinformation ("This car was driven only by my 87-year-old grandmother"). Nonetheless, our reactions to manipulation are more complex than that first familiar negative burst of emotion. We must briefly consider these complex reactions before returning to behavior control in psychology. To anticipate the punch line: this is much ado about nothing.

Our reactions to manipulation include several aspects. Perhaps most obvious is the implication that spontaneity is absent; one party is scheming or calculating in relation to the other. When we approve of this aspect, however, we are likely to use words like "plan," and we praise people who think before they act.

Manipulation is a word used in relation to machinery, that we control with knobs and levers. We resist the idea that someone can push the right buttons and thus elicit from us the desired responses. We often (though not always—see below) prefer to view ourselves as free or autonomous agents who choose their actions. "Flattery will get you nowhere," we say defiantly, even while sensing that we are perhaps overstating the case.

Manipulation also implies inequality between two parties, and presumptuousness on the part of the manipulators, who try to choose for themselves *and* for us. They want to make the decisions. The last thing they want to hear is, "I can think this through just as well as you can—and that is just what I am going to do." Manipulators doubt our competence ("There's a sucker born every minute"), or they seek to bypass it, perhaps because they think they have special privileges, or are unconcerned about us altogether (see below). No wonder we get angry when we sense that someone is trying to manipulate us!

But there are still other aspects. When we say that Joe manipulated (versus persuaded) Don to do X, we are stressing the basis on which Don is now doing X. Our concern is that Don was not persuaded, but rather, that intense emotions induced by Joe (such as fear of rejection) overpowered Don's normal tendencies. However, our reaction also depends in part on what Don's normal or typical pattern is. For example, many parents do not hesitate to manipulate a child by using threats to try to change some of that child's behaviors (such as throwing clothes on the floor), and they would defend such manipulation.

This points to another theme: our response to manipulation attempts may depend on what the goal is. We often suspect the goal is bad in some sense, since otherwise manipulation presumably would not be necessary. We normally do not need to interact with anyone to buy a real bargain. If someone is trying to con us, we suspect that we are not being offered a bargain at all. Thus, we often infer that the goal of manipulation is bad rather than good—an inference not always appropriate.

Efforts to manipulate others often strike us as expressions of extreme selfishness: the manipulators are interested only in their own welfare, and not in the welfare of others. This also is not always true, since the manipulators may be benevolent. For example, if your best friend were depressed to the point of withdrawing from social life, you might, after all else failed, resort to a combination of bribery, threat, and misinformation to get your friend to accompany you to a party: "I feel funny going alone. You'd help me a lot if you came, and anyway, it'll be a great party." The truth is that you would not feel funny going alone, your depressed friend would be a burden, and you have no idea how good the party will be. In other words, you are manipulating, but for your friend's sake, not your own; in fact, it's costing you. Thus, manipulation can involve using others for one's own gains, but it can also be benevolent and parentalistic.

Finally, our response to manipulation involves our knowledge that it can at times succeed. Otherwise, efforts to manipulate us would merely strike us as laughable and pathetic. We sometimes appropriately fear being made to do something now which we will regret later. We know all too well that we sometimes respond to situational pressures in unfortunate ways. But there is another aspect to this reaction: the realization that ordinarily nobody makes us do anything may confront us with our weaknesses. No one makes Gil grovel whenever the boss is around, even if it is true that the boss unfairly promotes unworthy grovelers. Even under such unpleasant circumstances, Gil has a clear choice. He can behave toward the boss in a manner that increases his probability of being promoted but simultaneously decreases his self-esteem—or he can be himself. It is sometimes easier to complain about what one is conned into doing (such as to get ahead) than to confront what one has chosen. In brief, sometimes we would rather believe that we were manipulated, that we had no choice, and that we are not responsible to our actions and our predicaments.

But control as manipulation is not the only interpretation we hear from people. One of the troubling phenomena of our times is that some people seem to be negative toward all behavior control, both internal and external, inner and outer. They believe that "nobody has a right to force me to do X." Such instant gratification (and its rationalizations) is a troubling phenomenon because social living simply cannot work that way, unless we choose to equate social living and incessant conflict. That statement is not intended as a prescription or a setting forth of ideals, but rather, as a description of social reality, or perhaps even as a tautology (as in, "By definition, a door cannot be both open and closed"). Others do not approve of my doing X; therefore, I cannot both do X and have their approval. If I do not enjoy constant, unresolvable tension, I must control either my actions or my need for approval or both.

Thus, behavior control is a prerequisite for both individual survival and social life. We learn to control ourselves, and to accept, even seek, a system of rules and sanctions. Behavior control is not manipulation, and psychologists, as a matter of moral principle, and in their professional code, reject using or scheming against clients for personal gain; this is true regardless of their theoretical orientation.

Within a therapeutic or counseling situation, behavior control is almost invariably a very basic concern. Some clients lack sufficient control; they may "act out" too often—act on impulse—with predictably disasterous results. Depressed people may weep uncontrollably. Some clients feel like straws in the wind—powerless, and at the mercy of others' control. They often fear expressing their needs and beliefs, because of low self-esteem ("I'm always wrong anyway") and fear of rejection. Some clients fear responsibility and want the psychologist to control them: tell me what to do.

The most common position of psychologists is not to make decisions for clients, but rather to help them develop awareness, self-trust, and self-control. One commonly accepted characteristic of a "mentally healthy" person is being able to express or not express needs, emotions, and ideas in a way appropriate to a situation—in other words, in a controlled fashion. Psychologists are likely to consider problematic (except under very trying circumstances) the passive view that "I have no choice" or "I really can't help it." These are widely shared values, and also, desirable ones morally. Indeed, it is difficult to see what moral goods could possibly result from inflicting on children feelings of mistrust, powerlessness, and low self-esteem.

Direct services are not the only applications of psychology. In industry, schools, prisons, the military, and other settings, psychologists serve as consultants, working directly with organization leaders and indirectly with subordinates. It is in this context that ambivalence about manipulation and behavior control are clearest. Surely anything that changes the undesirable behaviors of criminals is justified! And since when does one "reason" with nursery school children? And do military personnel not expect every minute of their lives to be controlled?

Indirect application of psychology touches on at least three issues. First, the goal of the application (for example, decreasing criminal behavior) is not the only morally relevant consideration. What we do to reach that goal should also be subjected to moral scrutiny. Furthermore, as a pragmatic matter, it should be noted that the means to our end often have other ends—by-products, as it were, from our chosen means, but not therefore insignificant. For example, it is conceivable that flogging children publicly in school would change targeted behaviors. It is inconceivable that this would be the only result. In fact, if we accepted such a procedure, many changes would already have occurred in society. The seductive notion "the ends justify the means" in simplistic both psychologically and morally.

Second, we sometimes assume that if organizational needs are being met, and/or if superordinates are benefiting, then subordinates are necessarily being harmed. This assumes necessarily adversarial relationships between workers and management or teachers and students. Such relationships can be full of conflict and strife, but they are not always like that.

Psychologists working for school systems and industry are not therefore automatically damaging children and workers!

Third, when there are serious conflicts between organizations and individuals, psychologists may face moral dilemmas. The questions that arise were discussed earlier (individual and/or environment). For example, what should a psychologist do when asked, "What is the best way for us to terminate these 137 workers?" Is there an obligation to still try to prevent their termination, to explore avenues that may have been missed, or only to answer the question as asked?

We have argued that manipulation involves trying to control behavior by:

Playing on emotions, bypassing reason, trying to counteract or bypass normal behavior, normal good judgment.

Getting people to do something immoral or harmful to themselves.

Using people selfishly, for personal gain, without concern for their welfare.

Scheming rather than thinking or planning.

Denying rather than enhancing *autonomy* (a sense of control of oneself and one's world).

Being parentalistic.

When, if ever, do psychologists manipulate? The answer to this complex question is not "never," but rather, "sometimes." For example, psychologists serving as consultants or researchers in advertising can accurately be described as using and refining manipulative techniques. Inducing people to become research subjects may involve manipulation, and this situation has appropriately disturbed many psychologists. Control of animals almost invariably involves manipulation, and as we have seen, not necessarily of the benevolently parentalistic variety. When dealing with young children, retarded people, and psychotics, psychologists (like relatives, physicians, and others) are often parentalistic, though certainly not malicious, nor scheming, nor only out for personal gain, nor seeking to induce such people to do something immoral or harmful to themselves. Benevolent parentalism is probably the most common kind of manipulation by psychologists, and, given the dictionary definition, should perhaps not be called that at all.

1984 still scares us, as indeed it should. Psychologists are not typically proponents of the social arrangements depicted in Orwell's terrible world, nor do they look forward to a *Brave New World*. Furthermore, they have little political or other power. We needlessly fear behavior control from psychologists, which we erroneously equate with whatever seems negative to us about "manipulation". Most psychologists recoil from the latter, and try to help people develop the kinds of inner controls necessary for peaceful social life and personal satisfaction.

APPLICATION AND COERCION

Psychology is usually applied with informed consent. For example, those who come for vocational counseling are informed about what can and cannot be expected from such counseling, and they then can choose to enter into it or not to. In some settings, however (like prisons), counseling and therapy may be mandatory, with negative consequences for refusal to participate.

The most basic question is whether or not such enforced therapy works. If not, it clearly would be pointless to force people into such therapy. The matter is not so simple, however, since this therapy sometimes is helpful. In that case, is such coercion justified? What are the bases for and the limits of such coercion?

It is helpful to compare mandatory driver training for reckless drivers with coercing heavy smokers to go to a smokers' clinic—even if a mandatory program might be successful. First, smoking harms primarily the smoker, and, therefore, seems to have less severe consequences for others than reckless driving. Second, society has no laws about the quantity of smoking, as it has about reckless driving behavior. Finally, heavy smokers may be addicted both physically and psychologically, and their smoking therefore resembles a compulsion more than a controllable choice. In contrast, we assume that drivers can control their behavior—that they know the law, and obey or violate it deliberately.

This last point needs clarification. If people are not in control of themselves, if they are not deliberately choosing and responsible for their actions, is this not evidence of incompetence, which is grounds for bypassing informed consent? The question as stated overgeneralizes the person's lack of control and competence. That one cannot stop smoking now does not mean that one is incompetent to decide whether or not to seek help in dealing with this currently uncontrollable behavior.

Thus, coercion should be limited to those instances when *(a)* it does not render the proposed mandatory program ineffective; *(b)* it does not produce unintended side effects that create problems more serious than the original one; *(c)* the person's behaviors are a danger to others; and *(d)* informed consent is inapplicable because the person cannot understand the particular program being considered. Informed consent is morally obligatory when it is applicable—which is most of the time. Coercion is only rarely both workable and justifiable.

THE RESPONSIBILITIES OF PSYCHOLOGISTS

Sometimes, those who do research are also those who apply the resulting knowledge. More commonly, however, psychological knowledge is in the public domain once a research project has been reported in professional journals or in the public media, and psychologists are sometimes as aghast as anyone at the ways in which such knowledge is (ab)used. For example, when the words "behavior modification" first became everyday English, one periodically read newspaper accounts of teachers who locked difficult children into closets or boxes, and were doing so in the name of "psychology"! Shall we hold psychologists responsible for such child abuse? Just what are the responsibilities of psychologists when everybody applies psychology?

In 1971, the *American Psychologist* published a provocative research report by Rokeach on "Long-range experimental modification of values, attitudes, and behavior," demonstrating that experimentally induced self-dissatisfaction could have long-term effects (Rokeach, 1971). College students were made aware of inconsistencies within their attitude and value systems. They were convinced that placing a far greater value on "freedom" than on "equality" meant being more interested in one's own freedom than in the freedom of other people. Not only did the students' values and attitudes change, but at least for some, the choices of major programs of study and donations to the National Association for the Advancement of Colored People were also affected—more than a year after self-dissatisfaction was induced! Rokeach concluded his report with the following sobering questions and discussion:

> If such socially important values as equality and freedom can be altered to become more important to human subjects, they can surely be altered to also become less important. Who shall decide which values are to be changed and who shall decide the direction of such change? Is it ethically possible to defend experimental work that may lead to relatively enduring changes in a person's values, attitudes, and behavior without his informed consent? To what extent should our educational institutions shape values as well as impart knowledge, and if so, which values and in which direction? If we have indeed learned how to bring about changes in values, attitudes, and behavior, as I think the experiments described here suggest, we must make certain that this kind of knowledge will be put to use for the benefit rather than the detriment of mankind. (pp. 458–459)

Psychologists are not alone in facing this problem. Knowledge of biochemistry can be used to advance medicine, or to develop germ warfare. Knowledge of physics was basic to the development of the atom bomb. Searching for new knowledge always entails taking risks, since we cannot predict all possible applications. Furthermore, we must accept the facts that almost all new knowledge can be abused morally, and that many applications have both good and bad consequences. Most of us would find it odd to hold the Wright brothers responsible for all plane disasters, since they only demonstrated that flying machines could be built. Are they at fault whenever a plane hits a mountain? Similarly, the names of Pavlov and Skinner are properly associated with research on conditioning. Do you consider them to be at fault whenever you believe that a conditioning technique is being abused? What are the moral responsibilities of psychologists in this matter?

1. Researchers should try to share information with nonpsychologists, as difficult as that may be (see Chapter 7). This sharing should include information and discussion about possible applications.
2. When application is intended from the start (as, for example, in much research on therapeutic techniques), Lewin's approach to *action research* is most defensible. Only when the researchers and the community cooperate is it possible to use research results as a basis for social action. This is so because psychologists do not have and should not have dictatorial powers. Recognized or not, acknowledged or not, values do inevitably enter into discussions between clients and psychologists, since both parties must in essence agree to the goals of their continued contracts, or they would (or should!) refuse to be involved.
3. If someone were to use research findings to try to increase prejudice in some group, that person would be responsible for that attempt, not the researcher. As is clear from Rokeach's article, however, psychologists can anticipate the possibility of such abuses. They therefore have an obligation to remain alert to actual applications and to try to take action against those which they consider to be immoral (through a school board or a legislative body).
4. The obligation to monitor and, if necessary, to protest the applications of psychological knowledge is shared by all psychologists, not just the few who are associated with a particular research project. Those few could not possibly keep track of every possible application all over the world! Thus, psychologists as a group must watch for immoral applications of psychological knowledge, and as citizens, should work with other citizens in this important area. It is not necessary that each and every psychologist be active socially and politically, but it is necessary that some be active in this way.
5. Psychologists are a heterogeneous group. Put 10 of them into a room, and you can expect arguments not only about what good research is, but also about moral goods. Since many moral issues have no simple answer, this is to be expected, and can, in fact, be to the advantage of everyone. Discussions about programs for retarded adults or about behavior modification in the classroom will be helpful both to psychologists and community members (who are also a heterogeneous group) as they seek to clarify the moral issues involved. The best that psychologists can do in such circumstances is to be explicit and clear about their moral views. The worst is to keep their views hidden and to try to manipulate others.

Rokeach's closing words are relevant here:

> But no scientist, in my opinion, should be permitted to decide such grave, ethical issues all by himself. I call on other scientists, professional associations, fund-granting agencies, universities, and other agencies of society to

enter into such deliberations in order to ensure that the knowledge gained will not be abused and that proper safeguards will be instituted to protect the fundamental rights and dignity of the individual. At the same time, it is also necessary to ensure that scientific research will continue to be encouraged on what is perhaps the most distinctively human of all human problems, namely, the nature of human value systems and how they affect social attitudes and social behavior. (p. 459)

CONCLUSION

When psychologists apply the knowledge of their discipline in new, real life settings, they make morally relevant decisions. Many of these are easy to make. In fact, in many situations, the morally defensible action may seem to be so obvious that we may even find it difficult to recognize that there is a choice.

Suppose that a diabetic man has just been told (again!) that losing weight is a matter of life and death. He finally goes to a weight control clinic. It is obvious that every effort should be made help him attain greater health, but here, as in other obvious situations, *it is important to know why*, so that the moral concepts and principles involved can be used in other situations (for example, behavior modification in the classroom, testing in industry). In this example, someone is seeking better health. To refuse him participation in clinic programs, or to contribute to his gaining weight would clearly violate both the principle or nonmaleficence and the principle of autonomy.

In other situations, it may be more difficult to determine just what is harmful to someone, whether someone has been informed, and/or whether someone has consented without coercion. Those who seek genetic counseling, for example, are psychologically in a situation very different from the diabetic's. They do not yet know a specific means (losing weight) to a specific end (becoming healthier). Rather, they are trying to learn what their alternatives are, and what would be the balance of positive and negative consequences of each one. Some of the information they need is technically or emotionally difficult. Therefore, informing them requires careful attention. For example, some people may need to deny or defend against the complex fact that a particular test may both provide critical information about the fetus and simultaneously expose the fetus to injury (at a given level of probability)—and yet they are not informed until they have understood and accepted that fact. The matter of coercion may also be problematic, if, for example, would-be grandparents or others exert psychological pressures on the expectant couple or woman. Questions will be raised in some instances about confidentiality, or about who shall make the final decision about amniocentesis or abortion—for example, when the pregnant female is 13 years old or moderately retarded.

Whether a situation appears to be morally simple or morally complex, psychologists need to be aware of the many ways in which moral values actually are involved. Analyzing the situation heightens one's awareness, and in addition, sometimes reveals that an apparently simple situation is not quite so simple after all. Simple or complex, the very least that we can assume is that in any relationship between psychologist and institution or individual, the psychologist views the client's goals as morally acceptable. If not, how would the psychologist justify helping the client toward those goals?

CHALLENGES

1. Pretend that you are a psychologist who has been invited to address a class of expectant parents, and to answer questions. Analyze the following questions and possible answers with respect to descriptive and prescriptive components:
   a. Should I pick up my baby whenever it cries?
   b. At what age do babies start to insist on having their own way? When do you really start to spoil a child?
   c. I really do not care for natural childbirth. Will I be harming my baby's emotional development if I go to a very traditional hospital?
2. Make a list of factors that contribute to your happiness. Which are within yourself? Which are in your environment? What kind of unhappiness might lead you to consult a psychologist? Why? What would or do you do about other kinds of unhappiness? Why?
3. Have you ever thought someone was trying to manipulate you? What did they do? Why did they do it? How did you feel? What did you do?
   Bring to class what you think is an example of psychologists manipulating or not manipulating people. Discuss the various examples in class. Analyze sources of agreement and disagreement about whether it was really manipulation, and about whether or not it was justified.
4. Do you think psychologists monitor the ever-expanding applications of psychology sufficiently? Explain your answer. What do you think are the obligations of psychologists in this matter?
5. Some people (especially students!) argue that too much of psychology is esoteric, useless—not applicable to real life situations. Others complain that psychology is used too much—that it is like a new religion that people use as a guide to living.
   In which areas or situations is psychology applied too much? Too little? Unusable? How can people apply psychology to their lives sensibly?

SPECIFIC AREAS OF CONTROVERSY

PART III

Part III discusses some of psychology's continuing and provocative ethical issues in the context of current areas of controversy.

Chapter 9 explores psychology's involvement with quality-of-life and life-and-death questions. Should psychologists stop a would-be-suicide? How should they think about aging? Retardation? Animal life? What are the morally relevant concerns in eugenics? Who is a person?

Chapter 10 discusses psychology's involvement and lack of involvement with the powerless, notably minority groups. Can psychology be value-free in addressing the concerns of powerless groups? Does psychology (should psychology) represent the interests of the dominant socioeconomic groups in society?

Chapter 11 discusses psychological testing within the framework of ethics. What purposes are tests designed to achieve, and why? What are the consequences of using tests?

Chapter 12 reviews the relationships between psychology and the law. Should psychologists become involved in the selection of juries? Should psychologists take sides in a legal dispute? What ethical questions arise when psychologists provide expert testimony?

These are not the only areas of controversy, yet they are representative of the moral questions and dilemmas which psychologists face in their work, whether with people or animals, with these people or those, in one social context or another.

9

LIFE AND DEATH

A chapter with this title may seem surprising in a book dealing not with medicine, but with psychology. However, two morally relevant sets of questions are explicitly or implicitly answered in the lives of all human beings, and psychologists are no exceptions.

1. When, if ever, is it obligatory to save a life? When, if ever, is it permissible or even obligatory to take a life, or to permit or even support the taking of a life? How, if at all, shall we differentiate between human beings and (other) animals in this matter?
2. What is an acceptable or a good or a high quality of life? To what quality of life shall psychologists aspire? For whom?

Even people who only rarely confront such questions directly have attitudes toward possible answers. A good way to experience these is to encounter repugnant attitudes and behaviors. As one tries to articulate what is repugnant, one begins to articulate one's opinions.

An instructive example is provided by Jacobo Timerman's book about his imprisonment in Argentina, which describes some Argentinians' ideas about the quality of life (Timerman, 1981). Whether these descriptions are accurate or not is not our concern. Rather, the question is how readers react to views like these:

> Juan Domingo Peron used to say that "violence from above engenders violence from below." Peronist youth understood at once what Peron was saying: he approved of violence and terrorism, and would lend his support to

169

any murder, kidnapping, or assault that fit into his goals for the conquest or reconquest of power. (pp. 24–25)

The doctor came to see me and removed the blindfold from my eyes. I asked him if he wasn't worried about my seeing his face. He acts surprised.

"I'm your friend. The one who takes care of you when they apply the machine. Have you had something to eat?"

"I have trouble eating. I'm drinking water. They gave me an apple."

"You're doing the right thing. Eat lightly. After all, Ghandi survived on much less. If you need something, call me."

"My gums hurt. They applied the machine to my mouth."

He examines my gums and advises me not to worry. I'm in perfect health. He tells me he's proud of the way I withstood it all. Some people die on their torturers, without a decision having been made to kill them; this is regarded as a professional failure. He indicates that I was once a friend of his father's, also a police doctor. His features do seem familiar. I mention his father's name; this is indeed the son. He assures me that I'm not going to be killed. I tell him that I haven't been tortured for two days, and he's pleased. (p. 54)

The interrogator was proud of having tortured [a journalist]. He spoke freely, knowing that he enjoyed impunity, convinced of his mission and never doubting that history would justify it. (p. 101)

Everyone who reads these passages reacts to them, whether positively or negatively. We chose them in the expectations that most readers of this book would react negatively. Furthermore, the attitudes underlying such reactions are at the core of our value systems, and these touch everything we do. These observations include psychologists. They, too, answer the questions posed above. In this chapter, we explore several difficult and challenging areas: threats to life; mental retardation; aging; eugenics; genetic counseling; and the evaluation of environments.

THREATS TO ONE'S OWN LIFE

Albert Camus once wrote, "There is but one truly serious philosophical problem, and that is suicide" (Camus, 1955, p. 3). Psychologists tend to assume that survival is a basic value, and that for everyone, including a suicidal person, life can almost always be improved, by changing either reality or the meaning ascribed to reality, or both. There is, then, some notion of a good life worth living, and of an obligation to maintain life and improve its quality. It is true that particular people sometimes welcome death, but with the possible exception of martyrdom, that is because they believe that a good life is no longer or never was possible. We do not need to know the details of the good life to have intuitive responses to this belief. Even without such details, we are almost universally moved by the tragic death of an 18-year-old whose suicide note mentions not getting into a particular college or being rejected in a romantic relationship.

There are difficult questions about what makes life worth living and whether suicide is ever justified. These questions, however, are rarely the main concern of psychologists, though they address them indirectly. In the clinical contexts in which psychologists usually encounter any threat to life—murder, suicide, anorexia nervosa—their paramount concern is to try to prevent the threatened or potential death. This obligation may even require the violation of another obligation, namely, to maintain confidentiality. This ranking is sound both morally and legally (see the discussion of the *Tarasoff* case in Part I and Chapter 12).

One very basic reason for this is that death is irreversible. If Ned kills himself, as he threatens to do, then the keeping of his confidences is of no further significance to him. On the other hand, if he is prevented from killing himself, probably against his stated wishes, he remains alive, though possibly troubled by the breaking of trust that literally saved his life, and for which he may nonetheless eventually be very grateful. Someone might want to counter this view with a quality of life argument. If Ned killed himself, at least he knew that he could trust someone (the psychologist), and this made the quality of his last days of life better than that of all his previous days. If the psychologist warned somebody of Ned's suicide threat, he once again felt betrayed, and although he then lived till the age of 96, the quality of his life was immeasurably poorer. This argument is not persuasive because it makes psychologically improbable assumptions. If Ned really did kill himself as he threatened to do, the last days of his life were probably extremely troubled, even though the psychologist did not break the promise of confidentiality. And if his life was saved, even against his wishes, it does not follow that he will view the efforts of people to save him as a betrayal of trust until he dies at 96. Ned may build a new life for himself, and he can, if he wants to, find another psychologist—but he can only do these things if he is alive. This commitment of psychologists to life does not, of course answer moral questions about why anyone (Ned or anyone else) should live, or whether we can be said to have a right to life, or to suicide, but it is a commitment which is rarely a point of argument within psychology.

It is also important to note that psychologists are rarely involved in the kinds of difficult cases which bioethicists discuss. May a severely burned, permanently handicapped, disfigured, suffering person commit suicide? May a terminal patient suffering severe pain beyond the reach of further medication? These are not typical of the person who threatens suicide in the course of psychotherapy. The assumption (prediction) which will best serve both client and psychologist is that Ned will eventually feel good about being alive. This prediction is justified on empirical grounds; Ned is experiencing an acute crisis, but he will eventually be able to cope with it, and will then feel good about being alive. Furthermore, the prediction becomes a self-fulfilling prophecy: the very making of the prediction contributes to its becoming true over time. Any other assumption would probably affect the therapeutic interaction negatively, and might even cost Ned his life. It would be as though the psychologists were saying, "I agree; your life is worthless now and in the future." Instead, they say, "Your life is precious, and worthy of our very best efforts."

Finally, in spite of the many important differences among the several prescriptions within psychology, almost all psychologists stress the social side of human existence: most people have families and friends. The depressed person's feeling that "nobody cares" or "I'm all alone" is likely to be viewed by a psychologist as an inaccurate description of the client's life, and above all, of what is attainable. If Ned claims that nobody cares, that is his description of his experiences within his current relationships, but his family and friends are probably very concerned about him, even if they cannot express their concerns in ways most helpful to him. Even if it is true that hardly anybody cares now, good relationships could be established in the future. The psychologist's belief that far better relationships are attainable for Ned is important for the outcome of the therapy, but it is also important in another sense. By viewing Ned as socially embedded both now and in the future, the psychologist is questioning the view of suicide as a private act—as one concerning only the person committing suicide. While the fact of our social embeddedness does not tell us what we morally may or should do, this fact does mean that suicides typically leave behind a number of bereaved people who, in addition, suffer from intense guilt. A moving, personal account was written by Anne-Grace Scheinin (*Newsweek*, February 7, 1983, p. 13), whose mother had committed suicide, and who had tried to kill herself several times.

> I saw the torment my mother's death caused others: my father, my brother, her neighbors and friends. When I saw their overwhelming grief, I knew I could never do the same thing she had done—force other people to take on the burden of pain I'd leave behind if I died by my own hand. Suicide is not a normal death. It is tragic beyond the most shattering experiences, and the ultimate form of abandonment. There is no fate on which to place the blame. It rests squarely on the shoulders of the victim and the people left behind, many of whom spend the rest of their lives wondering, never knowing, if there was anything they could have done to prevent such a tragedy, . . . There may be legitimate rationalizations for committing suicide. But my experiences have taught me that suicide, by and large, is a decision made by a desolate soul. The many suicidal patients I met in my hospital stays had no philosophy of death; their desire to die was not a condemnation of current socioeconomic or political realities. They were in profound emotional pain, and all they wanted was an end to that suffering.

Only rarely is suicide a rational act done in response to unchangeable, progressive, and agonizing physical and/or mental suffering. Even such cases are arguable, of course, but such argumentation is not our goal here. Rather, the point is that the psychologist's view of social reality is likely to differ from the client's when the latter is suicidal, and the latter is taken to be mistaken, not morally, but in a factual sense. First, it is probable that others do care. Second, suicide affects the client and these others. Finally, given the overpowering emotions of the client coupled with a distorted assessment of reality, the psychologist will view parentalism as morally justified, even obligatory. In fact, when clients verbalize their intentions to commit suicide, they can be viewed as asking for help since, presumably, if they really wanted to kill themselves, they would do it, not talk about it. As Scheinin put it:

> By the way: to all the doctors, nurses and psychiatrists who forced me to live when I didn't want to—thank you for keeping breath in my lungs and my heart beating and encouraging hope in me when I didn't have any hope. I'm glad I'm alive to say that.

THREATS TO ANOTHER'S LIFE

Threats to another person's life raise somewhat different questions. Primary among these is how seriously to take such threats. Fine gradations occur as one moves from, "I was so mad I could have killed him," to "I'm going to shoot my brother tomorrow morning." As with suicide, the most justifiable position may be to treat every statement that sounds like a threat as a real threat to a human life. After *Tarasoff*, psychologists are likely to do that either out of conviction or because a legal precedent has been established. One result of this is a new problem. Psychologists will inform clients about their policies, including a commitment to keep everything confidential except threats to life. Consequently, the rare clients who are thinking about killing someone may not share these thoughts with their psychologists, who certainly cannot prevent planned murders about which they do not know! Thus, clients should be informed about the psychologist's policies, because otherwise they cannot give informed consent to the therapeutic situation. But although this obligation is clear, its possible consequence is also clear; some clients may even wonder whether anything besides threats to life would cause the psychologist to violate confidentiality. As a result, clients may decide not to discuss certain areas of their lives that are, in fact, problematic for them.

That psychologists would try to prevent the death of someone who is not a client is one of those obvious moral intuitions that deserve discussion. It is true that we cannot be certain that a threat will be carried out, but that is not the question here. Rather, assume that when this client threatens to shoot his brother or the people next door, he intends to do so; the question then is, "What obligations do psychologists have toward nonclients with whom clients have intimate or casual contacts?" Consider the variety of threats possible: to kill, rob, deceive, insult. Psychologists are sometimes caught between two sets of obligations and commitments. On the one hand are obligations to the larger society. Foremost among these is the concern for life, since, as we pointed out above, this is the prerequisite for all other concerns. On the other hand are the obligations to particular clients. In most instances, it is not necessary to say "on the other hand," since clients only rarely threaten murder. But when clients state that they plan to act against moral principles, then the psychologist faces a moral dilemma. It is easy to say, "Let them work it out in therapy." Of course— but the client will be going home in 23 minutes! The threat to a nonclient's life takes precedence over confidentiality, but this would not be uniformly true for other threats. Psychologists do not say, "If lying to your children makes you feel better, go ahead," nor do they say, "You shouldn't lie, and I'm going to warn your children about this." Nonetheless, their choices express a commitment to those moral values they consider basic to a good quality of life for both clients and the larger society.

The possible consequences of the threatened act will determine whether or not anyone should be warned. Only when the possible consequences are very serious will psychologists break confidentiality. Most people can deal with insults, as unpleasant as they are, and it would seem strange to have psychologists warn family members that the client will soon be insulting them. On the other hand, we could imagine a lie that would have such tragic consequences that anyone able to identify it as a lie is obligated to do so. We are not describing a daily occurrence in therapy. Rather, our point is that psychologists bring their moral principles to all activities, since these are as important in their lives as they are in the lives of others.

Most lives end nonviolently, from natural causes, and increasingly, in old age. That old joke about growing old being preferable to the only alternative reflects our culture's low opinion of both old age and death. This view of aging has existed in psychology, too.

AGING

The psychological changes that accompany the processes of aging can be approached as a problem of either pure or applied science. Values are central in either case.

In 1979, Smyer and Gatz opened their *American Psychologist* article on "Aging and mental health: Business as usual?" with this sentence: "The aging of clinical psychology is a fairly recent phenomenon" (p. 240). In their 1980 article, "Life-span developmental psychology", Baltes, Reese, and Lipsitt footnoted its title as follows: "This is the first chapter in the *Annual Review of Psychology* on this subject" (p. 65). In their 1983 *Annual Review* article on "Psychology of adult development and aging", Birren, Cunningham, and Yamamoto wrote, "If the amount of material published and cited in APA journals defines the orthodoxy of psychology, then adult

development and aging is unorthodox and child development is orthodox''
(pp. 544–45).

Baltes et al. (1980) and Smyer and Gatz (1979) went on to consider possible reasons for psychology's relative neglect of the area of aging. Perhaps the strong emphasis on childhood during the middle of this century was a contributing factor, though that phenomenon, too, would have to be explained. The same could be said about the relatively late emergence of gerontology (the 1950s). Perhaps the prescription to be experimental and behavioristic precluded the study of the development of inner processes central to the study of adult development and aging. Perhaps the aging of society and the aging of those who became psychologists during and immediately after World War II are important factors. No doubt the reasons are many and complex, yet the fact remains that life span developmental psychology has only recently taken hold. Yet surely older human beings have always been there, even as children have.

Psychologists' stress on the experimental method and the study of behavior has been modified to include more observational and correlational methods as well as experimental and cognitive content. Furthermore, it has been convenient to study animals and college students, at times to the exclusion of other groups of human beings. This imbalance, too, is in the process of being corrected.

The interest in children is understandable. If the early years are truly critical for later life, then surely we want to know about them—though how such information could be helpful without an understanding of the later years is not clear. Much of commonsense child psychology was erroneous, and even now, we continue to be astonished as new information becomes available through research (Field, Woodson, Greenberg, & Cohen, 1982); however, the common sense psychology of aging is also full of errors. In a rapidly changing society, it is not surprising that veneration of the wisdom of the aged can give way to admiration of the know-how of the young, especially in the area of technology. The youth orientation of our society has become institutionalized, and therefore a factor for everyone to contend with eventually. Those who do not believe this need only speak to someone who became unemployed at the age of 47. Some people still believe that after 30 or 40, one becomes ugly and sexless, and many admire most what the young do best, notably in sports and athletics. Finally, as childhood and adult diseases and therefore mortality have been controlled, notably by immunization and antibiotics, we have come to associate aging with increased illness and of course death, both of which we value negatively.

Psychologists are not always immune to pervasive cultural values, though they are sometimes in the vanguard of change, notably in dealing with prejudice, altruism, and creativity. Within the last quarter century, however, a new orientation to conceptualizing development has taken hold: "Life-span developmental psychology is concerned with the description, explanation, and modification (optimization) of developmental processes in the human life course from conception to death" (Baltes, et al., 1980, p. 66). This orientation includes values in at least two ways:

1. The word "optimization" clearly implies a value framework—as would also the omission of either this word or "modification".
2. This orientation does not assume a certain endstate (such as early adulthood) of the developmental process, with subsequent changes viewed as deterioration; rather, "no special state of maturity is assumed as a general principle, and therefore, development is seen as a life-long process" (p. 70).

It is important to recognize the values in this orientation, rather than thinking that developmental psychology used to have undesirable values but is now value-free. Newer values may please us, but that does not mean that psychology is value-free! That no one phase of development should be singled out as best, and that optimization is a concept relevant to all phases of development are statements of values, not facts. Life, then, can be viewed as developing until death, and the continual optimization of its quality as everyone's moral responsibility.

This modified approach does not deny that psychological changes take place as human beings move from birth to death, nor even that evaluation of such changes will sometimes lead us to use words like "deficit" or "decline." Just as blindness (rather than sightedness) is evaluated as deficit, so, too, is an inability to recognize relatives. However, even absolute deficit (total deafness or blindness) permits people to give up in despair or to stress optimization, and data alone cannot guide this choice. This modified approach also suggests that traits need to be viewed in the contexts of people's lives, and this in turn leads to questions about how traits are measured.

All too frequently, older adults are tested with the kinds of materials that make up standardized intelligence tests. Using such materials, it is easy to conclude that the differences between older and younger testees represent deficits, but in fact, exclusive reliance on such materials represents a bias toward youth. What specific tasks demand of us is not good in a vacuum. Rather, we value certain skills because they are helpful in coping with the demands of living, and these change as we progress through life. What intelligence tests stress are skills important for the young in specific educational and occupational settings. If, instead, we asked 10-year-olds how to resolve neighborhood disputes, their answers might seem very deficient compared to those of 60-year-olds. The observed differences certainly exist, but which ones we single out for attention and judge to be important, so important perhaps that we set them up as the standard for intelligence, is a matter of our values, as these pertain to personality development and social institutions and practices. Perhaps in the future somebody will create a "wisdom" scale. As Birren et al. (1983) put it:

> Clayton and Birren (1980) developed the concept of wisdom in relation to age and culture. They concluded that characteristics attributed to wise persons are useful to both old and young. Wisdom clearly is an important topic to which insufficient attention has been paid. (p. 554)

In their discussion of aging and mental health, Smyer and Gatz (1979) pointed out that "one consistently overlooked element is the importance of preventive efforts when working with older adults" (p. 241). This oversight is unfortunate but easy to understand. If older adults are viewed as inexorably moving toward personalities of poor quality, then preventive efforts appear doomed, and resignation to an unfortunate fate seems to be the only sensible response. In contrast, Smyer and Gatz stress that human change is best viewed within the life span developmental orientation, and that the term "optimization" is preferable to "prevention." While the prevention of negative change is desirable, it is even better to think about optimizing one's life. All of us, young and old alike, solve problems actively, and have both skills and deficits in relation to the demands of life. At the same time, it is important to recognize that when people are powerless ("as is often the case with older adults, particularly poor and minority group members"), interventions "should focus on those systems and environmental factors that can give people options and therefore power" (p. 242). Two assumptions are made here. First, intervention should sometimes focus on the environment rather than the person, because the problem resides more in the former than in the latter. Second, powerlessness diminishes the quality of life, while having options and power enhances it. (So important is this point that we are devoting an entire chapter to it: see Chapter 10.)

The new perspective on development includes several themes related to the quality of life. We should deal with the entire life span, not one or two segments of it, in both research and application. Strength and weakness are defined as much by situations as by traits; no personality is the best one in all situations. It is possible to study changes during the life span both without denying their existence and without derogating anyone. Optimization and even prevention are concepts relevant to the entire life span. "My memory is gone" is usually an exaggeration. In any case, one can, at any age, write things down for later reference. But the phenomenon of aging also touches on beliefs about and attitudes toward the heterogeneity of humankind. Although all older people are human beings, what kinds of persons are they? We will return to these issues after we discuss mental retardation, another phenomenon to which they are relevant. The parallels in these fields are striking.

MENTAL RETARDATION

In the fourth edition (1969) of *Psychological problems in mental deficiency,* Sarason and Doris wrote,

> Expertise itself, a knowledge of facts and theories never leads to a social action program. It is only when the expertise interacts with a value system that social action programs arise. . . . We have strenuously to resist assuming, implicitly or explicitly, that our practices are the result of cold logic and scientific facts unmediated by the knotty problem of value. (p. 3)

They also pointed out that "the theories and practices that characterize a field at a particular point in time reflect the nature of that society at that time" (p. 4). They then cited *mental deficiency* as a particularly clear example of these points: both theory and practice reflect the ideas and values of society.

They raised the question of "why mental subnormality—as an area of professional practice as well as an area of basic and applied research— involved relatively few people and was barely represented in university centers of training and research" in the years before World War II (p. 6). They cited two points to begin to answer this question: lack of national concern and policy; and the view that little could be done for retarded people. The prevailing assumption was that everyone would be best off if retarded people were segregated in special institutions.

The preface to the second edition (1979) of Chinn, Drew, and Logan's *Mental retardation: A life cycle approach* touches on the same themes, and states that the first edition, published as recently as 1975, had noted a public awakening to mental retardation. This awakening was not a matter of noticing retardation but of a shift in attitudes, and terminological changes reflect this fact: mental "deficiency" and "subnormality" are being replaced by "retardation," while "moron," "idiot," and "imbecile" are being replaced by "Down's Syndrome" and "phenyketonuria." Efforts to define mental retardation have clarified both the nature of the concept and the purposes it serves. In most countries, the definition includes a reference to IQ. In addition, some countries, including Great Britain and the United States, include *adaptive behavior;* this refers to personal independence and social responsibility appropriate for the person's age and cultural group. The inclusion of adaptive behavior is controversial because this turns out to be an ill-defined, elusive concept. Even if it were clearly defined, however, it is a concept that not only describes but also prescribes, since it includes "the threshold of community tolerance" (Chinn et al., p. 7). It goes without saying that this also applies to the level of intellectual functioning considered problematic: why accept IQ 70 or 75 as a dividing line?

The mentally retarded can be divided into two large and heterogeneous groups: the clinically retarded and the socioculturally retarded (Edgerton,

1979). The clinically retarded are usually diagnosed at a young age, tend to have physiological defects and IQs below 55, are born about equally in all social classes, and parents typically seek treatment for the child. In contrast, the socioculturally retarded are typically not diagnosed until they go to school, and they rarely have physical abnormalities. Their adaptive behavior can be good; their school work, however, is not. They are born mostly to the socially disadvantaged. The parents may not seek help, and in fact, may be angry about the label attached to their child.

Edgerton points out that societies make problems through their needs and expectations; one could imagine, he argues, a society in which "gawkishness" is considered a serious problem. This phenomenon, which was discussed also in relation to aging—that a problem is the joint product of individual characteristics and social expectations—leads Edgerton to ask whether societies can also unmake problems. Could they, for example, ignore mental retardation? His answer is that they could not and do not. All societies demand some level of intellectual, social, and physical competency, so that clinical retardation is considered a problem in all, sociocultural retardation in most. This statement of the problem permits an important shift in perspective, however: all of us have many areas of incompetence. How much emphasis do we, as a society, want to place on school competency? Should we continue to call the socioculturally retarded "retarded"?

Our classifications will continue to change not only in relation to changing stress on schooling, as well as to changing schooling, but also in relation to technological advances. An obvious example is working as a cashier. A machine now informs cashiers how much change to give back to customers, while previously, they had to figure that out. The demands of the environment can also be simplified in other ways. In the past, many legal documents (such as leases) were written so as to be comprehensible to only a few (notably lawyers), while in recent years, they have been written in plain English. The basic points of such documents can probably be made clear to most people, including many of the socioculturally retarded: pay your rent on the first of the month and do not rip the walls apart. Thus, society has shifted from leases that rendered most of us incompetent to leases that most of us can understand. An important point is at stake here. Just as the way normal people are classified can change as a function of environmental demands (even when the people have not changed at all), so can it change for some retarded persons (even when they have not changed at all). The way people are classified can change many times in the course of their lives.

But in addition, retarded persons can and do change. As society's posture has changed, so have ideas about what retarded people can or cannot do. One issue confronted in recent years is the purpose of definition and classification or diagnosis. Do we want to predict who will inevitably be a failure, or do we want to find specific strengths and weaknesses because we want to help in specific ways? Achievements depend in part on training or education. As Allen and Allen (1979) pointed out,

> Severely retarded children, formerly thought untrainable, can now feed and dress themselves due to a comprehensive behavior-modification program. As psychologists crack the code of human learning, the complex mental steps other people learn automatically can be broken down and taught to persons who are mentally retarded. (p. 51)

The fields of aging and mental retardation have been and continue to be suffused with values. At one time, very few psychologists (and other professionals) were involved with these fields. In contrast, more professionals now choose these areas. The concepts in these fields reveal values: degenerate, deterioration, imbecile, senile, optimization. The same is true of hypotheses, especially insofar as stress on biological and hereditary causes have been correlated (unjustifiably) with defeatism: nothing can be done. (Even when there are hereditary factors, much can be done, as with insulin injections for diabetes and corrective lenses for myopia.) When can older and retarded people give informed consent? Who is the client—the person, the family, or both? To whom does confidentiality apply in the matter of sharing information about the client with others? What kind of helping, if any, is possible? Desirable? Many of these questions apply also to suicidal persons, since all of them are related to the two questions posed at the beginning of this chapter about the value and quality of life. We are now in a position to consider evaluations of human variety in a general way, though we will return frequently to the examples already considered. Why, for example, is retardation abnormal or subnormal?

EVALUATING MENTAL VARIETY

Judgments of normal-abnormal (unequal rather than equal) are made in one basic way, although it appears that there are two. One is the statistical approach: whatever is rare is away from the norm. If a characteristic is normally distributed in the population, then both ends of the curve will be abnormal; for example, adult heights of 3'2" and 7'8" are both abnormal in the United States. Sometimes, such statistical deviance can alert us to a problem, but as the example of height shows, *problem* has to be defined in relation to people's goals. A small, light person may excel in gymnastics, a tall one in basketball. Then again, they may both find that height has no bearing on anything they want to do, above all, on their acting responsibly towards others.

The second approach to abnormality posits a good or best state and then considers each person in relation to that. Some good states are chosen by the overwhelming majority of human beings. Perhaps the best example is being free of discomfort and pain. When we are intensely thirsty or sprain an ankle or develop strep throat, pain alerts us to a problem, but it is also experienced negatively. This, in fact, is one part of the judgment about what illness is: it can be life-threatening, incapacitating, and painful, which means that it takes us away from the ideal state of health. In some cases, however, the notion of an ideal state raises considerable argument, and therefore the ever-troubling question, If there are several points of view about this, which one is best? For example, are self-actualized people the best ones, as Maslow claimed? Is self-actualization what we should seek even as we seek good health? How about the ideal: capable of being a productive member of society?

The statistical approach is in fact one variant of the ideal state approach. We decide whether the current statistical norm is best, or whether we should move toward a new norm, one which is deviant today; we decide whether what everybody wants (like being without pain) is good; we decide whether an ideal to which only a few people are currently committed (like extreme authoritarianism) should be everyone's ideal. These decisions reflect our moral values, and are decisions we must and do make. Should we perhaps be striving to increase the number of retarded persons? These are the moral issues all of us address as we consider the future of human variety.

All societies make such judgments. Those who could barely, or not at all, take care of their own survival needs, and who could function only minimally as members of the community, placed special demands on others, and were likely to be viewed negatively throughout much of human history. When merely surviving was an almost daily struggle for a group, then those who threatened such survival—though we might welcome them today—were easily viewed as a menace. Someone who cannot walk—whether born that way or weak from illness—can, under particular circumstances, threaten the survival of those who can walk. The former have to be carried by the latter, and in addition, consume precious food. Even under less extreme conditions, every social group stresses some minimum level of competence. The markedly deviant are subnormal in the sense of never, or never again, being able to survive without special care from others, and also in the sense of not meeting an expected standard for contributing to the group—a standard often set by the (average) majority. The deviant are therefore also in the minority.

In technologically advanced countries, most people need not be preoccupied with survival. Food materializes magically, and so do cures for many diseases. Under conditions so benign for surviving, one can begin to wonder about negative attitudes toward those few unable to care for themselves. It is tempting to answer in terms of financial cost, but we must be careful about that. While mental retardation is costly, what we are discussing is the negative attitude toward spending money on mental retardation. For example, educating average to brilliant people is also costly, but it is widely accepted or favored. In order to understand this, we must consider a value-laden concept used by both psychologists and philosophers: personhood. We will argue for three points:

1. Personhood comes in degrees, and only under certain conditions can one say that a particular human being is not a person.
2. Several criteria for personhood exist, and each of them comes in degrees. A person who is close to zero on one continuum may not be close on another.
3. The moral relevance of each criterion must be considered for each situation. For example, how much and what kinds of personhood are relevant to decisions about training and education?

All moral agents are persons, but not all degrees of personhood imply moral agency. Many attributes (criteria) have been viewed as central to personhood (Kinget, 1975; Warren, 1973): consciousness, thought, rationality, morality, humor, self-awareness. First, most minimally but importantly, personhood implies some degree of consciousness, of experiencing. Of particular importance is the experiencing of pain, since the precept closest to a moral absolute is that it is morally wrong to inflict pain on other human beings without intending to benefit them and/or without their informed consent.

A second attribute of personhood is the capacity for making and using symbols, and this capacity is involved in all the other aspects listed above. Thus, our mental lives can be extraordinarily complex: consider our literature, our science, and the complexity of our emotional lives. Intimately related to our capacity for thought is our morality; presumably we stop for a red light not only because we do not want to risk getting a ticket, but also because we understand what could happen if we did not, or if nobody did! Also related to thought is our capacity for a concept of self that extends across a lifetime. We reflect about the meaning of our lives; we understand that some day we will die, and this affects how we live. We reflect about ourselves and our actions.

The claim that a particular human being has no personhood at all requires as proof that none of the characteristics mentioned exist in any degree—that there is no consciousness, not even experience of pain, and no thinking of any kind. Adult human beings with total nonpersonhood are rare (some comatose patients). Since personhood comes in degrees, we must be cautious about rigid categories of *person* and *nonperson*. If we stress consciousness, we will consider most human beings to be persons. If we stress a sense of self over time, we will include fewer, or we will say that fewer people display that aspect of personhood.

This approach to personhood has two important implications. First, once we accept these criteria for personhood, the kind and degree of personhood of any particular living being—human or animal, young or old, brilliant or retarded—becomes an empirical question. Second, the concept person not only describes, it also prescribes, since most of us clearly view personhood as something good, something valuable, something to be cherished and developed. How many of us would press a magic button which would render us instantly and irrevocably comatose?

If most of us do indeed view personhood as good, then we should do whatever we can to sustain and enhance it in ourselves and in others. This is one meaning of optimizing: arranging society so as to permit everyone to be as much person as they can be. This view differs from our society's stress on competition and productivity, according to which teaching retarded 17-year-olds to tie their shoe laces is a futile gesture, since they will still not be normally productive in society.

Two points are relevant to this way of evaluating mental variety. First, productivity is a continuum, and one is hard put to choose a dividing line between those who are good enough and those who are not. If we compared people of average achievement with the gifted, we would probably conclude that the latter are more productive than the former. It does not follow, however, that average people therefore should not develop their capacities. Second, we face a choice between viewing all human beings as ends to be served by the means of society, and viewing them as subunits within a larger entity (society) that is to be served. The psychologists who stress acceptance of self and others and optimization for everyone reflect the former view; those who believe that people have to produce at some level reflect the latter, and, unless they die young, they must eventually face an awesome truth: one day, by virtue of disease or accident, they themselves may no longer be productive enough. Then what? A world in which only material productivity counts is in the end a frightening world for everyone.

It is also important to look critically at productivity and its results. Many of them enrich our lives, but the same inventiveness that contributes to the development of medication can also contribute to the development of chemical warfare. Not only positive results, but many of our current problems and sorrows, too, were created by those of us who are normal persons. Surely no one could presume to blame the threat of another war, perhaps (unthinkably) a nuclear war, on the senile and the retarded.

Nothing in the last three paragraphs should be taken as a denial of facts. Yes, parents will be shaken when their child is diagnosed as clinically retarded. Yes, research and quality care cost money. Yes, although many of us are revising our beliefs and attitudes, we have a long way to go. Rather, this analysis of personhood has attempted to explore the implications of this concept for private and social life.

ARE ANIMALS PERSONS?

In Part II, we discussed moral arguments for and against using animals as research subjects. Researchers use procedures with animals that are forbidden with people; they hurt, harm, and kill them. Are animals persons to any degree? If so, why is it permissible to treat them in this fashion? The arguments "for" stress the humanly beneficial knowledge gained from well-designed research on animals. Implied or stated is the claim that procedures that are morally unacceptable with humans are permissible with animals. An excellent example is provided in the preface to *Helplessness* (Seligman, 1975):

> Since much of the subject matter of this book derives from experimentation, I must say a few words about ethics. Many of the experiments I shall describe may seem cruel, particularly to the non-scientist: pigeons are deprived of food, dogs are shocked, rats are plunged into cold water, infant monkeys are deprived of their mothers, and all experimental animals are deprived of their freedom by confinement to cages. Are such manipulations ethically justifiable? To my mind they are by and large not only justifiable, but, for scientists whose basic commitment is to the alleviation of human misery, not to do them would be unjustifiable. In my opinion, each scientist must ask himself one question before doing any experiment on an animal: Is it likely that the pain and deprivation that this animal is about to endure will be greatly outweighed by the resulting alleviation of human pain and deprivation? If the answer is yes, the experiment is justified. Anyone who has spent time with severely depressed patients or with schizophrenic adults can appreciate the degree of their misery; to argue, as some do, that people should not do experiments on animals, is to ignore the misery of their fellow human beings. Not to do such research is to consign millions of humans to continued misery. Most human beings, as well as household pets, are alive today because animal experiments with medical ends were carried out; without such studies, polio would still be rampant, smallpox widespread and almost always fatal, and phobias incurable. As for the studies discussed in this book, I believe that what we have learned about depression, anxiety, sudden death, and their cure and prevention justifies the animal experiments that have led us to these insights (p. xi)

We will not review our earlier arguments here, but rather, want to point out that psychological research has contributed to our understanding of personhood among animals. For as soon as we consider how we know about or test for personhood, we can see that this concept is relevant not only to human beings, but also, in some degree, to animals. We know about another human being's pain and an animal's pain in essentially similar ways: we interpret certain vocalizations and other behaviors in relation to certain situations. (As we specify these, we can distinguish between mild and severe pain, between feigned and real pain.) Thus, we cannot characterize *consciousness* or *having experiences* without including at least some animals; they show some degree of personhood by this standard, while comatose human beings may not.

Thought also cannot be defined without including infrahumans to some extent. Furthermore, some humans have very limited personhood by this standard—for example, those who are severely brain damaged or severely retarded. While the most dramatic examples of animal thinking seem to occur in apes, psychological research has repeatedly illustrated that more limited thinking may also be inferred in mice, rats, and dogs. Thus, animals display some degree of personhood by this standard, though as far as we know now, the human capacity for thinking is far greater than any animal's.

People sometimes even impute morality to animals, though they may of course be wrong in doing so. Pet owners, for example, may say that their dogs feel guilty when caught on a favorite but forbidden chair; they are then clearly attributing a moral capacity to their dogs. Cynics (and psychologists!) are quick to say that the dogs in question are probably only afraid of punishment, and they may well be right. What is critical here, however, is that the cynics' comment raises the question, "How, then, do we know that humans have a capacity for morality, that they too, are not merely acting out of fear of punishment or desire for reward?" This is not a frivolous question. According to Kohlberg (1964), moral development progresses through stages, but not everyone develops to the highest stage of principled autonomy; some people never progress beyond the fear of negative consequences or the desire to be well treated by those with power. Thus, depending on how we define moral behavior, and what we continue to learn about chimpanzees, gorillas, and dolphins, we may or may not conclude that infrahumans share morality with us in any degree at all, and that this aspect of personhood varies considerably among human beings.

Finally, as far as we know now, even chimpanzees with sign language do not contemplate the meaning of life and death. Having a sense of self that extends across a lifetime is not universal among humans, but it does seem to be unique to humans, though chimpanzees do have some degree of self-concept (Gallup, 1977).

Thus, the greatest potential for personhood is found among human beings. We could continue to reserve the word *person* for humans, but we cannot escape the fact that other creatures share with us some of the features of personhood in some degree, and these are always morally relevant. As Seligman put it, we are weighing human and animal pain; animals are not tormented for pleasure, but are hurt only to obtain knowledge about human and animal behavior. But why is human suffering weighted more than animal suffering? The answer may be that human beings, like most other creatures, are predisposed to favor their own species, and are thus committed to optimizing the personhood of humans, which typically far exceeds the potential personhood of other animals. Human beings can be and should be concerned about other creatures, but when a choice must be made they help people, even those low on personhood, and even at the expense of animals. That same concern for all human beings, regardless of level of personhood, commits moral people to the view that no human being should be subjected to the procedures which

Seligman described. Exceptions to that commitment are always morally objectionable, and correctly evoke images of Nazism.

In every era, including the present one, some psychologists have worried that society's and psychology's increasing concern and care for humans of lesser personhood would in the end prove harmful to humankind. Not only are such deviants not productive in this view, but they will have deviant children—and in greater number than normal people will have normal children. We must therefore turn our attention to eugenics and some psychologists' involvement in it.

EUGENICS

The value that has become prominent during approximately the last 25 years can be summarized as, "Bring out the best in each individual." The means to this end are viewed as environmental, and involve social change, personal change, or both. Eugenicists propose both different ends and different means. The end is improving humankind and the means is changing the gene pool. As Bajema (1976) put it, "The purpose of eugenics as a science is to ascertain the direction and rate of genetic change in human populations that is being brought about by natural selection or that might be brought about by selection if certain social changes occurred. The purpose of eugenics as a social movement is to modify in a eugenic direction the way in which natural selection is operating on human populations." (p. 3)

For some, this may evoke images of Hitler's "master race," while for others, it suggests the possibility of eliminating genetic diseases. The simple truth is that these two "improvements" are related: both involve attempts to change human kind by using knowledge about heredity. Such usage has sometimes been codified in laws—such as those that forbid siblings to marry. It would be most unfortunate if in this era of genetic engineering most people identified eugenics with Hitler. Instead, we have to learn to ask specific questions about what would be changed, how, for what purpose, and what the consequences would be for different groups or individuals. Eugenics is already with us, not only in the laws mentioned above, but also in selective abortions. The more we learn about controlling heredity, the more urgent it will be for all of us to reflect about the complex questions eugenics raises. This is so because whatever we do represents our choice among alternatives; this is true even on those occasions when we decide to leave well enough alone. Once we know how to do something, not doing it is as much a choice as doing it.

While medical specialists have been concerned about abnormalities like Tay Sachs, psychologists have been most interested in traits, notably those in the areas of intellect. This is understandable when you consider the significance of thinking to the concept of personhood. In fact, when someone is capable of only minimal thought, we quickly use expressions like "barely human" (barely a person) to describe that individual. Two kinds of questions are raised by eugenics, the technical and the moral, although, as pointed out in Part II, these quickly interact. Just what is inherited? Just what should we preserve, enhance, eliminate? Eugenics as a social movement has to be considered cautiously in both respects.

It has become a truism that people are the products of both heredity and environment. Eugenicists stress the importance of changing the human gene pool, without, however, claiming that environments can be neglected. But although it is clear that all human characteristics have a hereditary base, we do not yet fully understand how that base operates. It would be difficult indeed to predict the long-range consequences of breeding people (assuming we could) for positive characteristics like talent for music or mathematics or leadership. What else would be different in individuals besides that one characteristic? What would change in interactions among people?

At this time, scientists cannot answer these questions. Let us pretend, however, that we agree on some goal—for example, that we should raise the level of intelligence among human beings. One question is whether we would be able to accomplish this goal at all. A cautious answer is, "Possibly," but even if we could do so, the question is whether we should. As pointed out in Chapter 8, both ends and means should be subjected to moral scrutiny. We can question not only the goal, but also the policies required to reach it. Assuming intelligence is in part inherited, how many human beings are we willing to kill, incarcerate, or sterilize in order to prevent them from having children, which is precisely what eugenics would demand? Alternately, we could offer inducements to stupid people to have fewer or no children and to smart people to have many. It is difficult to imagine how such a policy could be implemented in a democracy, or even that it would become law in the first place. Consider a policy of awarding cash to males and females with IQs under 85 for not having children, and of providing free sterilization, birth control, and abortion. Since both males and females usually mature physically before they turn 18, this policy might tempt poor parents, in particular, to have their prepubescent children sterilized. But even more fundamentally, this policy singles out a particular group of people and stigmatizes them as a threat to all humanity! It is also a policy that would put us on a very slippery slope, since IQs are used to establish level of intelligence. It would be convenient if the behavior of those with IQs of 87 were dramatically different from those with IQs of 83, but such is not the case. A law of this kind would be picking some arbitrary IQ, be it 75 or 85; if 85 today, why not 90 tomorrow? Just where would one start, and where would one stop?

Although eugenicists have often stressed the intellective aspects of personhood, they have discussed other aspects as well. During the 19th century, many biological and social scientists, including some psychologists, believed in *degeneration theory,* according to which a variety of undesirable deviations were transmitted mainly by heredity but also by such environmental factors as disease and psychological shock in pregnant women. Degeneracy included not only retardation, but also psychosis, alcoholism, criminality, and poverty. As Saranson and Doris (1969) pointed out repeatedly, studying the theories proposed by past scientists serves to remind us of the interaction of the factual knowledge and the values of a given time period in explaining humanly important phenomena. Desirable (nondegenerate) people were intelligent, productive, well adjusted, and moral. They displayed one kind of personhood, and any deviation from this was intolerable and hereditary. Proposals for controlling human reproduction would seem to follow perforce.

Modern eugenic proposals are more modest, and we can drift into accepting them without giving them the thought they deserve. Consider the possible elimination of Down's Syndrome through the use of amniocentesis and abortion, and ongoing debates about reproduction among the retarded. Two assumptions are involved. The first is that it is bad that low IQ people exist. It is bad because they themselves may suffer, and because they are more dependent on others, or in different ways, than most of us. The second assumption is that their IQs are heritable, which would mean that overall, the children of retarded people would have lower IQs than the children of normal people, not to mention above average ones. The second assumption is still being hotly debated (see Eysenck & Kamin, 1981), and this alone should make us cautious. That Carl and Sue *might perhaps* have children with IQs lower than those of Tom and Linda seems meager ground indeed for forbidding Carl and Sue to have children.

The more difficult questions are raised by the first assumption—that human suffering could be decreased by decreasing the number of retarded people in the world. Even if we could all agree about the nature of suffering, which seems doubtful, it is far from clear that this prediction would turn out to be true. Of course, the goal of eugenics, as we pointed out above, is not to help every individual to develop optimally, but rather, to decrease the numbers of certain groups of individuals (for example, the retarded). It is not difficult to restate this as the goal of decreasing "our" suffering by eliminating "them." Why would we pay taxes to support them, when the same moneys could make life better for us? The simplest answer seems to be that eliminating people does not make life better for those remaining, because most means for doing so are extraordinarily frightening, the important exception being voluntary, individual decisions about abortion.

A national policy legally requiring abortion or sterilization under specified conditions would create much new suffering even as it sought to decrease existing suffering. The same would be true of a policy forbidding these under all circumstances. Far wiser, considering our ignorance about the heritability of traits and the multiple possible consequences of systematically changing the gene pool is a policy permitting individual choice. We normally permit parents to make many decisions. For example, they are free to raise their children at home or to send them to boarding school. Decisions about sterilization are somewhat more complex. First, they are discriminatory, since they pertain to only some children, not to all. Second, the issue of informed consent is involved. It is one thing to choose childlessness for oneself, quite another to choose it for someone else. While some retarded adults cannot be properly informed, some certainly can understand the idea that a particular procedure would make it impossible for them to have children. One unfortunate consequence of the widespread use of a single number to express intelligence is that people understandably overgeneralize: those with low IQs are stupid and therefore cannot learn or understand anything. But as we have seen, this simply is not true. A person who cannot master high school algebra may nonetheless deal capably with many other challenges, including those of parenthood—or at least, no less capably than average or above average IQ parents do! In particular cases, parents may have good reasons for choosing sterilization for a son or daughter, but the needs and wishes of that child deserve to be taken as seriously as the needs and wishes of their other children. Who will tell Sue and Carl that they may not have children because they are so stupid?

Modern eugenicists no longer sound as though they envision a world where everybody has an IQ of at least 95 (except for rare, unavoidable cases of clinical retardation), nobody ever hallucinates, and nobody ever commits a crime. They do, however, offer one perspective on what to do about specific genetic deviations from the norm: decrease their number for the sake of the future human gene pool. In addition, we must discuss one other point. It is difficult enough to suggest how much of which traits are particularly useful to individuals and society right now. Cultures continue to change in unpredictable ways, and the human use of the ecosystem is changing the physical world in unpredictable ways. It is therefore impossible to list which traits future human beings will find useful, and in what proportions. It is not even self-evident that high IQ is first on the list. Degeneracy was once a major concern to some, as IQs appear to be now. The people of the future will encounter their own joys and sorrows, and they may wish to measure traits with which we are not even acquainted— clusters of behaviors we have not even categorized in our current society. Then again, they may wish to stress traits we consider relatively unimportant in our current society.

For most prospective parents, the major concern is quite different: for both selfish and unselfish reasons, they want to have healthy, normal children. Amniocentesis and abortion are making it increasingly possible for parents to terminate particular pregnancies, and genetic counseling is therefore increasingly more common.

GENETIC COUNSELING

Genetic counseling deals with family planning in the light of information about genetically transmissable traits, notably those related to disease (such as Tay Sachs, hemophilia). Decisions to be made may pertain to marriage, pregnancy, or abortion. Such counseling always includes the sharing of information about the trait in question—about the probability that the child will be affected or about the consequences for the child and the others in the family of the child's being affected. It sometimes includes advice, though counselors range from the very nondirective, who believe that clients must make their own decisions in such matters, to the very directive, who believe that professional counselors should give advice because they are technically and emotionally in the best position to make the necessary decisions.

Genetic counseling clearly touches on many important questions. Some of these overlap with those in eugenics, like questions about which defects should be eliminated, and why. Others may be unique to genetic counseling, like questions about the morally relevant ways, if any, in which a fetus differs from an infant, a child, or an adult. Those who occasionally or continually do genetic counseling will surely have considered such questions in great detail, but in their role as counselors, their most basic question is what to do when their own moral beliefs differ from those of their client(s).

To answer this question, we must first differentiate between those who are prochoice and those who are antichoice. The latter could have one of two views: abortion should be legally forbidden or it should be legally compulsory. In either case, the individual would have no choice except by breaking a law. Prochoice, however, refers to a range of possible positions. Suppose that we asked 100 women, "Under what conditions would you choose abortion for yourself?" Some would undoubtedly answer, "Under no circumstances—not even if I had been raped." The remaining women would not, however, all answer, "Under all circumstances—even if I knew that the baby would have eyes of one color but I preferred another color." Instead, those who accept or favor abortion under some circumstances do not necessarily accept or favor it under any and all circumstances, and the acceptable circumstances may vary from person to person. Thus, prochoice refers to a range of possible positions; only to those who are absolutely against any choice does it appear to be just one position. Even when both counselor and client(s) are prochoice, then, there may be important differences between their views.

The antichoice position is a logically consistent one, and its implications for action are clear. This view begins with the thesis that a fetus is a human being who is murdered during an abortion. Whether or not you agree with that assumption, you should acknowledge that most people are not pro-choice about murder; they believe that murder should be illegal, and that an act of murder should be severely punished, or at least, that the murderer should be removed from society. An antichoice counselor can accept only one position, and feels obligated to state it as clearly and persuasively as possible. When an antichoice counselor acts on this obligation, clients can then decide whether or not to stay with this counselor, or to seek out someone else.

Prochoice counselors can either accept the client's decisions, whether or not these coincide with their own, or they can make a referral to someone whose views are closer to the client's. Suppose that Linda Brown, doing genetic counseling, believes that abortions are justified when it is highly probable that the baby will suffer greatly, but not when the family expects to be inconvenienced by a baby who will be dull. She is currently counseling the Marshalls, who are close to choosing an abortion for a Down's Syndrome fetus. Brown would not make the same choice for herself, unless she was convinced the baby would suffer. Under these conditions, it might seem unreasonable to expect Brown to take the position that "The decision is yours," or to make a referral to someone who takes a position different from her own on such an important matter.

But in fact, neither of these is unreasonable. Since Brown is not absolutely opposed to abortion, she would recognize that where to stop on a continuum between two extreme views is not easily decided, and that legitimate differences of opinion are possible and probable. Only someone consistently against choice (either, "Of course you should get an abortion" or "Under no circumstances should you get an abortion") would have difficulty recognizing that others, too, need and should have the freedom to think about their moral dilemmas in their own way. Accepting that others should have a choice (between carrying the fetus to term or aborting it) entails accepting that they will sometimes choose what you would not choose for yourself; if you cannot accept someone's choosing what you would not choose, then you are not prochoice. If Brown is uncomfortable, or believes the Marshalls are, then a referral to someone else may be advisable.

Other considerations are also morally relevant to Brown's prochoice position. Nobody can predict accurately what kind(s) of suffering this particular child will endure (for example, from a defective heart), nor the actual impact(s) of the child on the family. The Marshalls may not be thinking of their convenience, but rather, may be making (intuiting) a prediction different from Brown's about their future behavior toward each other and all their children. Furthermore, how can one decide where a family's inconvenience ends and its suffering begins? Because Brown is prochoice, she will view the problems of predicting the child's specific characteristics and their impact(s) on both child and family as morally relevant. Accepting the implications of such unpredictability is also consistent with Brown's position that one cannot find the one right answer to the predicament of the Marshalls, and that the choice should be theirs.

Why do prospective parents want healthy, normal children? Why might some choose abortion for a particular abnormality while others choose to have the child? Every new child affects the already existing family, and they affect the child. Even a healthy baby requires care, and thus makes demands on the family. When the child is viewed as a positive addition to the family, at least some of the work is experienced as enjoyable. Furthermore, other people admire the baby, and every small symbol of development is a source of joy, be it the first tooth or the first step. The arrival of a deviant baby is typically viewed as a tragedy. Such babies may require extraordinary kinds and amounts of care, thus disrupting the family greatly. Medical expenses may drain the family. Development will be slow, and rarely will anyone admire "that adorable baby." These negative factors are so well known that the sense of tragedy is all but universal. But family members are not concerned only for themselves; they anticipate that the children will suffer, perhaps from a series of operations forever beyond their comprehension, perhaps from the taunting of normal children. It is hardly surprising that many prospective parents avail themselves of abortion when faced with such prospects.

Of course, not everyone views the arrival of a baby with some abnormality in the same way. For some, it will be a matter of course that they will love and care for this child, and, without denying the negative aspects of this experience, they will stress the positive ones, the most basic being the gains in compassion and maturity. When neighborhood children tease a retarded child, his or her siblings experience the sort of challenging adversity that can promote the development of those traits related to wisdom. In an era when it is self-evident to some that every deviant fetus should be aborted, it is important to emphasize again that prochoice means that others may sometimes choose to do what you consider to be wrong. Thus, the moral obligation of prochoice counselors is to inform clients, and to help them to apply information to their own situation; this will involve dealing with emotions as much as dealing with statistics about a particular abnormality. Since no pat solutions are available none will be offered.

The concept of personhood is involved in this area, as in retardation, and aging, and the use of animals in research. It seems clear that one kind of deviancy about which prospective parents are concerned is limited potential for personhood; this concerns them both for the child and for themselves. In addition, questions arise about the beginnings of personhood. Which kinds of personhood, if any, emerge during which stage of pregnancy? At the earliest stages, personhood may be nonexistent. In that case, one can distinguish between existing persons (parents, other family members, other members of society) and future persons. Questions about obligations to future persons still provoke much debate, but they probably figure explicitly or implicitly in many cases of genetic counseling. Thus, one could express the dilemma of the prospective parents as trying to balance their obligations to already existing persons against their obligations to a future person, perhaps one with a limited potential for personhood.

EVALUATING AND CHANGING THE ENVIRONMENT

In several places, we have pointed out the significance of the situations people confront, as these are related to their goals and capabilities. We are accustomed to evaluating individual traits and actions; only rarely do we evaluate situations, and yet every action occurs within some context! This chapter was opened with some passages from a book about a truly horrifying imprisonment. When some people commit suicide under such conditions, it can be instructive to discuss whether or not this act was morally justified or permissible, but this response is incomplete if it does not include an evaluation of the situation. Some acts (even murder) may be judged to be permissible under the worst of human conditions. That is not an argument in favor of murder, but an argument against the situation.

This same perspective applies to the very retarded and the senile. It is easier for us to stress and judge their deficiencies than to focus our attention on their environment, because we are an important part of that environment; this pertains to our attitudes and our actions. Thus, optimizing refers to both people and environments: we should try to create social environments for each other that will bring out the best in each of us. Increased knowledge in the social sciences would permit us to do that better than we now do it—but we have to be willing to search for that knowledge and to use it for that purpose. If we feel uncomfortable in the presence of those who are senile or retarded, is that an argument for eliminating them, or for changing our attitude?

CONCLUSIONS

In a sense, every effort to solve a problem is an intervention. This chapter, has addressed problems related to the saving or taking of life, and to the quality of life. Psychologists act to preserve human life and to enhance its quality, which can refer to individuals or to humankind. Thus, some psychologists want to help individuals to maximize their personhood; this will contribute to mutually beneficial relationships with others and thus to everyone's happiness. Other psychologists evaluate the varieties of mental life in a hierarchic fashion, placing greater value upon some than upon others, and they want to act so as to improve the human gene pool. In our discussion, the former emphasis was favored. Interventions should generally benefit individuals, regardless of kind or degree of personhood, since it is individuals who experience suffering and joy, not groups.

Psychologists often help people modify traits and behaviors, and this is an important contribution to their lives. But it is an incomplete approach; traits and behaviors are evaluated with reference to situations, and situations contribute powerfully to well being. Therefore, modification must pertain not only to traits and behaviors, but also to situations. This is a tall order. In hard times, especially, people and governments can become all too eager to find good reasons for neglecting or even eliminating this or that group. As we have seen, psychologists have many good reasons for rejecting that approach.

10

PSYCHOLOGY AND
THE POWERLESS

Contrary to the ideology of the melting pot, our society is more like a collection of different groups of people in nearly constant struggle for the things that are valued in our society (jobs, housing, prestige). Furthermore, these groups differ in their power to control and have access to these resources. Because they have more economic and political power, some groups have more control than others over the distribution of resources in our society. The groups that traditionally have lacked significant levels of power in our society include not only ethnic and racial groups (blacks, Hispanics, native Americans), but also women, the elderly, and homosexuals. From this perspective one can define a collection of groups who can be classified as relatively powerless, and, who, because of their lack of power, have been historically subjected to discrimination and oppressive practices by the dominant groups in society.

In this chapter we explore the relevant ethical questions concerning psychology and the powerless. When psychologists study people, they often categorize them into the same groups that the society at large does. For example, psychologists study racial differences (IQ differences between blacks and whites), and sex differences (male-female differences in conformity). There are studies dealing with the causes of homosexuality and with memory deterioration in the elderly. In studying these groups and making group comparisons psychology does not and cannot remain value-free (see Part II). The way psychology studies, conceptualizes, or thinks about these groups cannot be neutral and, thus, psychology becomes a part of the intergroup struggle. Psychology can be used to serve the interests of the powerful or the interests of the powerless.

Furthermore, the activities of psychologists can, and frequently do, affect people's lives. As a matter of fact, when one looks at the social institutions that make use of psychology or psychologists, it is tempting to say that psychology affects everyone's lives. For example, the educational system, the legal system, and many of the government's social programs often make use of psychological knowledge. These are also the institutions that influence the distribution of power in society. When viewed from this perspective, ethical considerations become even more relevant.

We will examine the moral questions involved in psychology's treatment of powerless groups by dividing the activities of psychologists into the different components discussed in Part II.

CHOOSING AN AREA

We can examine how choosing an area of investigation is a source of ethical concern for psychology's treatment of powerless groups from three basic perspectives. First, many times psychologists choose an area of study for the purpose of alleviating a human, social problem. Sometimes this is the primary, explicit concern of an investigation (for example, how to structure an educational program to prevent drug usage among teenagers). However, even when solution of a problem is not the primary concern of an investigation, it is still a relevant consideration. For example, those who do research on alcoholism (or autism, or prejudice) do so, not simply to understand the phenomenon, but also, however indirectly, to prevent it or alleviate it. Thus, there is no research on how to increase alcoholism, but considerable research on how to cure it.

It could be said, then, that the areas of problems that psychologists choose to investigate tell us something about what psychologists consider to be important. However, as some observers have noted, psychological activity is, to a large extent, shaped by the concerns of the society at large (Shields, 1975; X, 1973). As Cedric X put it:

> To the extent that scientific activities are expensive, to that extent science will rely upon the public for support of its activities. And to that extent the wishes of the American public will be paid at least minimal attention. This results in a sociocultural shaping of scientific activity—not in terms of what evidence is found, *but in terms of what questions are asked.* (p. 116, emphasis added)

Words like *society* and the *public,* however, are rather broad. Our society is to a large extent a collection of different groups. Are these groups equally influential in defining what problems are worthy of attention? Clearly not, and for two reasons. First, investigation of a problem is dependent upon financial-political support. Legislators make up the budget that determines the amount of money going into research. By definition, powerless groups lack the economic and political power to influence the areas of research that get funded.

Secondly, as Kidder and Stewart (1975) point out, social science has been primarily the occupation of white, middle-class males. Therefore, they are unfamiliar with, or perhaps insensitive to, the problems of people whose life experiences are different from their own.

The area of drug addiction is a good example of how psychology has ignored the problems of powerless groups in society. Although in recent years there has been considerable research on drug addiction, research on some groups whose pattern of drug usage may be unique, continues to be virtually nonexistent. Marsh, Colten, and Tucker (1982) made this argument for women:

> Despite extremely negative reactions to women's substance use, and despite the fact that a large proportion of the female population has been engaged in the use of some kind of addictive drug and alcohol, substance use by women has been largely ignored as a valid domain of concern by policy-makers, practitioners, and social researchers. (p. 2)

The same argument can be made about blacks. Drug addiction was never really considered a major problem until drug use became prevalent among middle-class, white youth. Yet, drug addiction had been a problem in poor black neighborhoods long before that.

Another informative example deals with psychological research on the aged. For many years the elderly constituted a relatively powerless group in society. More recently, the percentage of elderly people in the population has increased and they have gained modest amounts of political power. One would expect then that this change in the status of the elderly would be reflected in psychology's concern with the elderly. To test this notion we looked at the proportion of studies dealing with the topic of aging listed in the *Psychological Abstracts* (a reference source for studies published in a wide variety of psychology journals) for the years 1972, 1975, 1978, and 1981. We found that in 1972 only .47 percent of all studies referenced dealt with the topic of aging. This proportion steadily increased until 1981 when 2 percent of the studies listed were concerned with aging; although still low, this figure represents a 425 percent increase. These figures are consistent with the idea that psychologists' concerns with social problems are not equally influenced by the different groups in society.

No one questions the morality of psychology when it attempts to address human problems. The ethical question that can be raised here, though, concerns the principle of equality. Should not the problems of the powerless groups be addressed as much as those of the powerful? Why should the latter get more attention than the former? According to the principle of equality it would be wrong to ignore (or pay less attention to) the problems of the disadvantaged groups, unless, of course, it can be shown that the different groups in our society are not equal on some dimension that would justify differential treatment. One argument that may be used, for example, is the alleged intellectual inferiority of blacks. Or a similar argument may be made about the "inferior" qualities of women (too emotional, not independent enough).

Yet, it is difficult to see how these differences, even if they exist (which we reject), would justify ignoring the problems of the groups included. It would simply mean that their problems are of a different nature. Let us take for example a group of people who are truly intellectually inferior, the mentally retarded. Research can be conducted to develop better methods of developing their skills or restructuring the environment so that it becomes less intellectually demanding. The problems of the retarded are undoubtedly different from ours, but this does not mean that psychology ought to ignore them.

A second way in which choosing an area of investigation can be a source of ethical concern for psychology's treatment of powerless groups has to do with how psychology can promote negative stereotypes about these groups.

After selecting a particular area of study an investigator can choose to focus on either the positive or the negative aspects of the issue being investigated. Take, for example, the black family. It is nearly impossible for any student of the social sciences not to be exposed to the vast literature on the unstable, matriarchal, divorce-ridden black family. Furthermore, it would be very hard for someone who becomes familiar with this "scientific" literature not to form a very negative impression of blacks, impressions which can easily be used to justify racist beliefs and practices. Clearly, the intent of social scientists who write about the black family is not to promote such negative stereotypes. Nevertheless, there has been undue emphasis on the negative side of the black family when one could just as easily focus on the positive aspects. Billingsley (1970) even argued that the black family has been distorted by "white social science" and that the relevant, necessary questions about the black family have not been asked. In his words:

> The plain fact is that in most communities of any size, most black families meet the American test of stability. Contrary to the impressions generally circulated by white students of the black family, most black families, even in the ghetto, are headed by men. And in most of these families, even the very poor ones, most of these men are still married to their original wives. Furthermore, most of these men and many of the women are employed full time and are still not able to pull their families out of poverty. What we need to know more about is how these families manage. How do they function? How do they manage to meet the needs of their children? (p. 132)

Billingsley does not argue that the black family has no problems, but rather, that an excessive concern with the negative aspects of black family life has produced a negative, distorted picture of black families. In addition, such research presents, by comparison, a distorted, positive portrayal of white families. Jones (1972) argued:

> By continually referring to the breakdown of the black family, the Moynihan Report seems to imply that the white American family is a stable, enviably competent producer of well-adjusted, achievement oriented youth. Yet in the early 1970's, a major problem of *white* America is described as the "generation gap," a euphemism for social problems such as alienation, drug use and abuse, violence, and crisis in confidence. (p. 49)

The example of the black family is not a unique one. Other writers have noted how psychological research with Mexican-Americans (Padilla, 1971) and Puerto Ricans (Padilla & Ruiz, 1974) has tended to focus on the pathological aspects of minority groups.

It may seem contradictory to argue on the one hand, that social science has ignored the problems faced by many powerless groups and then, on the other hand, to argue that the research has focused on the negative aspects of minority groups. However, to study the problems afflicting many minority groups does not necessarily imply a negative portrayal of minorities. Also, emphasizing the negative aspects of minorities does not mean that their problems are being addressed. For example, unemployment has been traditionally, though not exclusively, a problem faced by members of disadvantaged groups. Yet, to study the effects of unemployment on various indices of mental health does not necessarily reflect negatively on minority group members. Furthermore, studies on the negative aspects of the black family may do very little in alleviating or understanding the problems faced by blacks.

The tendency to negatively portray members of minority groups, who are already the object of prejudice and discrimination, adversely affects the members of these groups. The effect can be subtle: for example, research findings can be disseminated through the media where they reach the public's consciousness, and prejudices and stereotypes are then maintained or created. Even more seriously, research findings can be translated into public policy or used to justify existing discriminatory policies (Ryan, 1971). The potential harm for minority groups is real. The question for psychologists, then, is an ethical one. To be sure, there are problems with the black family and not everything that minorities do can be characterized as positive. But just as surely, the black family has many strengths, not everything that minorities do can be characterized as negative, and not presenting a more balanced picture of minority groups is ethically questionable.

It could be argued that psychologists' tendency to focus on the negative is not unique to powerless groups, that psychologists have tended to focus on the negative aspects of people, period. This is clearly revealed in the amount of research devoted to negative topics (aggression, psychosis) rather than the positive side of people (altruism, love). Still, there is some validity in our argument regarding powerless groups. Psychologists can study people as people in general or they can study people as members of particular groups. For example, depending on my research interests I can think of John as simply an individual, or I can classify him as a black (or white) individual. In the former instance whatever I conclude about John, no matter how negative, will not be associated with any racial or ethnic group. In the latter case whatever I study about John will reflect on his racial group. The implications for stereotypes and prejudices are very different in these two cases.

There is a third way in which choosing an area of investigation has ethical implications concerning powerless groups. Many times the area psychologists choose to study or the questions they ask are related to societal values regarding what is, or is not, a desirable goal. A good example of this is the area of intergroup relations. Much of this research has been conducted with the aim of reducing or eliminating intergroup conflict. Although no one would argue against such a goal, there are different models for the resolution of intergroup conflict and how we can function as a multiethnic society. Depending upon which model one adopts, different topics will be investigated and different questions will be asked.

At this point it may be helpful to describe briefly what the two major models of intergroup relations are, how the choice of models will lead to different research questions, and how they have guided social science research in the past.

An *assimilationist* model seeks the incorporation of an ethnic group into the culture of another group. In our case, it is the process whereby a minority group loses its identity and adopts the culture (values, beliefs, practices) of the dominant group. Assimilation can take place at three different levels and all three must be completed to achieve full assimilation. Initially, there is behavioral assimilation. This happens when the minority group chooses to behaviorally conform to the culture of the dominant group. Secondly, there is structural assimilation which can be subdivided into secondary and primary stages. Secondary structural assimilation refers to the dominant group's acceptance of minority group members in public institutional settings (schools, church, work). Primary structural assimilation refers to the dominant group's acceptance of minority individuals at the level of intimate relationships (friends, marriage partners). When this level is reached, one can say that a group has been completely assimilated into the dominant culture.

A second model for intergroup relations is *cultural pluralism*. According to this model a minority group would not lose its identity as it interacts with the dominant group. On the contrary, the minority group would try to maintain and promote its culture while, at the same time, trying to achieve equal status with the majority in the political and economic spheres.

Depending on which model of intergroup relations one adopts, different research questions will be investigated. For example, a researcher guided by an assimilationist perspective might stress the negative aspects of bilingualism, emphasize the similarities among individuals of different groups, or investigate the benefits of intergroup contact. On the other hand, if one is guided by a pluralist perspective one might stress the positive aspects of bilingualism, how people can learn to accept or enjoy cultural differences, or the drawbacks of intergroup contact.

In looking at the research that has been conducted on intergroup relations it is clear that it has been primarily guided by an assimilationist perspective. As Billingsley (1970) noted, social scientists tend to view other cultures primarily as groups to be assimilated. Thus, the Moynihan Report suggests that black families should be more like white families and the Coleman Report suggests that black students should be more like white students. In a similar vein, Beckman, Henthorn, Niyakawa-Howard, and Passin (1970) describe how too much research has concentrated on the negative effects of culture conflict within minority individuals while little has been done to investigate the advantages of being bicultural.

The assimilationist bias is also revealed by the research on prejudice. The great majority of the studies on prejudice have investigated the prejudices of the dominant groups toward members of minority groups. Very little has been done in the area of minority prejudices towards the dominant groups. This is consistent with an assimilationist model in which acceptance of the minorities by the dominant groups is of critical importance.

Although the term *culture* may not be applicable in this case, a good example of how an assimilationist philosophy has guided social science research in intergroup relations is the research on homosexuality. In a review of the literature on homosexuality Morin (1975) noted that over one half of the studies dealt with a search for the causes of homosexuality or the psychological adjustment of homosexuals. Such concern with homosexual etiology reveals a heterosexual bias on two grounds. First, although psychologists frequently search for the causes of homosexuality they rarely search for the causes of heterosexuality; that is, we accept heterosexuality and view homosexuality as problematic. Second, the search for the causes of homosexuality reflects the heterosexual society's anxieties regarding homosexuality. The implications of the research on homosexuality are clear: if we knew what caused homosexuality we could prevent young people from becoming homosexuals. Or, perhaps we could devise more effective methods for changing a homosexual orientation. Again the assimilationist philosophy is obvious: homosexuals should become heterosexuals.

Yet, there are many questions regarding homosexuality more important to homosexuals that have remained largely ignored. For example, what role does the presence of a gay community play in the social adjustment of homosexuals? How can homosexuals cope better with a primarily heterosexual world? These are research questions, however, that assume a pluralistic model in which a homosexual orientation is acceptable. It is true that in 1975 the American Psychiatric Association removed the diagnosis of homosexuality as a mental illness from its manual. However, society still shows a heterosexual bias which is reflected in psychological research on homosexuality.

Furthermore, it can be argued that an assimilationist model serves primarily the interests of the dominant majority. As Luhman and Gilman (1980) note:

> It is always in the interests of any ethnic group to promote its culture when it comes into contact with other ethnic groups. The more its culture comes to dominate a society, the more competitive advantage its members will have in that society. In the U.S., people of English descent had the power to promote their culture as the dominant one in the early days of the nation. The English culture has not lost that domination since; over 200 years later, it is still people of basically English descent who hold a competitive advantage in the United States. (p. 136)

In summary, one can conclude that, for the most part, psychology has shown a clear majority bias in choosing areas of investigation, either by ignoring some of the problems facing members of powerless groups, or by promoting negative stereotypes about minority groups, or by the assumptions guiding the research on intergroup relations. In all these cases the questions that researchers have asked have not been guided by the interests of powerless groups.

CONCEPTUALIZING

In 1966 the United States Office of Education published a document titled *Equality of Educational Opportunity* (more popularly known as the Coleman Report) dealing with segregation in schools and its effect upon student achievement. One of the unexpected findings of this report was that black children were highly motivated to achieve in school and that parents of black children showed an exceptionally high level of interest in their children's education (as reported by Ryan, 1971). Simultaneously, the Coleman Report found that blacks had lower rates of school-completion and lower college-going rates. These are undisputed, observable facts. However, it is not enough for psychologists to simply report these facts and leave it at that. These facts beg for an explanation, for interpretation. Why this inconsistency in black children's motivation and achievement? Why not in white children?

In trying to answer these questions we begin to theorize about the relationship between motivation, achievement, the school system, and racial differences. We also develop and use concepts. For example, in trying to interpret this finding from the Coleman Report some social scientists may begin to talk about racial differences in intelligence. Thus, we use the concepts of race and of intelligence.

Concepts and theories are, of course, not value-free (see Chapter 5). The concept of intelligence itself has been accused of being culturally biased in that it reflects white, middle-class values (Garcia, 1981). Furthermore, consider the explanation provided by the Coleman Report regarding the inconsistency between black children's motivation and their achievement. According to the Report, the discrepancy is due to a lack of realism in the aspirations of black children and their parents. That is, their expectations are too high, out of touch with social reality. Contrast this to the explanation stating that the discrepancy is due to the school's discriminatory practices against black students. It should be readily apparent to the reader that these two explanations reflect very different values regarding blacks and the school system. One explanation implies that the school system ought to be changed in relation to its treatment of black students, while the other explanation says nothing about the school system. If they were translated into public policy, these two explanations would have radically different effects upon the school-related experiences of black children.

There are two basic perspectives from which to examine the values in the concepts and theories that deal with the powerless.

Different versus Deficient

Stereotypes aside, many intergroup differences are real. That is, there are many differences among social, ethnic, and racial groups across a variety of variables. For example, there are language differences between middle-class white children and lower-class black children (Cazden, 1970), and between Anglos and Hispanics (Ruiz, Padilla & Alvarez, 1978). Chinese Americans express more external locus-of-control beliefs and are less extroverted than Anglo Americans (Hsieh, Shybut, & Lotsof, 1969; Sue, 1981). The entire value system of Native Americans is almost diametrically opposed to Anglo values (Sue, 1981). There are, of course, many other examples.

Differences among groups, however are rarely left alone for what they are—differences in styles and preferences. In conceptualizing about these differences it is very hard, if not impossible, not to evaluate them, however subtly. Thus we speak, not of how two groups have different personality styles, but how individuals of one group are better adjusted than individuals of another group. In addition, such evaluations, not surprisingly, exhibit a clear majority bias. That is, behaviors, beliefs, or values that differ from those of the dominant group are conceptualized as being somehow inferior or deficient.

Perhaps the most widely acknowledged example of this tendency is in the concept of the *culturally deprived* child. Riessman (1962) proposed this concept to explain why middle-class children perform better than lower-class children in the classroom. According to Riessman, middle-class children outperform lower-class children because of a superior cultural background; they have more toys, more access to books, and better verbal interactions with their parents. While some of these factors may, in part, account for the better performance of middle-class children, it still shows a majority bias to talk about a culturally deprived child because no one, by definition, lacks a culture. What is really meant, of course, is that lower-class children are brought up in an environment that differs from accepted middle-class standards. But, if we all agree that school achievement is a desirable goal and, furthermore, the cultural background of middle-class children prepares them for school better than the background of lower-class children, can one not say then that the middle-class background is superior to the lower-class background? Again, it is a matter of perspective. As Ryan (1971) points out, it makes just as much sense to say that lower-class children do not do as well in school because the school system is not prepared to deal with lower-class children as saying that the lower-class child lacks the preparation (culture) to succeed in the school system.

Bilingual education is a good example of how a school system can adapt to culturally different children. A child who is raised in a home where Spanish is the primary language will probably have a more difficult time in an English-speaking school than a child who is raised in an English-speaking home. However, the bilingual child's difficulty can be viewed as a deficiency in his background (little or incorrect English spoken at home) or as a deficiency in the school (no programs especially designed for bilingual children). Our argument is not that a bilingual program is the best way to deal with children whose primary language is not English. What we wish to emphasize is that a cultural difference need not be necessarily conceptualized as a deficiency.

No concepts in psychology, however, exemplify the different versus deficient distinction as much as those related to mental health. As Szasz (1970) pointed out, mental health is defined by whatever traits and behaviors are valued in a society. It would not be too surprising, then, to find that popular definitions of mental health typically reflect white, male, middle-class values. For example, one popular method of defining mental health is in terms of an ideal set of psychological traits. According to Sue (1981):

> Such an approach stresses the importance of attaining some ideal goal such as a consciousness-balance of psychic forces (Freud, 1960; Jung, 1960), self-actualization-creativity (Rogers, 1961; Maslow, 1968), or competence, autonomy, and resistance to stress (Allport, 1961; White, 1963). The discriminatory

nature of such approaches is grounded in the belief of a universal application (all populations and all situations) and a failure to recognize the value base from which the criteria derive. The particular goal or ideal used is intimately linked to a theoretical frame of reference and values held by the practitioner.

Furthermore, definitions of mental health such as competence, autonomy, and resistance to stress are related to white middle-class notions of "individual" maturity. (p. 6)

The classic example of this phenomenon is the double standard of mental health for males and females (Broverman, Broverman, Clarkson, Rosenkratz, & Vogel, 1970). In this study a group of clinicians was asked to describe, through the use of trait-adjectives, a mature, healthy, socially competent male; a second group of clinicians was asked to describe a mature, healthy, socially competent female; and a third group was asked to describe a mature, healthy, socially competent, adult. The results revealed a clear double standard of mental health. There was very little difference in the descriptions of a healthy man and a healthy adult. However, the traits that were used to describe a healthy adult were different from those used to describe a healthy woman. These findings clearly show "that the traits which make up the male criterion are the norm for the healthy adult and are more highly valued in this society" (Williams, 1977, p. 341).

A second popular method of defining mental health is through the use of tests. Because tests are not persons they may seem to bypass values altogether. However, as is pointed out in Chapter 11, tests reflect the value system of the test makers. If a particular psychologist (or society) values autonomy as an indicator of mental health, this psychologist will develop a test in which responses indicating a lack of autonomy are scored as indicating a deficiency. Thus, the psychologist's values become incorporated into the test.

Another way in which a test can be scored is through the use of statistical norms. For example, if the great majority of people respond No to the question "Are you easily embarrassed when meeting people for the first time?" then anyone who answers Yes is considered deviant or abnormal. Values are involved in conceptualizing anything that is different as deficient or undesirable. Since members of powerless groups usually constitute a statistical minority, this approach to testing becomes biased against these groups.

In view of these biases, it is not surprising that Sue (1981) concludes: "When we seriously study the 'scientific' literature of the past relating to the culturally different, we are immediately impressed with how an implicit equation of minorities and pathology is a common theme" (p. 12).

Internal versus External

Consider these two approaches at understanding the racial riots that occurred in many American cities during the late 1960s. One could try to explain the riots by looking at the rioters—their personality or emotions.

One conclusion that may be drawn is that the riots occurred because the rioters felt relatively deprived, or because of unrealistic expectations about progress, or as a displacement of frustration. One the other hand, one can look for the causes of the riots in the social, political, and economic structure of American ghettos. According to this approach one may conclude that the people rioted because of economic deprivation and racist practices that people in ghettos face in their everyday lives.

One significant way in which these two explanations differ is in their locus of causality: internal versus external. An internal explanation is one that looks for the causes of behavior in the person. An external explanation, on the other hand, looks at the situation the person is in. Thus, explaining the riots in terms of the psychological makeup of the rioters (versus nonrioters) is an internal explanation while explaining the riots in terms of prejudice and discrimination is an external explanation. According to the latter explanation most people, not just those who rioted, would react to injustice in the same manner.

Ryan (1971) vividly portrayed how this distinction is the primary mechanism used by social scientists in what he termed "blaming the victim." This process involved blaming the victims of social conditions for their own misfortunes by providing internal explanations of their status. As Ryan explains it:

> We must particularly ask, "To whom are social problems a problem?" And usually, if truth were to be told, we would have to admit that we mean they are a problem to those of us who are outside the boundaries of what we have defined as the problem. Negroes are a problem to racist whites, welfare is a problem to stingy taxpayers, delinquency is a problem to nervous property owners. Now, if this is the quality of our assumptions about social problems, we are led unerringly to certain beliefs about the causes of these problems. We cannot comfortably believe that we are the cause of that which is problematic to us; therefore, we are almost compelled to believe that they—the problematic ones—are the cause. (pp. 12–13)

Simply, if we are unwilling to believe that we may be partly responsible for another person's poverty, then we must put the blame on the poor people themselves. One way of achieving this is to develop internal explanations of poverty. As a matter of fact, according to Ryan, the study of poverty is one of the prime examples of blaming the victim.

One popular concept in the social science literature on poverty has been that of the culture of poverty. In short, it states that the poor are socialized in such a way that they develop characteristics (such as low expectations for success or an inability to delay gratification) that impair their economic progress. Again, notice that the explanation for poverty is to be found in poor people themselves.

One important ethical issue involved here is the relationship between explanation and justification (see Chapter 13). To be sure, explaining something is not the same thing as justifying it. To say that someone is poor because he/she cannot delay gratification does not, of logical necessity, mean that he/she ought to be poor, or that there ought to be poverty. On the other hand, explanations and justifications are not completely divorced. Some explanations prompt, or invite, a particular justification more readily than others. Thus, it becomes easier to say that someone deserves to be poor if they are poor because they cannot delay gratification than if they are poor because the economic structure denies them access to avenues of economic advancement. By simply shifting the locus of causality an explanation becomes more compatible with a justification.

In a more subtle manner, the field of mental health presents the same bias in relation to minorities. As pointed out by Smith, Burlew, Mosley, and Whitney (1978), personal development and adjustment have been primarily studied from three basic viewpoints: psychoanalytic, behavioral, and humanistic. Despite their theoretical differences on a number of issues, all three viewpoints view mental illness primarily as an individual (rather than social) problem. Yet, the authors point out:

> An awareness of the situation of blacks and other minorities in the United States should make it evident that something is wrong with the belief that minority mental health problems are primarily intrapsychic. It should be apparent that the issue of race intrudes all through the psychosexual, psychodynamic, behavioral, and self-awareness development process. (p. 6)

The authors go on to argue that most mental health problems afflicting the powerless come from prejudice and discrimination, unemployment, and poverty. That is, the problems are social-psychological (external) rather than individual (internal).

Chesler (1972) makes similar claims regarding women and mental health. In addition to criticizing the prevailing double standard of mental health (previously discussed) she charges that many of the typically female mental health problems, such as depression, are the result of a woman's adherence to the traditional female role that fosters helplessness, powerlessness, and dependency. This is in contrast to the traditional professional view of depression that looks at depression as an individual response to some personal loss. Notice the difference in the locus of causality of these two explanations; whereas one encourages women to look outside of themselves (societal sex roles) for the source of their problems, the other one encourages women to look inside themselves for their problems. This is not to say that explanations must be either internal or external, or that one is necessarily better than the other. As a matter of fact, it is becoming widely recognized that most behaviors can best be explained by the interaction between a person and the environment. Still, most theoretical explanations of human behavior tend to emphasize one or the other. Next, we turn to the ethical implications of these conceptualizations about human behavior.

Change versus the Status Quo

One very important ethical implication of deficient (versus different) and internal (versus external) conceptualizations has to do with the extent to which they support the status quo—politically, economically, and professionally.

Many of the significant social-political issues of our times are related, however indirectly, to the inequalities that exist among different racial, ethnic, and social groups in our society. For example, race relations is itself an important issue; women have mounted a significant social movement that has made society question many of its traditional beliefs and, in addition, forced many legislative changes; the elderly and homosexuals, among others, have begun similar movements; poverty and unemployment are disproportionately, though not exclusively, a problem for minority groups. The list could go on.

The way society as a whole, and government in particular, deals with these problems depends on the way they are conceptualized. If we view the lack of achievement of lower-class children as a product of cultural deprivation then it follows that we should develop programs to change these children's socialization process, not the school system. Or, if we view women's subordinate social status in society as a function of their biological makeup then we need not talk about developing the economic independence of women, or affirmative action, or other similar programs. Different conceptualizations have radically different implications for social change, or lack thereof. Furthermore, these implications often reach the level of formal public policy recommendation and implementation. For example, the Moynihan Report, which viewed the instability of the black family as the root of many of the problems of black people, formally advised the federal government to develop programs designed to promote stability in the black family.

Gurin and Gurin (1970) note how federal programs designed to deal with poverty and unemployment have been guided by the conceptualization that poverty is the result of the psychological characteristics of poor people. According to the authors the early programs for the hard-core unemployed often devoted more energy on resocialization than on skill training and job placement.

The consequences for members of disadvantaged groups, then, are very real. The systems and social forces (the status quo) that shape these individuals' lives are influenced, however indirectly, by the way social scientists think about these social issues.

Albee (1982) also noted the political-economic implications in the field of mental health. As we previously pointed out, mental health problems have been conceptualized primarily in individual-internal terms while ignoring the detrimental impact that social forces can have in people's lives, especially the powerless. In Albee's words:

> Unfortunately, an explanation of the high rate of mental disturbance among the poor in terms of defects is less costly to society than a social-learning explanation. We can spend a modest amount of public funds to support biomedical research, looking for the "twisted molecules" that will explain the twisted behavior. We can promise to develop a pill or injection, an operation, or some other new individual organic treatment that will cure by correcting the defect. Or we can wring our hands at the evidence that certain people are defective and take no action.

> Each alternative is relatively inexpensive. If we were to acknowledge that much of the emotional distress and mental disturbance in our society is due to dehumanizing social influences, such a position would call for widespread and expensive social reform. (p. 1044)

As the author noted, the relationship between theorizing and social reform is clear. Furthermore, it is irrelevant whether an explanation points to a person's genes or to his/her personality traits. Both explanations imply that it is futile to alter social conditions because the problem resides in the person.

Truth and Values

One popular view of science (including social science) is that it searches for Truth; social scientists develop hypotheses and after conducting research they either discard or accept a hypothesis or theory. Thus, if an experiment is well designed and the scientist is honest, then the data, not the social scientist's values or ideology, will determine the validity of a hypothesis. For example, according to this view, whether blacks have not achieved equality with whites because they are not as intelligent as whites is an empirical question, not an ideological one. It is true that the results may end up supporting one side of an ideological debate, but that is beyond the control of the social scientist.

There are, however, a number of problems with this overly strict, scientific view of social science. First of all, the nature of the social issues we have discussed so far is such that a critical series of experiments cannot be conducted. It is simply impossible to experimentally manipulate prejudice in societies to observe what would happen to a black family, or to homosexuals, under an experimental and a control condition. We must, therefore, rely on very indirect sources of data which leave much room for extrapolation, speculation, and values.

Second, the way in which the problem is conceptualized, before an experiment is even conducted, influences the evidence that is collected. Miller (1970) illustrates this in discussing psychological research on poverty:

> The issue is inequality, not poverty. To say poverty implies a fairly fixed line, defined by some pretentiously scientific standards, to which all families should be brought. Inequality asserts that the issue is the relative position of

individuals. Therefore, it forces attention to the relationships and relativities of different groups in society. We can discuss inequality without discussing the better-off. I cannot pinpoint the consequences of the shift in terms, but I have the very strong feeling that if one is concerned with inequality rather than poverty, different issues and different ways of studying old issues emerge. (p. 171)

Finally, in building theories we need concepts, concepts constructed by humans and as such influenced by cultural factors. It is just not possible to develop a value-free definition of intelligence, or mental health, or poverty. Concepts such as these are hopelessly culture-bound and any definition will, of necessity, favor one group over another.

GATHERING INFORMATION

Chapter 6 discussed the major ethical issues pertaining to the gathering of information: informed consent and parentalism. Although Williams (1974) has documented cases of gross abuses of minority populations as research subjects, no one would really argue that ethical considerations such as informed consent or nonmaleficence should not apply equally to members of powerless groups, since to do so would imply that minorities are different from others with respect to moral agency or personhood.

There are some considerations, however, that are particularly relevant to minority populations and deserve further comment.

Utilization of Research Findings

Chapter 4 noted how most psychological research can be classified as either basic or applied. The former is only concerned with resolving theoretical issues while the latter emphasizes the utility of the research for problem solving. However, it is never the case that research dealing with minority groups is entirely basic. Any research result regarding group differences, no matter how innocent it may appear on the surface, can be interpreted to have implications for some social, educational, or political program. If nothing else, any finding regarding group differences can be used to support beliefs about the inferiority or superiority of a particular group. Since nearly all psychological concepts can be classified along a good-bad dimension, one group will always be portrayed as better than another. Also, it usually has been the powerless who have been portrayed in a negative light. Research in this area, then, will nearly always have consequences for members of powerless groups.

The principle of informed consent dictates that participants in a research project be informed about the risks and benefits of the procedure to be used in the experiment and then, after weighing these factors, freely consent or refuse to participate.

Ethical discussions about informed consent always seem to center on the experimental procedures themselves, like giving subjects false feedback about their abilities or exposing subjects to anxiety-provoking stimuli. Rarely is any thought given to the use or application of the findings as a potential risk to the subject. Yet, as we have noted, a good case can be made that for minority individuals this aspect of a research project can be a definite risk, perhaps not directly for the individual subjects, but indirectly through their membership in a group.

One possible objection that researchers may raise against this suggestion is that it would make research on minority groups practically impossible. Informing subjects about the purpose and the hypothesis of the study as well as the possible implications of the findings will bias the subjects in such a manner that the data will be meaningless.

There are, however, some possible solutions to this problem. One solution would be to discuss the research project (including the dissemination and utilization of the findings) with a variety of community leaders and/or agencies who would not necessarily be subjects in the study. Nevertheless, acting on their judgment of the community's best interest would encourage either participation or a boycott of the research project.

Another alternative is to give the relevant information to subjects after they have participated in the experiment and then provide them with the opportunity to withdraw their data if they object to implications the study findings may have.

Although these suggestions are not without their problems, the available evidence indicates that minorities are becoming increasingly concerned with this issue. For example, one of the recommendations of the *NAACP Report on Minority Testing* (1976) called for a moratorium on the uses of standardized testing with minorities. The reason is not that the administration of the test itself presents a harm (physical or psychological) to the subject. Instead, the concern is with how the findings are interpreted (or misinterpreted) and used in a variety of settings such as the school system.

Testing, however, is not the only area of concern. There has been in recent years a noticeable increase in the hostilities and suspicions expressed by minority populations towards all social science researchers (Rainwater & Pittman, 1967). One major reason is that minorities feel that in many instances they have been betrayed by social scientists. Many feel they have donated their time and effort participating in studies only to see the findings used in a manner detrimental to their struggle, or to see themselves portrayed in professional journals in a very negative manner. These legitimate concerns on the part of minorities present a good argument for mandatory inclusion of this information (such as purpose and interpretation) as a part of informed consent.

Representation in Research

Participation in research by minority individuals is not limited to research whose primary focus is the study of minorities per se. For example, minority individuals may participate in studies dealing with sexual arousal, achievement motivation, or any other area of psychology. Minority status in these cases is incidental to the study and the data from all subjects are freely combined.

One problem that may arise in this context stems from the fact that minorities are grossly underrepresented in most of these studies. Therefore, the findings are not representative of any particular group. Yet, more than likely the findings of the study will be generalized to all populations. Greenglass and Stewart (1973) found this to be true in the case of males and females. In an extensive review of the psychological literature they found that the results of studies that used only males were usually generalized to the population at large. When only females were used in the study, however, the experimenters tended to be more careful in their generalizations to the male population.

The result of this practice is that, in many instances, unfair generalizations are made to minority populations, many times with negative consequences for them. For example, one of the major complaints blacks and Hispanics have made about psychological testing is that standardization studies have been conducted primarily on white samples whose norms are then (unfairly) applied to all ethnic groups. The same can be said about research on mental health (Smith et al., 1978). Most of the research on mental health has been conducted on white, middle-class samples and generalized to everyone. Yet, as the authors point out, the mental health problems of minority populations are different from the mental health problems of middle-class populations.

Deaux (1976) notes that the early research on achievement motivation was done primarily with males even though the theory of achievement motivation was not restricted to males. The result was that "during all of this rapid period of development . . . the nature of achievement behavior in women remained shrouded in ignorance" (p. 48).

SHARING INFORMATION

Results of research regarding group differences or intergroup relations always have potential applications resulting in practices that can affect people's lives. It is important then that research findings not be misinterpreted. Misinterpretation can especially (though not exclusively) be a problem with those not sophisticated in experimental and statistical methods. For example, generalizations are made to populations not randomly sampled; results are generalized to real life situations without appropriate caution; or within group variation is usually ignored.

Given these potential misuses of research findings, what are the obligations of researchers in reporting the results of their studies? Some argue that social scientists have a moral obligation to guard against misuses of the data. Sue (1981) writes:

> A researcher cannot escape the moral and ethical implications of his/her research and must take responsibility for the outcome of his/her study. He/she should guard against misinterpretations and take into account cultural factors and the limitations of his/her instruments. (p. 20)
>
> Similarly, Rainwater and Pittman (1967) argue: . . . though we do not feel a researcher must avoid telling the truth because it may hurt a group (problems of confidentiality aside) we do believe that he must take this possibility into account in presenting his findings and make every reasonable effort to deny weapons to potential misusers. (p. 362)

However, as is evident to readers of psychology journals, most researchers do not subscribe to this practice. More than likely this is due to fear that a concern for the welfare of a particular group may ultimately lead, in some cases, to a suppression of findings. This would be in direct contradiction to the traditional view of the scientific model whose primary value is the "search for and the report of the truth." Certainly, there are situations in which the obligation to tell the truth and nonmaleficence legitimately conflict and the psychologist faces a true dilemma (see Chapter 7). However, in reporting research findings about group differences, the conflict between truth telling and nonmaleficence is, for the most part, a pseudo-issue.

First of all, as we noted earlier, facts must be presented in some kind of context, both theoretical and cultural, before they have any substantive meaning. Again, to use the classic example, what does it mean to say that, on the average, blacks score 15 IQ points below whites? This statement is really meaningless until we start discussing the meaning of an IQ, different concepts of intelligence, and the validity of the concept of race. Or, take the example where 90 percent of upper-class parents, compared to 70 percent of lower-class parents, prefer a college education for their children (discussed by Ryan, 1971). Is the truth that poor people do not value an education? The great majority (70 percent) do prefer a college education for their children. Maybe not as much relative to the upper-class, but notice that this is a relative statement. Why must the upper-class be the standard of comparison? Besides, maybe this finding really means that 30 percent of the poor are being realistic and 70 percent are delusional. In this example then, what is the social scientist's obligation to report if the sole obligation is to report the truth? The only possible answer is that the social scientist is obligated to report the actual percentages (90 percent and 70 percent) that are in themselves quite meaningless. What may be harmful to the poor in this case is not whether the truth is told but how it is told. Thus, appeals to truth telling cannot be used to escape the responsibility of dealing with the moral implications of the research.

USING KNOWLEDGE

American minorities have, for the most part, a different world view than other groups in society, including psychologists. By this we mean that they have different beliefs, different values, and a different perspective about their position in and their relationship to, the rest of society. It is a world view that stems from life experiences not shared by other groups. It would not be too surprising, then, to find that American minorities have a different perspective about psychological research. As Sue (1981) explained it:

> Many members of ethnic minorities find it difficult to see the relevance or applicability of much research conducted on them. This is especially true when they view the researcher as a laboratory specialist dealing with abstract theoretical ideas rather than with the real human conditions. Much hostility is directed toward the researcher who is perceived in this way. There is a growing feeling among ethnic minorities that research should go beyond the mere explaining of human behavior. Research should contribute to the concerns and betterment of the groups being studied. This concern is not only voiced by minorities, but also by many students, scholars, and the public. (p. 18)

This view is quite different from the traditional position of the psychological establishment (Proshansky, 1972). In addition, even though debates about basic versus applied research have a long history in psychology, many American minorities are taking a more extreme position on this issue than most psychologists (even those with an applied orientation) would espouse. Spokespersons for minority groups are demanding more than just research relevant to their problem whose findings are then simply published in professional journals. They are asking for more direct involvement on the part of social scientists in directly applying psychological knowledge to solve their problems.

On the one hand this may seem like a selfish attitude on the part of minority groups. Traditionally, people are asked to participate in research programs to join the scientist in a common goal: the advancement of science and knowledge about human behavior. Yet, as we said, minorities' perspective of social science has been shaped by their position in society and their life experiences. With a long history of deprivation (economic politically) and always on the lower rung of the economic ladder, furthering the goals of social science is understandably not a high priority among minority individuals. This is not meant as an apology for the attitudes of American minorities. On the contrary, we will argue that what minorities are asking for is an equitable relationship with social science. If anything, the selfishness may be on the part of all scientists who have gone into minority communities, "done their studies, and left—leaving everything the same except their own academic careers" (Couchman, 1973). As Couchman hinted, social scientists are not solely interested in altruistically advancing our knowledge of human behavior. The fact is that researchers obtain many personal gains from their research. They are not simply advancing science, they are also advancing themselves while giving little in return to the people being studied.

Gordon (1973) went so far as to accuse psychology of unethical conduct in its relations with the black community (and the same argument could be made for other minority groups). He wrote:

> Even a casual examination of white psychology as an investigatory business reveals that enormous amounts of information are extracted annually from the black community without adequate explanation, justification, or community-relevant follow-up services. Black people are used indiscriminately as human guinea pigs to further the "scholarly" ambitions and success strivings of white social science. . . . Contracts, grants, degrees, consultantships, publications, tenures, prestigious appointments, careers, and "expert" reputations are carried home to suburbia on the backs of the poor and the black. Under the guise of scholarly detachment and objectivity, social science research has consistently demonstrated an unwillingness to contribute its political leverage, employment potential, energy, skills, and funds to the uplift and long term betterment of the black community. . . . Social scientists have refused to become social *advocates* of the often powerless persons they insist upon studying. (Emphasis in the original, pp. 88–89)

Gordon's charge is exploitation; researchers use the resources of minority populations for their own benefit while giving little if anything, in return. Of course, it can always be argued that sound psychological knowledge about social problems and intergroup behavior will guide policy makers in developing more effective programs to deal with the problems of minorities. One often cited example is the 1954 Supreme Court decision *Brown* v. *the Board of Education* that outlawed segregated classrooms in the United States. In a footnote to the decision the Supreme Court noted some social science research (Clark & Clark, 1947) that documented the possible detrimental effects of segregation on the self-esteem of black children. Although the actual impact of psychological research on the Supreme Court is debatable, there have been some instances when social scientists conducted their research with a commitment towards utilizing research findings for the betterment of powerless groups. A good example of this is the early social-psychological research on prejudice. Brazziell (1973), in writing about the negative attitude towards social science by minority communities commented:

> The nub of the problem is the type of investigator doing race-related research. The old research cadres consisted of men who were staunchly com-

mitted to the concept of human rights and racial justice. These men abhorred racism, recognized its impact on the children in their studies, and built their work on the premise that successful programs to overcome the ravages of bigotry must include the elimination, or at least the harnessing, of bigotry itself. (p. 42)

Lewin's (1948) concept of action research is also very similar to minority groups' vision for social science research. Lewin advocated the involvement of social science in the resolution of social conflicts, not only through the application of existing psychological knowledge, but as a means of developing theories. In other words, building and applying theories go hand in hand.

Still, these have been the exception rather than the rule and, as Deutsch (1975) points out, most psychologists have turned towards the development of theory in laboratory settings with little concern for application.

Outside of social policy, knowledge developed through research can also benefit people through direct services offered by psychologists (therapy and counseling). However, minority individuals are frequently unable to benefit from such services. This underutilization of mental health services results primarily from economic factors (many minority individuals cannot afford such services) and from cultural factors, such as language barriers. It is true that in response to the lack of mental health services available to minorities and the poor a congressional commission on mental health developed the concept of community mental health centers, designed specifically to deal with the mental health problems of minority individuals at little or no cost to the client. Yet, as Albee (1982) points out, less than 5 percent of the total mental budget is spent on community mental health center interventions. Also, in some cases these community mental health centers have not been very responsive to the needs of minority populations (Padilla, Ruiz, & Alvarez, 1975).

In short, psychology can be "used" to benefit individuals in one of two manners: by influencing public policy in the development of social programs and through the use of direct services provided by psychologists. In both cases it can be argued that psychology (psychologists) has benefited more from minority groups than the other way around.

SUMMARY AND CONCLUSIONS

As psychology becomes involved in the study of racial, ethnic, and social groups it cannot remain a neutral observer of the struggle between the dominant and the subordinate groups in our society. In this chapter we have tried to show, specifically, how the activities of psychologists inevitably reflects one set of values (cultural, political) over another and therefore supports either the interests of the dominant or the disadvantaged groups. Furthermore, psychology has shown a clear bias in supporting the interests of the powerful and the status quo, many times in the name of scientific objectivity.

To correct this bias a number of psychologists (Goering & Cummins, 1970; Gordon, 1973; Brazziell, 1973) have proposed several solutions. The one common theme among all of these is collaboration between researcher and minority communities at all levels of research (defining the problem, designing the study and so forth). This would not mean that minority groups would dictate to researchers how to design a study or interpret its findings. It would mean that psychologists would be sensitized to the values implicit in their research, they would be familiar with the interests of minority groups, and minority communities would be protected against exploitation by researchers (Gordon, 1973).

We do not wish to suggest that psychologists simply and automatically take sides with the disadvantaged and the powerless. We do wish to point out that under the guise of scientific objectivity social scientists have often served the interests of the dominant groups and institutions. As a result psychologists should increasingly question the value base of their activities and openly discuss questions of fairness and justice.

11

TESTING

Many people think of two activities in relation to psychologists: therapy and testing. Almost no one in the western world grows up without tests, although most of these are teacher-made and used in the classroom, rather than being created and used by psychologists.

Testing is almost inevitably an emotion-laden topic. First, every test situation reveals us to ourselves (Schafer, 1948). When we unexpectedly get a 95 in biology, or when we discover that we can still roller skate after several years of not doing so, we are pleased; when we fail or fall, we are perturbed. Our reactions to the results of the testing are also revealed in another way: if we are very elated or upset by them, then clearly we cared a great deal—no matter what we may have thought or said before the testing occurred. Questionnaires or other personality tests also produce self-confrontation, as when a testee thinks, while responding to the test material, "I guess I really am weird."

Second, test results are available to at least one other person, the tester, and at times to several or even many other people, as when National Merit finalists are named in a local paper.

Third, testing situations frequently arouse anxiety, sometimes very intense anxiety, as when a semester grade, or a promotion, or a prison placement is at stake. In other words; testing arouses anxiety because the results can have a great impact on our future lives.

Finally, testing situations may arouse anger, typically when it seems that the results will be used in a manner which is unfair to a group of people or to some individual.

Our feelings about tests are thus related to several moral issues which arise in relation to testing. What are the goals of a particular testing situation: who is testing whom, and why? Who, if anyone, will be benefited? Who, if anyone, will be harmed? Is the test valid? Are the testees being coerced? If so, is the coercion justified? Who will know the results? Are tests an example of technology guiding moral (and other) choices—the tail wagging the dog?

THE NATURE OF TESTS

Tests try to do systematically and quantitatively what all of us do informally: observe behavior and draw inferences from the observations. You may try to size up a new acquaintance, or to figure out whether you have what it takes to become a dentist or a teacher or a systems analyst. A graduate school may try to decide whether or not to admit you, or a business whether or not to hire you or in what area to train you.

In some situations, informal observation is accurate and fair enough. If you have ever helped a child to conquer roller skating, you know that every new attempt by the child is both a learning experience and a test situation which permits both of you to gauge the child's progress. Furthermore, it probably enables you to observe the child's responses, both useful and erroneous ones, and this in turn enables you to help the child. Without thinking about it, you were "scoring" the child's "test responses": how long did the child skate before falling or having to grab your arm?

In other situations, such informal procedures simply cannot serve the purpose at hand. There may be too much to observe, with the result that we make errors. Furthermore, in the absence of a formal procedure, our personal biases may intrude themselves. Tests were developed to deal with such problems.

Tests are carefully chosen samples of behavior that are used to make inferences about other behaviors or about traits; more specifically, a test is "an objective and standardized measure of a sample of behavior" (Anastasi, 1976, p. 23). If we put this definition into a moral context, it could be said to stress that everyone should be observed under as nearly identical conditions as can be arranged, and that everyone's test responses should be treated as identically as possible; objectivity and standardization may thus be viewed as *moral ideals* for those who construct and use tests. We would certainly complain about faulty conclusions and unfair practices if John's job performances were observed while he was fresh and energetic, while Doug's were observed when he was exhausted, and then John was promoted on the grounds that he is the better worker. Or again, all of us can recall being angry, perhaps morally outraged, when the teacher's pet kept getting undeserved A's. Tests try to get around these important concerns: people are to be observed under similar conditions; their responses are to be scored without favoritism; and deviations from these ideals are to be reported and considered in the interpretation of the test results.

To give a specific example, we can return to Joe, the child who was being evaluated because of difficulties in school (see Chapter 6). Suppose Joe takes an intelligence test. If the time permitted for work on a particular puzzle is two minutes, then Joe, too, is to be permitted two minutes, not one or three, no matter how the psychologist feels about him. If Joe puts two pieces in upside down, the psychologist is to look up how many points Joe's solution should get, rather than deciding that because Joe is deserving of sympathy, he should get full credit in spite of these errors. The interpretation of Joe's test results will depend in part on more than his answers to test questions. For example, it will be important to note how anxious he was during the testing, since his anxiety may have affected his performance adversely. This sounds more nebulous than it actually is. If Joe was pacing the room during a timed puzzle, for example, or repeatedly berating himself ("I'm just no good at this stuff"), then he was not concentrating on the puzzle as he could have if he were a relaxed, confident child, and his performance will reflect these physical and mental interferences with his work on the puzzle. In other words, the psychologist tries to create a standard testing situation and to score without bias, but cannot always succeed; these facts must be reported and considered along with the facts of Joe's test responses and his scores.

THE PURPOSE OF TESTING

The behaviors and traits measured by psychologists often reflect the concepts and thus the values of our society (see Chapter 5). For example, aptitude and achievement tests are used extensively, a fact which should surprise no one, since our society prizes potential and actual accomplishments. Such accomplishments, furthermore, are admired and rewarded in particular areas and in particular amounts—intelligence rather than kindness, more rather than less intelligence.

The basic purpose of testing is to be able to *compare individuals, or the same individual at different time periods, in behaviors and traits that are of importance in society* (Anastasi, 1976). Such comparisons can be part of pure research, applied research, or application. It is the last context that has received most attention.

Why do we make comparisons? Because these give meaning to our measures (see below), and because we consider them helpful to the goals of accuracy and fairness. Does Mike finally understand long division? Grades of 52, 78, and 96 on three successive long division tests suggest that he does. Which 10 people out of 33 would most benefit from a particular training program? We will try to select the 10 people who are better suited to the program than the other 23. Is it "normal" for a four-year-old to do X?

Not if hardly any four-year-olds do it, but most one-year-olds do. In all these cases, we are making comparisons on traits or behaviors. We are also expressing values: it is good to learn long division; the most (rather than the least) likely to succeed should be chosen for a training program; it is good to be a typical four-year-old, or it is bad if development is "slow."

Comparisons are used for selection, placement, and diagnosis. People may or may not be selected for a training program, they may be placed into French I or French II, or they may be diagnosed as schizophrenic rather than as depressive or normal. In all these uses, predictions are involved. The people selected are the ones expected (predicted) to do best. A placement test shows that Jim resembles those in French I, but that his score is far lower than those going into French II. Severe difficulty or even failure is therefore predicted if Jim were to be placed into French II. Diagnosis resembles placement, since it essentially involves predicting the probable responses to and outcomes of particular "treatments" (hospitalization versus ordinary daily life, instead of French I versus French II).

TESTS AS MEASURES

Test responses can be quantified within one of two perspectives. One involves *comparing each person's performance with some standard*—an ideal or perfect or useful performance. For example, the best possible performance on a classroom test, and therefore the ideal, is 100 percent correct, and each student can be considered in relation to this standard. This standard need not be set at 100 percent, however; for example, a score of 90 percent or better may indicate sufficient mastery to permit success on the next unit of study. On a particular test, an entire class could get 100 percent, or they could all fail.

The second perspective involves *comparing each person's performance with the performances of others*. A particular test may be so difficult that no one ever scores 100 percent, nor did the developers of the test intend them to. Instead, the test will have been constructed so that the scores will range from very low to very high, in order to reveal individual differences. Then, for each person, we will be able to answer the question, How many people do better? Even if Marge only scored 78 percent correct, her score may be among the highest ones, with only 1.2 percent scoring higher. It will *never* be the case that an entire class scores in the top 1 percent—only 1 percent can do that!

Not all tests have right and wrong answers. If the question is "6 × 3 = ?," then 18 is right, 63 is wrong. In contrast, if the question is, "Would you rather go to a party or read a book?" or "Tell a story about this picture," then right and wrong have a different meaning, and the quantification of responses must be different. If a picture shows someone staring into space, for example, then an answer like, "This airplane is going fast" would be startlingly wrong in some sense (for example, in being unrelated to the picture), but most answers would be about the thoughts, ideas, dreams, or wishes of the person pictured, and one story would be as right (related to the picture) as the next one. Similarly, it is not "correct" to prefer parties to books or vice versa. One story or preference, could, however, be better than another *in relation to the nontest behavior* of concern. For example, those who tell happy stories or prefer parties might be more successful salespeople than those who tell sad ones or prefer books. To quantify test responses in these cases, we might use as the standard the maximum number of "good salesperson" responses possible within that test, or we may compare people on the number of "good salesperson" responses they make to the test materials.

Neither of these approaches is better for every situation. For basic skills in elementary school, perhaps we should emphasize the importance of striving for the most complete mastery of which each child is capable. In the best of all possible worlds, most children would eventually score close to 100%. On the other hand, in order to select just a few applicants for some difficult training program, we may want tests that permit us to select the best 12 percent.

Each of these approaches to quantifying scores touches on moral concerns. That test scores often involve comparing testees with each other may be a tragic reflection of society's worst values rather than a virtue. Even if a test could ensure a fair race, why should life be a race at all? Why should our ability to afford dental care depend on how fast we can run, or how well we play the bassoon, or how rapidly we master algebra or calculus in comparison to others? This important criticism refers to the basis on which goods and rewards are distributed in our society, and the use of testing to support the current system of distribution. In their professional role (as distinct from their role as citizens), psychologists could be involved with both of these, especially the second.

Many clients accept the view that "Life is a race" as the basis for a good society, one in which talents and ambition are developed as fully as possible for the good of all, including the testees. Psychologists do not preach this view to reluctant clients, yet their use of comparative scoring (and their use of tests to select "the best") supports this view. Many students seem to share this view; they are quite willing to leave the $300,000 salaries and the Nobel prizes to others, provided only that they, too, can lead middle-class lives.

Just as comparing people to each other can be evaluated, so can scoring each person individually in relation to a standard. In some testing situations, this is the best approach; in others, however, it raises problems. Suppose that a teacher expects everyone in the class to score 85 percent correct or better. In that case, the test may be extremely easy. If so, standards for excellence are perhaps being neglected, and one then hears complaints about lowered standards. On the other hand, if the test is not easy, then the expectation of 85 percent or better may place unreasonble pressures on some students to do what they cannot do. It is true that high expectations communicate "I have faith in you," and such faith may contribute to a student's effort and interest and therefore also achievement. On the other hand, if a student cannot attain a particular level of achievement, even positive expectations can produce anxiety, and such anxiety may interfere with learning. Furthermore, individual differences cannot be eradicated and should not be disguised or hidden by the use of "6 × 3" questions for college students, who will, of course, all get high grades on such a test. We cannot all score 85 percent in Physics 523 or American Literature 562 and easy tests cannot alter that reality, and should not be used to hide it. Nor is it likely that tomorrow everyone will be performing at the level which is the top 1 percent today.

VALIDITY

This is not a book about psychological tests, but test validity must be considered here to clarify questions about morally permissible use of tests. This topic is an outstanding example of something in psychology that is difficult to share with nonpsychologists. In part, this is because it seems obvious and simple to judge a test on the basis of its appearance—to look a test over and then say that it looks like a good test or a poor one. Thus, it seems strange that being able to make designs out of blocks has any bearing on any trait, let alone an important one like intelligence. And how could the perception of ink blots possibly tell anything about personality? Furthermore, the topic of validity is a difficult one because to understand in detail what psychologists do when they validate a test requires an understanding of at least some statistical concepts. In the following presentation the basic rationale of validation will be presented without details, and therefore, without statistics.

A test is valid insofar as it fulfills its purpose. In the present context, this points to an obligation to validate tests and to use only those which are valid for particular groups or situations. This statement parallels, "Do not use broken thermometers," or "Do not use a thermometer to measure height." While this certainly sounds like gratuitous advice, problems actually arise in two areas. First, when do tests fulfill their purpose? In other words, when does an instrument tell temperature? Second, what are morally defensible uses of tests? In other words, when may or should we measure temperature? There is one point of contact between these two: under no circumstances could we defend taking people's temperatures with a broken thermometer. To put it as sharply as possible: either we may or should take people's temperatures under given circumstances, or not. If not, we should not use any thermometer, but if temperatures are to be taken, then we are obligated to seek accurate measurements.

It would probably never occur to you to judge a thermometer on the basis of whether it simply looks to you like something that could give information about body temperature. Similarly, psychologists do not judge the validity of a test by its appearance. Instead, *tests are judged by their observed relationships to nontest behaviors or to traits.* These will be discussed separately.

Assume that workers on a particular job differ from one another in their work-related behaviors (the number of errors per unit; the number of units per hour; the number of absences per month). Suppose management wanted to understand these behaviors in order to change them in a good direction (such as fewer absences), or to hire better people (those less likely to be absent). A test may become part of the information gathering process if scores on it turn out to be related to absenteeism—if, for example, it turns out that the lower the test score, the lower the rate of absenteeism. If a useful degree of relationship is found between scores on a test and absenteeism, then that test will have *predictive validity* for a particular purpose. It could be used as one source of information about job applicants desiring this kind of work because it could be used to predict one work-related behavior. Using the test would then be technically appropriate, even if its materials looked strange to nonpsychologists. We would then have evidence that the thermometer works (it is not broken), and that it measures temperature (not height). This is the basic procedure in test validation; test scores are related to the behaviors of interest: scholastic aptitude test scores are related to grade point averages, personality test scores are related to recidivism rates for those convicted of crimes.

The rationale is somewhat more complicated when traits are to be measured, but the procedures are similar. Basically, we look for several different ways the trait might express itself. One of these is through the test, the others through behaviors outside the test situation. For example, people seem to differ in ability to handle stressful situations. At one extreme are those who bounce back quickly, at the other, those who are easily overwhelmed. Eager to measure this trait, we try to develop a "Coping Test," or a "Coping Score" based on responses to an existing test (for example, the famous ink blots). But what shall we relate to these test scores? We are attempting to measure a *trait,* which means that it ought to reveal itself in several situations—that is what we ordinarily mean when we say that Sue is "friendlier" or "less ambitious" than Ann. Therefore, we will try to find several important expressions of "coping." One very basic expression might be how much time people of a particular age group have spent in a mental hospital in the course of their lives. Another might be recovery from the effects of a major trauma, like the loss of a loved one. In other words, in this case we will seek relationships between test scores and several quite different behaviors, all of which we take to be related to coping.

It should be apparent from these examples that trait validation at its best is a *process of progressive approximation,* and that no measure used is perfectly accurate—nor are the thermometers in our medicine chests. The question will be: do they serve the purpose? All psychological measures and/or inferences are somewhat inaccurate, whether we are talking about how or why someone comes to enter a mental hospital, why someone explodes at work, or why someone gets a particular score on a particular test. Our observations may fluctuate somewhat from one occasion to another. Furthermore, coping is not the only factor involved in any of these, though it may be one factor common to all of them. And that is a matter of interpretation, not measurement.

THE PROBLEM OF TEST NAMES

What a test measures is thus always a matter of interpretation; it is expressed in the name of the test: reading readiness, mechanical aptitude, personality, intelligence, interest, femininity. Since these names refer to characteristics or traits, it is implied that the test has been trait validated, and that all the available data have been interpreted. In fact, this is what it means to say that we know what trait the test measures.

Consider this example. An arithmetic test consists only of word problems, the kind which say, "A man earns $... per year. He spends $... How much does he have left?" In this test, scores will depend not only on arithmetic comprehension, but also on reading skills. We might therefore anticipate that it would turn out to be an arithmetic reasoning test for those who can read at grade level, but not for those with reading difficulties. In other words, the test will be valid only under specified conditions— namely, for those who can read at a certain level. If we wanted to know about the arithmetic comprehension of a child who had arrived two weeks ago from Spain or China, it would be a very poor test to choose: it would be invalid for this child and others in similar circumstances.

Someone might say, "Why don't we use a test that has on it only numbers and universally used signs like +? Surely that would be an arithmetic test for everyone, though somewhat different from the other one." But we can quickly come up with an exception to that statement; for example, a blind child could not display arithmetic achievement on that test. Nonetheless, we are more likely to call the test an arithmetic test than a vision test, because we know what the test measures under specifiable conditions, and therefore will not use the test for blind children. (And as a vision test, it would have its own defects!) Scores on this test express the trait of arithmetic achievement only under certain conditions, but the name does not make this clear; it is simply called an arithmetic test. There is no way around this. The name of a test cannot include a list of conditions under which it works and may be used.

The problem of naming the test, of stating what it measures, is thus a matter of trait validation. The more we know about the conditions under which test scores do express the trait named in the test, the more validly we can use it. We say that thermometers measure temperature even though we all know about the enterprising children who want a day off from school and who therefore rinse their mouths with hot water before their temperatures are taken so that they will seem to have a fever. We all understand what we mean, for everyday purposes, when we say that a thermometer measures body temperatures. We also know that someone who has never used one before must be given full instructions about how to take temperatures correctly—in other words, about the conditions under which valid readings are obtained.

THE PROBLEM OF DEALING WITH INDIVIDUAL EVENTS

You have applied for a job advertised in the newspaper. You soon discover that about 80 people have applied for 12 openings. At that instant, your only concern may well be whether or not you will be one of the 12 hired, but at some other time, you may wonder whether the hiring process will make incorrect judgments (predictions) about some of the 80 applicants. The same situation would prevail if 80 students had applied for 12 openings in a graduate program. Applicant 26 may be totally unqualified— like someone applying for a typist position who types with two fingers. Applicant 57 may be outstanding in every way. And so on. But since all psychological measures are somewhat inaccurate, could it come to pass that you are judged qualified when in fact you are not, or vice versa?

The answer is yes, it could and does happen. It is possible that the applicant ranked 11th is actually not as qualified as the one ranked 14th among these 80. To understand this, consider two people who take their temperatures with ordinary thermometers. One has a temperature of 98.5, the other 98.8. Since these measures are not "dead accurate," it is certainly possible that their (almost identical) scores might be reversed two minutes later. But what if the last person selected had a score of 98.7? Then these people are now experiencing the consequences (one pleasantly, the other unpleasantly) of our inability to measure with total accuracy and our inability to predict any behavior with total accuracy.

No matter how many tests and other sources of information are used, the selection process will almost always choose a few who will fail and/or reject a few who would have succeeded. Our anger is understandable if we are among the rejected ones, as is our inclination to believe firmly that we would have succeeded on the job. *But there is no intent here to harm or be unjust to any particular individual.* Rather, the situation is inevitable because no test is perfectly reliable.

This means that each person's test score is really only one score out of a certain probable range—just like a temperature reading. If you took your temperature three minutes ago and read "98.5," and I take it now and read "98.8," we do not accuse each other of either stupidity or malice; rather, we both think of your current temperature as fluctuating within the normal range, perhaps between 98.5 and 98.9. The reason we are not disturbed by this degree of *unreliability* is simple: for most of our uses of such a thermometer, it does not make any difference what the temperature is within that range. This would be true even if you were trying to decide whether or not to call the doctor; surely 99.8 versus 100.0 would not be the deciding factor!

When tests are used to predict nontest behaviors, however, the situation is different. If people with scores below 70 percent are said to fail, and if you scored 68 percent, your probable range might well be 67–72. You surely did not do as well as someone who scored 95 percent, but it is possible that if you had taken the test two hours later, you would have scored 71.

Notice that the fluctuations are small: a good test is highly reliable. If the test is also valid—if scores on this test are related to job or school performance—then we have every reason to predict that more of those who scored 95 percent will be successful than of those who scored 73 percent; if test scores are completely unrelated to the performance in question, the test should not be used at all. The same is true if the test is low on reliability; what could one possibly do with a thermometer which registered 98.3 now and 104.8 two minutes later?

The fluctuations we have been describing occur also in the nontest performance which we are using to validate the test. Consider classroom grades or grade point average. If John is doing straight A work in a course, he will get an A (we hope!), but if the final will be the deciding factor between an A and a B, then unreliability of the sort we have been discussing will enter in. Yesterday John felt wonderful, but today he does not; yesterday he might have made that A (and a slightly higher grade point average), while today he may get a B (and a slightly lower grade point average).

These unavoidable fluctuations mean that for any group of people, it is very likely that predictions of nontest behavior based on any number of tests and other information will make incorrect decisions for at least some people. This is especially true because if the matter were clear-cut, we would not need a test. You will not make any mistakes at all if you do not hire as translators those people who speak only one language; the only test you needed for that decision was the one which established them as monolingual! On the other hand, if 20 people show up who all seem to be fluent in French, you will find a valid test useful, yet perhaps reject someone who would have done well on the job and hire someone who will not. The test will be useful because it will decrease the number of such mistakes; more correct decisions will be made. But the percent of correct and incorrect decisions is a statistic which pertains to a group, not to a particular person.

MORAL ISSUES: INTRODUCTION

It should be easy to see by now why in application, testing presents moral dilemmas; in fact, we have already mentioned some of these. Whether psychologists like it or not, institutions (schools, prisons, mental hospitals, industries) will continue to compare people to themselves and to others in order to select and place them—to categorize them as in or out of an institution or a program, and to predict that they will do better in this placement than in that one. How should psychologists respond to this reality?

One option is to help institutions to select and place as accurately and fairly as possible. In other words, some psychologists choose to contribute to doing better and more fairly what would otherwise be done more poorly and less fairly. On the other hand, our society is far from perfect, which means that immoral practices have sometimes become institutionalized and legal (for example, "Irish need not apply"). If some psychologists judge the goals or practices of an institution to be immoral, they ought not be in the position of helping someone to do better what they believe they ought not to be done at all! Thus, perhaps these psychologists should refuse to participate in developing selection procedures for industry, and should instead use their skills to further goals they consider morally defensible (reducing unemployment, poor job performance, and low morale). As will be discussed in later sections, psychologists sometimes must either support or change existing values, must serve either institutions or individuals.

Self-Confrontation

Testees confront themselves as they interpret testing procedures and materials in their own ways. This occurs in all contexts, even when tests are used in pure research. Participants may be told truthfully that the research is in its beginning stages, and that the test is only now being developed, so that it cannot give useful information about anyone; they may nonetheless compare their performance to some standard they set for themselves or to the performances of others in the room. In our competi-

tive society, people become ego-involved easily, so that even in pure research on learning, they may worry about their mastery of finger mazes or
nonsense syllables. Personality testing may elicit considerable self-inter-
pretation, much of it incorrect. Psychologists cannot prevent people from
doing this. They can, however, anticipate this very common reaction, and
try to make sure that before people leave, erroneous ideas about themselves have been corrected. The best way to do this is to create a climate in
which people will be free to express themselves and to ask questions about
their concerns.

Informed Consent

In Chapter 4, we explored the concepts important to an understanding
of informed consent. In the present context, this means that testees should
be informed about the nature and purpose of a test; how others, if any, will
be able to obtain the results; what the results will be used for; and the
period of time for which the results will remain on record. To consent
freely means to consider this information in relation to one's needs or
predicament, and then to be able to decide without external coercion
whether or not to take the test. Whenever negative consequences would be
imposed on a testee by someone else, it is appropriate to speak of coercion.
For example, executives being considered for promotion know that if they
refuse to participate in the extensive testing that is often a part of the
evaluation, they will no longer be considered for the promotion; they are
thus being coerced.

Testing has become such an established part of certain situations that
many people accept or approve of such coerced testing, or at least prefer it
to available alternatives. Thus, students know that being absent on the day
of an examination has negative consequences, yet if they agree that
achievement should be evaluated, they may prefer tests to other, possibly
less accurate and more biased methods. Coercive testing seems to be most
accepted when tests seem clearly related to the nontest behavior or the trait
being measured (knowledge of Chemistry I). Achievement testing,
whether in school or industry, is the best example of this. If you were
learning to repair certain machines, it would appear reasonable to you that
your teacher and future employers would want to know how well you are
progressing; in fact, you would want to know this, too, and might even
consider it obligatory for the teacher to give tests. On the other hand,
attitude and other personality testing is less accepted, since it is often
viewed as an invasion of privacy even when the responses bear some
relation to job performance or other nontest behavior. If you were applying
for a bookkeeper position with a private utility company, you might become very angry at questions that ask about your views on private versus
public ownership of utilities. You would probably feel very coerced, as

indeed, you probably would be: if you did not answer these questions, you would not be hired.

Adherence to informed consent is greatest whenever someone comes to a psychologist with a problem and seeks or agrees to testing as part of the search for possible solutions. Within a voluntary clinical-counseling context, clients are likely to be maximally informed and uncoerced. Informed consent is violated when information about the test is deliberately withheld and when refusal to take the test will result in externally imposed negative consequences. In between are the situations in which we agree in advance that periodic coerced testing is preferable to other methods, given the need for evaluation of performance.

Confidentiality

Informed consent is important in relation to confidentiality; basically, test results ought to be held in strictest confidence by testers unless a testee has agreed to sharing them with others. Testees (or their guardians) do this willingly whenever they are convinced that these others will try to be helpful. For example, parents may be eager to have a teacher or a pediatrician know about the results of their child's testing. Testees should never be deceived into believing that the results will be kept confidential when in fact the tester plans to share them with others in a way that identifies the testees. While never is a strong word, it is difficult to even imagine a realistic scenario (whether in research or in application) in which such deceit would be morally justified.

Confidentiality is sometimes violated, perhaps considered not applicable, within certain settings. Within judicial and correctional systems, for example, many testees probably anticipate violations of both informed consent and confidentiality; they may receive little information about the testing, they are coerced into being tested, and they expect the results to be available to many of the people working within those systems. One very basic consideration in such instances is whether or not the tests used are valid under these conditions. Someone accused of a crime may or may not consider it advantageous to try to appear stupid or crazy or out of it. To say the very least, the testing conditions are not standard, and the results will therefore be particularly difficult to interpret.

Confidentiality may also be violated in educational settings, as when teachers or professors post grades for an entire class, identifying each student by name rather than by secret code. Many students, not only those who failed a test or a course, would not agree to this practice if they were asked; they prefer to share their grades selectively (with friends), if at all. Some teachers may argue that this practice benefits students, since it heightens competition and (they hope) embarrasses those who did poorly into working harder. This view is parentalistic, and assumes that it is permissible to inflict pain (embarrassment) on students, either as a punishment or to change their behavior. The practice of publicizing outstanding performances seems acceptable because one assumes that most people would agree to it if asked. Since that assumption may be incorrect, it would be preferable to ask people about it. Test booklets could ask, "If your score is in the top X percent, do you agree to have your name published in the newspaper?

Trait Validation in a Moral Context

While discussing validation, it was pointed out that the name of the test tells us what psychologists believe it measures. Before they can say that this test measures "coping," not "reading," they must do a series of interrelated studies. The slow process of trait validation is a challenging technical and scientific problem; in addition, ideas about what the test measures also impinge on people's lives when the tests are used.

For at least some traits, psychologists cannot completely agree on the meaning of the trait-word before they even begin to construct a test. In these cases, there is usually some basic sense of what the trait-word means, but it is not as clear as "fourth grade arithmetic achievement." Consider "intelligence." Almost everyone has an intuitive feel for this word, but that is unfortunately not enough for creating, evaluating, and using a test. Most of us would not even consider including "hopping on one foot" as an item in an intelligence test for adolescents, but we would soon be arguing about items asking for information about and manipulation of particular objects, words or situations. What we call intelligence is in part a reflection of our values. For example, why is one intelligent insofar as one can learn arithmetic or acquire a large vocabulary, but not insofar as one can create or interpret poetry? Why is one intelligent when one can do various block or picture puzzles but not when one is outstanding at resolving conflicts in the workplace?

Even if we were to give up the word "intelligence," and talk instead about narrower traits like "scholastic aptitude" (the ability to do well in school), we would be left with a fairly long list of conditions under which a vocabulary test, for example, would not validly measure someone's aptitude for acquiring a large and rich vocabulary, and therefore should not be used. It would not measure this aptitude for those who are so anxious that they freeze during testing, nor for those who have never been exposed to the words on the test, nor for those who do not take the test seriously and therefore do not even try. A test is *mis*used whenever interpretations of its scores are based on false assumptions. If we must not assume that a blind child can see the printed page, we also should not assume that one and all have been exposed to words like "derogate" or "exacerbate," or that if they have not been, it was because they made choices in life which were based on and reveal their low intelligence.

It is easy to see that misinterpretations of scores lead to erroneous decisions. A thermometer score of 102.6 has to be interpreted correctly before it can be used correctly, or else a parent may attribute "the virus" to a healthy child who wants to avoid school. Similarly, IQs have to be interpreted correctly, or else we will make serious errors like attributing poor learning aptitude (low intelligence) to many capable children. But the matter does not end there. Not only will such children be described incorrectly, but they will also be placed incorrectly into special classes, educational settings likely to harm them. And that incorrect placement will not even be the only source of harm, for in a society that emphasizes academic achievement as much as ours does, the label attached to the placement will also be damaging. It is bad enough to be categorized and labeled as a low achiever; at least that term refers only to one setting—school. Far worse, are labels related to intelligence (slow, dull, retarded). First, intelligence refers to functioning in so many situations—school, work, even social relationships. Second, some people still believe that "you're born that way"—that an IQ is like eye color. In fact, no test score is fixed like eye color. Finally, intelligence tests seem to measure this unchangeable, innate entity precisely—not in inches or pounds but in scientifically established IQ points. "Low intelligence" is indeed a devastating label!

In the face of these problems, what should psychologists do? Should they perhaps refuse to give tests names, saying instead, "This is Test 37"? That would be a futile effort: surely everyone with any interest at all in Test 37 would want to know what it measures! Better approaches would be to make sure tests are not misused and scores misinterpreted, to point out such errors when they occur, and to continue to educate the public about both the nature of tests and human traits.

The Problem of Bias in Testing

We all have ideas about fairness. One of these is that it is a virtue—that it is morally wrong to treat people unfairly. Another is that fairness and equality are related.

Consider the following example. Ann was hired as a secretary, but Joan was not. Was the decision fair? This question is different from asking, "Did the decision hurt Joan?" It is probable that Joan experienced pain in this situation, not only in the form of damage to her self-esteem, but also because she may still be jobless. No one hurt Joan intentionally, however: no one denied her the job for the purpose of causing her pain.

But was the decision fair? This depends on whether or not we can establish morally relevant differences between those who were selected (hired) and those who were not. If all those taller than 5'9" had been rejected, or if all those with wealthy parents had been hired, we would be morally outraged, but what if the company maintains that it tries to select those most likely to do good work? Difficult questions arise about the meaning of fairness in testing, especially in relation to minority groups, but not only in relation to them. Again, the most basic distinction to be made is between *test validity* and *test use*. The latter should always be of central concern, since we ought not to use (valid) tests in morally wrong ways. But what is morally right and wrong here?

Consider this hypothetical extension of the Ann-Joan example. Scores on the typing tests which they both took are related to (can predict) typing speed and accuracy on the job, and the test is therefore used as one source of information in the hiring of typists. Since it is a typing test, its predictive validity was probably established for women since very few typists are men. Now pretend that the salary for typists has just tripled, and that men are suddenly applying for typing jobs. We do what it seems we should do: we observe the relationship between test scores and job performance for a sample of male typists. Now assume that our data show that the test can serve its intended purpose with men: for them, too, test scores are related to job performance. But assume also that there is another striking finding: overall, men perform more poorly than women on both the test and the job!

What shall we do now? One possibility is to combine the data for men and women, since the test has equal predictive validity for both. This means that companies will hire those with the highest test scores, assuming that these individuals are also courteous and punctual. Most of these will turn out to be women, since women tend to get better scores on this test than men. The companies may want to argue that this is justifiable, given their need for fast and accurate typists and the (validity) information about the test. But men (and social critics) may take a different view: since men have never been encouraged to develop typing skills, and since they may in fact have been ridiculed if they said that they were planning to become typists, it is not surprising that they cannot suddenly compete with women—neither on the test nor on the job. Joan and Ann, on the other hand, are both women; they may even have attended the same secretarial school. (On the other hand, they may not; perhaps Joan could not afford to get such training.)

Notice that the key issue in this example is not predictive validity; were the test useless for men (unable to predict their job performance), nobody would defend its use with male applicants. But once we know that it has as much predictive validity for them as for women, the critical questions are about the uses to which the test is put. We have two basic options: use the test at the request of individuals who are considering becoming typists, or use it at the request of organizations screening applicants. In the first instance, the test is used for the testees, who will decide for themselves, perhaps within the context of vocational counseling, what to do about their particular scores; in the second instance, the test is for the companies, the survival of which is of great importance to their current employees, stockholders, and customers. Because the interests of job applicants and organizations sometimes conflict, these critical questions are far harder to answer than, "Is this test valid?"

This example makes clear that fairness involves

1. Questions about the validity of a test for particular groups and/or situations.
2. Questions about the opportunities of different groups to acquire the behaviors, opinions, and/or skills judged to be good or right both on the test and in the critical nontest situation (job, school).
3. Questions about *conflicting interests:* is the test for the benefit of testees or organizations?

A fourth important factor is the trait or nontest behavior to be measured by the test. Most commonly, several measures are combined for the purpose of selecting those who are most likely to become good students, physicians, machine operators, electricians, or clerical workers. Or perhaps the testing is intended to clarify the (good) personality strengths and (bad) weaknesses of particular clients. In all these instances, choices will be made about what good means in relation to students or electricians or personalities—in other words, in relation to various complex real-life functioning.

Unfortunately, such goodness may be defined with an eye on ease of measurement rather than the complex demands of daily life. Thus, student goodness becomes the grade point average and typist goodness becomes a speed and accuracy measure. Psychologists face a true dilemma here. Everyone knows that "good doctor" is not synonymous with "somebody who gets good grades." To be sure, doctors have to learn a considerable amount of complex material, but on a day-to-day basis, patients look not only for medical knowledge, but also for support, caring, concern, integrity, and honesty. (Thus, we hear bitterness expressed because a physician did not discuss available alternate treatment modes, or dealt coldly, harshly, or condescendingly with an aging person.) The goodness of human personality and human functioning in particular settings is always a complex business. But the more psychologists stress that complexity, the less likely are they to come up with measures against which to check the validity of the tests! Grades in school and lateness on the job do provide such measures, but these give limited information about people; as indices of goodness, they seem simpleminded and incomplete. To state the dilemma sharply: in the absence of measures of important nontest behaviors, the validation process becomes nonquantitative and may even begin to approach, "The test *looks* valid"; on the other hand, the measures typically used tap only a segment (at times an alarmingly small segment) of the complex functioning about which we are actually concerned.

What does this dilemma have to do with fairness? Consider admission to medical school. We could admit those with the highest grades, or we could admit those with a certain necessary grade point average who will also bring medical care to those areas which need it most and will go into family practice instead of an overcrowded specialty. Many charges of unfairness deal with precisely this issue. The main charge here (again) is not that a particular test is not valid for predicting grade point average in medical school, but rather, that the entire selection process is a search for the wrong people, insofar as it rejects those who would be "good doctors" in important ways other than "tops in school." Rejected applicants and social critics claim, in essence, that the selection process unfairly and (unwisely) eliminates far too many of those whom they consider to be the best future doctors. Is it fair that only medical schools decide for all of us what a good doctor is?

Twenty years ago, Banesh Hoffman, a mathematician, attacked multiple choice questions for several reasons, including the following:

> The tests deny the creative person a significant opportunity to demonstrate his creativity, and favor the shrewd and facile candidate over the one who has something of his own to say. They penalize the candidate who perceives subtle points unnoticed by less able people, including the test-makers. (Barnette, 1964, pp. 326–327)

Questions about fairness to minority groups involve these same four factors:

1. Easiest to answer are questions about the predictive validity of a test for a particular group (for example, Hispanics). Thus, statistical analyses of the appropriate data can establish how well or how poorly high school rank in class and/or SAT scores predict freshman grade point averages for each group.

2. Questions about the opportunities of different groups to acquire important test and real-life behaviors provoke some debate, but the basic issues are clear. How much, if any, of the schooling of this or that group is inferior? How much difference does schooling make for the behavior in question? Overall, however, it is clear that minority groups continue to lack equality of opportunity in both education and employment, in part because of the misuse of tests. As a result, a specific score may have different meanings for members of different groups. This was of course the case in the hypothetical example of male applicants for typist positions, and would also be the case if Joan could not afford to go to secretarial school. If Ann could not ride a bike after days of practice and Joan cannot ride on her first try, we know we must not

compare them; we also know that we cannot infer that Joan has "poor potential." It is unjustifiable to ignore these basic points simply because a test is involved.

3. A conflict of interests is often glaring in these cases. A business organization may in essence take the position that its basic obligation is to run a profitable business, and that it can only function as a "social service agency" (which trains the untrained) insofar as such activity does not conflict with its basic obligation. A minority group member may stress that organizations ought to exist to benefit individuals, and that testing should be used only at the request of individuals, and only for their benefit: informed consent and beneficence, or at least nonmaleficence, are as important in this context as in others.

4. Members of minority groups may have conceptions very different from the traditional or majority ones of what makes a good personality or a good lawyer. What is masculinity, and how much of it is good? How much drivenness (ambition)? What is intelligence? What intellectual styles are good in what contexts? Why is freshman grade point average so important? (These questions are explored in greater detail in Chapter 10).

We cannot refuse to face these important questions, nor can we afford to caricature possible answers. No one suggests that those whose only grades were C's and D's should be admitted to graduate school, nor that outstanding talent in one area entitles one to admission in an unrelated graduate program. If only the issues were that simple! Instead, the debates about the moral use of tests involve complex issues that reflect the major problems of society, as do also, inevitably, debates about nuclear energy and scarce medical resources.

So far, this discussion of fairness has alluded to but has not explored the hard-nosed answers to these challenges. Some people might wish to argue as follows. Life is rarely fair to anyone, no matter what the era or background or immediate situation. Joe wants to win the Boston Marathon, but his knees hurt whenever he runs six miles. Arnold has a special fondness for caviar, but he cannot afford to indulge it. Brad was born with a major irremediable physical handicap. Are any of these "fair"? Furthermore, institutions do not care and should not care why anyone can or cannot type fast enough or solve difficult engineering problems; what they do and should care about is that people's special skills be used for their own and others' benefits. It is not fair that Joan cannot afford to go to secretarial school, but we all have problems like that. Joan should accept reality; let her find a job and go to school at night. If she cannot do this because she has less energy than other people, that may not be fair, but it is her problem; she should solve the problems presented by her traits instead of expecting other people to solve them for her.

This view deserves serious analysis and consideration.

1. It is necessary to distinguish between uncontrollable inequities created biologically (Brad's handicap), and controllable ones created by particular social arrangements (some people have annual incomes of $100,000, while others earn $8,000). No one knew Brad would be born with this incurable handicap; either he dies, is killed at birth, or lives with it. Salaries, on the other hand, could be changed.

2. We must try to distinguish among the hardships that different people have. Very few of us, perhaps no one, would vote to give Arnold extra money for caviar; we can only hope that he, too, recognizes the difference between the absence of caviar and the absence of a job.

3. People's problems typically grow out of the interaction of their characteristics and their environment. Thus, Arnold earns $11,000 per year because (for example) particular pay scales exist at this time and because (for example) he has certain skills. At some other time, his skills might be worth much more. Joan's problem therefore should not be attributed only to her traits. (And whether or not she can control her traits is a difficult and complex question we will return to in Part IV.)

4. In what settings, if any, is it justified to consider only an end state (a test score) and not its causes? Suppose a theater group is about to perform, and one of the stars arrives with laryngitis. In that situation, no one will ask about either causes or responsibility; whether or not the star contributed to the development of the laryngitis, the stand-in will play the lead. The others in the group may be very sympathetic and full of advice about cures, but "the show must go on." It is probable that even the star (unhappily) accepts this decision.

Tests are used for selection, placement, and diagnosis in schools, mental hospitals, counseling centers, prisons, the armed services, and industry. Consideration of only an end state (test score) makes no sense at all when the reason for testing is to help the testee. Carleen failed this test; that is a fact. If a training or educational setting is designed to help her, the first question will have to be: Why? She might tell us that she studied and thought she understood the material; then again, she might confess that she had barely studied. Any help that she receives must be keyed to the "diagnosis." When the welfare of an organization is the primary consideration, however, its members may say, "It doesn't matter to us why Carleen failed; it matters only that she did, and that we can find others to fit our needs. If we select people like her, we will function less efficiently, and this is true whether she failed because she becomes very anxious under stress or because she has had little opportunity to learn the skills required by the test. This organization isn't a counseling center, nor is it a school."

Industry is the setting where this view is most firmly entrenched. Whether industry itself can survive with this view is an important question. A provocative book (Mankin, 1978) with a long but revealing title (*Toward a post-industrial psychology: Emerging perspectives on technology, work, education, and leisure*), reviews the assumptions of early industrial psychology. One of these is "a view of the worker as a factor to be manipulated to increase productivity" (p. 5). He calls the emerging view "the humanistic application of technology." It would be easy to substitute "moral" for "humanistic," since this view stresses respect for each human being.

> Technology should be used to serve humanity in general, not just some humans; future generations and not just those interested in their own advantage. . . . Humanistic technology also means that those individuals who are most likely to experience the negative consequences of a particular technology should be able to have some influence over the decisions concerning its implementation. In more general terms, technological change should be subject to human control and not inevitably structure our values, purposes, and behavior to conform to its requirements and function; it should be used as an instrument to increase our influence over our lives and not as a means to dominate them. (Mankin, 1978, pp. 8–9)

Finally, we ask why is a harsh, competitive world, in which each person is an isolated unit ("That's *your* problem") morally superior to a compassionate one in which people are linked by concern for each other?

PSYCHOLOGISTS IN SOCIETY

Some people have argued (Sowell, 1973; Anastasi, 1976) that the same test that seems to contribute to labeling and unfairness can also discover talents where established biases might deny or neglect them. Thus, a timid, impoverished child who never asks or answers questions in school may, to everyone's surprise, achieve far above grade level on a standardized test, and turn out to have an IQ of 127. Surely, then, runs this argument, tests are far more accurate and objective than the casual observations of teachers, employees, or others, and therefore to the advantage of minorities. Sowell is empathetic on this point:

> Moreover, it is precisely the black students who need IQ tests most of all, for it is precisely with black students that alternative methods of spotting intellectual ability have failed. Dr. Martin Jenkins, who has conducted more studies of high-IQ black children than anyone else, has commented on how frequently even children with IQ's of 150 have not been spotted as outstanding by their teachers. My experiences confirm this. A vivid example is a black mother in Los Angeles who asked a teacher if her child had any special ability, and was told: "Mrs. B., David is just average. He will never be anything more than average." Later, when David was tested, his IQ was 155. I have even more painful memories from my own childhood in Harlem, when I was assigned to a class for backward children, and then—a year later, after taking IQ and other tests—was assigned to a class for advanced children. Anyone familiar with the pathetically inadequate counseling available in most ghetto schools will know that the subjective judgments of the staff

are not to be relied on. Here and there, certainly one finds isolated individuals whose sensitivity and experience enable them to make shrewd assessments of children, but a system of selection cannot depend on such rare persons turning up when needed. (Sowell, 1973, p. 37)

As was pointed out earlier, there is merit in this point, which is at the core of test construction and use, and that undoubtedly contributes to our acceptance of tests and testing in our lives. But this point does not deal with some of the criticisms raised in relation to the issues of labeling and fairness. Most critical, perhaps, is the point that an IQ of 127 is good, and the timidity of the child is bad, in the context of society as it is now. The particular skills that make possible the score of 127 are not equally important in all social contexts or settings, and timidity or shyness is not necessarily viewed as a handicap that must be overcome; in fact, in females, such behavior has typically been considered charming, admirable, or even virtuous.

A second point becomes clear if one thinks about the uses to which test scores are put. Sowell reports that he was first placed into a class for below-average children. Almost any teacher would say that ideally, a child's curriculum is related to that child's achievements. Given the constraints of teaching many children, however, and the financial constraints on almost all school systems, such tailoring is available (often grudgingly) only for the children at the extremes; the regular classroom is the mold available for the vast majority of nonextreme children. Ideally, there would be no such mold, since achievement testing reveals each child's individuality; while some children are uniformly average, others are slow to acquire certain skills, quick to acquire others. Since each child is a unique configuration of talents, interests, and skills, the question ought not to be, "Does this child fit into the mold?" but rather, "How can we best help this child to develop her or his talents?"

Psychologists do not always defend society as it is. Psychologists were studying prejudice long before the term *racism* became fashionable, because they viewed it as morally wrong, and because they were therefore looking for ways to decrease or eliminate it. Similarly, psychologists have been in the forefront of ideas, research, and application in the areas of gender role behavior and creativity. In many instances, however, test scores are judged to be good or bad in relation to nontest behavior, and this behavior is usually chosen because of its importance within an existing system. Thus, if those scoring high or in the middle of the range turn out to be the best workers, then high or mid-range scores become "good."

On many occasions, then, our purpose in constructing and using tests reflect and support existing values and institutions. And some of these deserve support! Psychologists must and do judge when to support the status quo, and when it ought to be changed; even those who do not consider such issues in depth reveal in their actions what their positions are.

CONCLUSION

Let us restate the basic point: the purpose of testing is to measure behaviors and traits more accurately and fairly than we would be able to without tests. It is difficult to argue against accuracy and fairness, since both of these are virtues once we grant the desirability of observing or measuring the variable in question. For example, once we decide to reward those people with the lowest rates of absence and lateness, we have a moral obligation to make the relevant observations as accurately and fairly as possible. This statement need not be imposed on the people involved; they themselves are likely to insist on it—with the possible exception of the few who think that they could cheat their way to the reward, and even they might not want to defend what they are thinking of doing as "moral."

The most extreme response to current tests and testing would be the suggestion that we do away with them altogether. This is improbable, of course; in addition, it would be undesirable, since testing in principle represents an effort to be accurate and fair. Although this chapter has explored ethically relevant problems in the use of tests, it is not difficult to characterize morally justified testing: the tests should be valid, and should be used in research and/or at the request of clients and for their benefit. And such testing does exist! Unfortunately, morally problematic testing also continues to exist. The response to this should not be to abandon all testing, but rather, to correct misuses and abuses. This will not be easy, since much of what is wrong with testing reflects what is wrong in society.

Successful technologies seem to have a life of their own; they become a force to be reckoned with. Half of the United States seem to have been paved with asphalt and concrete because cars are so useful, though perhaps the closest analogy may be the excessive use of new medical tests. We sometimes seem to forget why psychological tests were created in the first place. They were created in order to measure important traits and/or behaviors as accurately and impartially as possible. Over time, we begin to act as though we believed that the test exhaustively defined the trait or behavior, though we know that this is not true. High scores on certain tests become so important that we "teach to the test" instead of concerning ourselves with the trait that it was intended to measure. Students sometimes define their learning domains in this way: Will this be on the test? Our infatuation with quantification results in questions like, How long does this paper have to be? Would you take off points if I had an extra page? If I were one page short? Once we have tests for screening professional school applicants, we forget (repress?) the fact that we never came to grips with the fundamental issue of what good professionals are, or if we did, that the test covers only one segment of their significant activity.

Sometimes we seem to be like a family who bought a vacation house because they enjoy being outdoors in that area, but who are now spending all their spare time taking care of the house. One step toward finding a better balance is for testers and testees alike to repeatedly ask and then answer the question, Why am I doing this? The most important steps, however, will continue to involve legal and other challenges to questionable practices.

12

PSYCHOLOGY AND THE LAW

The potential use of psychology in the courtroom has been advocated since the turn of the century (Munsterberg, 1908) and by a number of others since (Burtt, 1931; Kolasa, 1972; Stern, 1939; Toch, 1961). In many ways such use would only seem natural, since many of the assumptions and questions faced by those involved in the legal profession are concerned with human behavior. Consider the following: Are jurors X and Y prejudiced? If so, will it interfere with their ability to evaluate the evidence? Is segregation detrimental to the educational experience of black children? Is a criminal too dangerous to be released on parole? These and other similar questions are faced every day by those in the legal system, and they are questions in which the expertise of psychologists would be useful. In spite of the obvious overlap between the two disciplines, it has only been recently that psychologists and other social scientists have become significantly involved in the courtroom. Three areas in which social sciences are playing an increasingly larger, and controversial, role are those of scientific jury selection, the use of psychologists as expert witnesses, and providing psychological services to prisoners. In this chapter we examine some of the major ethical questions confronting psychologists when they become involved in the judicial system.

JURY SELECTION

Description

While most readers are familiar with the traditional activities of psychologists—doing research and therapy—they are probably not familiar with how social scientists are involved in the jury selection process; a brief description is therefore presented.

The composition of a jury is determined by two selection stages. The first stage involves selecting a pool of prospective jurors from the eligible population to serve for a set period of time. This initial pool, called the venire, is supposed to be representative of the population at large. The selection procedures, however, sometimes results in venires that are not representative of the community. For example, randomly selecting persons from voter registration lists may result in underrepresentation of some ethnic minorities. The involvement of social scientists at this stage has consisted of the use of surveys and statistical methods; the resulting data are then presented by attorneys as evidence that the selection process resulted in an unrepresentative jury pool. The second stage, called the voir dire, consists of questioning the individual jurors about personal biases that may disqualify them from serving in the jury. Attorneys may challenge the seating of a particular juror "for cause," that is, the attorney can try to convince the judge that a particular juror is biased. In addition, attorneys are given a set number of preemptory challenges which they can use to exclude a juror without having to offer any reasons. It is through the use of such challenges that an attorney can significantly affect the final composition of the jury.

Clearly, attorneys try to select jurors who will be favorable to their side and to dismiss those they consider unfavorable. In the past attorneys have relied on their intuitive or common sense knowledge about human behavior to predict how favorable a given juror will be. It is in dealing with this issue that attorneys have begun to use social scientists. By systematically determining the social and psychological characteristics of jurors that are associated with a pro or anti-defendant predisposition, social scientists can determine the favorability of the juror for one side or the other.

Jury Research

The involvement of social scientists in jury selection was, in many ways, a direct outgrowth of the research that social scientists had been conducting on the workings of the jury. As noted in the introduction, many of the questions faced by the legal profession are questions about human behavior. Many of the assumptions the legal profession made about human behavior, however, were based on intuitions and common sense notions about human nature, not on empirical knowledge. One of the assumptions that social scientists have been particularly concerned with is the general competence of juries. Erlanger (1970) points out that most of the research on juries has been an attempt to empirically determine whether juries render judgments based on the evidence and the judge's instructions, or on their own intuitions about the law and other legally irrelevant considerations. The implication is, of course, that such knowledge could be employed by legal professionals to enact changes that could bring about better justice. As Gerbasi, Zuckerman, and Reis (1977) explained: "Such research will facilitate the development of legal methods that in practice are consistent with their original underlying philosophies and will bring us closer to the ideal of blind justice" (p. 343). The underlying idea, then, is that acting with knowledge is superior to actions based on simple intuition.

While the merits of any research enterprise are always subject to debate, most people would argue that bringing us "closer to the ideals of blind justice" is a worthwhile goal to which social scientists should direct their efforts. It is, however, when we delve into specifics that controversies emerge. For starters, we need to have some idea of what is meant by justice (in the judicial context) and how this knowledge is to be used.

In one sense, judicial justice is defined as persons receiving their deserved outcomes: a person who is guilty of committing an unlawful act should be convicted, while an innocent person should be acquitted. However, just who is guilty or innocent is impossible to determine independently. If it were possible there would be no need for trials! But justice is also defined by our notion of what constitutes a fair trial, that is, a set of procedures that will hopefully result in the guilty being convicted and the innocent being acquitted. This includes defining the proper role of the jury and the attorneys. Traditionally there have been two views on what the proper role of the jury is. One view holds that a jury should be impartial: it should put aside its prejudices, evaluate the evidence, and make a decision based solely on the evidence and the law. While this is the most popularly recognized ideal of a jury, there is a second view regarding the jury's proper function. According to Brooks and Doob (1975), a jury can be seen as having the right to ignore the written law if it conflicts with the "notions of justice and fairness prevailing in the community." According to this second perspective, the function of the jury is to serve as the "conscience of the community," and it may therefore choose to ignore a particular law if it deems it unfair. For example, if a defendant is being tried for violation of a law which happens to be unpopular, as gambling laws usually are, it would be "just" to acquit the defendant regardless of how incriminating the evidence is.

The ideal, then is to select a jury that is representative of the community. But does this mean that if a black defendant is being tried in a generally racist community one should strive to select a jury representative of that community, and that it would be fair for such a jury to ignore the evidence and convict the defendant? No, according to this view the jurors may ignore laws they view as unfair, but feelings about the defendant's race are not to enter into the decision. This brings up another point regarding fairness: every defendant should be treated equally regardless of race or any other characteristic that is irrelevant to the question of guilt or innocence. This is consistent with the ethical principle of equality that equals should be treated alike. Since blacks and whites (or any other racial or social classifications) are equal in relation to moral agency, then it follows that they should be treated equally before the law.

Finally, our notion of what constitutes a fair trial is described in the following quote from Cohn and Udolf (1979):

> Our legal system is based on the premise that the best way to arrive at the truth is to have two able advocates for the opposing positions fight it out before an impartial judge or jury. The idea that ours is an adversary system is fundamental to an understanding of the operation of our legal system. Attorneys and prosecutors are not impartial sifters of objective evidence but advocates of particular positions. It is their duty to present their side of the case in the most favorable light possible consistent with the facts and the rules of procedure. Indeed the entire system is based on the supposition that they will do just that. (p. 10)

One implication of this adversary system is that both sides are equally able to present the evidence and their client in a favorable light to the jury. To the extent that one side is more able than the other, then, justice may not be achieved.

Our question now is, how does the participation of social scientists in the jury selection process fit in with these notions of justice and fairness? Let us first take the issue of the proper function of the jury. While the merits and drawbacks of the two points of view can be debated, social scientists could probably help in selecting more impartial and representative juries. However, the adversary nature of the judicial system leads social scientists to abandon the goals of either impartiality or representativeness. As stated above, the system is based on the supposition that each side will do its best to win the case. From the client's perspective, then, the purpose is not to select an impartial or representative jury but one favorable or biased for the client's side. It is reasonable to assume that the "other side" will do the opposite. Thus, unless you do the same, your client may have a jury biased against him/her.

At this point, it is clear that social scientists involved in jury selection have to choose sides. Yet, to openly choose sides in a dispute is foreign to most social scientists, whose training emphasizes an objective search for truth without personal preferences. Our question is: What principle(s) should be used in guiding this decision? The political and personal values of the scientists? Schulman, Shaver, Coleman, Emrich, and Christie (1973) are social scientists who have frequently been involved in jury selection, including the well known Harrisburg Seven trial, in which they worked for the defense. They defended their partisanship as follows:

> Is it ethical, for instance, for social scientists to take sides in a dispute, in negotiations, or in any social interaction? The question has already been answered positively by market researchers, military and industrial psychologists, private political pollsters, and many other social scientists engaged in applied research. But we cannot settle ethical questions by precedent. In the Harrisburg trial, we believed strongly that the defendants' right to presumption of innocence was seriously threatened. The Government chose a conservative location for the trial. J. Edgar Hoover proclaimed the defendants' guilt long before the trial began. William Lynch made public some of the controversial Berrigan-McAlister letters. As in most criminal and political trials, the investigatory and financial resources of the Government far outweighed those of the defendants. And the trial raised a host of constitutional questions, from wire-tapping to conspiracy laws. For these reasons we believed, and still believe, that our partisanship was proper. (p. 84)

It is for similar reasons that Ellison and Buckhout (1981) support the use of scientific jury selection for the defense. The judicial system holds that convicting an innocent person is a greater wrong than letting a guilty one go free. This is reflected in the principle of *presumption of innocence* that places the burden of proof on the prosecution. It is also true that the majority of prospective jurors enter into court with a presumption of guilt and put the burden of proof on the defendant (see Buckhout & Baker, 1977). It could then be argued that the involvement of social scientists can help and has helped to preserve this principle.

Still, a number of criticisms can and have been made regarding scientific jury selection. First of all, while the defendant is entitled to presumption of innocence, justice demands that a jury remain impartial. Suppose, for example, that a Ku Klux Klan member is on trial for murdering a black youth. Would it be fair to have 12 KKK sympathizers sit on the jury? Clearly these jurors would enter the courtroom with a presumption of innocence, but more than that, they would probably acquit the defendant regardless of the evidence. Obviously it would be in the best interests of the defendant to try to select a jury, but it would not be in the best interest of justice. Proponents of scientific jury selection would argue that an able prosecutor would not allow that. While this may be an extreme example, is it not the purpose of scientific jury selection to give one side an advantage?

A second point of controversy deals with the social scientists' right to refuse their services to some defendants. Some trials, especially the highly celebrated and political ones, arouse very strong emotions in people, emotions to which social scientists are also subject, and which may enter into their judgment as to whether or not to get involved in helping a particular defendant. It is conceivable that a social scientist with very liberal political values may have had some personal qualms about getting involved in the defense of, let's say, John Mitchell. And yet, it would be wrong to conclude that some defendants do not have a right to justice or the best possible defense. Again, this would be inconsistent with the principle of equality.

Finally, a related and the most serious, criticism leveled at the use of scientific jury selection is that some defendants will have more access to these services than others and this will amplify the inequities that presently exist in our judicial system. Etzioni (1974) pointed out that the average defendant will not be able to obtain such aid, and therefore only the wealthy or those with a following will have an advantage.

No one can deny that some groups of people, like the wealthy, have greater resources available to them. Because of financial considerations, or the fact that only celebrated cases will come to the attention of the social scientists, these services will most probably only be available to the rich and the celebrated, thus increasing the inequities in the administration of justice.

Saks (1976) acknowledges this and responds that "it does not demonstrate some evil inherent in scientific jury selection. It points, instead, to a fundamental inequity in our courts" (p. 12). He adds:

> The problem lies not in each service and invention but in the system in which these things are used. The critics of scientific jury selection, to keep existing inequities from becoming more pronounced, would keep this new technique out of the courtroom or restructure court proceedings to minimize its potential impact. But, next year or decade they will have to rally again to ban yet another innovation and then another and another after that. I suggest that these energies would be more efficiently directed at reforming the system which fosters all of these inequities. (p. 13)

It is true that social scientists and scientific jury selection did not create these inequities, that they are part of the judicial system and society in general. One could argue that "that's the way things are," that there are and there will always be inequities, and that the services of social scientists, or anyone else, will always be more accessible to some groups of people than to others. To some extent this is being realistic. Because of the distribution of wealth in our society the rich will have, and many argue rightfully so, better homes and better cars. But we need to distinguish between a description of reality and a prescription for justice. There are areas in which inequities should not exist, and one of these is justice. Saks suggests that critics direct their energies at changing the system itself. One reason why social scientists may resist the suggestion is that the legal system is not their province, that the legal system "belongs" to judges and legislators, and it is their responsibility to enact the changes necessary to eliminate the inequities in the system. This argument ignores the fact that by working in the judicial system one becomes part of the system. Furthermore, to work within the system is not to remain value free; it is, rather, to accept the values and practices espoused by that system. As the Task Force on the Role of Psychology in the Criminal Justice System (1978) puts it:

> To accept the criminal and juvenile justice systems on their own terms may be to settle for "first order" or cosmetic, change rather than "second order," or more fundamental, improvement in how we conceptualize the roles and ethics of psychologists. (p. 1102)

At the heart of the matter is the question of the role of social scientists as agents of change in our society. While the traditional role of the social scientists has not been that of a social or political activist, there is no reason why everyone has to follow the traditional model forever. As was pointed out in Part I, the concern of moral reflection is what we ought to do rather than what we actually do. Social science is what social scientists do and they have choices in the matter of what to do. Ring (1971) has proposed a model for a politically active psychology. As he explained it:

> The principal research task of the psychologist would be to investigate how institutions and bureaucracies function, with particular reference to the effects of institutional practices on one's clients. Examples of institutions and bureaucracies that might be profitably studied in this way would include law enforcement agencies such as the police courts, and prisons; schools; the welfare bureaucracy; governmental agencies; the military services; mental institutions; institutions of higher education; and so on. (pp. 8–9)

Furthermore, he points out that "the investigator must see to it that his research is used to help bring about the recommended institutional changes which his work has led him to propose" (p. 12). To be sure, this viewpoint has its detractors (Walker, 1970), who argue that political activism is incompatible with the intellectual objectivity that is necessary to achieve the basic goal of psychology, the understanding of behavior. But if being objective means remaining detached or neutral, then it is a mistake to equate activism with advocacy. Social scientists who are involved with the legal system either accept and serve existing institutional practices or they work to change them. Clearly, it would be impossible to fully debate here the merits of these two professional roles for social scientists. It is our intent, rather, to point out that first, one approach is no more objective than the other, and second, that the question is not only a professional one but also an ethical one.

Gathering Information about Potential Jurors

The process of selecting favorable jurors involves gathering information. Two major methods have been used. One is to select a sample of persons from the community where the trial is to take place and to interview these persons about a number of background characteristics (age, political affiliation) and their attitudes on topics such as justice, the police, and in well-publicized trials, their attitudes toward the defendant. By intercorrelating these measures, the social scientist can then more or less determine the characteristics of a favorable juror. For example, one may find that the ideal favorable juror would be a young, well-educated, highly religious female. The accuracy of this prediction is of course affected by the accuracy of the information obtained from the respondents.

One problem that arises, especially in well-publicized trials, is that if the respondents know that the researcher is working for one side, they may distort their answers or refuse to cooperate altogether. As a result, some social scientists have kept this information from the respondent (Schulman et al., 1973). These investigators admit to having some concerns about this ethical issue, but they defend their practice on the grounds that the interview does not harm the respondent in any way, the respondents should be aware that any information they give could be put to uses that they do not approve of, and the same methods are available to the "other side."

Let us analyze these individually. The first deals with the concept of *harm*. It is true that the respondents are not harmed, in the sense that they do not suffer any physical harm, nor are they subjected to procedures that in themselves are anxiety-provoking or emotionally upsetting. However, this is a very narrow definition of harm. It is conceivable, perhaps even probable, that some persons will become angry, upset, or morally outraged upon finding out that their answers were used for something of which they do not approve. Is this not a form of harm? Besides, as was pointed out in Chapter 6, the end state of the people observed should not be the only morally relevant consideration.

The second reason the authors gave in justifying the deception of the respondents is the following:

> The public should consider that today a person can be interviewed without knowing whether his answers will help elect a candidate that he favors or opposes, promote a product that will help or harm him, design TV programs that will entertain or deceive him, or assist the cause of antiwar activists whose freedom he might like to restrict. (p. 84)

The fact that TV programmers, market researchers, poll takers, and others use deception, however, does not justify its use. Again, we should note the difference between description and prescription. Also, whether the respondent should be aware of possible deception is irrelevant, as it is the obligation of the scientist to inform the respondent.

Finally, the fact that the other side is willing or able to employ the same methods may or may not be relevant, depending upon how it is interpreted. Taken at face value, this argument does not address the researcher's obligation to the respondent. As was pointed out earlier, the fact that someone else will deceive a person does not justify my doing so. However, suppose that our side does not, and that this results in the defendant not receiving a fair trial. If this situation could be anticipated with high probability, then helping the defendant may be a more compelling obligation than telling the truth; however, the social scientist should always consider whether other methods that do not involve deception could result in the same outcome.

A second method of gathering information is through the use of information networks. This consists of obtaining information about prospective jurors through the use of "informants," persons (other than family members) who are in a position to provide information about the prospective jurors (for example, statements that they might have made at a meeting). Schulman, Kairys, Harring, Borona, and Christie (1976) recommended that it is better to inform the prospective jurors of the investigation, since they are likely to find out anyway and feel resentful, therefore prejudicing them against your case. But should this be the only relevant consideration?

One argument that could be made for withholding informed consent is that such information is already part of the public domain and thus should be available to anyone who wants to use it. The critical question here is what is meant by "public." We need to distinguish between obtaining information about a person through direct information and the use of informants. People expect, and rightly so, a certain degree of trust in their interactions with others, and violation of this trust is not something that should be prompted by social scientists. Another problem is that information obtained through this method identifies the prospective jurors and thus violates their privacy. In light of these considerations, informed consent should be mandatory.

A third method, the voir dire, is the traditional manner of obtaining information from prospective jurors. This is the procedure the judicial system has provided for attorneys to question the jurors. In this case the jurors are aware of why they are being questioned and the use to which such information will be put, so the issue of informed consent does not present a problem. Unfortunately, this is also a very unreliable method of obtaining information from jurors. In a voir dire, few people will admit publicly to, for example, racial prejudice. Bush (1976) even presented evidence indicating that in some cases prospective jurors have lied about their prejudices in order to sit in the jury and convict a defendant.

In summary, most of these information-gathering techniques involve some ethically questionable procedures, especially on the issue of informed consent. A deontological moral code would ignore other considerations and say that these procedures are morally wrong. A consequentalist theory would consider the defendant's right to a fair trial, thus making an ethical judgment more problematic. On the one hand a deontological theory seems too inflexible to deal with all the issues involved. On the other hand, it would be too easy to justify an "anything goes" attitude in the name of justice. What the ethically correct approach is should be determined after careful consideration of the moral issues involved in any one case.

EXPERT TESTIMONY

A second role that psychologists are increasingly playing in the legal system is in providing testimony about psychological research findings that are relevant to criminal or civil cases. These cases can range anywhere from a routine rape trial to a Supreme Court case that will determine national legal policy. To most people this may seem a clear-cut, noncontroversial activity free of any ethical dilemma. After all, what could be more straightforward than experts reporting their knowledge? A closer analysis of the question, however, reveals that many ethically-relevant issues are involved. Loftus and Monahan (1980), who have themselves frequently been involved as expert witnesses, pointed out some of the ethical questions faced by psychologists who are asked to present expert testimony, questions that take on great social significance considering the consequences involved.

Questions about the Validity of the Research

Any research finding is only as good as the methodology that produced it. It is not enough to report, for example, that a number of studies have found that intelligence testing of minorities has a detrimental effect on their educational development. There are well designed and bad studies that produce respectively, interpretable and worthless findings. This means that the psychologists serving as witnesses must also evaluate the studies and present only those they consider worthy. Evaluation, however, is a fairly subjective enterprise affected by a number of factors that ideally would not play a role in this process. It should come as no surprise that many times judgments about the validity of a study are affected by whether the findings support a point of view to which the psychologist is intellectually and/or emotionally committed. In the case of presenting expert testimony, this problem is amplified by the fact that the expert witnesses are usually those who have conducted the research themselves. It is clear that when placed in this situation, psychologists would ideally try to put aside their personal and ideological preferences and to evaluate the research on more objective, standard criteria. Although this is much easier said than done, being aware of this bias could help psychologists reduce or eliminate it.

Questions about Presenting Both Sides

In many cases, it is likely that studies on the same question yield different findings. This may not be due so much to the unreliability of social
science data, nor even to the fact that some studies are poorly conducted,
as it is to the fact that different researchers use different methods in collect-
ing their data. There is, for example, more than one way to define intelligence or educational experience. As a result, there is often more than one
reasonable side and the question thus becomes: Do expert witnesses have
an obligation to present both sides of an issue? One position is that they
should present both sides regardless of their own position. Loftus and
Monahan (1980) explained:

> If good, solid evidence exists to support the other position, the expert may
> have an ethical, even if not a legal, obligation to discuss it. In our opinion, *the
> expert who has taken an oath to tell the "whole truth" may have an obligation to bring
> up research evidence that runs counter to the thrust of his or her testimony.* (p. 280)

This view is couched in the traditional model of the objective, disinter-
ested scientist. Some however, disagree (Rivlin, 1973; Wolfgang, 1974).
They would have the psychologist play the role of adversary for a particular position. Their position is based primarily on two arguments. First of
all, they argue that since the judicial system is based on an adversary
system, impartiality has no place in court. Expert witnesses should present
their testimony, and it is then up to the other side to critique the evidence
or present its own supportive evidence. This means, of course, that the
psychologist would consciously ignore findings, not because they are
deemed unworthy, but because they do not support one side of the dispute. This is something that runs contrary to the scientific ideal. The question here, then, is whether one supports the values and methods of the
judicial system or those of science. Whenever one opts for playing the role
of adversary however, one should be up front about it. To present yourself
as an objective witness while playing the role of adversary would be deceitful.

A second argument that is made for the position of psychologist-as-
adversary is that science is not, and cannot be value-free. Thus, to pretend
to be objective in presenting evidence is merely to hide one's biases. As
was pointed out in Section II, social scientists cannot be value-free in
choosing a research problem, nor in the way they conceptualize the problem. However, it may be possible, though not easy, to be complete rather
than selective in reporting research findings. Even Ring (discussed above)
who argued for psychologists to become political advocates, stressed that
psychologists should not ignore research findings unsupportive of their
position.

The Question of Personal Values

There may be times when findings support only one side of a research question and yet the psychologist may be faced with an ethical problem. Loftus and Monahan presented one case in which one of the authors was asked to testify on behalf of a defendant accused of rape, a crime for which it is very difficult to obtain convictions, and the expert testimony would have reduced the chances of a conviction. The author explained her decision as follows:

> In this particular example, the personal dilemma was resolved when she reasoned that although obtaining convictions of actual rapists is of crucial importance, avoiding the mistaken conviction of innocent people is equally important. If the expert testimony serves to make the jurors better able to evaluate the eyewitness testimony so that both of these goals are served, then, in her opinion, justice is improved. (p. 281)

If one believes that every defendant is entitled to have the best evidence presented on his/her behalf, then this reasoning is correct.

The Question of Predictability

Perhaps the most serious ethical problem for psychologists, though, comes when they are asked to testify regarding the dangerousness of individuals. Predictions of the probability of an individual's dangerous behavior are used by the courts to make decisions about bail, parole, involuntary commitment of the mentally ill, and even as a basis for the use of capital punishment (Shah, 1978). In light of the importance of these decisions we would want to be certain that psychologists are accurate in their predictions. Yet, in recent years, the evidence clearly indicates that predictions about dangerous behavior are largely inaccurate, and that the mistakes that occur are mostly due to overprediction—that is, predictions that individuals will be dangerous when in fact they will not be. In part, overprediction results from the way in which psychologists have conceptualized dangerousness. According to Shah (1978), behavior is often viewed as being a reflection of someone's personality—that is, something permanent. Thus, once dangerousness is attributed to the person, dangerous behavior is likely to be overpredicted.

There are other reasons for overprediction, however, more directly relevant to the question of values. In predicting dangerousness, two types of errors can be made: predicting dangerousness when in fact the person is not dangerous, and not predicting dangerousness when the person is truly dangerous. Now consider the consequences of these two errors for the psychologist. In the first case, the person may be incarcerated and the error is likely to go undetected. On the other hand, commission of a violent act by a person who was not judged to be dangerous could have negative consequences for the psychologist. To make judgments that affect the lives of individuals on the basis of personal, professional consequences rather than on factors relevant to a valid prediction is clearly ethically questionable. Yet, that these personal considerations play a role in the prediction of dangerousness has been admitted by psychologists working in the criminal justice system (Clingempeel, Mulvey, & Repucci, 1980).

Another question faced by psychologists has to do, not with professional considerations, but with the consequences of their decisions for the individuals being judged and the community at large. Clearly any kind of error will result in an injustice for the individual being judged, while underprediction may result in a danger to the community. Is there any way to morally balance these two? To a large extent, the answer depends on the purpose of the prediction. For example, overprediction may be more morally justifiable in the case of a prisoner being considered for parole than in the case when a prediction of dangerousness would result in the death sentence. Outside of such general comparative statements, it is clear that there is no one answer to this question.

The problem stems from the fact that, given our present state of knowledge about human behavior, it is impossible to accurately predict dangerousness. The question should then be raised: Why do it at all? When asked to do something that you cannot do, the most obvious answer, as well as the most moral one, would be to refuse. After all, it would be immoral to make decisions affecting the lives of people when such decisions are based on ignorance. However, as some psychologists have pointed out (Clingempeel, et al, 1980), if the courts find it necessary to make these decisions then others, who may be even less qualified (and might therefore make even more incorrect decisions) than psychologists, will make them. While this may be true, the basic question, again, revolves around how psychologists conceptualize their position in the legal system. An alternative would be to take the responsibility for educating those in the system about the limitations of predicting behavior, in this case the prediction of dangerousness, so that they may act in a more enlightened manner.

CONFIDENTIALITY

According to a survey conducted on psychologists working in correctional institutions (Clingempeel et al., 1980), the most frequently mentioned ethical problem was "Who is the client?" and often this problem revolved around the issue of confidentiality. For example, suppose you are a therapist, and while conducting therapy with a prisoner you learn that he or she is involved in smuggling drugs into prison. Should you inform the prison officials? They obviously would want to know, and they are the ones paying for your services. On the other hand, informing the prison officials would constitute a breach of confidentiality to the prisoner, who is the recipient of your services and the person whom you are trying to help. Furthermore, some degree of confidentiality is necessary for any therapy to be successful. Or, to take a more serious example, suppose a prisoner reveals during the course of therapy that he or she is planning to seriously harm or kill another person. It is these types of dilemmas that involve questions concerning the psychologist's loyalties, not only to the prison system and the offender, but to society at large.

One factor that makes these dilemmas very difficult for psychologists is the ability to judge the veracity or validity of the clients' statements. Sometimes people in therapy (or outside therapy) make threats without really meaning them, and the therapist has no adequate way of assessing the real intent of the patient. Yet, this assessment has very important ethical implications. Should the therapist decide to breach confidentiality on the mistaken assumption that the patient intends to carry out the threat, the therapist will have unnecessarily betrayed the trust of the patient. On the other hand, should the therapist wrongly assume that the patient does not plan to actualize the threat, then a person's life may realistically be in danger.

Even assuming that therapists can correctly predict that the patient will carry out a threat, an ethical question remains: should the therapist breach confidentiality and inform on the patient? One argument that can be made for not breaching confidentiality is that the psychologist has made a promise to the patient and promises, ideally, ought not to be broken. Secondly, the client is the person in need of help and the purpose of therapy, as well as the responsibility of the therapist, is to provide such help. Breaching confidentiality would obviously hurt the therapeutic relationship. Therefore, the loyalties of the psychologist should lie with the recipient of the services. Siegel (1977) has even argued that a break of confidentiality is tantamount to a violation of the patients' civil rights. It may also be interesting to note that a survey conducted by the Task Force on the Role of Psychology in the Criminal Justice System (Clingempeel et al., 1980) concluded that psychologists tended to prefer not to break confidentiality. According to the authors: "Their (the psychologists') concern for the potential harm to their clients given a confidentiality breach appeared to overshadow any commitment to law enforcement, punishment, protection of society, or other institutional values" (p. 146). This is not really surprising considering psychologists training, which strongly emphasizes commitment and responsibility to their clients' welfare.

However, not everyone in the profession agrees. The *Ethical Principles of Psychologists* (1981) recommends that confidentiality be breached when there is a clear danger to an individual or to society. The Task Force also agrees that there may be situations when confidentiality may be breached, as, for example, when a "life threatening act is imminent." Shah (1977) argued that even though confidentiality and the patients' welfare is a value central to psychology, psychologists should not demand that society accept their values, especially since the public's safety may be involved. It should also be noted that the California Supreme Court (*Tarasoff* v. *Regents of the University of California*) has ruled that confidentiality must yield in cases where there is the possibility of danger to others.

The overriding question seems to be one of the psychologist's obligations. Clearly, psychologists have obligations to their clients, namely to help them. Psychologists, however, do not practice their trade (therapy, research) in isolation from the rest of society and thus should be sensitive to societal concerns. An absolutist position on the issue of confidentiality ignores the psychologist's obligations to the rest of society and the possible suffering of other individuals. For example, a prisoner who smuggles drugs into prisons may be selling to (and thus hurting) other prisoners, some of whom may also be under treatment. This is not to say that confidentiality should be readily breached but that other obligations should also be taken into account.

One way to avoid this dilemma altogether is to anticipate it and inform people beforehand of the level of confidentiality the therapist is willing to provide. Then, the individual has the choice of what information to reveal to the therapist. Of course, this approach is not without its problems, since when not assured of complete confidentiality, the individual may feel reluctant to disclose information or discuss matters necessary for therapy to be successful. The question of what level of confidentiality to grant to people seems especially problematic for psychologists working in correctional institutions. The reason is that prison officials, as payers of the psychologist's services, may demand a certain degree of access to information disclosed during therapy, information not necessarily critical to anyone's safety but that may pertain to prison regulations or discipline. In this case psychologists have a conflict of loyalties: loyalties to the prison officials who are the payers of their services, and loyalties to the prisoners who are the recipients of the services.

In approaching this problem it may be useful to try to elucidate why this confusion over loyalties arises in the first place. A client is a person who pays for the services offered by a psychologist. Normally, the one who pays for and receives the services is the same person, in which case no conflict takes place. However, on occasion, a person may employ a psychologist to provide services for someone else. Common examples are a parent who employs a psychologist to provide services for a child, or a prison official for prisoners. A psychologist who accepts the terms of such an arrangement should be willing to make some assumptions regarding the relationship between the two parties. The first is that the psychologist recognizes the authority of the paying client to make decisions for the recipient of the services. This authority may be grounded on the incompetence of the recipient (a child) or on the legitimate powers of the state (a prisoner). A psychologist who does not recognize this authority should refuse to participate in this arrangement. A second assumption is that the paying client is acting in the recipient's best interest, thst is, the services are conducted for the benefit of the person who receives them. If this is the case, and if the privilege of confidentiality is a necessary aspect of these services, then the paying client should be willing to accord this privilege to the psychologist. As such, no conflict would take place regarding the psychologist's loyalties because both clients would have the same interest. This point is in agreement with the recommendation of the Task Force which states that the level of confidentiality in criminal justice settings should be the same as the level that exists in voluntary, noninstitutional settings.

SUMMARY

As was pointed out in Part II, when psychologists pursue their scholarly activities of doing research, building theories, and applying their findings, they are confronted with a number of choices with moral implications. When psychologists become involved in systems and institutions with practices and traditions different from those of their disciple, they are faced with additional moral problems. In this chapter we have examined the major ethical problems for those involved in the legal system. The principal factor in such problems is that the values expressed and practiced by the legal system frequently differ from those in psychology. One cannot, under the pretense of "objectivity," accept systems and institutions as they exist, since to do so would be to condone and perpetuate their values and practices. Legal professionals have a conception of the role that psychologists should play in the legal system. Psychologists should realize, however, that they have a choice in defining their role and should recognize the ethical implications of their choice.

PSYCHOLOGY
AND
ETHICS

PART IV

We have focused most of our attention so far on the ways in which the activities of psychologists, as teachers, researchers, counselors, and resource persons are open to moral valuation and inquiry. At the same time, we have made some suggestions about ways in which moral philosophers might profit from reflecting on the contributions of psychologists. It is probably fair to say that both ethicists and psychologists have a tendency to think and work in relative isolation from each other. Most moral philosophers are inclined to think that observations about motivations, feelings, and attitudes are merely psychological features of human conduct that can be safely ignored in deliberations on ethics. Most psychologists, on the other hand, tend to think that value-related issues fall outside the scope of their scientific inquiries and activities. If what we have said so far has any validity at all, then both of these extreme perspectives are mistaken.

We are not claiming that "doing ethics," on the one hand, and "doing psychology," on the other, amount to the same thing. We do not even wish to claim that these two areas ought to be merged into one. Both ethics and psychology are, in their own rights, full-time endeavors, and the uniqueness of each should not be undermined. What we are attempting to show is the pointlessness, if not the impossibility, of doing one in complete isolation from the other. The challenge we are issuing, and hope to make explicit and defend in the following chapters, is a challenge to both psychologists and ethicists. It is the challenge to combine their efforts in working toward a better understanding of human conduct. We will argue against both psychology divorced from ethical reflection and ethics divorced from psychological insights. Ethics and psychology share concepts and hypotheses; both, for example, interpret rationality and human nature. Thus, insights from both disciplines are essential for a more comprehensive approach to understanding human behavior, and for using that understanding wisely.

Any human activity can be viewed from a variety of perspectives or points of view. Something as simple and ordinary as walking in the park can be viewed as a way of getting some exercise, reaching a destination, escaping the pressures of work, protesting an unjust social policy, spending leisure time, engaging in deep reflection, or abandoning someone. How we view a person walking through a park will depend on the total context of the walk and upon our purposes in observing, understanding, and/or evaluating it. Moreover, the moral evaluation we might make of a particular instance of walking through the park depends in large measure on the moral framework we adopt and our knowledge (facts and theories) of human behavior. Let us, therefore, consider the many and various ways in which the ethical and the psychological are integrally related in our understanding of human conduct.

OVERLAPS BETWEEN ETHICS AND PSYCHOLOGY

In this chapter, we explore three widely accepted ways of differentiating between ethics and psychology, show weaknesses in each, and discuss the overlap between these two disciplines. The three possible differences between ethics and psychology are that psychologists try to describe and explain, while ethicists are concerned about evaluation and justification; psychologists deal with nonmoral values, goals, and behaviors, while ethicists deal with moral ones; and that psychologists deal with what transpires within single individuals, while ethicists deal with relationships among individuals. We will deal with each of these in some detail, and as we do so, will attempt to further delineate the field of ethics beyond what was possible in the beginning of this book.

EXPLANATION AND JUSTIFICATION

A good way to begin to see the interactions between psychological and ethical issues is by reflecting on the ways in which we explain and justify human actions. Traditionally, psychology is said to describe and explain, giving the causes of behavior, while ethics is said to consider possible justifications for behavior, evaluating possible reasons for engaging in it. Thus, the ethicist might ask whether lying is justified under particular conditions, while the psychologist might ask for explanations of people's lying under those conditions.

But the distinction is not that clear. If Jim believes that he is morally obligated to do X, then that belief is acting as one cause of his doing X, and is thus part of an explanation. At the same time, an examination of moral obligations and moral justification involves the use of concepts included not only in ethical theories, but also in the explanations of modern psychology—concepts like *excuses, good reasons, rationality, equality,* and *human nature.* While there is something to be said for a division of labor based on the traditional distinction, a deeper examination of the interrelationships between explaining and justifying is clearly needed.

Are Explanations Sufficient Justification?

Suppose we witness a man striking a child. The question, "Why is he hitting the child?" seems to request an explanation of the man's conduct. A possible answer might be, "Because the child has just lied to him again." In contrast, the question, "Should he hit the child?" seems to invite assertions about justification or the lack thereof. Possible responses might be, "Yes, because it would teach the child right from wrong," or "No, because the child's hostility will increase." These tell us that this man's belief was one cause of his action, and what his (good) reasons might be for hitting or not hitting children. He might be saying, for example, "Children should be taught not to lie, and spanking is one good way to teach this."

Giving a correct explanation is usually not the same thing as giving a sufficient justification. The man's belief may be one cause of his actions, but this fact does not justify his trying to teach the child not to lie or his use of corporal punishment. Or to use a different example, it may be correct that she ate dinner because certain physiological processes were occurring within her, or because it was 6:00 P.M., but to justify her action, we must shift perspective, and explore the question, "Under what circumstances, if any, should we eat when hungry or at a certain time?"

While explanations are not sufficient justifications, these often overlap. Our everyday explanations of behavior often imply moral values, something we pointed out earlier about psychologists' explanations of behavior, too. In the domain of human action, it is difficult, perhaps impossible, to explain without assuming or implying values, and the question "Why?" often refers to both. When people ask a question like, "Why is he hitting the child?", they are in part looking for causes, in part for justification. They understand from the answer, "Because the child just lied to him again" both what triggered (caused) his action and that he would (probably) justify it by referring to his obligation to teach the child not to lie. Notice that justifications may include assumptions or statements about cause-and-effect relationships (for example, "Spanking causes children to change their ideas and/or behavior"), but in addition, they always assume or state what is good, what ought to be ("Children should tell the truth"; "Parents should teach their children").

What Explanation and Justification Share

It is possible to challenge both explanations and justifications. If you were certain that the child had not lied, for example, you would search for other explanations of the man's behavior: "He is becoming more and more paranoid," or "He is constantly losing control of himself and then offering excuses." Perhaps you do not believe that spanking is a good teaching technique, because it does not produce the desired result, or because you oppose corporal punishment on moral grounds. Finally, perhaps someone believes that in a rotten world, children should learn lying, not truth telling, as a survival technique.

Clearly, some procedures are needed for establishing the validity or worth of various claims in both psychology and ethics. All the above examples involve preliminary *definitions, observations, reasoning, and interpretation in overlapping domains.* Whether or not the man is paranoid or making excuses will not be as simple to establish as whether or not he is wearing a sweater. Clear definitions will be harder to come by, it will be harder to specify what the relevant observations are, and the values will be harder to articulate, though there seems to be wide agreement that paranoia is "sick" or "dysfunctional." If he falsely believes that his wife is poisoning him, it will be relatively simple, but what if he worries about foreign agents, conspiracies, or "my enemies"? Similarly, it will not be easy to specify when a statement is only an excuse or rationalization, though these have to be distinguished from good reasons in both ethics and psychology.

Defining, observing, reasoning, and interpreting will also be involved in arguing that telling the truth is a better moral ideal than telling lies. Although this seems to involve only ethics, notice that the distinction between lying and truth telling involves psychological concepts. For example, if the man were paranoid, he might be telling the truth as he sees it, and not intentionally trying to mislead anyone. The distinction between these is psychological in nature: did he intend to deceive anyone or not? Furthermore, the concept of paranoia raises questions about whether or not the man could do otherwise. Thus, as we explain, we include value judgments; as we evaluate, we include psychological concepts.

What Do We Explain? Justify?

It is instructive that we usually do not ask for justifications of physical events (a flat tire), only for explanations of them. To be sure, many people try to give meaning to floods or bountiful harvests, notably by referring to punishments or rewards given by God. But when people ask someone to justify the hitting of a child, they ordinarily believe that this act may or may not be justifiable, that both are possible. Furthermore, people do not ask this question about all human actions, but only about those which are intentional. Thus, if someone accidentally steps on your foot, you do not normally think that this action needs justification. On the other hand, if someone deliberately steps on your foot, you may assume that this person could have chosen not to, and you may think or say, "How dare you?", or "Who do you think you are?", or "What gives you the right?" But whether the act was accidental or deliberate, we might seek an explanation.

The concepts *accidental, deliberate,* and *intentional* are of major importance in both ethics and psychology, as well as in the field of law. When is an action "deliberate"? Since the time of Freud, we all smile knowingly at the expression "accidentally on purpose": is anything an accident? Should you after all ask the person who accidentally stepped on your foot to justify that action? If all our actions have causes, can we ever be held responsible for them? We will return to these questions in Chapter 15.

Value-Free Explanation

We saw earlier that in their efforts to give value-free explanations of behavior, psychologists may try to bypass moral values altogether. At times, the resulting explanations unfortunately sound as though they were excusing the behavior (although this is not and should not be their purpose). Consider a familiar example: the delinquent stole because . . . We then hear a sad life story, involving a broken home or even abandonment, poor schooling, and run-down neighborhoods. In the light of the child's burdens, how can we sit in judgment? In fact, the impact of the life history may be to make us feel guilty for judging; we may be sensitive enough to recognize ourselves in this other. The often-repeated, "There but for the grace of God go I" captures this: under the same circumstances, I might or would have stolen, too. How, then, we may be tempted to say, can we sit in judgment, as it were, and say that the stealing is bad?

First, we cannot help but make such judgments, or we would be unable to decide what to do next: should we encourage the child not to steal, or to steal more?

Second, it is important to remember that we are not judging a person, but rather, a particular action. We certainly need not, in fact should not, talk about "that rotten kid"; rather, we may conclude that stealing is or is not justified under those conditions.

Third, one can be sympathetic to someone's plight, including one's own, and yet disapprove of something that person did. Our hearts may go out to certain children and yet we are not forced to condone or support their stealing—nor, it is important to stress, the unfortunate circumstances of their lives.

Thus, in psychology and in daily life, both explanations and evaluations are necessary, and this is worth stating again, even though explanations and evaluations will in any case overlap and influence each other. Although psychological explanations often imply values, it is easy to get the impressions that they do not, or even that they seem to excuse almost any behavior. Two factors seem to be involved in this.

First, there are cases in which people want explicit statements about the values that are involved, but do not get them. As was pointed out above, when we ask, "Why?", we are often seeking both explanation and justification. It is unfortunate that some psychologists continue to think that their concepts are value-free, but this certainly does not mean that psychologists excuse or approve of anything and everything. An explanation for one person's torturing another does not mean that psychologists have no opinion about torture merely because they do not state it. In fact, it is probable that the explanation will include value-laden terms related to mental illness, or to an unhealthy environment, and that recommendations will be made about how to eliminate such behavior, not how to increase it. Causes apart, psychologists are no more likely than anyone else to condone torture. There would be less misunderstanding on this point if psychologists were explicit about their values.

Second, there are cases in which the explanation implies or states that people are not responsible for their actions. It is as though no distinction were being made between intended (deliberate) and unintended (accidental) actions, or between being in control of oneself and being out of control ("blind with rage"). Suppose we asked, "Why did June do X?," and received the answer, "Because she has been rewarded many times in the past for doing X." If her actions were not her under control, we might conclude that she is not responsible for them, but past rewards do not imply a present inability to choose between doing X and not doing X. Even though June has been praised in the past for doing X, she could still decide not to do X now, perhaps on the grounds that this would be the more moral choice. Therefore, we are still likely to develop some ideas about whether or not her actions are justifiable, regardless of how often they were rewarded in the past. This example, too, raises questions about concepts that are relevant to both ethics and psychology: moral agency, intention, responsibility, and determinism. Some of these have been discussed earlier; we will return to them in Chapter 15.

Two Kinds of Explanation

Both psychologists and lay people offer two kinds of explanations. These tell what in the past contributes to the present actions, and to what end or purpose the person is engaged in these actions. "Because she has been rewarded in the past," is an example of the first kind, while, "In order to earn money," would be an example of the second kind. Both kinds are subject to moral scrutiny. This point was already made above in relation to June's past rewards. It is equally true of the second kind of explanation, since both purposes and the means for achieving them are subject to moral scrutiny. Suppose that someone explains an action by saying, "I lied in court in order to get this innocent person, whom I hate, imprisoned." That may or may not be a correct explanation (second kind), but it seems clear that both the purpose and the means of reaching it are morally unjustified. When people or psychologists give reasons for actions, we can still ask, "But are those good reasons—that is, reasons which justify the action?"

In Conclusion

The interplay of explanation and justification shows how the perspectives of the psychologist and the ethicist overlap. Together, they offer a more complete and coherent account of everyday activities than separately. Both the psychologist who tries to explain behavior in morally neutral terms and the ethicist who tries to justify judgments about the moral rightness or wrongness of an action independent of any psychological considerations are denying the inevitable overlap of their two disciplines. Furthermore, they are bound to overlook some vitally important features of the activity in question, and some ideas that will prove helpful in their respective disciplines.

MORAL AND NONMORAL

A second attempt to establish an absolute division between psychology and ethics involves saying that the psychologist is only interested in nonmoral values, goals, and actions, the ethicist only in morally relevant ones. At the same time, ethicists might say that only moral reasons count when one is reasoning about ethical issues.

If what we have been saying is correct, however, then it is probably impossible to divide values, goals, and actions into two categories, the morally relevant and the morally nonrelevant. Let us return to that walk in the park. Shall we say that sometimes that walk has nothing to do with morality (when one walks to exercise), while at other times it does (when one walks away from someone)? This seems to us to be an indefensible distinction. Instead, our position is that it is better to consider moral scrutiny as one single, important frame of reference or perspective, and that we may view any goal or value or action from that vantage point. We must therefore ask what this frame of reference is—in other words, to what does "moral scrutiny" refer?

Consider this example. A shopper, admiring a particular sweater, knows that one can obtain sweaters in a store by either buying or stealing them; the shopper also knows the consequences of each act. In the end, the shopper has to make a choice: buy the sweater, steal it, or leave the store without it.

From the point of view of "what achieves what," the shopper and we can probably answer some factual questions like how to obtain sweaters and what happens to those caught shoplifting. But this is not the only perspective possible; we can also subject the shopper's choice to moral scrutiny. We are in the moral domain when someone's actions affect others in certain ways (to be specified below) and the person is aware of this fact, and when that person could physically and psychologically have done otherwise. The shopper's actions affect others, and the shopper knows this; furthermore, the action taken is the result of a choice. We may even consider breathing behavior from this perspective. You know that when you exhale, you affect the air around you. If you were just starting a cold, you could not stop exhaling, but you could choose to be very careful about breathing on others, in an effort to keep them from catching your cold.

The Last Survivor

Thus, our moral concerns grow out of our interactions with other living beings. Imagine for a moment that you are the only survivor on earth: all other human and animal life has died. Under these circumstances, could you do anything immoral? Would using up natural resources be immoral? Burning great works of art? Drugging yourself with heroin or alcohol? Committing suicide?

Some theorists (for instance, Kant) have argued that we have *duties to ourselves*, but there are problems with this idea. A duty or obligation is something owed, not unlike a financial debt. And just as we are not at liberty to declare that we have no debt to someone from whom we have borrowed money, we are not at liberty to simply declare that we have no duties or obligations to others (if, for example, we have made a promise). At the same time, consider how odd it seems to say that we owe ourselves money. Can we really borrow money from ourselves in anything but a figurative sense in which we "borrow" from our savings account? If we can declare that we do not have to pay back the money (as we do not have to when we borrow from ourselves), then we do not have a genuine debt. Only the lender can forgive the debt. When we borrow from ourselves, the lender and the borrower are one and the same person. Hence, we cannot have a genuine indebtedness to ourselves. By a parallel line of reasoning, we can say that there are no genuine moral duties or obligations to oneself (Singer, 1959). Morality, then, involves others.

Another way to look at duties to oneself is to see them as means to chosen ends. For example, if you said, "I owe it to myself to eat well-balanced meals," you would mean, "If I want to remain healthy, I should eat well-balanced meals." But the question that arises for the hypothetical last survivor is, "Am I morally obligated to try to remain healthy?" Would it make any sense for this person to think, "I owe it to myself to remain healthy, to remain alive"?

In the case of the last survivor, it could be argued that there is a moral obligation to do and not do certain things because of the commandments of God. But this situation is covered by the extension of the term "others" to all "others," including whatever living entities we might think exist. In other words, as long as God exists, the last survivor is not the last one after all.

For nontheists, the last surviving human may only have obligations to animal life and perhaps even to vegetative life, but if these have also been extinguished, then the last survivor's moral duties and obligations are indeed minimal, if not totally nonexistent. This is at least part of what it means to say that *ethics can be described as the discipline which deals with any one person's interests in relation to the interests of others.* The last survivor case is quite hypothetical, but it helps us to see what ethics deals with, and this, in turn, forces us to ask *which interests* (survival, well being, happiness) and *which others* (humans, other mammals, insects, plants, marine life) should be considered when we decide on the rightness or wrongness of our actions and the good or evil they might produce.

A Definition of Morality

Gewirth (1978) has offered the following definition of morality, which includes the above considerations: "a morality is a set of categorically obligatory requirements for action that are addressed at least in part to every actual or prospective agent, and that are concerned with furthering the interests, especially the most important interests, of persons and recipients other than or in addition to the agent or the speaker." (p. 1)

It may seem at first glance that this definition severely limits the domain that can be viewed from the perspective of ethics, but in fact, it does not. Much of what we do alone and privately is "social behavior" involving past or present others, and represents a choice among socially important alternatives. We watch John taking that walk in the park. What has that to do with the above definition? John has chosen to walk for pleasure or to think about apologizing to someone; he might instead be peeling the dinner potatoes or mowing the lawn or cheering up a depressed friend. He may be alone at this time, but his behavior is nonetheless socially embedded, and under some circumstances, we might judge his decision to keep walking rather harshly (if, for example, someone were screaming for help after an accident). Thus, we can subject John's taking a walk to moral scrutiny. That does not mean that this activity will be condemned, but only that it is appropriate to ask certain questions about it.

In Conclusion

Acts, values, and goals are not easily divided into the morally relevant and the morally nonrelevant. Rather, to take the moral perspective is to ask certain questions rather than or in addition to others: "Should John be walking right now?" rather than or in addition to, "What else is John doing as he walks?", or "Why does John prefer walking to lying down?" If the division between moral and nonmoral acts, values, and goals is not as sharp as it is often thought to be, it would seem that an absolute differentiation between ethics and psychology cannot be based on that distinction.

CONFLICTS OF INTEREST

A third distinction between the concerns of the psychologist and those of the ethicist has to do with the way each deals with human interests and the conflicts that frequently occur between any two such interests. The word *interest*, in the sense of something being in someone's interest, is close in meaning to *benefit*. "This is or isn't in your interest," means much the same as, "This is or isn't to your benefit."

It could be argued that psychologists are exclusively concerned with conflicts of interest within the individual (intrapsychic motives and cognitions), whereas conflicts among individuals are dealt with by ethicists, lawyers, and political scientists. But here again, the matter is not quite so simple.

Psychology's Stress on the Individual

In recent years, some psychologists (Pepitone, 1981; Sampson, 1982) have argued that psychologists study events (physiological and/or psychological) which mainly occur inside the individual, and that this is wrong. These critiques involve three related points. First, psychologists stress insufficiently or omit important human realities. We are all socially embedded, and therefore one cannot understand what is inside the person without understanding what is outside (social institutions and rules). Furthermore, many important activities (cooperating and helping, to name just two) are by their very nature inter (rather than intra) personal, and therefore, psychologists distort their nature by looking at one person's motives or cognitions at a time. Finally, critics argue that studying the person rather than the-person-in-a-social-context makes psychologists perpetuators of the status quo, in that they think about attitude or personality change rather than or in addition to social change. While some of these critiques are overstated (Is everyone who studies the effects of drugs on emotions really an ideological conservative and potential fascist?), they make the important point that an exclusively intraindividual psychology would be unsatisfactory from the points of view of both psychology and ethics. And in fact, psychology is not as intraindividual as these critics imply. Social psychology in particular has always emphasized the causal potency of the immediate social environment, including of course what other people present say and do. "Conflict of interests" is not the expression social psychologists use most often, but prejudice, discrimination, cooperation and resolution of intergroup conflicts are traditional areas within social psychology. Thus, while some psychologists do and should concern themselves mainly with intraindividual processes, this is certainly not true of all of them.

What Interests?

Both ethics and psychology, then, deal with conflicts of interests, and the most basic question therefore is, "*What* interests conflict as people live together?" The ones most commonly mentioned seem to be related to the important but nebulous concept of happiness, and several are psychological in nature: gratification, pleasure, avoidance of pain; freedom, liberty; health, well being, welfare; wealth; fame; reputation; self-respect; survival of the individual.

A conflict of interests often occurs within one person, and is often morally relevant, though, as was pointed out above, only insofar as it impinges on others. If you were the last surviving human being, you might find that doing X had both benefits and costs for you (it might get you something you want, but it would also exhaust you); it is not clear, however, that this inner conflict about whether or not to do X would be morally relevant. In many, probably most, real life situations, however, inner conflict is morally relevant, since each of the conflicting interests is probably socially embedded. (This is probably one reason why the field of social psychology keeps expanding, to the point that it seems to encompass most of psychology.)

A conflict of interests between or among people is morally relevant by definition. We see such conflicts when two individuals express incompatible needs or goals (I want to take a short cut across your property, but you do not want me to). Such conflicts can also occur between individual needs or goals and group rules, as when a child wants to hit someone but has learned the rule that we should not hit others. Notice that what appear to be private, individual conflicts are often actually embedded in social rules; for example, we may want to get even with someone in a nasty fashion, yet believe that we would and should feel guilty if we did, because we have internalized certain moral rules.

How Do We Know What Is in Anyone's Interest?

Since the concept *interests* is so important in Gewirth's definition of morality, we have to ask how we know about people's interests. In fact, to answer this question, we have to become amateur natural and social scientists, especially psychologists. The subjective approach relies on our verbalizations; thus, I may say that soda and potato chips give me pleasure, so that it is "in my interest" to consume them. The objective approach relies on facts; thus, these foods are in fact enjoyed by many people, but they are also in fact junk foods, the excessive consumption of which increases the probability of damaging one's health—and so it is not in anyone's interest to enjoy them too often.

Two points must be considered in this context. First, it is not always easy to establish what the facts are. At times, as in the matter of foods, science can supply the needed information, but not always. Suppose that it is a question of "pleasant" music. What do we know about people's musical preferences and about the actual effects of their choices in music?

Second, even when facts are available, the conflict of interests may involve questions of priorities, which represent the different subjective rankings of different people. Suppose two people accept the facts about soda and potato chips. One may say, "It is in my interest to eat them because I choose food more on the basis of what gives me pleasure now than on the basis of what may happen 10 years from now." In contrast, the other may say, "It is in my interest to put later health ahead of current pleasures." Such prioritizing is not based on facts alone.

Who Decides?

If several competent adults come to different decisions, can we judge some decisions to be morally superior to others? In part, this depends on our conception of *competent* (another concept important in both ethics and psychology). For example, if someone were to say first, "I enjoy life and want to go on living," and then, "I want to eat this poisonous mushroom because I enjoy new foods," we would not be struck by that person's priorities, but rather, by the contradictory nature of the stated interests. In other words, we would question the person's rationality, and might even consider treating the person parentalistically: we will not let you eat the mushroom, no matter what you say.

When adults are competent, or at least are not incompetent, perhaps each person's decisions should be respected, no matter how preposterous they seem to others. To return to the junk food example, if both are competent, perhaps the best they can do is to respect each other's decision: one will eat potato chips, the other will not.

But morality, as was pointed out earlier, deals with socially embedded interests; the fact is that each of us is not the last surviving human being! Suppose that Jerry keeps eating salty snacks, develops high blood pressure that remains undetected because he does not have it checked, and finally has a stroke. He is now suffering, and in addition, may be causing others to suffer: his family, friends, and perhaps the many (other) taxpayers who contribute to his medical care if he cannot pay for it fully. Why others are suffering is an important consideration. They may be concerned mainly about Jerry—about his health or even survival. On the other hand, they may be concerned mainly about themselves—about their disappointment or embarrassment. In any case, these others are probably also finding it in their interest to engage in various behaviors which increase the probability of later illness, and we may all have a mutual (if only partly explicit) agreement to care for each other if and when our assorted excesses catch up with us. But if not, others may have good reasons both to respect our decisions about junk food and not to respect them.

If most of our interests are socially embedded, and if it is not possible to isolate either purely moral or purely nonmoral aspects of human behavior, then it would seem that both the psychologist and the ethicist are destined to enter the same arena. Far from providing a basis for separating the two disciplines, our analysis of the nature of human interests seems only to bring these disciplines closer together.

CONCLUSION

We have argued that differences between explanation and justification, between moral and nonmoral values, goals, and actions, and between individual versus socially embedded interests do not completely divide the activities of psychologists from those of ethicists. On the contrary, these overlap considerably and therefore, the effort to understand human conduct calls for the combined efforts of these two disciplines. We will now show how such cooperation might clarify our thoughts about human conduct.

14

MORAL PRINCIPLES
AND ORIENTATIONS

The activities of psychologists from the ethicist's perspective have been discussed in earlier chapters. In the following pages, we reverse: we discuss "doing ethics" from a psychological perspective. While doing so, we consider the nature and functions of moral principles, as well as the significance of approaches to human nature. Ultimately, this will lead to questions about such issues as validating moral principles and the nature of moral relativism.

In his *Essays in Common-Sense Philosophy* (1920), C. E. M. Joad argues that

> the sort of creed you hold, the philosophic school you belong to, the view you take in purely intellectual matters, is to some extent conditioned by your character as a whole, and by your general outlook on life intellectual, emotional, and instinctive. (p. 221)

Joad maintains that the influence of temperament and character on our intellectual processes is considerable, and that this influence should not be discounted when evaluating the positions or theories people embrace. All too often, in both moral philosophy and in psychology, we tend to disregard, view negatively, or be suspicious of the close connections between the intellectual and the emotional. Character conditions beliefs, and this psychological truth cannot be neglected. On the other hand, we still need to evaluate the beliefs per se, as is true in any other area (art, science), where beliefs and/or tastes are also expressive of personality.

An example of a particularly sharp division between the conceptual and the emotional occurs in relation to suicide. Moral philosophers tend to focus on the rationality and justification of suicide, while psychologists tend to emphasize the impulsive, depressive, or ambivalent emotional state of the suicidal person.

To counter this trend, Motto (1972), a psychiatrist, takes great pains to point out the importance of taking the intellectual or rational elements into consideration. To deal with suicide as either a purely emotional or a purely intellectual problem would be a mistake. In the following pages, we show how the intellectual and the emotional aspects of our personalities are interrelated and jointly significant not in suicide, but in "doing ethics."

COMMONSENSE BELIEFS

Most people have commonsense psychologies and philosophies that are, to some extent, related to the professional varieties. Ethics often deals in a systematic way with moral intuitions and gut reactions. For example, most people strongly reject torture. If, hypothetically, a psychologist said that torture was approved more by those at "higher" stages of moral development than those at "lower" stages, we would probably question those moral stages rather than incorporating this research result into our thinking. If an ethical theory led to the conclusion that torture was rarely wrong morally, we would similarly question the theory. This example illustrates that we all bring strong gut reactions, moral intuitions, and commonsense beliefs to our formal study of ethics and the psychology of moral behavior and beliefs, reactions which we do not, and perhaps should not, easily give up.

Our commonsense views must be right or workable for us in some way, or we would modify them; they help us to deal with our daily lives by providing answers to problems (how to vote or to react to job pressures), and by permitting us to maintain workable relationships with others (harmony, silent disagreement, argument). Nonetheless, we learn at an early age that we might be wrong, since many views exist on any topic, and the moral domain is certainly no exception! How can we evaluate the many opinions we hear about abortion, capital punishment, euthanasia, or about whether our company should have become involved in a particular business transaction? Whose views are morally right, and why? More specifically, are psychologists and philosophers different from others, so that their views are better than the commonsense views of others?

WHY MORAL PRINCIPLES, AND WHOSE?

Most adults are capable, at least occasionally, of thinking about themselves as they would think about someone else, or "objectively." For example, Mark may be unable to shake a particular prejudice, yet he may also be able to recognize it as such. This tells us that although Mark still has a certain gut reaction, a belief that still sometimes seems commonsense to him, he also has evaluated it and judged it wrong; he would not, for example, deliberately teach it to his children, and might, in fact, teach them the very opposite.

This objectivity, of which most of us are capable, has been refined and developed by philosophers and psychologists in different ways, and is what makes their approaches and ideas somewhat different from those of others. They are neither more nor less moral in their actions than others, nor have they found The One True Morality; they, too, disagree with one another about abortion and other issues. But, in their professional capacities, they can approach moral ideals more systematically and impersonally than most people are able to under the pressures of their daily lives. For example, most of us have views about lying; examples would be, "I don't lie unless I have to," and "You should never tell a lie." A moral philosopher would point out that we are far less likely to say "I never tell the truth unless I have to," and would then explore truth telling as a moral ideal. A philosopher would also discuss the issue of absolutes ("never"). In fact, one philosopher has written an entire book on lying (Bok, 1978), that discusses these and many other questions.

What is good about being systematic and impersonal? Does that mean that being immersed in particular situations in a committed, caring way is bad, that we should think about life, not live it? That one should sometimes stand back and subject problems to critical thinking does not imply that one should not commit oneself to action or to having joyful experiences. Exploring a question objectively is good because it represents an effort to get beyond our very personal, at times overly emotional views. If you have ever failed a test but have nonetheless acknowledged that both the questions and the grading were fair, you understand this point. It means that you have some conception of justice, and can apply it to your own situation even if you would feel better if you could believe that your "F" resulted from the unfairness of the professor. We probably could not live together if each of us kept shifting our ideas about fairness as a function of how we felt in each situation.

Who, then, is best equipped to discover and evaluate moral ideals, and under what conditions? Perhaps philosophers and psychologists, in their professional capacities, could best distinguish between good reasons and (bad) rationalizations; on the other hand, perhaps such impersonal rationality is impossible and, even if possible, too far removed from the realities of people's predicaments, thoughts, and emotions. Furthermore, history teaches us the sad lesson that intellectuals are not always on the side of the angels; they have defended (rationalized?) a variety of abuses of the powerless, whether in the form of slavery, discrimination, colonialism, or dictatorship.

The alternative idea that all individuals, while coping with their daily lives, are best equipped to discover moral ideals, deserves consideration, therefore, and it is certainly more democratic. Unfortunately, history is not uniformly encouraging here, either. With hindsight, we know that even a consensus among most or all citizens can be morally wrong. What if a country's laws permit or encourage slavery or discrimination, yet are supported by most of its citizens? Must we conclude that these laws are therefore moral? Might we not want to persuade those to whom slavery or discrimination is common sense that there are morally superior alternatives?

If we try to do so, we will eventually appeal to *moral* principles like autonomy and nonmaleficence, as well as to facts about human beings. For example, "You shouldn't discriminate because discrimination unfairly harms people" appeals to the principles of justice and nonmaleficence, and is based on our knowledge of what harms or hurts people. We do indeed discover and learn common sense in the process of living, but we can and must continually modify our common sense beliefs in accordance with new (often scientific) information, and evaluate them within a higher, more universal moral perspective. *Not to do so is to treat our current views as true and morally acceptable, if only by implication.*

ARE MORAL PRINCIPLES ENOUGH?

Are moral principles, by themselves, a sufficient guarantee that our conduct will actually be good or right? Can we simply write a computer program that, combining psychological information, moral principles, and specifics about various situations, will produce solutions to all the practical and perplexing problems of daily life?

If we view this computer in isolation from the programmer, we see a machine that calculates and operates in a purely logical fashion for any and all subject matter; it does not matter to this machine whether it is solving a problem about growing carrots or starting a war. Nothing matters to this machine: there is no emotional element, no compassion, no experiential history of the sort which contributes to character, temperament, and common sense. A person who tries to think about human conduct in this computer-like fashion will rarely, perhaps never, succeed in being moral. We cannot step out of our skins, so to speak, and this means that we cannot escape the compassional, personal, and interpersonal character of our human situations. As important as moral theories and principles are to our thinking about ethics, they cannot be the whole story.

Each situation has its own meaning for each of the people involved in it, and reasoning is not the best way to learn in what ways a situation matters to someone else. Rather, one needs to be sensitive to others—to know, for example, that this is one occasion when a friend cannot face a particular truth. Situations often combine rational and empathic components. Parents understand that babies need preventive shots, and they usually weight this understanding more heavily than their empathy for the help-less, noncomprehending baby who is about to be jabbed in the arm.

This example makes clear why a computer cannot be moral. Even if we know (in a variety of ways) what would and would not cause someone else to experience pain now and in the future, knowledge alone does not result in any particular action. We might, after all, use our knowledge about the vulnerabilities of others to hurt them, rather than to spare them pain. While intellect can describe the consequences of diphtheria and injections, it cannot account for our choices among alternatives. Without compassion, caring, and concern, we are not moved by the immediate (the shot) or the potential (diphtheria) suffering and pain of others. And why would we have programmed the principle of nonmaleficence into the computer in the first place? (We will return to this question when we discuss rationality in Chapter 15.)

BASIC ATTITUDINAL ORIENTATIONS

The claim that temperament influences thought tempts us to use, with modifications, the distinction James (1907) made between "tough-minded" and "tender-minded" people. According to him, the tender-minded are "rationalistic, intellectualistic, idealistic, optimistic, religious, free willist, monistic, and dogmatical" (p. 22). The tough-minded, on the other hand, are "empiricist, sensationalistic, materialistic, pessimistic, irreligious, fatal-istic, pluralistic, and skeptical" (p. 22). It is not very likely that any one individual actually fits completely into either of these two categories—to say nothing of most people fitting into one or the other. There may, how-ever, be a range of basic attitudes that determine our orientation toward the world and the way people behave in it (Wrightsman, 1972). By taking several liberties with the categories James introduced, and by understand-ing the terms *tough* and *tender* to refer to the extremes of these basic attitu-dinal orientations, we can explore two very different outlooks.

What we will call the tough view includes several themes. Be realistic. Hierarchies always exist in human social arrangements, as they do among animals. These hierarchies are related to individual differences in vision or height or talent, since such characteristics have consequences in our lives. Perhaps you deserve what you have (your amounts and kinds of happi-ness, well being), or perhaps it is just fate or luck. Some deer just run faster than others, and therefore they have certain advantages. We have to accept such realities. Some variety of Social Darwinism is inevitable, natural, and/ or desirable. It is natural (inherent in human nature) for each of us to be concerned about and take care of ourselves; self-interest "is" and "ought to be." The preferred moral theory is ethical egoism.

What we call the tender view, in contrast, stresses moral equality despite the many differences among people in vision, or height, or talent. We could have been poor instead of rich, or vice versa: in any case, we deserve no credit or rewards for having particular parents, since we did not choose them, yet they gave us both genes and environment! We should be concerned about and take care of ourselves and others; even enlightened self-interest is not enough. Be compassionate. We can help each other to move toward greater happiness and well being. We must evaluate what we are surviving in and for, and change the world as desirable, necessary, and possible. Be realistic, but be idealistic, too.

These two extremes can probably be found among psychologists, philosophers, and any other group of people. Thus, some say that we should help one and all to achieve their maximum potential, while others maintain that this is impossible or undesirable, given certain inevitable human characteristics and hierarchies. Some say that criminals should be rehabilitated, while others say they should be punished. Some say we should rely on experts and leaders, in other words, on those at the tops of certain hierarchies; others say we should encourage everyone's participation, since everyone contributes, and since we therefore learn from one another. Many people are tough in certain areas, tender in others; we are talking about a complex continuum. Still, the contrasting themes are recognizable in the people we meet every day.

IS ONE ORIENTATION BETTER?

Evaluating these two orientations is difficult, but several points can be made. As we have seen, tough-minded people tend to stress that they are realistic, and that their values are natural—that is, in tune with nature, perhaps developed during ages of evolution. This claim misses an important point: descriptions of reality do not force us to say, "Whatever is, is good." It may be natural in some sense for an angry child to throw sand or stones at others, but we are not therefore obligated to praise that child! Instead, we will probably try to help children deal with their anger differently even when they find it very difficult not to be physically aggressive. We will do so because we are concerned for the safety of others, for the future happiness of the children, and for the quality of social life. Chronic interpersonal violence is a singularly unattractive social ideal which typically appeals to neither tough nor tender people. While we ignore reality at our peril, reality nonetheless leaves us many morally relevant choices; one does not have to accept whatever exists.

The tender-minded, who tend to stress ideals, may therefore deliberately challenge existing realities. For example, insofar as they seek to realize everyone's potential, they will have to recommend that many social changes be made. But ideals too far removed from current reality can begin to sound as though they are asking for the impossible; an extreme example would be, "Let us create a perfect society." A moral theory should not say, "Do what you cannot do," since this contradicts itself. Ideas about just what can be changed are related to conceptions of human nature (see Chapter 15).

Tough-minded people also often seem to favor ethical egoism over other moral theories. "Looking out for #1" is a tough-minded attitude. As we saw earlier, ethical egoism is the view that we ought to do what is in our interest, which is of course different from saying that we do act self-interestedly. This view does not lead to the conclusion that we should act on every impulse; after all, we are enlightened or realistic enough to realize what would happen if we did. Thus, while ethical egoism may sound as though it preaches selfishness or thoughtless impulsivity, it actually does not, since people can anticipate that such conduct would often have negative consequences, and would therefore not be in their interest. But when no negative consequences appear to be forthcoming, ethical egoism may lead to conclusions many people find morally repugnant. Suppose a man wanted to commit a perfect murder. He chooses a derelict, whom he would kill instantaneously without warning or struggle. Thus, the murderer would cause neither anxiety nor pain; nobody would miss the dead person, so that the murderer has not hurt others, and he would have no reason to anticipate retribution; finally, assume the murderer experiences no guilt feelings. Ethical egoism would then say, "You should commit this murder, since you want to, and careful consideration of all the consequences shows there will be no bad ones for you."

Aside from such dramatically counterintuitive conclusions, ethical egoism has another failing. Since we ought to do what is in our interest, it follows that we must be able to determine the potential costs and benefits of our actions. We would have to know, for example, not just that we feel like listening to loud music at 2:00 A.M., but also how we will feel when the neighbors descend upon us in a rage or call the police. As we all know from personal experience, it can be difficult to correctly anticipate one's own reactions to a situation. Insofar as this is impossible or even improbable, egoism requires people to do something which they (probably) cannot do.

One sometimes hears people try to defend ethical egoism by arguing that all of us are always acting on the basis of self-interest, that in fact, that is all we can do. Even if we were helping others, our behavior would be self-interested. Implied or stated explicitly is the companion idea that altruism, compassion, kindness, and generosity are actually all misnamed selfishness. This line of argument confuses the contexts of explanation and justification. It is true that the explanation for your actions will be found in your needs and beliefs, not in someone else's; you are eating to take care of your hunger, not another person's! But when people bemoan "me-ism," they are evaluating; their perspective is moral scrutiny, and they are saying, essentially, "It is morally wrong for these people to do X under these conditions because they are satisfying their needs at the expense of others." And social arrangements that support doing that are more likely to be acceptable to the tough-minded since to them, pecking orders among humans seem as natural as those among animals.

But while certain problems can be identified in both tough and tender views, we cannot conclude that one is consistently better than the other. Instead, when people with such different world views discuss the fundamentals of moral theory, they ultimately come to an unbridgable gap— unbridgable, that is, by facts and reason. People at one point on the tough-tender continuum may find it hard to even grasp that anyone could be cold enough or unrealistic enough to be at a very different point, and they usually feel that way long before they formally study either psychology or philosophy. If this is true, argument may do little to change their minds, especially if their orientation is extreme, since they may then be motivated to defend their one and only true world view against attack, and some of them are very adept indeed at doing so. The situation is similar to trying to decrease prejudice by providing information. An extremely prejudiced person, who may sound almost ridiculous to others, may be able to explain or incorporate virtually any information that seems to others to clearly argue against the prejudice. This is why some people maintain that they do not like to argue about politics and religion; they probably would not succeed in changing anyone's mind anyway, they say, and they might even lose a few friends.

At times or at some level, perhaps the best we can hope for is a comprehension of differences, and an effort to find common ground and even common conclusions in discussions of specific issues (like the use of animals in research). In addition, all of us, regardless of orientation, need to remain alert to possible weaknesses in all world views, even, perhaps especially, our own. If it is foolish to say "We should all try to be perfect," it is even more foolish to say, "I am already perfect."

MORAL RELATIVISM AND ABSOLUTISM

These two very different, perhaps irreconcilable, ways of looking at the universe bring us back to questions about moral relativism and moral absolutism, previously discussed in Chapter 3. Most commonly, the tension between them stems from a consideration of cultural differences, but as we have just seen, different moralities are parts of the different world views that exist within our own culture. If the validity of such world views cannot be determined by reason and observation, does that have to mean that "anything goes"? Our answer to this question is a resounding No. Perhaps the most basic consideration is that no point on the tough-tender continuum offers the moral perspective that anything goes. But there are other considerations.

We said earlier that intent is an important factor in moral judgments. We evaluate John and Ned differently if John accidentally harmed someone because he could not possibly have known X while Ned deliberately used his knowledge of X to harm someone. Piaget reported in the 1920s that young children judge on the basis of end results, while older children judge on the basis of intentions (Piaget, 1932). He demonstrated this by telling children stories which pitted intentions and end results against each other. For example, one child was helping a parent (intent) and broke many cups (result), while another child was disobeying a parent (intent) and broke one cup (result). All the children can repeat the details of the story, but the young child judges according to the number of cups broken, the older child according to helping versus disobeying parents. The older child is on the right track, but we may hesitate when we begin to think about infanticide and torture.

We could say about these, too, that intention is critical. It is one thing if someone kills a baby because, "I didn't want it"; it is another when killing infants is a culture's way of controlling overpopulation or mass starvation—or is it? Similarly, it is one thing if someone tortures because seeing helpless others suffer is pleasurable; it is quite another if an enemy soldier has important information which could reduce the subsequent carnage on both sides—or is it? Just as we would like to live in a world where resources are never scarce, we would like a world in which starvation and war do not exist. But reality does not match our wishes, and so these difficult and disturbing questions continue to confront us.

Absolutists claim that such behaviors as the taking of life, torture, lying, stealing are always wrong, never justifiable. Relativists claim that it depends—on the meaning of the act, on the intentions of the doer. Consider research on pain-killing drugs, which are typically tested on animals and later on human volunteers. Is it morally permissible for researchers to create pain in animals in order to then test the drugs? The researchers intend to better alleviate suffering in animals and humans; they are not torturing these animals in order to enjoy their suffering, yet the inflicting of pain is deliberate. Is such intentional creation of pain ever justifiable?

In our society, we encounter conflicting themes about this side by side. We smile at the responses of Piaget's young children, yet also say, "The road to Hell is paved with good intentions." We do not mean only that things sometimes turn out differently from what was expected or intended; we mean also that we are disturbed by the killing of healthy infants regardless of cultural context.

We ought not to squelch such absolutism too easily, but even if we do, the relativism of intent or context or meaning or situation discussed by no means requires that we shrug our shoulders at atrocities like those committed in concentration and slave labor camps. One should not compare those horrors to infanticide that is responsive to famine or to torture of an enemy soldier during war. Thus, to take one example, the murder of the Jews in Europe did not save anyone, did not help the country's war efforts, were not based on any good intentions, cannot be excused by any absence of information—in brief, cannot be morally justified at all. It was very clear after World War II that most Germans agreed with this view, since they did not brag about what they had done, but rather, denied it; as has been pointed out bitterly many times, apparently "no one" in Hitler's Germany knew anything about or approved of the slaughter of the Jews! Yet surely we are proud if we have done something laudable (like fighting the good fight), even if our conquerers do not quite appreciate it.

If a relativism related to intentions does not mean that "anything goes," why not squelch whatever absolutism is within us? Surely it is just a remnant from those moments of childhood when some adult sharply said No! Perhaps that is true to some extent, but it is not the whole story. We ought to recoil from all torture, and even if we conclude, regretfully, that its use is justified (perhaps even obligatory) on some very rare occasions, we ought to remind ourselves that those occasions represent the worst in human situations, not the best. We ought to recoil from torturing because that reaction will decrease the probability of our actually doing a morally reprehensible thing in any particular situation. Along with whatever makes us think we ought to do it in that situation, however reluctantly, we will still also be pulled in the direction of not doing it. This attitude has enormous social utility: would we really prefer to live in a world where people might torture each other at the drop of a hat, so to speak? Thus, moral principles stated as absolutes (*always, never*) are vulnerable because we can quickly think up exceptions, except, perhaps, if we build the exceptions into the statements (We should never do X except under conditions Y.). Nonetheless, such principles serve as statements of valuable ideals, of worthy aspirations, for people and their institutions.

The psychological impacts of moral relativism also need to be considered. On the one hand, relativism is correlated in some people with increasing openmindedness, as they consider, for example, that one or another form of euthanasia may be defensible in one or another cultural context. On the other hand, those who interpret relativism as "anything goes" or "to each his/her own" sometimes believe that one has no right to try to alter anyone's behavior, or even to teach children about right and wrong; presumably, children will discover that is right for them as or when they grow up. Actually, the children do (inevitably) make discoveries. They find a variety of beliefs and behaviors, and in the absence of guidance, develop their own strategies for handling conflicts of interest, many of which probably involve struggles for power. This is the point which "relativistic" parents miss: their children will not act impulsively, without thinking, and they will develop some ideas ("Might is right"). The question is whether the parents really believe that the child's impulsive acts or ideas are as good as their own ("It's not nice to grab everything; let them have some, too."). Will children automatically move into belief systems acceptable to their parents and to society? In fact, "To each his/her own" usually turns out to mean "within certain limits." The situation is comparable to children's career choices. The professional parents may say, "Anything—just so they're happy and self-supporting." Then one child chooses to work in a factory, and the parents' reactions make it clear that factory work was not included in "anything." And so it often is with morality—only here the matter is more serious: the child may end up a hated and dangerous bully or in prison instead of that (perfectly respectable) factory.

What is wrong with parents and other caretakers professing and applying a distorted "anything goes" relativism is that they do not and should not believe it, and that they may end up alienated from their now strange, grown-up children. The children, meanwhile, have grown up without the direction the parents would have given if only they had not tried so hard to be "good" parents; furthermore, the children's own moral code may make it difficult for them to live among other people. Similarly, professionals who either verbalize or model "anything goes—it's all relative," should not be surprised when some of the activities of their former students truly shock them.

Perhaps it is not amiss to conclude this section by pointing out that the obligations of specialists to share their knowledge with nonspecialists in nondestructive ways apply not only to psychologists (Chapter 7), but also to philosophers. Many people are perplexed about moral issues, and therefore, one of the more encouraging developments in recent years is the availability of good mass market ethics books, articles, and TV programs, as well as "values clarification" programs in the schools.

EQUALITY

Conceptions of equality and inequality are always important in ethics, and are included in both tough and tender views. It has become a cliché that human beings are alike in certain respects, but that each of us is also unique—that is, different from all others. The question therefore arises: what are the moral implications of similarities and differences among people?

In Chapter 3, we pointed out that many (but not all) people are equal as moral agents, and that moral principles, such as nonmaleficence, may be taken to be relevant to all those who are equal with respect to some characteristics ("capable of being harmed"). Such categories involve both theoretical and factual knowledge; we can ask of any one person (say, Ted), "Is he a moral agent?" and, "In what ways, if any, can he be harmed?" But such knowledge is not usable unless we also have moral ideals like, "We shouldn't harm the 'harmable' simply to enjoy their suffering." In addition, in order to treat equals equally, or to make sure that informed consent has been obtained, we need knowledge about how to implement these ideals. Moral equality does not imply identical treatment for everyone. Ted and Joe may feel coerced under different circumstances, and it may take fewer and different words to inform one than the other. The natural and social sciences contribute to our knowledge about differences and similarities among humans and animals—among individuals, species, nationalities, genders, races, and ages. Philosophers contribute to our thinking about and understanding of the moral relevance of such knowledge.

When differences are used in a manner we judge to be unjust, we speak of discrimination. Those who discriminate usually justify their actions by arguing that the A's and the B's are different, with one group being superior to the other, and that these differences are morally relevant. They do not argue that no differences exist between the A's and the B's, but that they may or should be treated differently anyway; thus, discriminators, too, believe that only unequals may be treated unequally. They also do not argue that although differences exist, they are not a justifiable basis for favoring one group over another. Racists, for example, argue that Race A differs from Race B on trait X, and that this difference justifies favoring one of the races, the one they consider superior. Notice that racists thus make two claims, one about factual information, the other about arguments of justification. The same is true of sexism and agism: men and women, or older and younger people differ in that . . . and this difference justifies . . .

Either or both claims can be challenged. Does the claimed difference actually exist? If so, what bearing has it on a particular morally relevant decision? The differences sought, found, stressed, and used are sometimes the same for the tough and the tender, but not always. In addition, some types of faulty reasoning are very widespread, cutting across world views and moral theories. It is best to begin with these.

First, it is important to remember that the differences between the A's and the B's do not necessarily apply to each and every comparison between a particular A and a particular B. This is true because individual differences exist in every group, and the group ranges overlap. On the average, men can lift more weight than women; since the ranges overlap, however, not every man can lift more than every woman. Thus, a particular woman may be able to do a loading-unloading job better than a particular man. Second, even if there were no overlap whatsoever between men and women on this characteristic, global judgments of inferior-superior would not follow, since many other characteristics are also morally relevant, and the sexes may not differ on these.

It may seem, and some might wish to argue, that it is natural to make global judgments of superior-inferior on the basis of limited information; for better or worse, we do evaluate individuals and groups. The reasons why such evaluation is widespread are not hard to find. The traits we use to compare people are the socially important ones—the ones that influence how people cope with their problems or with their interpersonal relationships: honesty, intelligence, manipulativeness, and talent. Virtually everyone in our society has ideas about which end of each of these continua is "best"; for example, more talent is better than less talent. Furthermore, we expect people good in one area to be good in other areas; so widespread is this phenomenon that it even has a name: halo effect. These continua, then, are not value-free. If Don is characterized as "deceitful," we have received information to which we react negatively, and which, furthermore, leads us to suspect or believe that Don has other negative characteristics. In brief, we have made an overall negative evaluation of Don. Although this is natural, in the sense that it comes easily to us, it is not therefore correct or justifiable. While Don may be deceitful, he probably also has positive attributes. Furthermore, being uneasy with someone given to deception is not the same as making the we-they distinction familiar in discrimination: we are good, they are bad. Instead, if it is justified to treat people who constantly deceive others differently from those who are usually honest, such differential treatment is justified even when it also applies to some of "us"; the morally relevant distinction (inequality) is not "we-they," but "hard-easy to trust."

But the differences sought and stressed are also related to one's world view. It was stated above that scientists provide information about groups and individual characteristics. While this is true, stating it that way obscures an important point, developed in chapters 4 and 5: we seek and interpret such information not only in relation to scientific theory, but also in relation to our values. Specifically, because we live in a competitive society, we often try to bring out differences among people rather than similarities, and to use this information to justify their different positions in the existing socioeconomic hierarchy (see Chapters 10 and 11). Thus, we may say that Linda deserves this promotion because she is better than or has more of something than Jennie; that both are in fact doing excellent work predictive of success at the higher level is not helpful information if they are competing for one position. We can also cherish differences and uniqueness in noncompetitive contexts. Thus, it adds much to our lives that our friends are not our clones!

Even when we have concluded that a particular difference is important, we still face some difficult choices. We may decide that reading skills are very important, and that we must therefore deal with individual differences in this characteristic. What shall we do about a child who is having much trouble learning to read? What about the five-year-old who reads at the third grade level? In an era of limited resources, and given the unique needs of each child (since each child also has other talents, not to mention interests), as well as the needs of the society in which they all live, who shall receive what resources? When not everyone can have diagnostic testing (for example, in reading), who should get it? Who should have what reading instruction? Possible answers are that resources should go to: those who need them most; those who would benefit most; those who deserve them most; and those who present the greatest future threat to the welfare of others. The poorest readers need special instruction most; the average and the gifted may benefit most; those who try hardest deserve it most; those who might become unemployable or turn to a life of crime present the greatest danger to others. All of these are morally relevant considerations, and were resources not in short supply, all of them would be considered very seriously; in fact, taken together, they suggest that we ought to do the best we can for each and every individual! It is important that we recognize this: our basic problem is the lack of resources, not our total inability to figure out what might benefit individual children or society.

But resources are often limited, and then we find that tough- and tender-minded individuals may make different choices. The tough-minded may more readily give up on those at the low end of a continuum, either because they see individual differences as inevitable, perhaps innate, or because they blame the victims, holding poor readers, for example, responsible for their low reading level and for whatever difficulties stem from this. The tender-minded are more likely to continue to help the poor readers, perhaps on the assumptions that they had fewer resources in the past, and that the various advantages of the better readers will in any case permit them to cope with life with less help. Most arguments about the allocation of scarce resources include problematic assumptions about cause-and-effect relationships and about moral justification.

CONCLUSION

World views, including morality, involve more than intellect; they are attitudes and values rather than beliefs. To act morally towards others we need not only moral principles but also the desire to do so and the sensitivity to these others to be able to do so. Moral orientations differ in beliefs about equality/inequality (hierarchy) and realism/idealism. Such differences cannot be resolved by appeals to facts and reason; people can, however, try to understand these differences, search for and act on shared conclusions, and maintain a critical stance in relation to all world views, including their own. This does not mean that "anything goes," that whatever any person or group does is acceptable merely because it is done; both orientations permit and demand moral scrutiny of our actions. In the next chapter, we will explore the relationships among reason, compassion, and responsibility.

15

REASON, COMPASSION, AND RESPONSIBILITY

If our moral concerns grow out of our interactions with others, and if our moral orientations are included in our world views, then the root meaning of the term *moral responsibility* must lie in the notion of our response to others. A morally responsible person responds in morally significant ways to others—what they are, what they feel, what they say, and what they do. Being morally responsible means being "able to choose for oneself between right and wrong" and being "able to answer for one's conduct and obligations" (Webster, 1976). How we choose what we think is right and wrong and how we answer for our responses to others will depend on the view we take of human nature, and this is part of our overall world view. As Stevenson (1974) pointed out:

> This is surely one of the most important questions of all. For so much depends on our view of human nature. The meaning and purpose of life, what we ought to do, and what we hope to achieve—all these are fundamentally affected by whatever we think is the "real" or true nature of man. . . . Different views about human nature lead naturally to different conclusions about what we ought to do and how we can do it. (p. 3)

Because most of us are only vaguely aware even of our own view of human nature, it is important to get an idea of the rich variety of such theories. Stevenson's account covers the views of Plato, Christianity,

Marx, Freud, Sartre, Skinner, and Lorenz as major theories, and he alludes to several others as well. We recommend this book to the interested reader, since we cannot immerse ourselves in this comparative study here. But, since the way we respond to others morally is so heavily influenced by our view of human nature, we would do well to look briefly at Stevenson's major conclusions.

Stevenson sees compatibility among the seven theories he chose, in part because they are each "emphasizing different aspects of the total truth" about human beings (Stevenson, 1974, p. 121). Plato and the early Greeks emphasized the rational aspect of human nature; Christianity sees people primarily in relation to God; Marx stressed our essentially economic nature; Freud saw human nature as the interplay of the id, ego and superego throughout several developmental stages; Sartre maintained that there is no universal human nature but only our individual nature which we create for ourselves through our choices of actions and values; Skinner deemphasized human nature as he studied the impact of conditions in our environment, notably rewards and punishments, on our behavior; and Lorenz emphasized innate (evolved) behavioral tendencies released by appropriate environmental cues.

Two central issues emerge from the study of human nature: the extent to which what we ascribe to human nature is innate and fixed as opposed to learned within the social environment; and the separate question of determinism versus free will. It should be noted that environmentalists, hereditarians, and interactionists alike are typically determinists, since they all stress the causes of behavior, including the behavior of choosing; none stress free will. Our answers to these two questions will affect how optimistic we are about the prospects for improving human life. Also significantly affected is the extent to which we hold people responsible for what they are or for becoming what we think they should be.

THE TOUGH AND TENDER VIEWS

The tough view, as we have seen, depicts a dog-eat-dog world in which all of us are out for ourselves, and where the strong dominate the weak; this state of affairs is presumably acceptable to everyone, since "it's human nature"—innate. Thus, each of us is concerned about our own interests, and about the interests of others only insofar as these impinge on ours. Each of us would try to "get away with murder"; the tough view therefore leans toward "law and order," and stresses the need for controls from without when controls are needed.

The tender view depicts a world in which each of us could move toward principled and compassionate action, though not all of us do. Human nature is thus at least potentially good, though we all also have the capacity to become oriented toward the dog-eat-dog view; our development in our social environments is thus the deciding factor. Since, in this view, principled and compassionate action is morally and psychologically superior to action based on the tough philosophy, we should try to build a world in which more people, perhaps all, can develop in the good direction. Such a world would permit greater, though not exclusive reliance on inner controls.

The most striking thing about these two views is that we cannot easily put them to an empirical test, even though they sound like testable hypotheses. Instead, each of them functions as a self-fulfilling prophecy: those who believe the tough view of human nature find it to fit the facts, to be true, while those who believe the tender view find it to be true. That makes good sense psychologically. If you suspect people you meet of trying to do you in or to use you, they will respond to the messages you are sending. If you trust people, and expect them to be decent and kind, they respond to those messages. The responses of these others are related not only to their view of human nature, but also to yours.

When people say, "That can't be helped; it's just human nature," they are usually talking about something negative, and that expression, not surprisingly, is usually heard as part of the tough view. This points to a major difference between the two views. The tough view stresses characteristics which are inevitable because they are our nature, rather like our having two rather than three eyes. The tender view, in contrast, stresses that human beings are modifiable within certain limits. We will all need to eat and sleep, but we could grow up to believe that others will "use" us unless we constantly watch out, or we could grow up to believe that others can usually be trusted to be decent.

It should be clear that the tender view is optimistic and oriented toward humans controlling their own destinies; a sense of responsibility is seen as developing from within rather than from obedience to laws being imposed from without. The tender minded understand what sorts of social, political, and economic environments are needed for people to become the best of which they are capable; a sense of responsibility cannot develop under all conditions. The tough view, in contrast, tends to be pessimistic. What societies can and must do is to impose controls on those behaviors which would make social life difficult or impossible, and to channel inevitable aggression into constructive areas (economics, which naturally, inevitably, would have certain attributes).

FLEXIBILITY AND RESPONSIBILITY

It is helpful to consider the relationship between *is* and *ought* in this context. We take it for granted that human beings walk; no one suggests that walking is morally wrong, and a proposal that we all move from stroller to wheelchair would not even get a hearing. It is our nature to walk, to breathe, to eat—and, perhaps, to compete, to aggress, and to act on self-interest. Whenever we accept the inevitability of certain human attributes and activities, proposals for alternatives sound downright silly—rather like saying that we should have three eyes. Who would waste time thinking about that? But ideas about what is inevitable for human beings continue to change. As new situations either emerge in society or are deliberately introduced, notably by new technologies, we conclude that there was no inevitable *is* in those areas after all, and that we have every reason to think about possible *oughts*. Try to imagine, for a moment, the impact of a simple operation which could install a third eye in the backs of our heads.

Just how much flexibility exists, and in what areas, are questions that yield to research to some extent. For example, suppose we believed that humans will or must inevitably do X. If we then discovered human groups who never do X, we would have compelling data to consider: clearly, doing X is not inevitable. We are continually learning more about just how flexible humankind can be. First, we have learned about many different cultures from anthropological research. Second, we have seen dramatic changes in our own society. The point here is not to discuss whether these changes are desirable, but merely to note that they have occurred. For example, what was once called the "maternal instinct" clearly does not guarantee certain behaviors in the way that the eye-blink reflex does. In *Beast and man: the roots of human nature,* Midgley (1978) wrote, "Things that are natural in the minimal sense—widely practiced, emotionally seductive, hard to eradicate—do not have to be so in the strong sense in which we are called upon to approve them." (p. 328), or, we might add, resign ourselves to them. Even small amounts of flexibility mean that we can make choices, that there is no inevitable connection between is and ought.

If there is even a small measure of flexibility in human nature and in human actions, there will be a place for ethical reflection and for responsibility for one's actions. This is where moral theories, moral principles, and our model of moral reasoning come into play. This is the proper arena for ascribing moral responsibility to genuine moral agents for what they have done or failed to do.

It could be argued that those who view human nature and the universe as unchangeable are actually trying to avoid moral responsibility altogether. According to Ross (1958):

> The driving force of metaphysics in the field of morals and religion is the fear of the vicissitudes of life, the transitoriness of all things; the inexorability of death; or conversely, the desire for the absolute, the eternally immutable which defies the law of corruption. This fear, in moral matters, is associated with the fear of having to make choices and decisions under changing circumstances and on one's own responsibility. Therefore, by seeking justification for our actions in immutable principles outside ourselves, we try to relieve ourselves of the burden of responsibility. (p. 261)

In identifying the moral point of view with a reasoned and reflective outlook, we are not saying that moral responsibility is a purely rational or reasoned response. But reason does play a very significant role in our responses to moral situations, and we must therefore examine the nature of *rationality*.

MEANINGS OF *RATIONAL*

Rationality turns out to be multifaceted. As with the word *intelligence*, we might do well to avoid using it altogether, and to substitute words that refer to its several, more specific meanings. Sometimes being rational is associated with being logical. People who reason very clearly and precisely from premises to conclusions, avoiding formal and informal fallacies, might be described as rational. Their conclusions follow logically from their premises, and the law of contradiction is carefully followed. Whether or not anyone could be rational in this sense at all times and under all circumstances is doubtful, but most people, most of the time, seem to abjure contradictions in their thinking. We can say, then, that logical consistency in one's beliefs and judgment is prized by the reasonable, reflective individual.

Being rational is also associated with having certain beliefs about the real world. We should be using this second meaning if we called a person irrational for turning down a free trip around the world on an ocean liner because he or she believed that the earth is flat. Many people continue to hold erroneous beliefs which they learned as children. Depending on when they were born, they may continue to believe that telephones emit dangerous rays or electricity; that one will become ill if one eats X and Y simultaneously; or that it is absolutely impossible for humans to land on the moon. Being rational in this sense requires a certain amount of ordinary and scientific understanding of the world.

Being rational is also associated with acting in accordance with certain norms. A person may think logically and see the world in a generally accurate way, but at the same time, may engage in self-defeating behaviors, have unusual priorities, or take unusual risks. Such departures from commonly accepted norms may prompt people to call certain acts or even persons irrational, but as we shall see, these three are more difficult to apply than the first two, and deviations from a norm are not necessarily irrational.

Consider those who engage in self-defeating behaviors. It is irrational to tell everyone that I want to live, and then knowingly take a lethal dose of a poison "for the novel experience." This concept resembles the first one (being logical), but differs in that it stresses contradictions between conscious intentions and actual behavior. While the example above is clear but frivolous, this kind of irrationality is actually quite common; when it ruins a person's life, and/or seems startling to observers, we may nontechnically speak of craziness or irrationality. Thus, Ron may insist he wants good grades in college, but may, during counseling, reveal that he can't help playing pool all day and half the night. The contradiction between conscious intent and action in such cases is often resolvable in terms of intentions of which the person is not aware; thus, it might emerge that, for various reasons, Ron also intends to punish his parents by flunking out of college. Most of us engage in such self-defeating behaviors at least occasionally.

Some people have unusual priorities, or priorities unlike our own. We may judge them to be irrational if they eat food X even though they know that it will give them an ugly, itchy rash. When someone acts like that, others may be tempted to say, "How can you be so unreasonable?" The key to this kind of irrationality is the various weightings of pro's and con's. Everyone, including the eater, agrees that the eater is allergic to food X, and the eater enjoys eating food X, but does not enjoy the rash. The disagreement is in the priorities. Most people probably prefer to avoid the allergenic substance, but some prefer to enjoy it and then endure the consequences.

Some people take unusual risks, or risks we would not take. The food X example assumed that the eater was certain to get a rash, but in many cases, the consequences of our actions have various probabilities of occurring. Many people might say that it is irrational to jog when you have a virus. The rule of thumb is to try to take it easy when you are ill; most physicians would probably advise us not to jog for a day or two. Suppose Lionel said, "I'll take my chances. I've done it before. Once it got to me, but a couple of other times it didn't." Again, we are dealing with priorities (jogging versus feeling worse), but we are also dealing with taking risks. How much risk-taking is "rational?"

REASON AND MORALITY

All of these concepts of rationality, but especially the first two, may be involved in Gewirth's arguments in *Reason and Morality* (1978), in which he tries to answer three questions he views as central to moral philosophy: Why should we consider the interests of others? Whose interests? Which interests? His method combines reasoning with assumptions about the human mind. He first analyzes the nature of action and reason, and then proceeds to establish a supreme moral principle that, he argues, one can deny only on pain of self-contradiction. His thesis is worth reviewing and analyzing.

The action that is relevant to moral choice is both voluntary (uncoerced either mutually or physically) and purposive (intentional, goal directed). To hand over one's money on hearing "Your money or your life" is to do so under coercion. If one stumbles over a fascinating bookstore while strolling in a city, one's purpose was to take a walk; finding the store was accidental. Gewirth thus uses the terms *voluntary* and *purposive* in their conventional, everyday meanings. To be rational, according to Gewirth, is to apply deductive and inductive logic; this corresponds approximately to the first two conceptions of rationality discussed above. Rational agents understand that certain actions logically entail certain beliefs.

At times, such agents can tell us their beliefs, but in any case, we can infer them. This assumption is probably safer in certain instances than in others. When we repeatedly see people entering rooms through open doors rather than trying to enter through closed ones, we are probably safe in inferring their beliefs about what one can and cannot do in relation to solid objects. On the other hand, if we see someone steal a watch, we have to be fairly cautious. Maybe the person thought, "I don't want to get caught, and I won't be," but then again, the person may have wanted and expected to be caught. The watch itself may or may not have been the real goal; perhaps it or the act of stealing it symbolized something other than itself, such as masculinity.

Gewirth introduces this assumption for an important reason. He argues that each of us acts voluntarily and purposively as we take care of our important interests. From such action, he infers that we are in essence claiming certain rights for ourselves; these pertain to our freedom (which is by definition necessary for voluntary control) and to our well being (which is the goal of our purposive action). Since we must grant, if we observe other agents, that they are *just like us in these generic respects* (though not in specific tastes or inclinations), and since it is contradictory to claim these rights for ourselves but deny them to identical others, it follows that we must accept this supreme moral principle, which he calls the "Principle of Generic Consistency" (PGC): "Act in accord with the generic rights of your recipients as well as yourself" (Gewirth, 1978, p. 135). (Recipients are those who "receive" the actions of the agents.) "The PGC is an egalitarian universalist moral principle since it requires an equal distribution of the most general rights of action" (p. 140).

Gewirth thus argues that this PGC can only be denied irrationally. You could not, for example, say, "I need food to live. I claim for myself the right to plan for my food needs and to act on these plans without interference (coercion from others). You are like me in this respect; you, too, need food, but you have no right to plan for it and/or to act on your plans." It is irrational to find no relevant differences between you and me, and then to claim rights for myself but to deny them to you. It would also be an irrational denial of reality for you to contend, "I am claiming nothing for myself," when we can all watch you shop for food and then prepare your meal, and when we could all see your incredulous, outraged expression, and hear your tirade, if someone were to inform you that you no longer had a right to shop for food or to eat it!

Although it is not always correct to infer, "This person is assuming" or "thinking", it would appear that Gewirth has a good case overall, if we grant him his basic assumptions. But under certain conditions he could be wrong, and perhaps these instances reveal that he is assuming to start with that people are what he would consider moral, or that they see and understand the world as he does, or that they prioritize as he does. Suppose that a food shortage occurred. It is likely that some people would begin to stress ways in which others are not like them: "Yes, we both get hungry, but I do much more important work, so I should get more food." Neither deductive nor inductive reasoning will take care of the contention that one kind of work is more important than another, nor of the claim that one's job is morally relevant to the amount of food to which one is entitled during a shortage. These are value judgments. We would not all rank (prioritize) all jobs identically, nor would we agree on the moral relevance of jobs to food rations; some of us would no doubt consider the judgments of others to be irrational. Nonetheless, these are the kinds of value judgments we cannot easily stop making, and they affect the way we reason about moral issues.

In one sense, then, Gewirth's point is well taken: *if* we start with certain premises, and *if* we think in certain ways, we are all likely to come to the same conclusions. The problems reside in those ifs. We need not even go to other cultures; we need only consider the many different philosophies that have developed within Western civilization, even within any one country, during any one time period. Philosophers, as we have seen, do emphasize rationality, the development of good arguments for or against some thesis. How, then, in a field like ethics, can there be any disagreement? Obviously, the development of moral theories involves more than being able to think carefully and well. Consider the following quotation from Spinoza's *Ethics*: "It is plain that the law against the slaughtering of animals is founded rather on vain superstition and womanly pity than on sound reason." (Quoted in Midgley, 1978, p. 351) Must we now conclude that either those who argue for animal rights or Spinoza are irrational? If those whose special training places so much emphasis on reasoning can nonetheless reason their ways to such different views, it is very difficult to believe that good reasoning alone can always lead us to the best or the correct answer in ethics.

When we discussed the several concepts of rationality, we alluded to factors that can move us in irrational directions. It is sometimes even hard to be logical, especially when arguments are more involved than, "All A's are B. This is B. Therefore . . ." We are influenced by the specific details about those A's and B's, and often are influenced by a gut-level reaction (conclusion) we are not prepared to give up (See the section on: Whose moral principles?). Apart from the first concept of rationality (the purely logical), mathematics and ethics share little or no common ground; the other conceptions do not apply to mathematics at all, yet are probably relevant to almost any argument about morality.

In brief, the human capacities for thinking logically and observing the world have not provided us with moral theories comparable to mathematical ones, nor should we expect that, since ethics involves more kinds of rationality than mathematics and science do. In addition, we must consider an important point made by Gibson (1977):

> The basic idea motivating this paper is that rationality should be thought of as a human good and as a social goal. Two implications of this idea are (1) that a value-neutral conception of rationality is inadequate and (2) that moral, social, and political theories should treat rationality as a value to be promoted rather than as a property automatically attributed to all normal persons. (p. 193)

In other words, rationality should be viewed as a goal or positive value, whether or not it is in fact characteristic of every human being. This does not mean that one should always try to be logical, since being logical is not always an appropriate goal; while watching a beautiful sunset, for example, one may not want to reason at all. But we must qualify Gibson's important point even further. It is easier to be specific about the positive value of the first two concepts of rationality than of the last three. Logicians can teach us about logic, scientists about the natural world, but how can we find out what self-defeating behavior is, and what reasonable priorities and risks are? Answers to these questions involve values not only in setting goals, but also in trying to reach them. If we want to be logical (positively valued goal), we must understand that if all A's are B, and this is an A, then this A is also B; we cannot logically affirm the premises and deny the conclusion. But if we want good priorities (positively valued goal), we must have good values in addition to being able to think inductively and deductively.

COMPASSION

We pointed out earlier that even if a computer could deal logically with moral propositions, it nonetheless could not be empathic or compassionate. Compassion involves the capacity to experience vicariously someone else's feelings, volitions, or ideas, and, where there is suffering or misery, the desire to eliminate these, perhaps at some cost to oneself. People cannot literally feel someone else's experiences. Rather, some people seem to seek and pick up hints subtler than those most of us notice, and to act on these.

Periodically we learn from the media about killers who seem to have no remorse, and who never seem to have felt any compassion for their victims. They seem to have acted exclusively on the basis of their own, immediate impulses. If we were thinking about rehabilitation, what would we want to recommend for such killers? We probably would not first mention reason, knowledge, information, or ideas (rationality), since the killers no doubt knew murder was against the law, heard their victims plead or scream, and understood that doing X was virtually certain to kill their victims. Instead, we would probably fantasize miraculously infusing these killers with compassion. This choice would be based on our ideas about what makes people act; both need or desire and belief are necessary. Thus, you drink water because you are thirsty and because you believe water will quench your thirst. Neither the belief alone nor the need alone would cause you to drink the water. Wanting to infuse such killers with compassion reflects our idea that they have the relevant beliefs, but not the relevant desires (to avoid harming others, or even to protect them).

If our ordinary belief-desire explanatory model of action has as much utility as its long history might suggest, then it may help to put reason and compassion into this perspective: what we call reason is related to belief, what we call compassion, to desire. Reason alone does not energize us. Deductive and inductive reasoning may convince us that we should not do X if we want Y, yet we all know that we may do X nonetheless. Like the murderers discussed above, those caught shoplifting can probably tell us why their action was bad both morally and in terms of immediate negative consequences to themselves, and yet they did it. Knowing about people's beliefs is important, but it is not enough; we also need information about their feelings or desires. Some psychologists seem to stress the former in their theories (Piaget, Kohlberg), while others stress the latter (Freud).

We do have some of this information. Just as people's beliefs about moral rights and wrongs are related to their age and gender, so, too, is their compassion. It is becoming common lore, for example, that many males mellow with age; what left them cold or could not touch them at 20 may move them deeply when they are 45 or 70. Research on sex role stereotypes reveals that compassion is viewed as essentially feminine, a view clearly shared by Spinoza ("womanly pity"). A division of labor once traditional might have resulted in actual gender differences; women nurtured the family, but how would a warrior behave if he felt compassion for the enemy into whom he was about to shoot an arrow or a bullet? But these are not traditional times, and perhaps all of us need compassion when we review the facts about a possible nuclear war.

So far, we have been discussing compassion as an immediate feeling comparable, for example to hunger: we would feel hungry, and similarly, would feel empathic with a child who had just had a nasty spill while skating. In addition, however, we develop beliefs about the importance and proper role of compassion. Bloom (1977) found two dimensions of moral reasoning. He called one *social principledness*; it refers to determining a morally appropriate response through individually derived principles rather than through unquestioning obedience to external authority. He called the other *social humanism*; it refers to granting priority to the consequences of alternative actions for the people involved, and to resisting abstract theoretical justifications that direct attention away from the impact on individuals. Bloom tested several nationalities, and found that in most, these two dimensions were not related. This means that one could score high or low on both, or high on one, low on the other. Insofar as they are related, it is at the upper ends of both, as in Kohlberg's highest stage; those high on principledness may use humanism as a justifying principle, while those high on humanism may question authority. Gilligan's analysis of gender differences in moral perspectives (Gilligan, 1982) suggests that men are more likely to stress what Bloom called principledness (that each of us has the right to do certain things without interference from others), while women are more likely to stress humanism (they judge in terms of mutual responsibility and caring in human relationships).

It is important to take into account individual and group differences in compassion and in beliefs about compassion if we want to understand people's actions. Age, gender, and other group differences in compassion should be of as much concern to ethics and psychology as comparable group differences in reason or belief. Such differences challenge us to think about how much compassion is good in different situations, and how to help people strike a good balance between compassion and reason when these, taken singly, would lead them in different directions.

While psychologists and philosophers tend to use different terms (*cognition* and *motive* versus *belief* and *desire*), their explanations of human actions are alike in that they include both of these. While psychological and philosophical analyses of belief are important, this does not mean that only belief is important. One of the major challenges for both disciplines is to study human motives better and to incorporate the resulting understanding into their approaches to human behavior. When we think about programming that computer, we think about including a principle of nonmaleficence not only because we have good reasons for doing so, but also because empathy and compassion may make it impossible for us to say instead, "Always harm others as much as you can."

ACCOUNTABILITY

Earlier we said that being responsible means being responsive to others in certain ways, and also being answerable for our conduct and obligations. Being responsible, then, means being held accountable. Let us look more closely now at the concept of accountability.

The view of most psychologists that all behavior is determined (caused by heredity and environment) may appear to lead to a diminished notion of accountability, but this is not an essential consequence of believing that all behavior is caused, or of being a determinist. The critical question is, Could the person have done otherwise?

First, we can distinguish among causes. Suppose that Don is a passenger in a car. The driver deliberately drives into and destroys part of someone's property, then speeds off. How do we decide whether Don shares responsibility? We will want to know whether he entered that car willingly, or whether, instead, he was knocked unconscious, tied up, and then dragged into the car. Notice that in both cases, we are citing the causes of Don's being there (we are explaining it), but only in one case do we hold him responsible. If physical coercion was among the causes for his presence, he is not responsible, since he could not escape (do otherwise); if he participated in this act without coercion (some people might want to say "of his own free will"), he is responsible and can be held accountable.

Second, we can distinguish among both temporary and long-lasting inner states in terms of the extent to which the person has an experience of inner compulsion or coercion. Suppose Marcia feels coerced by inner voices to beat her children; she hears those voices—they are real for her and she cannot shut them off the way she can shut off the television set. The inner states which we single out for special consideration are those related to being able to either do or not do something. In no case do we have to approve of those children being beaten, but under certain conditions, we may think of Marcia as unable to stop beating her children.

This psychological interpretation presents real difficulties. We may say, "She cannot help it." Shortly thereafter, she begins therapy, and this eventually helps her to stop, thus demonstrating that she can indeed stop! We can answer this by comparing it to someone untying Don. Both he and Marcia were helpless at one point in time (though from different causes), but now they no longer are. The basic question is, "If all our actions are caused, can we ever help what we are doing?" Are we in a sense always under compulsion? This line of argument equates causation with inner compulsion or coercion, or with a feeling of helplessness. In fact, most of the time, most of us seem to feel in control of ourselves. We can and do shift gears, as we respond to new circumstances on the basis of our feelings and thoughts. Our being able to do X or not do X describes a psychological state—a very desirable state from the point of view of social living and personal happiness. It is precisely because we know something about the causes of behavior that we can help Marcia to acquire this state, so that she can stop compulsively beating her children, and over time, come to grips with the urge to do so.

Some theorists (Sartre and Szasz), and some nonprofessionals, argue that we ought not to describe people in terms of the degree of their inner freedom-compulsion, but rather, should assume that all of us are at the inner freedom end of this continuum, or that we at least have some desirable minimum of inner freedom. We would thus be attributing the best to everyone, and they would hopefully rise to the occasion. There is always some merit in this suggestion. It is far better for strangers to assume first, "Each of us can choose" than for them to assume, "Each of us cannot choose." But the workability of this suggestion is constrained by reality: at a particular moment of her life, under her particular circumstances, Marcia cannot stop beating those children, even though she anticipates feelings of guilt and possible legal actions against her. Our next question is likely to be one that, fortunately, research can answer over time: which techniques will best help Marcia to attain inner freedom?

Because any human activity is part of a long chain of events, we must be very specific when we talk about any compulsion, inner or outer. It is true that Don is tied into a car right now, and is not strong enough to break his bonds. We might, however, ask about his being in this predicament: could we hold him accountable for associating with certain people? When we say that someone is or is not responsible for an act, we have to specify carefully what act, over what period of time. We may agree that in one sense, a person addicted to drugs is not responsible for using the drugs; to be addicted is to be compelled in some sense. In another sense, however, we could argue that the person should not have turned to drugs in the first place, and that in a perhaps rare but lucid moment, the person could turn to the appropriate resources for help. That is a very difficult question psychologically: are we responsible for saying, "I can no longer help myself in this matter; I am out of control; I am no longer responsible for my actions"? In other words, can we be held accountable if we do not recognize or admit this when it correctly describes us?

The role of psychology in determining whether a person should be held accountable or not is obviously very major. The demand for moral action, for reasons, for moral principles that justify our actions assumes that the person is competent to make certain kinds of judgments and capable of acting on the basis of these judgments. When there is doubt about these psychological factors, the whole enterprise of rational justification (applying the model of moral reasoning described in Chapter 2) must be temporarily suspended, pending the outcome of psychological inquiry. In this regard, then, the application of moral philosophy is dependent upon the agents' accountability in the psychological sense. At the same time, accountability in the sense established by the psychologist is not complete, in that we can still ask for rational justification for the psychologically accountable action and for valuing accountability positively. In a sense, then, psychology can be seen to be dependent on moral theory as well. Very often, the person's ability to give good moral reasons is a determining factor in deciding questions of competence and accountability. Hence, taking these complexities into consideration, we must conclude that accountability is a matter in which psychology and ethics must work together if a more complete story is to be told.

TEMPTATION

Suppose that Jennie faces a situation in which she is accountable in the psychological sense, and assume further that she is reflective enough to have determined what her obligations are (what she ought to do). She has just found a wallet full of money, and knows she should return it with the money still in it. But she also has an urgent financial need that the found money would satisfy (she has to pay her rent), and no one else would know if she kept the wallet. Unlike the moral dilemmas we discussed in Chapter 2, the conflict here is not between opposing principles or even opposing moral intuitions. Rather, it is a tension between doing something one believes to be morally right, and not doing it, or even doing the opposite. Temptations of the sort that Jennie faces are a very real part of the moral life; in fact, they are probably far more common than moral dilemmas. This is probably true also for some psychologists, for whom deceiving people, for example, may be more temptation than moral dilemma.

Such temptations are basically double approach-avoidance conflicts. We may try to resolve them by rationalizing—that is, by making up phony reasons which suit a particular situation and allow us to override what we normally believe about right and wrong (when we are not tempted). Such rationalizations are usually detectable by others who know what our moral beliefs are. Furthermore, they are usually unsuccessful in ridding us of guilt for doing what we believe to be morally wrong, unless we lapse deeply into self-deception.

The conflict facing Jennie in the wallet example is the classic conflict between duty and desire. Before discussing it further, we must point out that this way of describing the conflict is actually quite incomplete. The experience of having a duty involves both cognitions and motives. Jennie knows or believes that she should return the wallet, and she is motivated to do so; she expects to feel good if she does, guilty if she does not. She may feel compassion for the unknown owner of the wallet. What we call desire or temptation also involves both cognitions and motives. Jennie knows that she must pay her rent, and that she has just found 800 real, not toy, dollars. She wants to keep that money. Notice that no matter what she decides to do, it will cost her something and she will gain something. The alternatives are money with guilt or poverty with "feeling good." When this conflict is described as one between duty and desire, we may mistakenly conclude that only one motive and one cognition are involved, but that does not do justice to the psychological richness of the conflict, and the many possibilities it presents for both reasoning and rationalizing.

As we contemplate Jennie's situation, we might say, with Kant, that doing one's duty when desire pulls one in the opposite direction, doing one's duty because it is one's duty, is more morally praiseworthy than doing one's duty when it is in line with one's desire. This is so because the former is clearly more difficult (costly) than the latter. Had Jennie found gloves she considered ugly, and which she therefore had no desire to own, we would be less impressed if she turned in what she had found.

Doing what it is difficult to do tends to build what used to be called "character." As Aristotle pointed out, each time we do a particular good deed, it becomes easier and easier to do it in subsequent situations. Building character is thus both a psychological and a philosophical matter; strength of character can be taken as a personal moral ideal. Teaching children to do what is right even when no authority figures are watching, and no matter how difficult it is, is an essential ingredient of a moral education; in fact, this is a basic responsibility of those in positions of influence, especially where young children are involved. This supports what we said earlier about parents who interpret relativism to mean that their children should receive no moral guidance at all!

SUMMARY AND CONCLUDING REFLECTIONS

We began by showing how psychology and ethics share complementary concerns about human behavior. Explanations of human conduct are not the same as justifications for it, but both explanation and justification have interrelated and overlapping features and concerns. It is often difficult and sometimes impossible to isolate the moral from the nonmoral aspects of human behavior. Rather, moral scrutiny is one particular perspective or frame of reference in terms of which one can and often should view human conduct. Ethics deals with "conflicts of interests" among people, a concept which can only be understood by taking both ethical and psychological notions into account.

We have also seen that philosophy (ethics) can help us to understand the process of moral reflection, whether we are thinking about the mundane matters of daily life or about highly complex moral dilemmas. The study of ethics broadens our conceptual horizons and encourages us to adopt the moral point of view. Psychology, on the other hand, gives us descriptions and analyses of the moral views of different individuals and groups, and of how these views fit into their lives. Psychologists offer us explanations of different views and how they develop, as well as information on how moral views might be changed. Only jointly can they answer the questions, "How can we improve our own conduct, and that of our children?," and more broadly, "How can we move toward a society of competent, compassionate moral agents?"

Psychologists do not all approach human conduct in the same way. Some are particularly interested in understanding inner processes as these relate to behavior. Others stress the immediate context and therefore study the person within a social and/or physical environment. That second emphasis is as relevant to ethical concerns as the first. There are some attempts to describe environments, but this turns out to be a difficult task. Questions about the nature and development of characteristics like rationality are and will continue to be important. In addition, however, ethicists and psychologists should work together on the description and evaluation of environments, not only of traits and behaviors. If one grants that different environments contribute to the development and expression of different traits and behaviors (which does not mean denying the influence of heredity), then it is clearly as necessary to evaluate the former as the latter. We asked above, "How can we move toward a society of competent, compassionate moral agents?" We cannot even begin to answer that question until we take seriously the reality that human beings always have an environment. Can we describe it? Do we understand when or for whom it is more nearly harmful or more nearly beneficial? These questions remain major challenges for both disciplines.

Both reason and temperament influence our moral perspective. Theories of human nature that stress heredity and social hierarchy are part of tougher moral perspectives, while theories of human nature which stress flexibility, environment, and equality are parts of more tender ones. No moral perspective is oriented to softening people, to making them weak, as it talks about the kinds of social change, if any, which would make goodness more probable. Life always gives us problems enough without our refusing to try to create a better world for ourselves.

When people with very different world views discuss moral issues, they may find that reasoning can help them only to understand their differences, not to erase or reconcile them. This is so because world views are anchored in all parts of the personality, not in reason alone. A change of world views would be like a religious conversion. But understanding each other is no small achievement, and it is of great importance for social life in a heterogeneous world. Although some differences may be irreconcilable and profound, no moral theory or perspective concludes that anything and everything is morally permissible simply because someone or some group believes it or does it. Ethical questions and answers should thus remain a central concern for all.

Rationality is one characteristic of human nature on which everyone agrees, though not everyone agrees on its importance: we do think better than any other living creature. Lions can maul us without even trying hard, but we can outthink them. We need to learn more about how to use that advantage to advantage (to ours and theirs)! We can reflect about our problems, including moral ones, before we act, and thus can cut down on the number of costly mistakes we make. Experience will, however, always remain a necessary and good teacher.

No group has the one and only best approach to moral problems, even when, or perhaps especially when, it thinks it does. Professionals, for better and worse, use a reflective, impersonal, intellectual approach. In contrast, for better and worse, lay people enter the domain of ethics in their daily lives in an inevitably more personal, involved, emotional way. As we contemplate the history of humankind with the benefits of hindsight, we can see that no approach produces the true answers that can be carefully preserved, intact, forever. This does not reveal that ethical inquiry is a failure, but rather, that our expectations are somewhat distorted. In this regard, ethics is like science. Many people continue to view science as a collection of facts. In reality, science is an approach to asking and trying to answer questions—with occasional brilliant leaps, but mainly with small, hard-won gains. And always, today's big gain can appear rather small, or even incorrect, tomorrow. A particularly instructive exercise is to pretend one is looking back at today from the year 2000 or 2100. What would appear then to be morally reprehensible and laudable that we are doing today?

Ethics, like science, is a human activity, and as such, filled with human strengths and weaknesses. Our strengths are not restricted to the cognitive domain; they include our capacity to empathize with others. Concepts like moral agency, competence, compassion, intention, and rationality are of central importance in both ethics and psychology. This is hardly surprising, given their central place in human life. Such concepts simultaneously describe and evaluate; psychology tends to stress the former, ethics the latter, but both disciplines use definition, observation, reasoning, and interpretation in relation to human conduct.

Moral reasoning is not an empty intellectual exercise, since moral concerns are a vital part of social living. But people learn from each other not only by precept. Above all, they learn through imitation and through the rewards and punishments they experience in relation to their conduct.

Responsible action and the willingness to be held accountable are therefore also central concerns in ethics and psychology; both disciplines do and must ask, "When are people accountable for their actions? What conduct shall we teach and model? How? What conduct shall we reward and punish? How?"

Now we have come full circle, since the thinking and conduct of professionals is included, as a matter of course, in what we have been saying. Thus, we come back to the ethics of doing psychology. In all that psychologists do, their values are involved: they ask certain questions; they collect certain data in certain ways. That does not mean that most of what they do is morally reprehensible. What it does mean is that their professional activity, like all human conduct, can be subjected to moral scrutiny, the nature of which must itself be examined. These are the things which we have tried to do in this book.

SUGGESTED FURTHER READINGS

Arnold, W. J. (Ed.). *Nebraska Symposium of Motivation, 1975.* Lincoln: University of Nebraska Press, 1976.

According to William J. Arnold's introduction, "In effect, this is a symposium on metatheoretical psychology, that is, on theories regarding the kinds of theories or explanatory systems psychology should have. As we shall see, such questions are not answered merely by running more experiments and gathering more 'facts.' Rather, they are questions of choice among differing conceptual frameworks where the decisions that we make will define what are to be regarded as psychological 'facts,' how they are to be determined, and what they mean" (p. viii). Especially relevant to the topics discussed in this book are the papers by Joseph R. Royce (Psychology is multi-: Methodological, variate, epistemic, world view, systemic, paradigmatic, theoretic, and disciplinary), Theodore Mischel (Psychological explanations and their vicissitudes), Joseph F. Rychlak (Psychological science as a humanist views it), and Sigmund Koch (Language communities, search cells, and the psychological studies). No paper in this volume is for beginners, and all demand careful, critical thinking. They are well worth the effort.

Beauchamp, Tom L. *Philosophical ethics.* New York: McGraw-Hill, 1982.

This is an excellent full-length introduction to philosophical theories in ethics. After a consideration of the fundamental questions of morality (e.g., what *is* morality?), Beauchamp presents an excellent account of the major ethical theories, supplemented by generous selections of primary sources. A section on rights, justice, and liberty is designed to deepen the reader's grasp of current issues involving these notions. The final sections of the book will greatly enhance the reader's understanding of the fact/value issue and the problem of justifying our moral beliefs. A highly commendable feature of this book is its balanced blend of explication by the author and his perceptive use of primary sources to illustrate key perspectives.

Bok, Sissela. *Lying: Moral choice in public and private life.* New York: Random House Vintage Books, 1979.

In this work, a moral philosopher looks at the ethical issues involved in the use of lies and deception as a means to achieving ends in government, medicine, academia, the law, and so forth, as well as our use of lying and deception in personal and private affairs. The various ways we try to justify lies and whether lying itself can ever really be justified is a central focus of Bok's fascinating book. This work will be of particular interest to those whose professional activities raise the question of lying and deception in research involving humans, as well as to those who must face the moral dilemmas stemming from the temptation of lying to clients and patients.

Frankena, William. *Ethics* (2nd ed.). Englewood Cliffs, N.J.: Prentice-Hall, 1973.

In this widely read account of the nature of ethics and the method of moral reasoning, key concepts and distinctions in ethics are carefully explained. To understand this work is to have a solid grasp of the conceptual framework employed in much contemporary moral thinking. Designed as a secondary source in ethical theory, Frankena's little book is already something of a classic in the field. Its widespread acceptance is perhaps due in part to the impartiality of Frankena's treatment of opposing ethical perspectives.

Gilligan, C. *In a different voice.* Cambridge, Mass.: Harvard University Press, 1982.

Gilligan argues that the moral perspective of women stresses obligation (the maintenance of relationships, with minimal pain to self and others), while that of men stresses rights (the maintenance of separateness, with minimal invasion of privacy, etc.). The mature adult integrates these two perspectives, with the progression toward such integration being different for men and women. Gilligan's interpretations are both illuminating and disturbing. Will women and men inevitably have different moral perspectives? Is sexual relativism comparable to cultural relativism?

Hilgard, E. R. Consciousness in contemporary psychology. *Annual Review of Psychology*, 1980, **31,** 1–26.

In this tightly organized but far-ranging essay, Hilgard traces some of the history of psychology, emphasizing the recent reemergence of the study of mind. This reemergence has affected many, perhaps most, areas of psychology and raises again questions about freedom and determinism, the relationship between mind and body, and the nature of "self." Hilgard argues that *(a)* attention to empirical methods continues to be and should be important in psychology, and *(b)* this need not and does not preclude studying mental processes.

Kendler, H. H. *Psychology: A science in conflict.* New York: Oxford University Press, 1981.

The title of Kendler's book describes it well, since it deals with conflicts about subject matter, method, explanation, values, and application. His brief postscript begins, "The unity of psychology has all but collapsed. Psychology is a multidisciplinary field with different segments employing irreconcilable orientations" (p. 371). These are carefully explored, both abstractly and in detail. Two chapters deal with psychology and values. While Kendler rejects both "Science is value-free" and "Science and values are inextricably intertwined" (p. 218), he supports what he calls the logical dissociation between values and facts more than we do. Concerned mainly with methodology, Kendler's book explores many fundamental issues related to philosophy of science in psychology. This book will be most helpful to those with a broad background in psychology.

Mappes, T. A., & Zembaty, J. S. (Eds.). *Social ethics.* (2nd ed.) New York: McGraw Hill, 1982.

An interdisciplinary collection of contemporary writings on current moral problems, this carefully edited work presents a rich variety of perspectives on such issues as abortion, euthanasia, the death penalty, sexual morality and sexual equality, discrimination and reverse discrimination, pornography and censorship, mental illness and individual liberty, world hunger, and issues in environmental ethics. Very good introductions to each essay are provided throughout the book. A highly commendable effort has been made at a balanced presentation of competing major perspectives on each issue.

Monahan, J. (Ed.). *Who is the client? The ethics of psychological intervention in the criminal justice system.* Washington, D.C.: American Psychological Association, 1980.

This series of readings presents a comprehensive overview of the ethical questions faced by psychologists in the criminal justice system, including police agencies, the courts, correctional institutions, and the juvenile justice system. The ethical issues are well defined, and the discussion is clear. The introductory chapter offers a series of recommendations for resolving the major ethical dilemmas confronting psychologists in the legal system.

Robinson, D. N. *Psychology and the law*. New York: Oxford University Press, 1980.

Robinson discusses the influence that the social sciences, particularly psychology, have had on the concept of justice and its administration. Specifically, he reviews the insanity defense, involuntary commitment, psychological testing, and the nature of persons. The author argues that on these issues, the psychological perspective usually conflicts with the traditional conceptions of justice. Robinson's arguments and discussions require careful and thoughtful reading.

Stevenson, Leslie. *Seven theories of human nature*. New York: Oxford University Press, 1974.

An interdisciplinary account of major theories on human nature, this little volume takes up Plato, Christianity, Marx, Freud, Sartre, Skinner, and Konrad Lorenz. Stevenson examines the view of the universe, our place in it, what being human means, and some account of how to better our human situation—all from the vantage points of these seven theories. The comparisons and interrelationships of the various theories are most instructive.

Taylor, P. W. (Ed.). *Problems of moral philosophy* (3rd Ed.). Belmont, Calif.: Wadsworth Publishing Company, 1978.

This collection of primary sources in ethical theory represents the entire spectrum of moral thought. The editor makes use of classical and contemporary sources in an effort to provide an in-depth study of such topics as ethical relativism, egoism (both psychological and ethical), moral responsibility, and the concept of moral choice. The selections on taking the moral point of view are particularly helpful.

Warnock, G. J. *Contemporary moral philosophy*. New York: St. Martin's Press, 1967.

Warnock's book is a brief (77 pp.) survey of major trends in moral philosophy in the English-speaking world in this century. Intuitionism, Emotivism, and Prescriptivism are considered in some detail, but the author considers these theories to be somewhat limited in their abilities to address current ethical dilemmas. This is a good background source for present-day reflection.

X, Cedric (Ed.). The white researcher in black society. *Journal of Social Issues*, 1973, 29(1).

This entire issue is devoted to a discussion of how social science, whose researchers are primarily white, has dealt with black society. This series of articles offers the black or minority perspective on a number of issues ranging from IQ tests to how white psychologists contribute to the maintenance of the status quo. Although the examples used in some of the articles are outdated, the ethical questions raised are still relevant today.

REFERENCES

Albee, G. W. Preventing psychopathology and promoting human potential. *American Psychologist*, 1982, *37*, 1043–1050.

Allen, D. F., & Allen, V. S. *Ethical issues in mental retardation*. Nashville, Tenn.: Parthenon, 1979.

Allport, C. W. *Pattern and growth in personality*. New York: Holt, Rinehart & Winston, 1961.

Allport, F. H. The J-curve hypothesis of conforming behavior. *Journal of Social Psychology*, 1934, *5*, 141–183.

Anastasi, A. *Psychological testing* (4th ed.). New York: Macmillan, 1976.

Aristotle. *Nicomachean ethics* (McKeon ed.). New York: Random House, 1941.

Asch, S. E. *Social psychology*. Englewood Cliffs, N.J.: Prentice-Hall, 1952.

Bajema, C. J. (Ed.). *Eugenics: Then and now*. New York: Halstead, 1976.

Bakan, D. The mystery-mastery complex in contemporary psychology. *American Psychologist*, 1965, *20*, 186–191.

Baltes, P. B., Reese, H. W., & Lipsitt, L. P. Life-span developmental psychology. *Annual Review of Psychology*, 1980, *31*, 65–110.

Bandura, A. Behavior theory and the models of man. *American Psychologist*, 1974, *29*, 859–869.

Barker, R. G. *Ecological psychology: Concepts and methods for studying the environment of human behavior*. Stanford, Calif.: Stanford University Press, 1968.

309

Barnette, W. L., Jr. (Ed.). *Readings in psychological tests and measurements.* Homewood, Ill.: Dorsey Press, 1964.

Beckman, G., Henthorn, W. E., Niyakawa-Howard, A., & Passin, H. *Culture learning program proposal.* Honolulu: East-West Center, 1970.

Beit-Hallahmi, B. Salvation and its vicissitudes: Clinical psychology and political values. *American Psychologist,* 1974, *29,* 124–129.

Bem, D. J., & Funder, D. Predicting more of the people more of the time: Assessing the personality of situations. *Psychological Review,* 1978, *85,* 485–501.

Benbow, C. P., & Stanley, J. C. Sex differences in mathematical ability: Fact or artifact? *Science,* 1980, *210,* 1262–1264.

Benbow, C. P., & Stanley, J. C. Letters. *Science,* 1981, *212,* 118–121.

Bennett, C. C. What price privacy? *American Psychologist,* 1967, 22, 371–376.

Billingsley, A. Black families and white social science. *Journal of Social Issues,* 1970, *26,* 127–142.

Birren, J. E., Cunningham, W. R., & Yamamoto, K. Psychology of adult development and aging. *Annual Review of Psychology,* 1983, *34,* 543–575.

Blackstone, W. T. The American Psychological Association code of ethics for research involving human participants: An appraisal. *The Southern Journal of Philosophy,* 1975, *13,* 407–418.

Block, N. J., & Dworkin, G. I.Q., heritability and inequality, Part II. *Philosophy and Public Affairs,* 1974, *4,* 40–99.

Bloom, A. H. Two dimensions of moral reasoning: Social principledness and social humanism in cross-cultural perspective. *Journal of Social Psychology,* 1977, *101,* 29–44.

Bok, S. *Lying: Moral choice in public and private life.* New York: Pantheon Books, 1978.

Bordin, E. S. Curiosity, compassion, and doubt: The dilemma of the psychologist. *American Psychologist,* 1966, *21,* 116–121.

Bowd, A. D. Ethics and animal experimentation. *American Psychologist,* 1980, *35,* 224–225.

Brazziell, W. F. White research in black communities: When solutions become part of the problem. *Journal of Social Issues,* 1973, *29,* 41–52.

Bronowski, J. *Science and human values.* New York: Harper & Row, 1956.

Brooks, W., & Doob, A. Justice and the jury. *Journal of Social Issues,* 1975, *31,* 171–182.

Broverman, I. K., Broverman, D. M., Clarkson, F. E., Rosenkratz, P. S., & Vogel, S. R. Sex-role stereotypes and clinical judgments of mental health. *Journal of Consulting and Clinical Psychology,* 1970, *34,* 1–7.

Brunner, E. *The divine imperative.* Philadelphia, Pa.: Westminster Press, 1932.

Brunswik, E. Systematic and representative design of psychological experiments. Berkeley, Calif.: *University of California Press, 1947.*

Buckhout, R., & Baker, E. Surveying the attitudes of seated jurors. *Social Action and the Law,* 1977, 4, (6), 98–101.

Burtt, H. E. *Legal psychology.* Englewood Cliffs, N.J.: Prentice-Hall, 1931.

Bush, N. The case for expansive *Voir Dire. Law and Psychology Review,* 1976, 2, 9–26.

Bush, R. *When a child needs help.* New York: Laurel, 1982.

Campbell, D. T. On the conflicts between biological and social evolution and between psychology and moral tradition. *American Psychologist,* 1975, 30, 1103–1126.

Camus, A. *The myth of Sisyphus and other essays.* New York: Alfred A. Knopf, 1955.

Carlsmith, J. M., Ellsworth, P. C., & Aronson, E. *Methods of research in social psychology.* Reading, Mass.: Addison-Wesley Publishing, 1976.

Carlsmith, J. M., Lepper, M. R., & Landauer, T. K. Children's obedience to adult requests: Interactive effects of anxiety arousal and apparent punitiveness of the adult. *Journal of Personality and Social Psychology,* 1974, 30, 822–828.

Casebook on Ethical Standards of Psychologists. Washington, D.C.: American Psychological Association, 1974.

Cazden, C. B. The situation: A neglected source of social class differences in language use. *Journal of Social Issues,* 1970, 26, 35–60.

Chesler, P. *Women and madness.* New York: Doubleday Publishing, 1972.

Chinn, P. C., Drew, C. J., & Logan, D. R. *Mental retardation: A life cycle approach* (2nd ed.) St. Louis, Mo.: C. V. Mosby, 1979.

Christie, R., & Geiss, F. L. *Studies in Machiavellianism.* New York: Academic Press, 1970.

Clark, K. B., & Clark, M. P. Racial identification and preference in Negro children. In T. M. Newcomb & E. L. Hartley (Eds.). *Readings in social psychology.* New York: Holt, Rinehart & Winston, 1947.

Clayton, V. P., & Birren, J. E. The development of wisdom across the lifespan: A reexamination of an ancient topic. Chapter 3 in *Life-span development and behavior,* P. B. Baltes & O. G. Brim, Jr. (Eds.). New York: Academic Press, 1980.

Clingempeel, W. G., Mulvey, E., & Repucci, N. D. A National study of ethical dilemmas of psychologists in the criminal justice system. In J. Monahan (Ed.). *Who Is the Client?* Washington, D.C. American Psychological Association, 1980.

Coan, R. W. Toward a psychological interpretation of psychology. *Journal of the History of the Behavioral Sciences*, 1973, *9*, 313–327.

Cohn, A., & Udolf, R. *The criminal justice system and its psychology*. New York: Van Nostrand Reinhold, 1979.

Coleman, J. S. *Equality of educational opportunity*. Washington, D.C.: U.S. Office of Education, 1966.

Collins, B. E. *Social psychology*. Reading, Mass.: Addison-Wesley Publishing, 1970.

Copi, I. M. *Introduction to logic* (6th ed.) New York: Macmillan, 1982.

Couchman, I. S. B. Notes from a white researcher in black society. *Journal of Social Issues*, 1973, *29*, 45–52.

Cronbach, L. J. Beyond the two disciplines of scientific psychology. *American Psychologist*, 1975, *30*, 116–127.

Cronbach, L. J. Test validation. In R. L. Thorndike (Ed.). *Educational Measurement*. Washington, D.C.: American Council on Education, 1971.

Cronbach, L. J., & Meehl, P. E. Construct validation in psychological tests. *Psychological Bulletin*, 1955, *52*, 281–302. Copyright 1955 by the American Psychological Association. Reprinted by permission of the publisher and author.

Dawkins, R. *The selfish gene*. New York: Oxford University Press, 1976.

Deaux, K. *The behavior of women and men*. Monterey, Calif.: Brooks/Cole Publishing, 1976.

Deutsch, M. Introduction. In M. Deutsch & H. A. Hornstein (Eds.). *Applying social psychology: Implications for research, practice, and training*. Hillsdale, N.J.: Erlbaum, 1975.

Diener, E., & Crandall, R. *Ethics in social and behavioral research*. Chicago: University of Chicago Press, 1978.

Edgerton, R. B. *Mental retardation*. Cambridge, Mass.: Harvard University Press, 1979.

Egelman, E., Alper, J., Leibowitz, L., Beckwith, J., Levine, R., & Leeds, A. Letters. *Science*, 1981, *212*, 116.

Ellison, K. W., & Buckhout, R. *Psychology and criminal justice*. New York: Harper & Row, 1981.

Erlanger, H. Jury research in America: Its past and future. *Law and Society Review*, 1970, *4*, 345–370.

Ethical Principles of Psychologists. Washington, D.C.: American Psychological Association, 1981.

Etzioni, A. Creating an imbalance. *Trial*, 1974, *10*, 28–30.

Eysenck, H. J., & Kamin, L. *The intelligence controversy*. New York: John Wiley & Sons, 1981.

Field, T. M., Woodson, R., Greenberg, R., & Cohen, D. Discrimination and imitation of facial expressions by neonates. *Science*, 1982, *218*, 179–181.

Flew, A. *A dictionary of philosophy*. New York, St. Martin's Press, 1979, S. V. "relativism," p. 281.

Forer, B. The fallacy of personal validation: A classroom demonstration of gullibility. *Journal of Abnormal and Social Psychology*, 1949, *44*, 118–123.

Frank, J. D. *Persuasion and healing: A comparative study of psychotherapy*. Baltimore: The John Hopkins Press, 1961.

Frankena, W. *Ethics* (2nd ed.). Englewood Cliffs, N.J.: Prentice-Hall, 1973.

Freud, S. *Psychopathology of everyday life*. In Standard Edition, Vol. 6, London: Hogarth Press, 1960.

Fried, C. *Right and wrong*. Cambridge, Mass.: Harvard University Press, 1978.

Gallup, G. G. Self-recognition in primates: A comparative approach to the bidirectional properties of consciousness. *American Psychologist*, 1977, *32*, 329–338.

Garcia, J. The logic and limits of mental aptitude testing. *American Psychologist*, 1981, *36*, 1172–1180.

Garcia, J. Tilting at the paper mills of academe. *American Psychologist*, 1981, *36*, 149–158.

Gerbasi, K., Zuckerman, M., & Reis, H. Justice needs a new blindfold: A review of mock jury research. *Psychological Bulletin*, 1977, *84*, 323–345.

Gergen, K. J. Social psychology as history. *Journal of Personality and Social Psychology*, 1973, *26*, 309–320.

Gert, B. *The moral rules: A new rational foundation for morality*. New York: Harper & Row, 1970.

Gewirth, A. *Reason and morality*. Chicago: University of Chicago Press, 1978.

Gibson, M. Rationality. *Philosophy and Public Affairs*, 1977, *6*, 193–225.

Gilligan, C. *In a different voice*. Cambridge, Mass.: Harvard University Press, 1982.

Glass, G. V. The wisdom of scientific inquiry on education. *Journal of Research in Science Teaching*, 1972, *9*, 3–18.

Goering, J. M., & Cummins, M. Intervention research and the survey process. *Journal of Social Issues*, 1970, *26*, 49–55.

Gomberg, P. I.Q. and race: A discussion of some confusions. *Ethics*, 1975, *85*, 258–266.

Gordon, T. Notes on white and black psychology. *Journal of Social Issues*, 1973, *29*, 87–95.

Gould, S. J. Morton's ranking of races by cranial capacity. *Science*, 1978, *200*, 503–509. Copyright 1978 by the American Association for the Advancement of Science.

Gould, S. J. Jensen's last stand. (Review of Jensen, A. R. *Bias in mental testing*. New York: Free Press, 1979) *New York Review of Books*, 1980, *27*(7), 38–44.

Greeley, A. M., & McCready, W. C. Are we a nation of mystics? *New York Times Magazine*, January 26, 1975, pp. 12–13.

Greenglass, E., & Stewart, M. The under-representation of women in social psychological research. *Ontario Psychologist*, 1973, *5*, 21–29.

Gurin, G. & Gurin, P. Expectancy theory of the study of poverty. *Journal of Social Issues*, 1970, *26*, 83–104.

Haan, N. *Coping and defending: Processes of self-environment organization.* New York: Academic Press, 1977.

Harris, G. W., & Levine, S. Sexual differentiation of the brain and its experimental control. *Journal of Physiology*, 1965, *181*, 379–400.

Hilgard, E. R. Consciousness in contemporary psychology. *Annual Review of Psychology*, 1980, *31*, 1–26.

Hobbes, T. *The leviathan.* New York: Collier Books, 1962. (Original, 1651).

Hsieh, T., Shybut, J., & Larsof, E. Internal versus external control and ethnic group membership: A cross-cultural comparison. *Journal of Consulting and Clinical Psychology*, 1969, *33*, 122–124.

Hume, D. *A treatise of human nature.* 1740. Book 3, Part I, Section I, Paragraph 27.

Hunt, M. A fraud that shook the world. *New York Times Magazine*, November 1, 1981, p. 42.

Ireland, R. R. The relevance of race research. *Ethics*, 1974, *84*, 140–145.

James, W. *Pragmatism.* New York: Longmans, Green & Co., 1907.

Jensen, A. R. How much can we boost I.Q. and scholastic achievement? *Harvard Educational Review*, 1969, *39*, 1–123.

Jensen, A. R. The strange case of Dr. Jensen and Mr. Hyde? *American Psychologist*, 1974, *29*, 467–468.

Joad, C. E. M. *Essays in common-sense philosophy.* Port Washington, N.Y.: Kennikat Press, 1920.

Jones, J. *Prejudice and racism.* Reading, Mass.: Addison-Wesley, 1972.

Jung, C. G. The structure and dynamics of the psyche. In *Collected Works.* Vol. 8. Princeton, N.J.: Princeton University Press, 1960.

Kelman, H. C. Manipulation of human behavior: An ethical dilemma for the social scientist. *Journal of Social Issues*, 1965, *21*, 31–46.

Kemeny, J. G. *A philosopher looks at science.* New York: Van Nostrand Reinhold, 1959.

Kidder, L., & Stewart, V. M. *The psychology of intergroup relations: Conflict and consciousness.* New York: McGraw-Hill, 1975.

Kinget, G. M. *On being human*. New York: Harcourt Brace Jovanovich, 1975.

Kohlberg, L. Development of moral character and moral ideology. In M. L. Hoffman & L. W. Hoffman (Eds.). *Review of Child Development Research*, Vol. I, pp. 383–431. New York: Russell Sage Foundation, 1964.

Kolasa, B. Psychology and law. *American Psychologist*, 1972, *27*, 499–503.

Kroeber, A., & Kluckholm, C. *Culture: A critical review of concepts and definitions*. The Peabody Museum, 1952.

Kuhn, T. S. *The structure of scientific revolutions*. Chicago: University of Chicago Press, 1962.

Larson, C. Media psychology: New rules and new responses. *APA Monitor*, 1982, *12*(12), 3.

Lewin, K. *Resolving social conflicts*. New York: Harper & Row, 1948.

Lipsey, M. W. Research and relevance: A survey of graduate students and faculty in psychology. *American Psychologist*, 1974, *29*, 541–553.

Loftus, E., & Monahan, J. Trial by data: Psychological research as legal evidence. *American Psychologist*, 1980, *35*, 270–283.

Lovell, V. R. The human use of personality tests: A dissenting view. *American Psychologist*, 1967, *22*, 383–393.

Luhman, R., & Gilman, S. *Race and ethnic relations: The social and political experience of minority groups*. Belmont, Calif.: Wadsworth, 1980.

Luria, S. E. Biological aspects of ethical principles. *Journal of Medicine and Philosophy*, 1976, *1*, 332–336.

MacIntyre, A. *After virtue: A study in moral theory*. Notre Dame, Ind.: University of Notre Dame Press, 1981.

Mankin, D. *Toward a post-industrial psychology: Emerging perspectives on technology, work, education and leisure*. New York: John Wiley & Sons, 1978.

Margolis, J. *Values and conduct*. New York: Oxford University Press, 1971.

Marsh, J. C., Colten, M. E., & Tucker, B. Women's use of drugs and alcohol: New perspectives. *Journal of Social Issues*, 1982, *38*, 1–8.

Maslow, A. H. *Toward a psychology of being* (2nd ed.). New York: Van Nostrand Reinhold, 1968.

Maslow, A. H. Toward a humanistic biology. *American Psychologist*, 1969, *24*, 724–735.

May, R. *Psychology and the human dilemma*. New York: Van Nostrand Reinhold, 1967.

Medlin, B. Ultimate principles and ethical egoism. *The Australasian Journal of Philosophy*, 1957, *35*, 208–214.

Midgley, M. *Beast and man: The roots of human nature*. Ithaca, N.Y.: Cornell University Press, 1978.

Milgram, S. Behavioral study of obedience. *Journal of Abnormal and Social Psychology*, 1963, *67*, 371–378.

Milgram, S. Issues in the study of obedience: A reply to Baumrind. *American Psychologist*, 1964, *19*, 843–852.

Miller, G. A. Psychology as a means of promoting human welfare. *American Psychologist*, 1969, *24*, 1063–1075.

Miller, S. M. Poverty research in the seventies. *Journal of Social Issues*, 1970, *26*, 169–173.

Money, J. Sexual dimorphism and homosexual gender identity. *Psychological Bulletin*, 1970, *74*, 425–440.

Moriarty, A. E. *Constancy and I.Q. change.* Springfield, Ill.: Charles C Thomas, 1966.

Morin, S. F. An annotated bibliography of research on lesbianism and male homosexuality. Paper presented at the meeting of the American Psychological Association, Chicago, 1975.

Motto, J. A. The right to suicide: a psychiatrist's view. *Life Threatening Behavior*, 1972, *2*, 225–231.

Munsterberg, H. *On the witness stand: Essays on psychology and crime.* New York: Clark Boardman, 1908.

NAACP Report on Minority Testing (1976). NAACP Special Contribution Fund, May, 1976.

Padilla, A. M., & Ruiz, R. A. *Latino mental health,* Washington, D.C.: U.S. Department of Health, Education, and Welfare, 1974.

Padilla, A. M., Ruiz, R. A., & Alvarez, R. Community mental services for the Spanish-speaking/surnamed population. *American Psychologist*, 1975, *30*, 897–905.

Padilla, E. R. The relationship between psychology and Chicanos: Failures and possibilities. In N. N. Wagner & M. R. Haug (Eds.). *Chicanos: Social and psychological perspectives.* St. Louis, Mo.: C. V. Mosby, 1971.

Passmore, J. The treatment of animals. *Journal of the History of Ideas*, 1975, *36*, 195–218.

Pepitone, A. Lessons from the history of social psychology. *American Psychologist*, 1981, *36*, 972–985.

Piaget, J. *The moral judgment of the child.* London: Kegan Paul, 1932.

Plato *The republic* (Cornford Ed.) Oxford: Oxford University Press, 1945.

Portuges, S. Media ethics. *APA Monitor*, 1981, *12*, No. 12, 2.

Proshansky, H. M. For what are we training our graduate students? *American Psychologist*, 1972, *27*, 205–212.

Rainwater, L., & Pittman, D. J. Ethical problems in studying a politically sensitive community. *Social Problems*, 1967, *14*, 357–366.

Ramsey, P. *The ethics of fetal research*. New Haven, Conn.: Yale University Press, 1975.

Rawls, J. *A theory of justice*. Cambridge, Mass.: Harvard University Press, 1971.

Reid, T. *Essays on the intellectual powers of man*. Boston: Phillips, Sampson, & Co., 1857.

Report of the task force on the role of psychology in the criminal justice system. *American Psychologist*, 1978, *33*, 1099–1113.

Riessman, F. *The culturally deprived child*. New York: Harper and Row, 1962.

Ring, K. Let's get started: An appeal to what's left in psychology. Unpublished manuscript. Storrs, Conn.: University of Connecticut, 1971.

Rivlin, A. Forensic social science. *Harvard Educational Review*, 1973, *43*, 61–75.

Rogers, C. R. *On becoming a person*. Boston: Houghton Mifflin, 1961.

Rokeach, M. Long-range experimental modification of values, attitudes, and behavior. *American Psychologist*, 1971, *26*, 453–459.

Rosenzweig, M. R. Environmental complexity, cerebral change, and behavior. *American Psychologist*, 1966, *21*, 321–332.

Ross, A. *On law and justice*. London: Stevens and Sons, 1958.

Ross, W. D. *The right and the good*. Oxford: Oxford University Press, 1930.

Ruiz, R. A., Padilla, A. M., & Alvarez, R. Issues in the counseling of Spanish speaking/surname clients: Recommendations for therapeutic services. In C. R. Walz & L. Benjamin (Eds.). *Transcultural counseling: Needs, programs, and techniques*. New York: Human Sciences Press, 1978.

Russo, A. Straight talk on gays. *A.P.A. Monitor*, 1982, *13* (6), 6.

Ryan, W. *Blaming the victim*. New York: Pantheon Books, 1971.

Saks, M. J. The limits of scientific jury selection: Ethical and empirical. *Jurimetrics Journal*, 1976, *17*, 3–22.

Sampson, E. E. Psychology and the American ideal. *Journal of Personality and Social Psychology*, 1977, *35*, 767–782.

Sampson, E. E. Cognitive psychology as ideology. *American Psychologist*, 1982, *37*, 593–594.

Sarason, S. B., & Doris, J. *Psychological problems in mental deficiency* (4th ed.). New York: Harper & Row, 1969.

Sartre, J. P. *Existentialism and human emotions*. New York: Philosophical Library, 1957.

Scarr-Salapatek, S. Race, social class, and I.Q. *Science*, 1971, *174*, 1285–1295.

Schafer, A. T., & Gray, M. W. Sex and mathematics. *Science*, 1981, *211*, 231.

Schafer, R. *The clinical application of psychological tests*. New York: International Universities Press, 1948.

Scheibe, K. E. The psychologist's advantage and its nullification: Limits of human predictability. *American Psychologist*, 1978, *33*, 869–881.

Scheinin, A. G. The burden of suicide. *Newsweek*, February 7, 1983.

Schlenker, B. R. Social psychology and science. *Journal of Personality and Social Psychology*, 1974, *29*, 1–15.

Schulman, J., Kairys, D., Harring, S., Borona, B., & Christie, R. Systematic jury selection. *Law and Psychology Review*, 1976, *3*, 31–42.

Schulman, J., Shaver, P., Colman, R., Emrich, B., & Christie, R. Recipe for a jury. *Psychology Today*, 1973, *6*, 37–44; 78–84. Copyright 1973 by the American Psychological Association. Reprinted by permission of the publisher and author.

Scriven, M. Truisms as the grounds for historical explanation. In P. L. Gardiner (Ed.). *Theories of History*. New York: Free Press, 1959.

Seligman, M. E. P. *Helplessness*. San Francisco: W. H. Freeman, 1975.

Shah, S., Editorial. *A.P.A. Monitor*, 1977, 8(2), p. 2.

Shah, S. Dangerousness: A paradigm for exploring some issues in law and psychology. *American Psychologist*, 1978, *33*, 224–238.

Shields, S. A. Functionalism, Darwinism, and the psychology of women. *American Psychologist*, 1975, *30*, 739–754.

Sidgwick, H. *The methods of ethics*. New York: Macmillan, 1874.

Sidgwick, H. *Philosophy: Its scope and relations*. New York: Macmillan, 1902.

Siegel, M. Editorial. *A.P.A. Monitor*, 1977, 8(2), p. 5.

Simon, S. B., Howe, L. W., & Kirschenbaum, H. *Value clarification: A handbook of practical strategies for teachers and students* (rev. ed.). New York: Hart, 1978.

Singer, M. G. Duties to oneself. *Ethics*, 1959, *69*, 202–205.

Singer, P. *Practical ethics*. Cambridge in ENGLAND: Cambridge University Press, 1979

Skinner, B. F. *Beyond freedom and dignity*. New York: Alfred A. Knopf, 1971.

Skinner, B. F. The steep and thorny way to a science of behavior. *American Psychologist*, 1975, *30*, 42–49

Smith, D. H. Scientific knowledge and forbidden truths—are there things we should not know? *Hastings Center Report*, 1978, *8*(6), 30–35.

Smith, N. C., Jr. Replication studies: A neglected aspect of psychological research. *American Psychologist*, 1970, *25*, 970–975.

Smith, W. D., Burlew, A. K., Mosley, M. H., & Whitney, W. *Minority issues in mental health*. Reading, Mass.: Addison-Wesley Publishing, 1978.

Smyer, M. A., & Gatz, M. Aging and mental health: Business as usual? *American Psychologist*, 1979, *34*, 240–246.

Snyder, M. L., & Mentzer, S. Social psychological perspectives on the physician's feelings and behavior. *Personality and Social Psychology Bulletin*, 1978, *4*, 541–547.

Soble, A. Deception in social science research: Is informed consent possible? *Hastings Center Report*, 1978, *8*(5), 40–46. Reprinted with the permission of The Hastings Center © Institute of Society, Ethics, and the Life Sciences, 360 Broadway, Hastings-on-Hudson, N.Y. 10706.

Sowell, T. The great I.Q. controversy. *Change*, May, 1973, 33–37. A publication of the Helen Dwight Reid Educational Foundation.

Stage, E. K., & Karplus, R. Letters. *Science*, 1981, *212*, 114.

Stannard, U. Adam's rib, or the woman within. *Transaction*, 1970, *8*, 24–35.

Steininger, M., & Voegtlin, K. Personality variables and beliefs about psychological issues. *Teaching of Psychology*, 1976, *3*, 51–54.

Stern, W. The psychology of testimony. *Journal of Abnormal and Social Psychology*, 1939, *34*, 3–20.

Stevenson, L. *Seven theories of human nature.* Oxford: Clarendon Press, 1974.

Strupp, H. H., & Hadley, S. W. A tripartite model of mental health and therapeutic outcomes: With special reference to negative effects in psychotherapy. *American Psychologist*, 1977, *32*, 187–196.

Sue, D. W. *Counseling the culturally different.* New York: John Wiley & Sons, 1981.

Szasz, T. S. *Ideology and insanity.* New York: Doubleday Publishing, 1970.

Tarasoff v. *Reagents of the University of California*, 13 C. 3D 177; 529 p. 2D 553; 118 California Reporter, 129 (1974).

Thomson, J. J. Regulations governing research of human subjects: Academic freedom and the IRB. *Academe*, 1981, December, 358–370.

Timerman, J. *Prisoner without a name, cell without a number*, trans. Toby Talbot. New York: Alfred A. Knopf, 1981.

Toch, M. *Legal and criminal psychology.* New York: Holt, Rinehart & Winston, 1961.

Tyler, L. E. Design for a hopeful psychology. *American Psychologist*, 1973, *28*, 1021–1029.

Veatch, H. *Rational man.* Bloomington: Indiana University Press, 1962.

Walker, E. Relevant psychology is a snark. *American Psychologist*, 1970, *25*, 1081–1086.

Warren, M. A. On the moral and legal status of abortion. *The Monist*, 1973, *57*, 43–61.

Watson, R. I. Psychology: A prescriptive science. *American Psychologist*, 1967, *22*, 435–443.

Webster's *Third International dictionary.* Springfield, Mass.: Merriam, 1961.

Webster's *New Collegiate dictionary.* Philippines: Merriam, 1976.

Wellman, C. Consent to medical research on children. *Archives for Philosophy of Law and Social Philosophy*, 1978, *IV*(12), 85–105.

Williams, E. F. *Notes of a feminist therapist*. New York: Dell, 1976.

Williams, J. *The psychology of women: Behaviors in a biosocial context*. New York: W. W. Norton, 1977.

Williams, R. L. The death of white research in the black community. *Journal of Non-White Concerns in Personnel and Guidance*, 1974, *2*, 116–132.

White, R. W. Ego and reality in psychoanalytic theory: A proposal regarding independent ego energies. *Psychological Issues*, 1963, *3*, 1–210.

Wilson, E. O. *Sociobiology: The new synthesis*. Cambridge, Mass.: Harvard University Press, 1975.

Wittgenstein, L. *Philosophical investigations*. New York: Macmillan, 1953.

Wolfgang, M. E. The social scientist in court. *Journal of Criminal Law and Criminology*, 1974, *65*, 239–247.

Wrightsman, L. S. *Social psychology in the seventies*. Monterey, Calif.: Brooks/Cole Publishing, 1972.

X, Cedric. The role of the white researcher in black society: A futuristic look. *Journal of Social Issues*, 1973, *29*, 109–118.

AUTHOR INDEX

SUBJECT INDEX